THE FUTURE OF WAR: A HISTORY

THE FUTURE
OF WAR

A HISTORY

LAWRENCE FREEDMAN

PUBLICAFFAIRS
New York

PublicAffairs
Hachette Book Group
1290 Avenue of the Americas, New York, NY 10104
www.publicaffairsbooks.com
@public_affairs

First edition: October 2017

Published by PublicAffairs, an imprint of Perseus Books, LLC, a subsidiary of Hachette Book Group, Inc.

The Hachette Speakers Bureau provides a wide range of authors for speaking events. To find out more, go to www.hachettespeakersbureau.com or call (866) 376-6591.

The publisher is not responsible for websites (or their content) that are not owned by the publisher.

Library of Congress Cataloging-in-Publication Data has been applied for.
ISBN 978-1-61039-305-8 (HC)
ISBN 978-1-61039-306-5 (EB)

For Sir Michael Howard

Teacher, Mentor, Friend

CONTENTS

INTRODUCTION

My trade is courage and atrocities.

I look at them and do not condemn.

I write things down the way they happened,

as near as can be remembered.

I don't ask *why*, because it is mostly the same.

Wars happen because the ones who start them

think they can win.

—MARGARET ATWOOD,
The Loneliness of the Military Historian[1], 1995

In Greek mythology the gods of war brought misery and mayhem. Ares, once let loose, became dangerous and terrifying. His companion, Enyo, destroyed cities, and his children embodied strife, fear, and dread. From Enyo's brother Polemos came the rarely used word 'polemology' for the study of war and the more frequent 'polemic' for aggressive language. Polemos appeared in Greek literature as war's vicious personification. One of Aesop's Fables describes how, as the gods chose their mates, Polemos struggled to find a partner. Eventually only Hybris was left. She was the goddess of reckless, arrogant pride, from whom we get the word 'hubris'. Polemos fell madly in love with Hybris and followed her wherever she went. The moral of the story was that the nations of the world should never allow Hybris to come among them for if they did war would not be far behind.

The Romans also linked war with the intrigues of the gods. Virgil's *Aeneid* described how war can become all-consuming, its furies sparing neither side, especially when it erupts into *discordia*—a civil war. Yet they also could see nobility and purpose in war. As Ares transformed into the Roman god Mars, he gained dignity and praise as a guardian of the people rather than as a source of disruption. Enyo became Bellona, who came with shield and sword. She had her own temple for meeting foreign ambassadors, proclaiming victorious generals, and declaring wars. But Bellona was in no sense sedate. In early Roman times she was honoured by human sacrifices and drinking blood. Her role was to inspire and urge on the soldiers to violence. Virgil describes her as carrying a blood-stained whip.

Bellona's name derives from the Latin word for war, *bellum*. This word lives on when we talk of people inclined to war as being bellicose or belligerent. The English wordsmiths of the first millennium, however, considered *bellum* to be inappropriately close to the word for beauty, *bellus*. They therefore looked for alternatives. The term that came into use was an old English word for struggle or strife—*gewin*. This was eventually replaced by the German *werran*, which meant something similar, and is linked to our word *worse*. *Werran* became *weorre* and then *warre* in English, and *guerre* in French.

War therefore has a long association with confusion and discord, but also with honour and the defence of all that is most valued. This duality of war means that it is driven forward because something that really matters is at stake, yet shaped by means that are inherently destructive, unruly, hard to control and contain. This is why war invokes such contrary emotions. On the one hand it describes the grim consequences of conflict. War can tear the heart out of communities. On the other it can be a source of extraordinary solidarity. It tends to be filled with desperate moments of tragedy and sorrow, of cruelty and waste, but also of inspiring moments of heroism. The gadgetry of war fascinates just as much as its effects appal. States continue to prepare for war while professing to wish to legislate it out of existence. If they must fight, they insist, they will do so only for the most righteous of reasons, as a last resort, and in the most civilized manner. Western culture, not at all uniquely, is infused with a keen sense of this duality, of war as a terrible thing to happen but on occasion a noble and necessary thing to do. We define war through this duality, acknowledging its inescapable violence but requiring that at least this be organised and purposive. Random acts of violence or conflicts that are conducted without violence do not count as wars.

THE INDICTMENT OF WAR IS THAT THE PURPOSES SERVED can never justify the costs. While instances might be found to refute this charge attempts to defend war as a means of resolving disputes have struggled since the arrival of nuclear weapons in 1945. The possibility that they would be employed in a Third World War created a catastrophic prospect, and not only for the belligerents but also for humanity as a whole. In such a war there could be no nobility and no purpose, and the confusion and discord would reach unimaginable levels. This is one reason why the major powers held back from another great war, even as they kept up their military inventories and conducted research into new generations of weaponry. Without much difficulty, they looked into the likely character of a future war and decided that this was not one they could survive. Observing this in 1985, the historian John Gaddis coined the term 'the Long Peace' to describe the years since 1945. This was a period in which millions had died in violent conflicts. The great powers were often involved, but there was comfort to be drawn in the absence of war directly between them.[2] Perhaps by reaching such horrific peaks of destructiveness, great-power war had almost abolished itself.

Optimism on this score grew in the 1990s after the end of the Cold War. The Long Peace continued, leading to speculation that perhaps humankind had learnt something about war. The historian John Keegan wondered whether: 'War ... may well be ceasing to commend itself to human beings as a desirable or productive, let alone rational, means of reconciling their discontents.'[3] The political scientist John Mueller had long taken a similar view: 'like duelling and slavery, war does not appear to be one of life's necessities'. It was a 'social affliction, but in certain important respects it is also a social affectation that can be shrugged off.'[4] The cognitive psychologist Steven Pinker in his book *The Better Angels of Our Nature*, published in 2011, marshalled a great array of sources to offer an even more encouraging prospect. Slowly but surely over human history, he reported, there had been a steady move away from reliance on violence to settle disputes.[5] The reason for this was normative progress, for among 'influential constituencies in developed countries' there was a growing 'conviction that war is inherently immoral because of its costs to human well-being.' On this basis, he argued, interstate war among developed countries would surely go the way of those domestic customs that over time had moved from being 'unexceptionable to immoral to unthinkable to not-thought-about'. Here he had a long list of obnoxious practices, starting with slavery and serfdom, and moving on to include disembowelling and heretic-burning before concluding with flogging and keelhauling (a particularly nasty naval punishment).[6]

He had evidence to support his general thesis on the decline of violence. Fifteen per cent of our early ancestors met with a violent death; by the sixteenth century this was down to some 2 per cent; over the last century around 0.7 per cent of the world's population died in battle.[7] After the book's publication, the *Human Security Project*, based at Simon Fraser University in Canada, confirmed a positive trend. The number of interstate wars had shrunk from six a year during the 1950s (including anti-colonial wars) to barely one a year in the first decade of the twenty-first century. More startling was their report that the total number of all conflicts over this period had dropped by some 40 per cent while the deadliest had gone down by more than a half. In terms of fatalities the decline was even more remarkable. In 1950 the annual rate was approximately 240 reported battle-related deaths per million of the world's population; in 2007 it was less than 10 per million. Even taking account of the growth in the world's population, and noting that the trend has been far from linear, that was still an absolute and not just relative decline.[8] This positive conclusion was picked up not only by commentators but also by governments.[9] Pinker was careful not to promise that humankind was on the eve of an 'Age of Aquarius' in which violence had been abolished.[10] Combinations of personalities, circumstances, and chance could produce unexpected surges of death and destruction. Nonetheless the effect of his work was calming. He acknowledged that the situation might change, perhaps abruptly, but no reason was given to suppose that it would. '[F]rom where we sit on the trend line, most trends point peaceward.'[11]

The long-term decline in rates of homicides and state cruelty and in the incidence of all wars reflected, he argued, the progressive triumph of our 'better angels' of empathy, self-control, and morality over the 'inner demons' of instrumental violence, domination, revenge, sadism, and ideology. This had come together as a 'civilising process'.[12] The contributing factors were: 'gentle commerce' encouraging trusting relationships across boundaries; 'feminisation', as women were less belligerent than men; an 'expanding circle of sympathy', as more cosmopolitan societies could not dismiss the pain and feelings of others as irrelevant or demonize them as subhuman; and, lastly, 'the escalator of reason', allowing for an intelligent, educated critique of claims that might once have been used to justify appalling practices. Underlying his argument, therefore, was a liberal scepticism about state power, opposition to militarism, disdain for mercantilism, and support of co-operative action and internationalism.

There were two big problems with Pinker's thesis. The first was the methodology. His focus was not the actual number of violent acts but the chances that an individual alive at a particular time would suffer a violent death. The yardstick therefore was the proportion of the world's population affected by violence and homicides as well as wars, measured as the number of deaths per 100,000 people.[13] On this measure he wished to show that there had been a persistent trend over centuries, even including the Second World War, the worst bloodletting of our time. Though past acts of violence may have been less deadly in their time, they represented larger proportions of the global population. Here he got himself into a tangle. As we shall see there is an enormous range of casualty estimates for the Second World War, and he was by no means taking the highest. Moreover, the speed of killing matters. Some terrible violence took place in the past but was over an extended period.[14] More seriously, the decline in deaths was not only a measure of violence but also of improvements in medical and social care and therefore longevity. With more people living past their fifties, the proportion of the population prone to street fights and military service declined. Over time the risk of being killed in battle went down.[15] Recruits now are likely to be healthier, and so able to cope better with injury. The only violence Pinker consistently considered was fatalities, but his charts might look different if he had looked at attempts to inflict bodily harm. Death tolls from deliberate violence measure consequences rather than intentions.

Knowing the proportion of the total world's population killed by war (and violence more generally) is unhelpful if the aim is to understand social and political processes. Numbers need to be related to particular contexts. Even during the Second World War some parts of the world were barely affected by hostilities. Governments and individuals do not assess risks by reference to global possibilities but to actual situations. To know that one is living at a time when less than one per cent should expect to die in battle is of little value when facing a heavily armed enemy any more than it is of interest for a new mother in Africa to know the life expectancy of babies in North America.

The second problem with Pinker was his desire to demonstrate the progression of civilisation. With industrialisation and easier trade it was harder to see the gain in war, while the costs were invariably large and the risks high.[16] Imperial conquests once promised cheap acquisitions, but by the middle of the last century the urge to seek out more pieces of the earth's surface to control and exploit was largely spent, and by its conclusion most of those pieces taken as colonies had been handed back to local people. War imposed heavy demands in terms of debt, diverted industrial effort, and the loss of trading opportunities. Simply put, wars became not only more dangerous but also less profitable.

Pinker pushed this a step further, seeking to demonstrate that humankind was advancing on a long learning curve so that, with regrettable exceptions and occasional setbacks, it was getting progressively better at avoiding violence. When history was viewed as a sort of Manichean struggle between the angelic good and demonic evil, only the civilising process could explain war's decline. Armed force described the problem and so could never be part of the solution. Relying on balances of power was distasteful because they consigned nations to permanent anarchy by assuming leaders would 'act like psychopaths and consider only the national self-interest, unsoftened by sentimental (and suicidal) thoughts of morality.'[17] The idea that considerations of power might have recently worked to reduce violence by encouraging countries to avoid war out of common prudence was rejected. He saw no consistent effect at work and no correlation over history 'between the destructive power of weaponry and the human toll of deadly quarrels.'[18]

It is certainly now rare for states to come directly to blows, but it was also rare in earlier periods. The numbers of all interstate wars stayed low during the post-1945 period, and there was no major war involving the great powers (though the 1950 Korean War was close). The position on civil wars, however, was much more mixed. The recorded conflicts showed a progressive rise from 1945, peaking in the early 1990s. There were forty armed conflicts in the world in 2014, the highest number since 1999. The number had risen from thirty-four in 2013, and they were becoming more deadly, with about a quarter accounting for all but a few per cent of the casualties.[19] There was no consistent and reliable trend line. A few of the conflicts had an enormous effect on the amount of violence around at any given time, such as Vietnam during the 1960s, or the Democratic Republic of the Congo in the 1990s, or Syria in the 2010s.

In 2011, the year Pinker's book was published, five Norwegian researchers, taking account of all the available research, sought to develop a model to predict internal conflict. This was done with considerable precision. They considered 'the most important structural factors that explain the onset, risk and duration of armed conflict' as an aid to good policymaking. If, for example, there was a high probability of conflict in Tanzania around 2030 then, the authors argued, 'the UN should monitor the country closely in order to be able to move early if this conflict should happen, and seek measures to address the underlying causes of conflict.' Overall their conclusion was optimistic: by '2050, the proportion of countries in conflict will be reduced to half the present rate.'[20]

They looked at the factors prominent in analyses of origins of civil war and the persistence of conflict, such as size, demography, including the numbers of unemployed young people, and the rate of socio-economic development. With economic growth, improved education, and healthcare came a measure of internal stability. On this basis, the 'main driver of the reduction in conflict that we predict', they reported, was the 'poverty reduction that the UN expects to continue over the next decades'. Just a few years of peace could make a real difference to a battered country's chances of escaping forever from violence. They highlighted 'the importance of assistance to post-conflict countries in the form of peacekeeping operations and other interventions.' These interventions could involve a range of actions from peacekeeping forces monitoring ceasefire arrangements to more robust engagements to impose a settlement on recalcitrant parties.

Unfortunately a problem with the analysis was revealed quite quickly. The data stopped in 2010, so it did not include conflicts in countries not mentioned at all in the study, notably Syria. In an interview in late 2012 one of the leaders of the project acknowledged that conflicts in the Middle East had weakened the clear correlation between socio-economic development and the absence of civil war. The fighting in Syria and Libya had shown that 'we also have to include democratisation processes in the model'.[21] The problem was actually larger. By focusing on factors which made states prone to civil war the model could not take account of political developments, and in particular the upheavals within the Muslim world, which had unleashed a new wave of uncompromising, hard-line movements.

The incidence of war therefore is hard to predict. After a period of optimism at the start of the 2010s there was a turn to pessimism.

Vicious conflicts in Ukraine and Syria caught the headlines and reminded of war's terrible cost. The rise of China into full great-power
status promised turbulence in the international system. The attitude
of the Russian leadership hardened, with President Putin stressing the
importance of his country's military strength, while the replacement
of President Obama by President Trump also appeared to put the
United States on a more nationalist course. There were concerns
about how well states would cope with the stresses and strains of
economic downturns or climate change without coming apart in civil
wars or finding themselves clashing with neighbours in a struggle for
scarce resources.

QUESTIONS ABOUT THE RISKS AND LIKELY CHARACTER OF
future war have long preoccupied politicians, military practitioners,
diplomats, jurists, journalists, and novelists. They concern the ambitions of powerful states, the reliability of allies, potential performance
in battle, the attitudes of oppressed peoples, the likely impact of the
latest weaponry, means to mitigate war's harmful effects, and whether
much might be expected from the latest international conference.
These questions are now addressed with added professionalism in
specialist think tanks, university departments of international relations, planning staffs at the top of governments, dedicated cells in
command centres, and horizon-scanning groups reporting to the chief
executives of major defence contractors. How they answer deter-
mines whether their customers assume the risks of peace or anticipate
those of war, or get taken by surprise in either avoidable war or in a
fight that they might have expected to win.

A variety of agendas therefore have long informed writing on future war. The intent has rarely been deliberately predictive. This was
not only for the obvious reasons—prediction is difficult and likely to
be wrong—but also because the concern was often to make the audience aware of lurking dangers or exciting prospects. The aim was to
prescribe courses of action that would improve security or avert catastrophe, encouraging governments to put more resources into the
military, or shift priorities, or recognize the threat posed by some
rising power, or redouble their efforts to resolve the most pressing
disputes, or find a way to abolish categories of weapons or even outlaw war. Some were works of cool rationality, demonstrating the folly
of war. Others displayed passionate advocacy to alert people to war's

horrors. Some conveyed their message analytically, increasingly employing the methodologies of the social sciences, while others relied on more literary forms.

Whether we go back to what can now seem the naïve optimism from before the First World War, the fearful realism that preceded the Second World War, or the attempts to come to terms with the utterly terrifying prospect of a nuclear conflict, this literature is valuable for what it reveals about the assumptions of earlier times, what was feared and why, and the remedies proposed. It tells us what was thought about the sort of disputes that could trigger wars, the rivalries that mattered, and the critical capabilities that could make all the difference. Observing how our past appeared when it was the future can help us understand why events occurred as they did, how individuals became prisoners of their experiences and missed what was blindingly obvious to later generations, and occasionally saw with Cassandra-like clarity what was coming, only to be ignored by their contemporaries. In short, the future of war has a distinctive and revealing past.

There are examples of imaginative fiction that looked far ahead, most obviously the novels of H. G. Wells. Most writers on future war, however, described worlds resembling their own. They wrote about possibilities inherent in the current state of affairs. Whether or not these would be realised depended on whether the right measures were taken, be they prudent forms of military provision or sensible efforts to resolve conflicts. This is why books about war were often books about peace, including schemes to eliminate war forever. Lastly, they were also about the past, because they picked up on observable social, political, economic, and technical trends. A plausible prospectus referred to events and tendencies that readers would recognise.

Two larger themes recur in this literature. First, a growing appreciation of the difficulties of containing war so that its destructiveness could be bounded in time and space, and second, linked to this, a search for a form of decisive force that might inflict a knockout blow on an enemy and so end a war quickly and successfully. Thoughts of future war often quickly alighted on a compelling strategy that might bring it to a speedy conclusion, promising if followed by one's own country but dangerous if adopted by an enemy. Far less thought was given to the consequences of a first blow that failed to floor the opponent, or how a war's course might be increasingly determined by non-military factors, including the formation and breaking of alliances, underlying economic and demographic strength or the public's readiness to make sacrifices and tolerate casualties.

Explanations for why the first moves in a coming war might be more successful than those attempted in previous wars tended to point to new technologies or tactics. It was easier to anticipate the hardware than the politics, because there was normally some idea on what was in the developmental pipeline. Machine guns, submarines, aircraft, armoured vehicles, radar, missiles, nuclear weapons, precision guidance, digitisation and artificial intelligence all challenged in their time established ways of thinking about the forms battle might take and the effort required for victory.

Although technology was presented as the main driver of change in warfare, its influence was shaped by the political context. The dismantling of empires, and later the implosion of European communism, led to the creation of many new states, a number with fragile political institutions, undeveloped economies, and social divisions. Much contemporary conflict has been bound up with the efforts of the governments of these countries to cope in conditions of continuing instability, the regional reverberations of their inability to do so, and attempts by outsiders to identify and deal with the causes and consequences of these conflicts.

Compared with the continuing and intensive study of how a great-power war might come about and what would happen if it did, until the 1990s far less effort was expended on civil wars, although these were far more frequent and often extremely deadly. There were always available scripts for great-power war and even great-power peace: when it came to civil wars, and external interventions to soften their impact and bring them to a close, the scripts were almost entirely improvised. The more it became necessary to look into particular societies at the violence within them, the more the definitions of war came to be stretched. The category could include both a nuclear war of short duration destroying whole civilisations, and some vicious local combat that had continued for years while neighbours barely paid attention. It has become reasonable to ask whether the more ferocious forms of gang warfare, hidden from view in the slums of modern mega-cities, should now count as armed conflict.

The reason that the future is difficult to predict is that it depends on choices that have yet to be made, including by our governments, in circumstances that remain uncertain. We ask questions about the future to inform choices not to succumb to fatalism. By stressing this aspect of thinking about war, peace, and the use of armed force this book provides a reminder that history is made by people who do not know what is going to happen next. Many developments that were awaited, either fearfully or eagerly, never happened. Those things that did happen were sometimes seen to be inevitable in retrospect but they were rarely identified as inevitable in prospect. 'History', as John Comaroff has observed, can be usefully studied as 'any succession of rupturing events which together bring to light our misunderstandings and misrecognitions of the present'.[22]

This book locates the writing on future war in the concerns of the time. The aim is not just to assess how prescient different writers were, or whether they could have done better given what was known about new weaponry or the experience of recent wars, but to explore the prevailing understandings about the causes of war and their likely conduct and course. How people imagined the wars of the future affected the conduct and course of those wars when they finally arrived. Unanticipated wars, in forms that had not been imagined, left participants and commentators struggling to understand where they had come from and how they might best be fought. The focus is largely but not solely on the United Kingdom and the United States. These countries are chosen not just because they happen to be the two that I know the best but because they have been at the top of the international hierarchy for some time. Due to their position, they worried more than most about a range of threats: they had a global perspective, and they were anxious about any disruptive challenge to a status quo which suited them well.

The book is divided into three parts. The first looks at the period from the middle of the nineteenth century to the end of the Cold War from around 1990. During this period there were dramatic developments in the technology and practice of warfare, including two world wars and concern about an even more cataclysmic third. The starting point, however, was an idealised model of warfare geared towards decisive battles that could be used to regulate relations among the great powers. This model encouraged efforts to achieve the maximum effect with the first blow in the hope that the resulting conflict could be contained and kept short. This model came under strain not only because of the difficulty of keeping wars short but also because of the progressive importance of the civilian sphere—as a source of resistance but also as a target. Attacking civilians became a way of disrupting the enemy war effort, coercing a society into seeking peace terms, and, at the extremity, eradicating a hostile population. These tendencies all peaked in the Second World War, with the Nazis seeking to exterminate European Jewry, partisan warfare in occupied territories, and massive air raids against major cities, culminating in the two atomic bombs of August 1945. Nuclear technology raised the possibility of the obliteration of whole civilisations. The effect of this was to introduce great caution into great-power relations, as war became an extraordinarily high-risk venture, and to encourage searches for ways to fight using new technologies that would reduce dependence upon nuclear threats. Because these were the wars that Western countries had to prepare to fight they dominated writings on future war, in both imaginative fiction and professional commentary.

Part II covers the period after 1990. The great surprise turned out not to be the cunning ways that adversaries found to catch out the West but the speed with which the Soviet Union and its Warsaw Pact alliance fell apart. The Soviet Threat that had so dominated all considerations of future war was suddenly absent. With no obvious scenarios for major war, a whole intellectual and policy effort ground to a shuddering halt. Attention soon moved to civil wars, not so much because they were a new phenomenon but because they began to draw in Western powers. As this happened there was no body of theory to illuminate the character of civil wars and provide guidance on intervention. The supposition had to be that the pattern for the future was being established. In trying to make sense of present conflicts, academics and practitioners hoped to set the terms for future engagements. But they struggled to do this. A better understanding of the nature and character of these wars meant that they often appeared even more complicated and intractable than previously supposed.

It was not humanitarian considerations but the al-Qaeda attack on the United States of 11 September 2001 that created the strategic imperatives for intensive Western intervention in Afghanistan and Iraq. The experience was sobering. It proved difficult to find the right mix of armed force and social reform that would make it possible to defeat insurgencies and bring stability to war-torn countries. Somehow to escape from the trap of perpetual conflict it was necessary to address the sources of fragility in states, but this required levels of external support that in most cases was difficult to provide, especially without credible indigenous political leadership. The quarter century after the end of the Cold War thus combined an improving academic appreciation of the sources of conflict in non-Western conflicts, deeper and more realistic than anything available in 1990, with an arc of Western engagement. The arc began tentatively, fuelled by greater commitment and ambition, until disillusion set in, confirming the early inclination to stay clear of these conflicts. There had been a search for a new type of future for war, but it had not been found.

In Part III we see how as enthusiasm for overseas interventions waned, great-power conflict made a comeback. Russia asserted its distinctive interests while China's rapid economic growth began to put it in a position where American predominance in the Asia-Pacific region might be challenged. Technological advances in robotics and artificial intelligence gave credibility to visions of future battle populated by automatons and offered the prospect of sleek and almost dehumanised versions of the ideal type of classical warfare. The practice suggested continuing tentativeness by the major powers when contemplating war with each other, reflected in the adoption of forms of warfare short of all-out war—perhaps involving attacks on cyber-systems or using information warfare as much as armed force. At the same time, against these idealised models of future combat, or the persistent fears of a nuclear confrontation, there was the everyday reality of grim, grinding civil wars, drawing in outsiders whose interventions were as likely to keep them going as bring them to a conclusion. There is no longer a dominant model for future war, but instead a blurred concept and a range of speculative possibilities.

PART ONE

[1]

Decisive Battle

And yet we had plenty of warnings, if we had only made use of them. The danger did not come on us unawares. It burst upon us suddenly, 'tis true; but its coming was foreshadowed plainly enough to open our eyes, if we had not been wilfully blind.

GEORGE CHESNEY,
The Battle of Dorking, 1871[1]

On 1 September 1870 a French army, on its way to relieve another under siege at Metz, was enveloped and then overwhelmed at the battle of Sedan. A report described how 'the battle had commenced at five in the morning, and at five in the afternoon the apparition of a French general waving a flag on the summit of the parapet of Sedan announced to the Germans their astonishing victory.' The report continued with the subsequent note sent by the French Emperor Napoleon III to King Wilhelm of Prussia: 'My brother, having failed to die at the head of my troops, I lay my sword at the feet of Your Majesty'.[2]

This described a classical, textbook military victory. The power balance of Europe had been transformed in a clash of arms, culminating in a battle that was concluded in a single day. That defeated party accepted that conclusion and the political consequences—except that Napoleon III was soon in no position to honour his promises to Wilhelm. He was deposed and the Third Republic was declared on 2 September 1870. The new government refused to accept the verdict of battle and decided to continue the fight. As the Germans put Paris to siege, the French raised new armies in the rest of the country, including snipers, or *francs-tireurs* ('free shooters'), who caused heavy casualties and complicated the defence of lines of supply.

The German Chancellor Otto von Bismarck became increasingly anxious that prolonged resistance would encourage other countries to enter the war on France's behalf and so he demanded ruthless action. Yet even when Paris fell at the end of January 1871, after two months of siege, it then became the scene of a revolutionary uprising. The regular French Army in turn crushed the Paris Commune. Only then could Germany agree terms with the republican French government. These were harsher than they would have been had the initial verdict of battle been accepted, including the transfer of Alsace and part of Lorraine to Germany, as well as reparations of five billion gold francs.

Sedan demanded the attention of all those concerned with the military art. The German victory had been made possible by impressive mobilisation of its forces, appreciating the role of railroads in getting men to the front. By contrast France's chaotic response to its own declaration of war, into which Bismarck had goaded them, meant that it missed the chance to mount an early offensive. The power of modern artillery had been fully on display. The tactics of Field Marshal Helmuth von Moltke showed how to manoeuvre with modern armies in a way that inspired later generations of military strategists. But if order had not been restored in the chaotic aftermath of Sedan the war would have been remembered differently. The Germans drew two crucial lessons. First, good strategy really could produce guidance for a quick victory in a regular war. Second, unless ruthless steps were taken, this victory might be thwarted should irregular resistance develop in a defeated nation.

In this case the resistance failed. It was also viewed as being something uniquely French, reflecting the country's insurrectionary traditions. For the moment, the main conclusion was that Germany was a very powerful state and an accomplished military actor, capable of moving boldly and ruthlessly against its enemies. The European order was now unsettled, with the balance of power weighted in its favour though its long-term intentions were unclear. Von Moltke's stunning victory reinforced a classical model of warfare despite hinting at its limitations.

IN MAY 1871, THE MONTH IN WHICH THE TREATY OF FRANKFURT formally concluded the Franco-Prussian War, *Blackwood's Magazine* in London published an anonymous short story, *The Battle of Dorking*. Written by Sir George Tomkyns Chesney, a colonel in the Royal Engineers, it caused such a sensation that it was soon available as a stand-alone pamphlet. It sold over 80,000 copies and triggered a national debate on the state of Britain's preparedness for war. This was the author's purpose. As Chesney explained in his original submission to his publisher, he sought to encourage the reorganisation of the British military system by demonstrating how England might be invaded 'and the collapse of our power and commerce in consequence'. His effectiveness can be measured by the fact that the furore prompted the prime minister of the day, William Gladstone, to complain publicly about how such alarmist talk could lead to unnecessary military expenditure sufficient to ruin the public finances.

Those seeking to counter Chesney's arguments often did so with their own fictional accounts, demonstrating that when you invent the story you can at least decide who wins.[3] These stories about the future made it possible to make polemical points with more vigour than reasoned argument or dissections of old campaigns. *The Battle of Dorking*'s success meant that it became more than just a sensation of 1871: a whole literary genre was created that provided, in the years leading up to the First World War, one medium by which patriotic anxieties might be stirred, nationalism fed, military innovations described, and preparations assessed. Writing on the future of war was designed to demonstrate what might happen if governments failed to get the writer's message and then act upon it with urgency.

Chesney was not of course the first to write on this subject or to express his ideas in a fictional form. The Napoleonic Wars had produced a mass of literature imagining invasions in one direction or another, in which the unwary were caught by cunning schemes and devices. There was also a comforting 'desire to see the enemy as contemptible, inferior, and already defeated'.[4] What made a difference in Chesney's case was that he was a gifted writer and able to take advantage of the rise of the popular press, which had created a growing audience for such provocations. Discontent over the handling of the Crimean War in the 1850s had already helped to move issues of war and peace out of the area of elite consultations and into democratic debate. In addition, his timing was excellent and not coincidental. Coming just after the German victory it reflected the pervasive belief, in retrospect perfectly justified, that the old order had been destabilised. Great-power relations would be in a state of flux for some time.

If France with its famed army could be so defeated, who might be the victim of the next upset? In this uncertainty some vital development in weaponry or military methods might make all the difference, leaving the ill-prepared or faint-hearted badly caught out.

Chesney's story was about how Britain was invaded by a foreign power, not named but evidently Germany (the victorious invaders spoke German). The enemy had been hatching plans for some time. The moment to strike came when Britain's guard was down. The Royal Navy was more dispersed than usual on a variety of colonial duties, while the army was dealing with the Fenians in Ireland, an uprising in India, and a challenge to Canada from the United States. The Germans pounced, taking care to honour the formalities by at least declaring war. Telegraphic communication to Britain was cut off so there could be no real warning. A well-prepared invasion force was soon off across the channel, facing minimum resistance when it reached the shore. The narrator of the book was a volunteer, one of many called to a ridge between Guildford and Dorking where, with available regulars, they were to take on the enemy force. Unfortunately the enemy turned out to be far better organised and disciplined. The British fought, as one would expect, valiantly. But without decent intelligence, logistics, and leadership, they were overcome.

To get the requisite knockout blow Chesney had to ensure that everything went right for the aggressors, even before the point was reached where the unpreparedness of the British army made a real difference. The operational key to the German victory lay in overcoming the major problem facing any would-be invader of Britain, its double advantage of being an island and in possession of the world's most powerful navy. Those earlier anxieties about the possibility of Napoleon invading had supposed that the great moat of the English Channel could be overcome using methods such as tunnelling and balloons. In 1784 an anti-British American satirist imagined how 'if the English should venture to sea with their fleet, a host of balloons in a trice they shall meet'.[5] Long after Napoleon had been seen off, the British continued to fret about all possible challenges to their naval supremacy, including that posed by steamships which offered increased speed and a capacity to overcome the limitations hitherto set by weather and tides. Chesney had the Royal Navy being caught out by a deft manoeuvre by the German fleet and then, most dramatically, by 'fatal engines which sent our ships, one after the other, to the bottom'. These he makes clear were torpedoes, although at the time the term was used to refer to the floating bombs that later came to be known as mines. It was only in 1870 that the first Admiralty trials took place of the propelled bombs that we now call torpedoes.[6] During the next decade navies began to fit them to both their capital ships and smaller vessels, and set in motion a debate about the relationship between the long-range big guns upon which they had previously relied and the new torpedoes with extra range but also uncertain accuracy.

Chesney was therefore up to date but did not move much beyond recent experience. For example, he made no mention of submarines, yet these turned out to be the most important imminent innovation in naval warfare. A crude form of submarine had been in use during the recent American Civil War, although it took until the end of the century for a more reliable version to be introduced by the French. More seriously, he showed little interest in the gruelling nature of the American war. Along with other Europeans he tended to assume that there was little to learn from the supposedly ill-disciplined and alcoholic American armies, other than what might happen with a swift and improvised expansion of relatively small volunteer armies into something much larger.[7]

According to Chesney the consequences of Britain's defeat were enormous. A once-proud nation was stripped of its colonies, 'its trade gone, its factories silent, its harbours empty, a prey to pauperism and decay'. It had been obliged to hand over its position as a leading naval power to Germany. This dire conclusion was solely the result of an attack that had caught the British completely by surprise. It was a surprise not only because of a sly military operation but also a lack of a triggering crisis. German success depended on there being no obvious reason to attack when it did. The war just happened because of an aggressive and opportunistic enemy. As a result Britain's position in the international hierarchy was altered forever.

The Battle of Dorking, and its subsequent imitators, described an inglorious defeat but not a bloody slaughter or a long-drawn out, agonising conflict. All could be won or lost in a short time. A nation caught by surprise would have no hope of recovery from the first setbacks; once defeated it could expect no mercy.[8] Losing such a war meant a loss of sovereignty, a way of life, and a pattern of trade. In this melodramatic view, international affairs would be forever reconfigured by the decision of battle. When Prime Minister Gladstone denounced Chesney's pamphlet as alarmist and a scheme to spend public money, he observed, 'Depend upon it that there is not this astounding disposition on the part of all mankind to make us the objects of hatred.'⁹

Chesney, who eventually became a Conservative MP, did not share the liberal optimism of the free-traders, such as Gladstone, who looked forward to economic interdependence promoting peace by providing formidable disincentives to war. Chesney's world, shared by many of the military establishment, was one in which all could be lost in a misjudged campaign. This was a view of war which combined urgency with complacency. Military defeat would equal political disaster, but the war itself would not be so bad. The lesson to be drawn from this and similar tracts was that great powers must stay alert and prepare properly for the coming tests, but not that the whole character of war was undergoing a change.

THIS WAS A CLASSICAL MODEL OF WAR, SHARED BY THE POLiticians, generals, admirals, and commentators of the time. It was classical in that it was based on a deeply embedded understanding of what war was about and how it should be fought. This view could be traced back to the Greeks and Romans. It was an ideal type in that it was understood that in practice every war might not correspond to the model, and in some cases the deviations would be severe; but it was still the best guide to preparing for war. It was also normative in that it would serve the interests of governments best if war could be fought in this way. If war could be kept short and contained then it could be retained as a serviceable instrument of policy while limiting its wider, disruptive social and political effects. Lastly, it was empirical in that Germany's success at Sedan confirmed the model, in a way that flattered its continuing validity and played down how it might be adapted in the light of the enormous changes then underway in science, industrial methods, forms of political participation, and the development of a mass media.

The wars of German unification—those with Denmark in 1864 and Austria in 1866 as well as France in 1870—led to the conviction that von Moltke's swift victories were the strategic precedents for the future. The German General Staff held to this conviction fiercely, and took exception to those who warned that future wars might not turn out so well, with victory coming only after a gruelling campaign of attrition rather than a swift battle in which the enemy would be annihilated. The belief framed thinking about future war elsewhere in Europe, not necessarily because that was how a war was bound to turn out but because the Germans had shown how it could be done and they might well do it again.

THE MOST POWERFUL THEORIES OF WAR OF THE TIME WERE those drawn from the Napoleonic Wars. The most influential theorist was Baron de Jomini who had served with Napoleon's army and was recognised as the keenest exponent of those principles of warfare exemplified by the Emperor. Following early writings which explored the campaigns of Frederick the Great and Napoleon, his *The Art of War*, first published in 1838, was the most widely accepted textbook for the armed forces of Europe, and a major influence in the United States. Napoleon himself claimed that Jomini had revealed his closest secrets.[10] During his lifetime he was much more celebrated than his contemporary, the Prussian Carl von Clausewitz, who is now considered to be the greater theorist. Jomini also outlasted Clausewitz by almost four decades, passing away aged 90 only a couple of years before Chesney published his pamphlet. In his book,[11] Jomini explored the dynamics of war apart from its political context. His advice was geared to explaining how generals needed to mass their forces against weaker enemy forces at some decisive point. Clausewitz, who remained more influential in Germany, had a keener sense of why plans went awry and the varied forms warfare might take, but his was still essentially a theory of battle and the circumstances in which it could be decisive. From Napoleon through Jomini, confirmed by Clausewitz and then demonstrated by von Moltke, the core assumption was that a great commander would eliminate the enemy army in battle, and in so doing deliver the enemy state up for whatever humiliation and punishment the victorious sovereign thought appropriate. In their classical form battles would begin at first light and be over by the end of the day, when the winner would be the side occupying the battlefield. For a truly decisive victory the defeated army side would be so depleted by casualties and men taken prisoner that it could no longer serve as an effective fighting force. That being so, the enemy state would have to accept terms. When the Austro-Hungarian Emperor Franz Joseph was defeated by France and Sardinia in the 1859 Battle of Solferino, he conceded: 'I have lost a battle, I pay with a province.'[12]

The assumption that wars could be settled by a well-constructed campaign, culminating in a decisive battle, was the received wisdom of the time. In 1851 Sir Edward Creasy published *The Fifteen Deci-*

sive *Battles of the World: From Marathon to Waterloo*, which in its title and its premise confirmed the view that some battles were not only masterpieces of the military art but also, in their effects, a source of significant impact on world history. Creasy noted 'the undeniable greatness in the disciplined courage, and the love of honour, which makes the combatants confront agony and destruction', and also the intellectual power and daring of the most effective commanders. Unfortunately, he observed, these qualities were 'to be found in the basest as well as in the noblest of mankind.' He quoted the poet Byron: ''Tis the Cause makes all, Degrades or hallows courage in its fall.'

What mattered to Creasy was whether battles were part of

the chain of causes and effects, by which they have helped to make us what we are; and also while we speculate on what we probably should have been, if any one of those battles had come to a different termination.[13]

Turning points in history had regularly been marked by battles. There was no reason to assume that this pattern would not continue into the future. Creasy's book set a challenge for those with their own favourite yet neglected battles to make a case for inclusion. There were regular updates which included the more recent 'decisive battles'. Thus when the book was republished in 1899, Gettysburg from the American Civil War and Sedan were added, along with contemporary encounters from the Spanish-American War.[14]

The appeal of battle lay in the thought that a climacteric encounter between two armies or navies, expending resources accumulated over decades, might, in a matter of hours, change history's course. Battles offered concentrated and acute drama as the fate of civilisations came to depend on the weaponry, bravery, and tactical acuity of a few—'we happy few, we band of brothers', as Shakespeare had Henry V say in his speech before Agincourt. But for battles to be 'decisive' depended on their influence upon a wider chain of events and not just who walked away alive and triumphant at the end of the day's fighting. The word 'decisive' had an air of finality, confirming that some large matter had now been concluded, but in other respects—unlike words such as 'victory' and 'defeat'—it was quite neutral. The decision could take the form of a negotiated settlement that left neither side satisfied. The essential feature was that they both accepted the result and that it reflected a situation largely achieved by military means.

There were specific battles upon which history appeared to have pivoted. Posit a different result from Napoleon's stunning victory over the Russians and Austrians at Austerlitz in 1805 and almost everything that happened thereafter looked different, or suppose Gettysburg had been lost and wonder whether the Union could have recovered. But a truly decisive battle was unusual. It was a rare war that turned on a single encounter. More often the difference made by individual battles could be understood only in the context of a wider war effort. Some of the most important battles were essentially defensive so that a war which might have been over quickly instead dragged on. Others had a cumulative impact, as one side's resources, reserves, and morale were steadily depleted because of successive defeats. Some gained their impact as they interacted with sieges (potentially as important as actual battle in shaping wars) or with irregular, guerrilla combat. Once all the other factors that determined military superiority were acknowledged, then battle became a means by which these factors could be demonstrated, a way of proving a capacity that was always there. In this respect some battles deserved a 'landmark' status not because of the nudge given to history but more as revelations of a wider cultural and material superiority.[15] By confirming this superiority a battle was a form of 'proof' of what might otherwise only have been suspected, now presented starkly and without nuance so all would appreciate the message.[16]

The moment could still be fleeting, and the next battle might prove something else, perhaps about the previous loser's capacity for finding allies or reviving its national morale. The key question was not the difference made by individual battles but whether wars could be concluded quickly. For those starting wars this was always the hope and in some cases the expectation. If the enemy proved to be resilient then over time non-military factors would become progressively more important. When a decisive battle was being considered before a war as a speculative possibility or a planning directive, what was in mind was the first, designed with ingenuity, planned with care, and fought by fresh and fearless soldiers eager to do their duty, but not the very last, fought by exhausted and scared soldiers, wondering if they could survive the final encounter. A first battle catching the enemy by surprise and inflicting a blow from which there could be no recovery could help avoid a long war. This was the 'allure of battle' that led to states gambling on aggression. Few states knowingly entered into an attritional long war, yet that was often what they got, and they suffered as a result.[17]

[2]

Indecisive Battle

In this final struggle for Britain's freedom the invader had been crushed and his power broken; for, thanks to our gallant citizen soldiers, the enemy that had for weeks overrun our smiling land like packs of hungry wolves, wantonly burning our homes and massacring the innocent and unprotected, had at length met with their well-merited deserts, and now lay spread over the miles of pastures, cornfields, and forests, stark, cold, and dead.

WILLIAM LE QUEUX,
The Invasion of 1910[1]

The influence of the classical model was evident not only in *The Battle of Dorking* but also in numerous books that followed, up to the start of the Great War in 1914. Although the literature adapted to shifts in international politics and developments in military technology and tactics, the essential framework remained largely the same. 'Save for rare exceptions', I. F. Clarke observed, these publications were 'distinguished by a complete failure to foresee the form a modern war would take.' They held to the possibility that any future European war would be marked by brief battles and heroic deeds. The application of science would work here, as in so many other areas of human affairs, to make matters better rather than worse. The conflict might be more ferocious, but the methods would also be

[11]

more efficient so that the dispute would be concluded, one way or the other, quickly. The character of this war fiction was a 'compound of complacency, ignorance, and innocence'. The possibility of war seemed real enough, yet there were few guides as to its likely character; this allowed either wishful thinking or crude alarmism full play.[2]

With the rapid expansion of the audience for newspapers and journals, war stories were good for circulation. In 1891 a new venture, a serious-minded journal called *Black and White*, hit upon the idea of a serial outlining the course of the next European war in a documentary fashion, with fictitious but plausible dispatches from the front, official telegrams, and newspapers' editorials, laced with exciting narrative and technical detail. When this was announced at the start of the next year the editor introduced the series by explaining:

> The air is full of rumours of war. The European nations stand fully armed and prepared for instant mobilisation. Authorities are agreed that a GREAT WAR must break out in the immediate future, and that this War will be fought under novel and surprising conditions.[3]

To help explain how this war might unfold the editors had consulted the 'chief living authorities in international politics, in strategy, and in war', led by Admiral Sir Philip Colomb, a former officer who had published widely on issues of sea power. His team used established military units and existing dispositions of fleets. In terms of prediction the most impressive aspect was that the war was triggered by an assassination attempt in the Balkans on Prince Ferdinand (unlike 1914 it was unsuccessful and the Prince was Bulgarian and not Austrian), which showed some understanding of the possibility of wars developing out of a clash between small states that drew in larger powers. In this case Britain was on the side of Germany against France and Russia. Other than that the war followed known strategies, and was decided by a series of battles on land and at sea, with great generals manoeuvring into position to land a heavy blow on the weakest point in the enemy line. In terms of new technologies, the authors appreciated the importance of the telegraph (including the ability to impose a news blackout by preventing its use) but were tentative about other developments, including the machine gun.[4]

In 1894 journalist William Le Queux wrote a book for the new *Daily Mail* newspaper about *The Great War in England in 1897*, starting with a French and Russian invasion.[5] The credibility of such a clash was underlined by the Fashoda Incident of 1898 when Britain and France almost came to blows as their imperial agendas clashed in North Africa. Six years later with the Entente Cordiale these two countries agreed to make up, and instead of being Britain's ally Germany now took centre stage as its most likely enemy. This prospect was reinforced by the developing naval arms race between the two. So when in March 1906 Le Queux revisited the topic for the *Daily Mail* with the serialisation of *The Invasion of 1910*, the Germans were now the enemy. There was the same combination of letters and reports to develop a dramatic story. It was a great success, with a million copies sold and translations into twenty-seven languages. The story was much more elaborate and sensational, with images of German troops marching through a battered London. The underlying strategy was one of a quick knockout blow, taking London and then assuming that a broken country would quickly agree terms. The scenario was always incredible, both in terms of the modest size of the invading force and the low casualties it faced, even when it got into trouble. One of the major editorial changes demanded by the *Daily Mail* was that the fighting take place near the larger cities where their readers were to be found rather than out of the way places. Maps were published showing where the German army was due to turn up the next day.

One message readers would take away was the importance of spies who had mischievously insinuated themselves throughout British society. Le Queux here and elsewhere was instrumental in encouraging the development of the Secret Service. Spies had also been present in his 1894 book, as had vivid descriptions of innocents being slaughtered as their cities were shelled.[6] In the earlier book civilians did come forward to help resist the enemy, but as volunteers, supporting regular forces. In the new book the invasion was largely defeated by resistance forces developed as the 'League of Defenders', who became more substantial and effective as the fighting moved up the country, and were somewhat more successful than their French counterparts of 1870. In this respect, Le Queux's approach was inspired by Field Marshal Lord Roberts's campaign to prepare for war with universal conscription and step up military training for the country's young men.[7]

THE 1906 BOOK CONTRIBUTED TO ANTI-GERMAN FEELING (xenophobia was a general consequence of much of the war fiction of this period across Europe), but it did not prepare its readers for what was to come. The core criticism of this body of literature has been that it failed to anticipate the stalemate and trench warfare of the Great War and the possibility that a war could go on so long in the face of such carnage.

Was this actually possible to anticipate? In the decades since the Napoleonic War the growing range and lethality of weapons combined with more efficient forms of transport and communication. Mass armies with new defensive capabilities supported by vast reserves of men and machinery steadily undermined the prospects for brilliant and irresistible offensive thrusts. Early versions of the machine gun made their appearance during the American Civil War. The deadly Maxim gun was first deployed by British forces over 1893–1894 in the First Matabele War in Rhodesia. Yet remarkably few of these or any comparable guns were purchased before 1914. It was only after their defensive value became apparent in the early months of the First World War that this situation changed.[8] Improvements in the range, accuracy, and ease of use of rifles and artillery had already extended the amount of ground an attacking force must pass and the dangers faced before they could engage with the enemy. This killing zone of concentrated fire in front of the defender's position was some 150 metres in the Napoleonic era. By the time of the Franco-Prussian War it was some 400 metres, and was as much as 1,500 metres by the mid-1890s. There were also tactics to get round this, including directed artillery fire to force the defenders to keep their heads down, and the use of terrain to reduce the open ground the attackers had to traverse. With larger armies and more in reserve, generals might have to expect greater losses in battles, but in principle offensives could still succeed.[9]

The military did not so much ignore new developments as struggle to comprehend their implications. As the battlefield became more deadly, and improving forms of transport got more men and materiel to the front, it was going to be harder to achieve an early result against an enemy of similar size and capabilities. But as the exact form a future war would take was becoming increasingly speculative, all that could be hoped was that it would be sufficiently familiar to be manageable so long as prudent preparations were set in motion and a sufficient offensive spirit was nurtured.

The weakness of the theory lay in the claim that whatever the material balances and the quality of the weaponry, battle came down to motivation and will power. It was a test of character, a readiness to press forward, even in the face of likely death, a surge of bravery and dash that would propel sufficient men across the field of fire to engage with the enemy and rip into them. Thus, the British Cavalry training manual of 1907 said: 'It must be accepted as a principle that the rifle, effective as it is, cannot replace the effect produced by the speed of the horse, the magnetism of the charge, and the terror of cold steel.'[10] If all else failed, mass would make the difference. The defence would be spread thinly: the offence would choose where to attack.

It was possible to imagine a different sort of war. In 1898 Polish banker Ivan Stanislavovich Bloch published a dense, six-volume study, entitled *The Future of War in Its Technical, Economic and Political Relations*. The last volume was published in English under the more provocative title *Is War Now Impossible?* Bloch's basic ideas were set out at the front of the book in the form of an interview with the radical journalist William Stead. He mounted the most formidable challenge to the view that offensives could succeed under modern conditions, that troops with high morale and élan could storm through whatever obstacles were put in their way. Instead Bloch insisted that the balance of advantage was shifting from the offence to the defence in land war. When troops moved into the open they would be cut down before they could engage with the enemy. The defence would dig in. 'The spade will be as indispensable to the soldier as his rifle'. The future war would, therefore, be 'a great war of entrenchments.'

Bloch's research was assiduous and few commentators found fault with his technical analysis. It was a prognosis built upon the armaments of the time, which made it harder for those who disliked his message to dismiss. The critiques were often to the implications of his logic. When he came to London to demonstrate how the Boer War of 1899–1901 had reinforced his views on the strength of the defence, he was accused not only of 'so-called non-jingoism, or non-militarism, the namby-pamby so-called humanitarianism' but also more seriously of a stress on 'ballistics' at the expense of the 'qualifications and idiosyncrasies of the personnel.'[11] To the traditionalists his sin was to deny that cavalry charges and bayonets would still have their place against intense firepower.

The implications of Bloch's pessimistic assessment were profound: 'instead of war fought out to the bitter end in a series of decisive battles, we shall have as a substitute a long period of continually increasing strain upon the resources of the combatants.' The 'future of war' did not so much involve 'fighting, but famine, not the slaying of men, but the bankruptcy of nations and the breakup of the whole social organization.'[12] Thus Bloch assumed a war brought to a conclusion not by battle but by economic and social collapse. A great war might begin but there would soon be demands to bring the conflict to a conclusion.

> For the vital interests of nations are all closely interwoven as they never were before, and, like people joining hands with him who receives an electric spark into his body, they all feel the shock. As soon as they perceive that the hardship is more than they can reasonably be expected to bear they will find ways and means of putting a speedy end to the war, whatever the belligerents may think and feel on the subject.[13]

Here Bloch was assuming that societies could not cope with the privations of war and absorb costs. Yet there was already the example of the American Civil War as one in which even in the face of military setbacks governments continued the fight in preference to accepting the dire consequences of defeat. He understood why a war might settle down into one of mutual attrition but not why both sides might continue fighting despite the pain. At each stage the incremental costs of carrying on would seem less than the costs of admitting defeat. Governments could bring in reserves and step up industrial production to sustain the war effort.

THE REAL RISK, THEREFORE, WAS NOT JUST OF UNNECESSARY pain before the impossibility of a decisive victory became apparent, but also of wars dragging on for some time. The longer a war dragged on the more factors beyond the military's control would become important, most importantly the relative economic and demographic strength of the belligerents, the degree of popular support that could be sustained in the face of continuing hardships and sacrifices, and the ability to split alliances or draw in extra allies. Then there was the question of irregular forces. It was one thing to prevail in battle and quite another to occupy enemy territory in the face of local hostility.

Although they may have had only a limited grasp of how battle might develop under modern conditions, writers of war fiction did recognise the importance of these considerations. The whole theme of Le Queux's fiction was that a successful military campaign could be challenged by a popular uprising, tying down an occupying force at every turn, adopting guerrilla warfare and even terrorist methods, despite facing harsh reprisals. Such books showed more acuity than formal military strategy in picking up on the importance of political and social changes in deciding the future of war as much as on new technologies. This did not mean that the fiction writers approved— far from it. They were often appalled by democratic trends that led governments to placate the masses with populist policies that risked eroding national will and defences.

For example, although Chesney was well aware of the Paris Commune, underway as he was writing, he drew no conclusions from it about the potential importance of irregular forms of warfare or civil strife. This 'foolish communism', which 'ruined the rich without benefiting the poor', had brought down the French. Such tendencies led leaders to pander to popular, short-term, selfish demands at the expense of the nation's defences. He lamented the passing from power of 'the class which had been used to rule, and to face political dangers', and which had brought the nation with honour unsullied through former struggles. It was now moving 'into the hands of the lower classes, uneducated, untrained to the use of political rights, and swayed by demagogues'.[14] Tory despair over liberal weakness grew over the following decades, reflected in the laments in Le Queux's 1906 book about the decline in fighting spirit. He also deplored the loss of a strong aristocratic government to one 'swayed by every breath of popular impulse.' It was the mark of the harm done to the country by the German invasion that the country succumbed to

> socialism, with its creed of "Thou shalt have no other god but Thyself," and its doctrine, "Let us eat and drink, for tomorrow we die," had replaced the religious beliefs of a generation of Englishmen taught to suffer and to die sooner than surrender to wrong.[15]

Another follower of Lord Roberts and his campaign to get the country's youth ready for the struggle to come was General Baden-Powell. When he began the Boy Scouts movement in 1908 it was to address the problem as he saw it of a deteriorating race that was ill-equipped to cope with the demands of war and the defence of the empire. His famous motto for the scouting movement was 'BE PREPARED'.

The preparation required was 'to die for your country . . . so that when the time comes you may charge home with confidence, not caring whether you are to be killed or not.'[16]

From the other end of the political spectrum this militarism, xenophobia, and alarmism looked like the real danger, encouraging a war fever among people who had no reason to feel hostile to each other. This was the line taken in successive conferences of the Second Socialist International until class unity gave way to patriotism in August 1914. For those who saw in war only misery and futility the rational course was to demonstrate this prospect and hope that good sense would prevail. This meant confronting popular belligerence and deploring tendencies towards aggressive, nationalistic 'Jingoism'.[17] The risk was that in the face of such attitudes it was unrealistic to expect measured and calm responses at times of crisis. Popular enthusiasm might fan the flames rather than dampen them down. War could be even more destructive as rational restraints were overcome.

THE NOVELIST AND ESSAYIST H. G. WELLS WAS THE MOST influential writer on future war of his time. Although a socialist, his vision owed as much to a gloomy view of humanity under stress as it did to his fascination with the potential of new types of weapons. As an advocate of world government, Wells sought consistently through his futuristic novels to demonstrate just how bad war could be, and how its abolition could only take place once this came to be appreciated. He saw fiction as 'the only medium through which we can discuss the majority of the problems which are being raised in such bristling multitude by our contemporary social development.'[18] In 1902 he also issued a manifesto, *Anticipation of the Reaction of Mechanical and Scientific Progress on Human Life and Thought.* This was the basis for his claim to be recognised as the first exponent of futurology. It included a chapter on 'War in the Twentieth Century'.

For Wells, the ability to embrace science represented the dividing line between the ancient and the modern, between those wedded to old practices and those embracing the most advanced methods—people he called 'the efficients'. In his 1902 essay he saw how this might be reflected in the practice of war. Instead of a 'dramatic little general spouting his troops into the proper hysterics for charging', the efficient would be represented 'far in the rear' by a 'central organizer' who would 'sit at the telephonic centre of his vast front.'[19] The war would be won with the seizure of the 'vital apparatus of the urban regions', such as water supply, electricity generating stations, and food distribution, despite the efforts of guerrilla bands to prevent the advance.

If we concentrate only on Wells's prescience we will miss the point of his military imagination. He can be credited with the invention of the tank, although the 'ironclads' he envisaged in 1903 were enormous at over 100 feet long and in their size and armament more like battleships (from which he took the name) than the sort of vehicles that could make a mark in a land battle. And while he saw the potential of aircraft at first he assumed that they would take far longer to develop than was in fact the case. Meanwhile he could not take the submarine at all seriously, as it was unlikely to do little more than 'suffocate its crew and founder at sea'. He was very excited by balloons which he thought would be everywhere on the first day of a new war. The new weapons of his imagination rarely suffered mechanical breakdowns or fell victim to obvious countermeasures.

More impressive was Wells's ability to appreciate the problems the new weapons might be trying to solve and those they would create. While the generals were arguing with Bloch's claim that trench warfare might be the natural response to the strength of the defence, he was thinking about the next steps if Bloch was right. While others produced more realistic models of how armoured tracked vehicles might be made to work, Wells's visions became much better known; his concept had sufficient credibility to encourage those searching in the early months of the Great War for ways to deal with the stalemate on the Western Front.[20]

For futurists the most exciting prospect was that of flying machines. Some of the possibilities had been indicated by the military use of balloons. The beleaguered citizens during the siege of Paris used balloons then to move people and post in and out of the city, bombard the Germans with propaganda messages although not much else, and attempt to get in supplies. In his 1887 novel, *The Clipper of the Clouds*, Jules Verne had backward-looking balloon enthusiasts confounded by Robur, a mysterious hero who had actually built a 'heavier than air' machine, that was as much helicopter as winged aircraft. At the novel's end Robur left the scene, taking with him the secret of his machine, observing that he was 'before his time' and that the divided nations were not ready for union. He would return when people were educated enough to profit from the invention and not abuse it.[21] In a dark sequel, published in 1904, Robur returned with a new machine, ominously called the *Terror*, which operated as a speedboat, submarine, automobile, or aircraft. The book's title, *Master of the World*, now indicated the inventor's intention. It would allow him, he proclaimed, to 'hold control of the entire world, and there lies no force within the reach of humanity which is able to resist me, under any circumstances whatsoever'. Yet before exercising control, he died with his machine, and its secrets, in a massive thunderstorm.[22]

1904 was the year of the Wright Brothers' first manned flight. Wells, who had already anticipated that aircraft would play a role in future war,[23] published in 1908 *The War in the Air*. In this story German airships terrorised American cities until surrender terms were accepted. Instead of New Yorkers being cowed into submission, however, they became angry and warlike, defying the Germans and so inviting their own destruction. This reflected Wells's view that war triggered intense, violent, and contagious emotions, so that once begun it was uncontrollable. 'Nation rose against nation and air-fleet grappled air-fleet, cities blazed and men died in multitudes.'[24] Thus air power was not a means to a decisive victory but instead a means by which war would be spread across previously impassable borders and into all areas of life. It posed a challenge precisely because it took war away from the classic battle, 'inextricably involving civilians and homes and all the apparatus of social life.' This he saw, apocalyptically, as leading to complete chaos and the breakdown of civilisation.

Wells was not the only writer to consider how a terrible new experience of war might encourage humankind to accept that war was now obsolete. The year before the publication of *The War in the Air*, the American writer Roy Norton published *The Vanishing Fleets*.[25] As Wells did a few years later (although more accurately), Norton picked up on the recent discovery of radiation. Norton saw this being used as an anti-gravity weapon. He had the president of the United States exclaim that access to the 'most deadly engine ever conceived' created a responsibility to use it 'as a means for controlling and thereby ending war for all time'. The same year, another book, with the title *The Man Who Ended War*[26], also drew on radioactivity, with a pacifist scientist, John King, working out how to turn it into a death ray that could paralyse seamen and melt battleships. King travelled the world in a submarine taking out individual warships from each of the great powers until they agreed to end war, at which point he destroyed himself and his invention.

Wells therefore was not alone in his fascination with deadly scientific breakthroughs that would enable the folly of war to be driven home in a great confrontation. But he had the greater literary capacity and broader social imagination.[27] He appreciated the two key features of air power. The first was the unequal fight between the airmen and their victims: 'men who were neither excited . . . not in any danger, poured death and destruction upon homes and crowds below'.[28] Second, he recognised that while air power allowed for new levels of destruction it was limited in what it could achieve militarily. As he observed in a new preface to *The War in the Air* in 1921:

[W]ith the flying machine war alters its character; it ceases to be an affair of "fronts" and becomes an affair of "areas"; neither side, victor or loser, remains immune from the gravest injuries, and while there is a vast increase in the destructiveness of war, there is also an increased indecisiveness.[29]

Because they could not hold territory, aircraft could not on their own 'win' wars, a point that we shall see was generally missed by the air power enthusiasts of the interwar years.

The world's problems, for Wells, were the result of nations refusing to accept the 'wider coalescence', the 'reasonable synthesis', of world government. They were so consumed with their national interests and so suspicious of each other that they could not embrace such wisdom. Instead they were behaving 'like ill-bred people in a crowded public car, to squeeze against one another, elbow, thrust, dispute and quarrel.' These habits of mind, according to Wells, produced an almost instinctive urge to violence and vengeance once the fragile constraints of civilisation and peace were broken. His argument, therefore, was that without socialism and world government, there would be compulsive destruction. Men and even whole nations were unable to help themselves. He first set out his credo in his 1901 *Anticipations*, looking forward to 'a Republic that must ultimately become a World State of capable rational men, developing amidst the fading contours and colours of our existing nations and institutions', and until the end of his life was making this case.[30]

His approach reflected assumptions, not uncommon of his time, about the possible development of a rational, scientific society that would displace capitalism and the system of nation states. The message was that future wars would be run through an educated and disciplined population. 'The law that dominates the future is glaringly plain. A people must develop and consolidate its educated efficient classes or be beaten in war and give way upon all points where its interests conflict with the interests of more capable people.' This thought was combined with some alarming social engineering. Advantage would go to the 'nation that most resolutely picks over, educates, sterilizes, exports, or poisons its People of the Abyss', and the one that dealt with gambling and the 'moral decay' of women, extinguished 'incompetent rich families', and turned 'the greatest proportion of its irresponsible adiposity into social muscle'. He had little confidence in the ability of the masses to make sensible decisions about peace and war. He assumed that social order would soon break down when they were subject to attack. In his novels the dominant impression is often less future inventions or the guidance of a highly competent elite and more the supposed immaturity of public opinion, prey to dangerous passions.

THE LIKELY RESPONSES OF THE WORKING CLASSES TO WAR, whether in or out of uniform, was a subject of both fascination and anxiety at this time. Wells was very familiar with Gustave Le Bon's *The Crowd: A Study of the Popular Mind*,[31] published in 1895, which encouraged the view that ordinary, rational people could lose their reason once they got caught up in the mass psychology of the crowd. This influenced views about what soldiers might be persuaded to do in battle as well as what might happen to civilians under fire. The uncertainty about the future of war was less about the hazards of modern battle but how well men could be motivated to meet them. In this respect the greatest vulnerability as far as the military class was concerned was degeneracy and moral decay. Ivan Bloch shared the assumption that modern man lacked the stomach for war, except that he welcomed this as antidote to militarism. He assumed that the stalemate of war would be broken not by a military breakthrough but by popular disgust at its misery and cost. Behind many of the developing theories of war at this time therefore were assumptions about how people in the mass would react to the experience.

This was not the concern of the generals as they advised governments across Europe. They did not assume that war would be easy but only that somebody's offensive would succeed, and if not their own it would be the enemy's. Hence the focus on the speed of mobil-isation to get into position while the enemy was disorganised and imbuing troops with a spirit of patriotism and self-sacrifice that would propel them forward. Massive loss of life was envisaged but stalemate was not. A German military magazine in 1908 insisted that the 1904 Russo-Japanese war had 'proved that even well-defended fortifications and entrenchments can be taken, even across open ground, by courage and cunning exploitation of terrain ... The con-cept of states waging war to the point of absolute exhaustion is be-yond the European cultural experience'.[32] A Russian military commentator dismissed Bloch's claim that 'the resolution of such questions by arms in the presence of modern, colossal, peoples' armies, technologically sophisticated materiel and social relationships is impossible'.[33] At the time of the Boer War the humourist Hector Munro (known as Saki) wrote a parody of *Alice in Wonderland*. At one point he has the Secretary for War, caricatured as the White Knight, telling Alice:

> "You see, I had read a book ... written by someone to prove that warfare under modern conditions was impossible. You may imag-ine how disturbing that was to a man of my profession..."
>
> Alice pondered. "You went to war, of course —"
>
> "Yes; but not under modern conditions."[34]

Munro died in action in 1916.

[3]

The House of Strife

A day will come when bullets and bomb-shells will be replaced by votes, by the universal suffrage of nations, by the venerable arbitration of a great Sovereign Senate.

VICTOR HUGO,
address to the Second International
Peace Congress, 1849[1]

Wells's assumption that only the full experience of a catastrophic war would propel humankind to peace was discouraging to those who believed that all war was self-evidently wretched and futile. Those who populated the peace movement in the second half of the nineteenth century did not believe that there was much new to learn. New types of weapons only made matters worse. Enough was known to get on with the business of outlawing war and finding better means to resolve disputes.

In 1816, Quakers organised the first formal peace society as the British Society for the Promotion of Permanent and Universal Peace. This movement spread rapidly in Europe and North America. There was always tension between the absolute pacifists, who believed that all differences could be transcended, and those who could not see how an enduring peace would be possible without social justice, which to be achieved might require some violence. Their mainstream agenda, however, focused on avoiding disputes by means of a congress of nations and international arbitration.[2] It also required a sustained act of political will, based on a moral appreciation that it was wicked to prepare to slaughter other human beings as acts of policy. Such a dramatic departure from past practice might have seemed too much to hope for, but this was a time of a belief in progress and the advance of civilisation. With the growth of trade, nations were becoming bound together by shared economic interests; so common sense without the necessity for complex negotiations and new treaties might suffice to render war obsolete.

Ivan Bloch added to the case for war's obsolescence by pointing to the probability that a future war would not see quick victories through dashing offensives. Yet he was unconvinced that in making the case against war it was good enough to describe its 'appalling consequences'. In addition it was necessary to turn back the 'obstinate fanatics of militarism from the road which they have mapped out for themselves.'[3] Militarism meant allowing military figures, arms manufacturers, and patriotic themes to dominate public life. Those who would benefit from war had a stake in its perpetuation—the politicians dazzled by the prospect of national grandeur, the generals by the prospect of glory, and the manufacturers by the prospect of profits. The arms dealers were considered to be particularly culpable, viewing every new type of weapon, from machine guns to torpedoes to heavy artillery, as a business opportunity, ready to create faux crises to generate a war fever and then sell to both sides.[4]

It was therefore not enough to rely on war becoming obsolescent on its own accord. Action had to be taken at the highest level to ensure that this was so. In 1899, encouraged by Bloch, Tsar Nicholas II of Russia decided to convene an international peace conference to address the issue. Russia's Foreign Minister wrote to his counterparts to urge them to attend this conference. He referred to the 'grave problems' caused by the unproductive effort currently being put into armaments. As 'terrible engines of destruction' were acquired their value was neutralised by the similar efforts others were making to acquire their own, and then lost altogether as new scientific discoveries left them obsolescent.

That May delegates from twenty-six countries met in a royal chateau just outside The Hague. There they were joined not only by Bloch but also by representatives of the various peace societies that would now be described as non-governmental organisations claiming to speak for civil society. Although the initiative came from a surprising quarter, the peace movement hailed the gathering. Bertha von Suttner of the Austrian Peace Society, whose hotel flew a white flag in her honour while she attended the conference, confided to her diary that 'from this time on [our] movement is incalculably nearer its goal; new ways are opening up before it'. The British Peace society thanked 'Almighty God' for recognition that its ideals were 'practicable' and that 'such a proposal be made to carry them into effect by one of the great potentates of the world'. Leo Tolstoy, an ardent pacifist but also a foe of the Tsar, was less impressed by such a 'childish, silly and hypocritical project of universal peace' at a time when spending on the army was being increased.[5]

Similar scepticism, if not for the same reason, was expressed by the leader of the American delegation, Andrew White. He complained of being inundated with 'queer letters and crankish proposals', and an enormous number of people with 'plans, schemes, notions, nostrums, whimsies of all sorts who press upon us and try to take our time', which was combined with 'the pest of interviewers and photographers'. While surrounded by all this enthusiasm for peace he observed of the delegates that no such group had met 'in a spirit of more hopeless scepticism as to any good result'.[6] Delegations had turned up more because it would have been impolite not to than because they took the Tsar's views seriously.

This contrast between the enthusiasm for peace as a principle and a project on the one hand and the harsh realities of international politics limited what the first Hague Conference could achieve. It was not judged a success. To encourage states to seek arbitration instead of war to resolve disputes, the participating states agreed to establish a Court of Arbitration at The Hague (which still exists). It had some success, but there were no enforcement mechanisms, an issue which confused pacifists because enforcement implied force.[7] Nor were substantial restraints agreed on military expenditures or new armaments, another issue which troubled pacifists as it required distinguishing good from bad weapons. Only in the third area, agreeing a code for the conduct of war, was there progress. The first Hague Peace Conference of 1899 was followed by the second in 1907. This had been scheduled for 1904 but then delayed because of Russia's war with Japan. A Peace Palace was built for the third, scheduled for 1915, but owing to the First World War it unsurprisingly did not take place. The net effect of this considerable effort had been to confirm war's role in international affairs while doing little to mitigate its effects.

Joseph Conrad, a novelist with a sharp eye for the political currents of his day, provided a thunderous critique. In an essay written in 1905, as Russia was losing its war with Japan, he expressed his pessimism about the future. The moral infancy of mankind was contrasted with the pressing material interests that drove the great powers to become rivals and grind against each other. The European peace was no more than 'temporary', dependent upon alliances based on mutual distrust and preparations for war. Only the 'fear of wounds' acted as a restraint. Even though the 'speeches of Emperors, Kings, Presidents, and Ministers' were 'monotonous with ardent protestations of fidelity to peace,' in practice war had never before 'received so much homage at the lips of men, and reigned with less disputed sway in their minds.' Nor had 'the right of war been more fully admitted in the rounded periods of public speeches, in books, in public prints, in all the public works of peace'. Because this was the right of a sovereign state and must be protected, the humanitarian effort that might have been directed against the very institution of war had instead concentrated on limiting its effects. This process of codifying the laws of war had served, Conrad noted in a telling phrase, to acknowledge 'the Earth as a House of Strife'. Conrad recorded the 'alarming comicality' and 'touching ingenuity' with which this mitigation sought 'to steal one by one the thunderbolts of their Jupiter', transforming war from a scourge into 'a calm and regulated institution'. 'At first sight', he added, 'the change does not seem for the better. Jove's thunderbolt looks a most dangerous plaything in the hands of the people.'[8]

THE LOGIC OF THE HAGUE CONFERENCES, AS CONRAD RECOGNISED, was not to outlaw war but to make it more palatable by smoothing down its rougher edges. This was a time, as one historian notes, when war had reached its 'pinnacle of legal prestige'. There was

> an impressively detailed edifice of legal rules dealing with the entire phenomenon of war from the opening of hostilities to the signing of the peace, plus all stages in between—including conduct on the battlefield, the occupation of enemy territory, relations with neutral powers, treatment of prisoners and spies, medical treatment for the wounded and much else.[9]

So long as the rules were followed then acts rightly considered criminal in all other circumstances became legal and were even celebrated.

As the international system assumed the autonomy and sovereignty of states, there was no higher authority to adjudicate on whether a particular war was unjust or improper. Since the 1648 'Peace of Westphalia', which concluded the deadly Thirty Years War, it was understood that the best way to avoid war was for states to mind their own business. The interests of states would be interpreted by whoever happened to be in charge at any particular time, on the dictum *'cuius regio eius religio'* ('whose realm, his religion'). These interests, however, also had meaning and durability well beyond the personalities and whims of particular rulers. States acquired their own legal personalities, distinct from the person of their ruler. Thereafter strategic imperatives were more likely to be followed than moral advice, and alterations in the configuration of power mattered more than legal guidance. Because no hierarchy or precedence could be agreed then all states enjoyed in principle a similar status, even if their actual power varied enormously. The rationales for war were still left entirely to the discretion of sovereigns.

The justification for war could be opportunistic, a sense that a natural enemy was weak, a reaction to a perceived slight, or in honour of alliance obligations. All that was required, once a decision was made, was to notify the chosen enemy in a declaration. Once made, a 'state of war' was in place. At this point governments and their armed forces could engage in practices that would have been illegal, piratical, and objectionable moments earlier but were now noble and praiseworthy. A declaration might be coupled with an ultimatum, to offer the adversary a chance to agree to a last-minute deal to avert hostilities. Alternatively it might be almost coincidental with the first military action, to avoid giving the new enemy time to prepare defences. The requirement for a formal declaration was captured in Article 1 of the Hague Conventions of 1907, which stated that hostilities should 'not commence without previous and explicit warning, in the form either of a reasoned declaration of war or of an ultimatum with conditional declaration of war.'

Though the laws of war did not seek to make war illegal they did try instead to make it less miserable. Thus the 1868 Declaration of St Petersburg, an earlier initiative of the Tsar, produced a solemn declaration to eschew 'the employment by their military or naval troops of any projectile of a weight below 400 grams, which is either explosive or charged with fulminating or inflammable substances.' The preamble carried the following sentiments, conveying the underpinning philosophy demonstrating how what was in practice a somewhat futile measure was supposed to help contain war:

> That the progress of civilization should have the effect of alleviating as much as possible the calamities of war;
>
> That the only legitimate object which States should endeavour to accomplish during war is to weaken the military forces of the enemy;
>
> That for this purpose it is sufficient to disable the greatest possible number of men;
>
> That this object would be exceeded by the employment of arms which uselessly aggravate the sufferings of disabled men, or render their death inevitable;
>
> That the employment of such arms would, therefore, be contrary to the laws of humanity...

The contracting parties wished to set 'the technical limits at which the necessities of war ought to yield to the requirements of humanity.'[10]

The impetus for this lay in reports of the misery of combatants post-battle. In 1859 Swiss businessman Henry Dunant came across the aftermath of the Austro-French Battle of Solferino, in which some 40,000 men had been killed or wounded. Appalled at its 'chaotic disorder, despair unspeakable, and misery of every kind',[11] he urged that every effort should be made to bring relief to those suffering as a result of war, whether from the winning or losing side. This led to the formation in 1863 of the International Committee of the Red Cross as a permanent relief agency and the adoption of the first Geneva Convention 'for the Amelioration of the Condition of the Wounded and Sick in Armed Forces in the Field'. The next year the first Geneva Convention for 'Bettering the Condition of Wounded Soldiers' accepted this as a status that transformed combatants into suffering human beings. It required respect for the neutrality of those trying to help. This would now be recognised by the symbol of the Red Cross on a white ground.

These rules on the conduct of war should be applied even-handedly. The quality of the cause would be no excuse for ignoring the rules. Essentially, 'war would be fought with more than a trace of the sporting ethos—on the basis of strictly even-handed rules agreed by both sides prior to the conflict, with low practices such as deception kept to a minimum'.[12] This was a legacy of the practice of limited war. A limited war was an unfortunate but occasionally unavoidable mechanism for dispute resolution, undertaken between parties who would expect to have a degree of diplomatic intercourse once the unpleasantness was closed off by a treaty of some sort. A yearning for a return to this model was evident in Article 22 of the 1899 Convention: 'The right of belligerents to adopt means of injuring the enemy is not unlimited.'[13] There were conventions to minimise the suffering caused by war, and to ensure the appropriate treatment of prisoners and the wounded. These were legacies of the old chivalric code, matters of honour and mutual respect, and worth keeping in mind in a system in which today's enemy might be tomorrow's ally. Yet they did little to alleviate the worst effects of war, and this was why there had been pressure to develop new rules that would provide a degree of protection for those who were effectively *hors de combat*, no longer able to fight.

A systematic code for the conduct of war was developed for the Union Army at a critical stage in the American Civil War. The author was Francis Lieber, a professor of law at Columbia University. The occasion was President Lincoln's Emancipation Proclamation of 1 January 1863, which proclaimed the freedom of slaves in ten rebel states. Against the Confederacy's insistence that blacks serving for the Union side deserved to be shot as traitors, Lieber asserted that they were entitled to the same protections as any combatants. A belligerent must 'declare that enemies of a certain class, color, or condition, when properly organized as soldiers, will not be treated by him as public enemies.' This now seems obvious, yet it also went to the heart of the war's core issue; it meant that slaves could no longer be treated as private property.

Lieber had an unsentimental view of war.[14] Within its domain, it should be acknowledged as an unavoidably ferocious business. Beyond its domain, civilisation should be preserved. The question was where to draw the line, and here he was flexible. If victory was at risk, civilised values had to be put aside. His key concept for drawing the line was military necessity. What constituted military necessity, however, was hardly an objective test and, in the end, would depend on a military commander's judgement. The Emancipation Proclamation itself could be an example of military necessity as it was not just about why the war was being fought but also about how it might be won by galvanising a faltering war effort.

Lieber defined military necessity as 'those measures which are indispensable for securing the ends of the war, and which are lawful according to the modern law and usages of war.' It allowed for the 'direct destruction of life or limb of armed enemies' but also 'other persons whose destruction is incidentally unavoidable in the armed contests of the war'. Also permitted was the 'destruction of property, and obstruction of the ways and channels of traffic, travel, or communication, and of all withholding of sustenance or means of life from the enemy'.[15]

Indispensability should take the priority. So, for example, while prisoners of war should not be executed, Lieber allowed for an exception in extreme circumstances where there might be no other choice if an operation was to succeed. If the cause was just, humanitarian restraints should not be allowed to prevent victory. Lieber did not claim to have identified any absolute standards of conduct and could be quite tolerant of harsh practices.[16] Humanity was best served, in the end, if a war was short, 'and the way to ensure short wars was to fight them as fiercely as possible. The prospect of fierce wars might even prevent war from breaking out in the first place.' When the Geneva Convention was revived and expanded in 1906 the issue of military necessity was to the fore. The phrase 'so far as military exigencies permit' made regular appearances. The President of the Conference observed the principle: 'No rules whatever can absolutely bind generals; what binds them are the directions they have been given'.[17] This pointed to the flaw in the efforts to control the future of war through international legislation. Whatever the consensus on best practice and appropriate restraint the conduct of wars would be shaped by the strategic imperatives that set them in motion and what appeared to be militarily necessary at any time. Moreover, any restraints would now be tested in circumstances in which the stakes were higher than before and popular passions more engaged.

[4]

Victory Through Cruelty

Future years will never know the seething hell and the black infernal background of countless minor scenes and interiors, (not the official surface-courteousness of the Generals, not the few great battles) of the Secession war; and it is best they should not—the real war will never get in the books.

WALT WHITMAN,
'The Million Dead, Too, Summ'd Up', 1881[1]

The concept of the civilian as a distinct category from the military can be traced back to the start of the nineteenth century, but it was not in general use until its end. It was too broad to be of much value in making sense of war. Whole populations might be affected if a war was won or lost, but ordinary people were not supposed to be relevant to its actual conduct. It was true that they occasionally got in the way, even in wars between professional, regular armies. They might be unfortunate enough to be in the path of marauding armies, and see their land plundered and their homes requisitioned. Even worse they could be caught in a city under siege, subject to privations and bombardments, or in a country under naval blockade.

Little attention was paid to this in the laws of war. The key distinction was between those involved in combat and those who were not. The distinction followed naturally from the ideal of war as a specialist activity for military professionals, acting as champions for their respective states. The laws were largely about protecting those who might have been combatants but were now no longer in a position to be so, either because of their wounds or imprisonment. They had little to say to those with no role in fighting. The interest was in where and how the line between combatancy and non-combatancy might be blurred, and what sort of protections might be expected either side of this line. Lieber spoke of the citizen of a hostile country as an 'enemy' to be subjected to the 'hardships of war', yet if 'unarmed' to be 'spared person, property, and honor as much as the exigencies of war will admit'.[2]

The effort to contain war through international agreements depended on shared values. These values, however, were under strain as the inspirations for war became more ideological and nationalist. Greater democracy meant that popular feelings were becoming increasingly influential. Civilians were not really passive bystanders, observing the results of decisions taken by their governments. If they could urge a war could they then expect to be protected from its consequences? If their country faced defeat and they took up arms to resist foreign occupation, had they become part of the military sphere? This question of partisan warfare proved to be especially intractable, as irregular fighters looked to the civilian population for sanctuary and sustenance. The most famous example was the guerrillas of Spain who fought against Napoleon, but there was also the example of Mexicans who continued to fight after the defeat of their armies by the Americans in the war of 1846–8.

Before his code, Lieber had written a treatise on guerrilla warfare which expressed the common disdain among professionals for irregulars, who were assumed to be no better than mobs. The distinction between regular and irregular forces referred to whether or not they were subject to the laws of war. These required keeping up the appearance of military professionalism: wearing uniforms (some men had operated in full uniform behind enemy lines during the Civil War), having a command structure, and being able to cope with prisoners of war. He stressed that those who took up arms 'do not cease on this account to be moral beings, responsible to one another and to God' and his code proscribed pillage, rape, and murder of unarmed inhabitants, but 'military necessity' still trumped all, and provided a reason why people might be starved or moved from their homes.

THE HYPOTHETICAL WARS FOR WHICH PLANS WERE MADE AND codes of conduct developed were those between great powers, the ones that would involve huge armies with the most modern weapons engaging in climacteric battles for the highest political stakes. The wars in which a number of these great powers were actually engaged over the second half of the nineteenth century and into the twentieth were quite different. These were wars of conquest against people without the military technology and organisation enjoyed by the Europeans who found their lands occupied, their people subjugated, and their resources exploited. From 1837 to 1901 Britain fought more than 400 battles in some sixty colonial campaigns.[3] Sometimes the indigenous people managed to accommodate and adjust; sometimes they resisted and were suppressed. The Hague Treaties were not extended to colonial conflicts: at both the 1899 and 1907 conferences, all imperial issues were deliberately excluded.[4]

These wars were of a separate type, described as 'small wars', with their own logic and character, often exasperating but never requiring the same amount of effort and resource as a conflict with another great power. The term was popularised by Charles Callwell of the British Army, drawing on extensive colonial experience, first in an essay and then in an 1886 book.[5] Occasionally the colonial forces were embarrassed in an ambush, but in a straight fight their material superiority and, it was assumed, superior culture and intelligence would always win through. 'The way to deal with Asiatics', observed Callwell, is 'to go for them and cow them by sheer force of will.'[6]

In practice the development of military technology from steam ships, which aided supply, to machine guns, which meant firepower that was both superior and portable, made a considerable difference, although this can be exaggerated. Machine guns were not plentiful. Most colonial armies depended on rifles. The view at the time was that the real problem with small wars lay not with the opponents but the need to fight them in such inhospitable places creating problems of supply and movement, and vulnerabilities to disease. This is why Callwell described them as 'wars against nature', and why medical progress, including disease control, had often more impact than new military technologies. Over time as the colonialists became more embedded, they drew on the most supportive elements of the local population to help them deal with the more unruly.

Those who contemplated the future of war considered these small wars to be of little interest. Bloch dismissed the evidence of such campaigns. He expressed no interest in 'frontier incidents or punitive brawls', or 'such trumpery expeditions against semi-barbarous peoples'.[7] If they were relevant it was as a potential cause of a big war. In an argument later picked up by Lenin, the British liberal theorist John Hobson warned of the combination of unscrupulous arms manufacturers and colonialism. Reflecting on the Boer War, he argued in 1902 that capitalism could not be satisfied by domestic markets and so required the acquisition of new territories to plunder for their resources and as new sources of trade.[8] Colonialism was thus seen as a potential source of a great-power war but not really a guide to its conduct.

The experience of colonisation was often extremely violent. At times there were battles as local leaders sought to resist conquest by Europeans, but as often resistance was low level, spasmodic, and not very effective. A study of Queensland, Australia over the nineteenth century concluded that over 65,000 Aboriginal Australians were killed from the 1820s until the early 1900s as a result of mass killings that were 'profligate, furtive and unprosecuted'.[9] In Tasmania, the native community fought a vicious war with settlers (the 'Black War') in the late 1820s. This, coupled with a lack of immunity to diseases brought in by the settlers, led to them being virtually wiped out.

The case of the Tasmanians led Wells to one of his greatest novels. In his 1897 masterpiece *War of the Worlds*, he invited his readers to imagine what it would be like if an alien power came to conquer as it had conquered others. In his story those on Earth had no answer to the superior power of the aliens. This was one step ahead of the invasion literature with which it is naturally compared because of the complete helplessness of the population in the face of the methods used, which included a 'black smoke', a form of poison gas. People had no choice but to flee from the devastating methods. In the end the Martians were brought down not by human resistance but by microscopic bacteria against which they had no immunity. Yet while Wells could show sympathy with the fate of colonised people, and often expressed anti-racist sentiments, a passage in *The War in the Air* from 1908 suggests that what was truly shocking about future war was that so-called civilised people might suffer the same fate as the colonised. He described the bombing of New York's Broadway: 'Below, they left ruins and blazing conflagrations and heaped and scattered dead; men, women and children mixed together as though they had been no more than Moors, or Zulus, or Chinese.'[10]

Colonialism established the idea of whole populations as legiti-mate targets. Such practices as massacring local people, destroying villages, eradicating crops, and slaughtering domesticated animals arose for largely strategic reasons—as the best available means West-ern armies had 'to defeat elusive, highly mobile peoples who were adept practitioners of guerrilla war'.[11] If that was the case when deal-ing with 'semi-barbarous peoples' then the same strategic logic would suggest that similar methods might work when used against suppos-edly more 'civilised' people.

This was demonstrated during the American Civil War. In the spring of 1864 the Confederacy was moving closer to defeat. It was pushing old men and young boys into its army. The Union's armies were beginning to move with freedom into its territory. As they did so they adopted a strategy that showed little regard for non-combat-ants. They had to live off the land which provided a rationale for plundering what they could. Among the troops, hostility towards the rebels ran deep, fortified by stories of maltreatment of slaves or the murder of soldiers when taken prisoners. The people of the Southern states were blamed for attempting secession and doing their best to sustain the war effort. Add to this mix General Sherman, who as a young officer had fought the Seminole Indians by avoiding their fighters and instead attacking crops and food supplies. He was con-vinced that measures directed against civilian life and property might compel the rebels to abandon the war at last. The scene was set for a punitive campaign.

The opportunity came when Sherman realised that the Confeder-ates had left Georgia undefended. The intent was not to massacre the inhabitants but for them to see their wealth destroyed as they were pushed back to a subsistence economy. Sherman wanted the Confed-eracy to 'fear and dread' the Union's forces. His explanation showed the shift in focus from a war against armies, which he saw as the common type of European war, to one against people: 'we are not only fighting hostile armies, but a hostile people, and must make old and young, rich and poor, feel the hard hand of war, as well as their organized armies.'[12] The destruction of Atlanta, the commercial centre of Georgia, was explained in terms of its role in the war: 'We have been fighting *Atlanta* all the time in the past: have been capturing guns, wagons, etc., etc., marked "*Atlanta*" and made here, all the time: and now since they have been doing so much to destroy us and our government, we have to destroy them, at least enough to prevent any more of that'. On the burning of Columbia, South Carolina, he observed that though he had neither wished nor ordered it, 'I have never shed many tears over the event, because I believe that it hastened what we all fought for, the end of the war.'[13] When all was done he told the people of Atlanta: 'War is cruelty and you cannot refine it. . . . You might as well appeal against the thunderstorm as these terrible hardships of war.' As he ordered their evacuation he urged them to look after their 'old and feeble' and wait until 'the mad passions of men cool down'.[14]

The important point about Sherman's strategy is that it worked. Taking Atlanta raised morale in the North and helped secure President Lincoln's re-election in 1864. The devastation caused by his troops moved the Confederacy, as its military position became increasingly hopeless, from defiance to surrender. This success influenced German strategy. We have already noted the frustration with French resistance after the 1870 defeat at Sedan. Initially von Moltke was complacent about this resistance, because he did not see it lasting, but the potential of 'People's War' began to make a deep impression on him. Chancellor Bismarck was frustrated from early on because of his anxieties over the French getting help from other countries unless the war was concluded swiftly. He took advice from an American general, Philip Sheridan, then in Berlin, who drew on the Civil War's merciless conclusion. Sheridan urged the need to cause the people 'so much suffering that they must long for peace, and force their governments to demand it. The people must be left nothing but their eyes to weep with over the war'. Bismarck was impressed and ordered villages to be raised and male inhabitants hung in areas where there had been guerrilla activity. There must be no 'laziness in killing'.[15] While von Moltke wanted to mount a traditional siege of Paris, waiting until exhaustion overtook the city, Bismarck did not want to wait and preferred bombardment. He got his way. His aim was coercion—to force the French into concessions. He then allowed the French government to hold Paris (in doing so they showed little mercy to the Commune) so long as they acceded to other German demands. He was prepared to act ruthlessly where necessary against civilians but then limit his demands on the French for the sake of political order. Von Moltke, by contrast, saw this pattern of warfare recurring, with France always likely to lend it encouragement, so wished to wage what would in effect have been total war against the French population to prevent them ever rising again.[16]

One German officer who had participated in this war, Colmar von der Goltz, saw in this the direction of future war as a 'life and death struggle' between whole nations, with the war ending with the subjugation of one by the other.[17] He followed Clausewitz explicitly, except that he now saw the 'absolute' not as an ideal to which war might tend but a new practical reality. A collision of interests might trigger a war, but it would be the 'passions of nations' that would be decisive. Goltz expressed his desire to shift strategy away from the excessive attention that had been given to the idea of 'generalship in battle' to future wars that would be decided only through the 'exhaustion of belligerent nations'. Even once defeated, the population might be so 'obstinate' that there could be a need to 'exert extreme pressure' upon them for a number of years.

It was away from Europe, in colonial wars, that this ruthless approach was most evident. Any restraints on inflicting suffering on whole populations if they refused to accept defeat were intentionally disregarded. During the Second Philippines War (1899–1902), as the Philippines Republic struggled to win independence from the United States, rebel support was undermined using internment camps, which led to large numbers of civilians dying in insanitary conditions. The United States lost some 4,000 troops and killed some 20,000 insurrectionists, but the war had a generally devastating effect on the local population as a whole, with some 200,000 dying largely because of the spread of disease.[18] At the same time the British were fighting the Second Boer War as the Afrikaner (Boer) South African Republic and the Orange Free State resisted incorporation into the British Empire. The British commander-in-chief, Herbert Kitchener, described his tactics as being to:

> flush out guerrillas in a series of systematic drives, organised like a sporting shoot, with success defined in a weekly "bag" of killed, captured and wounded, and to sweep the country bare of everything that could give sustenance to the guerrillas, including women and children … It was the clearance of civilians—uprooting a whole nation—that would come to dominate the last phase of the war.[19]

Some 28,000 women and children died in the British concentration camps, not because of a deliberate policy of extermination but because cramped conditions and poor sanitation, along with inadequate supplies of food and medicines, meant that malnutrition and disease were rife. They were not helped by primitive medical practices. The concept of military necessity was extended to genocide when German troops were sent to suppress the Herero Revolt in south-west Africa from 1904 to 1907, under orders to execute those captured and wounded, whether fighters or women and children, to the point where as many as three quarters of the population may have been killed.[20]

The enormous brutality shown in colonial territories was disconnected from the common view that any war fought among the European powers could be contained. In the event it was the practices developed in colonial wars that shaped the conduct of European war, just as Sherman's experience in dealing with the Seminole influenced his approach to the Confederacy. This tolerance of extreme violence in pursuit of the total annihilation of the enemy was taken through to the First World War.

The key principle was that if putting pressure on the population could get a war over quickly then that could be justified as military necessity. Von Moltke expressed this view succinctly in a letter of 1880:

> The greatest good deed in war is the speedy ending of the war, and every means to that end, so long as it is not *reprehensible*, must remain open. In no way can I declare myself in agreement with the Declaration of St. Petersburg that the sole justifiable measure in war is "the weakening of the enemy's military power." No, all the sources of support for the hostile government must be considered, its finances, railroads, foodstuffs, even its prestige.[21]

The safety and welfare of the army was the priority. At the second Hague Conference a German general observed, without irony, that 'soldiers also are men, and have a right to be treated with humanity.' When, exhausted by 'a long march or a battle', they 'come to rest in a village [they] have a right to be sure that the peaceful inhabitants shall not change suddenly into furious enemies.'[22] Smaller countries that could imagine needing to fight partisan wars objected. The compromise was that so long as civilians volunteered to serve in units that were essentially organised as if they were regular then their status could be recognised. A further dispensation was made to those who were defending their actual homes.[23]

The implications of this trend in thinking were not fully recognised. The idea of war as a sporting contest with rules to ensure fair play had yet to be banished. Ordinary people might be caught up in war, through no fault of their own, and suffer greatly, but the idea that they might be targeted as a deliberate strategy was widely considered repugnant, at least when it came to war between supposedly civilised countries. When Arthur Conan Doyle, known best for the Sherlock Holmes stories, published a story just before the start of the 1914 war in which eight German submarines sank merchant ships to starve Britain into submission, it was dismissed by admirals not so much because of any technical deficiencies but because they were unable to accept a form of warfare based on bringing down civilian ships: 'I do not think myself that any civilised nation will torpedo unarmed and defenceless merchant ships.'[24] Somehow, warfare was to be kept separate from wider social forces, though this begged the question of what civilised nations were doing fighting each other in the first place.

As the First World War began, the Germans remained anxious that every male capable of fighting might decide to do so. From the moment Belgium was invaded in August 1914 German forces were rounding up and executing civilians, as if they were certain to meet civilian resistance. These were pre-emptive reprisals against those not entitled to fight who might be tempted to do so. The fear of being sniped at by franc-tireurs, left hanging over from 1871, led to men of military age being executed for actions they had not taken. As some 5,500 were killed, and homes burnt, large sections of the Belgian population fled.[25]

THE COURSE OF THE WAR CONFOUNDED EXPECTATIONS. IT should have been evident that a war between two coalitions 'approaching equilibrium . . . would be long and evenly matched.'[26] The German war plan sought to escape the logic of this equilibrium by catching out French forces with a quick offensive. It honoured the spirit of 1870, relying on the speed of mobilisation to create an early winning position, but could not match the achievement. The main effect of the rush to mobilise was to impose urgency on the civilian leadership, leaving little time for any strategic discussion about whether the plans would work as advertised and the consequences if they did not, whether diplomacy might be given more time, and how well they related to political objectives. If the politicians had pushed harder they might have become more aware of the misgivings in the

military ranks. The German general staff knew that they were engaged in a gamble as they launched their massive offensive to take
out France, but they feared that the longer they waited the more of a
gamble it would become. In the event the gamble, with its violation
of Belgian neutrality, was sufficient to bring Britain into the war but
not enough to take France out. The demands the plan placed on German troops and their logistical support turned to be excessive.
Whether or not they really expected it to be over by Christmas, none
of the belligerents had prepared for a war that would be fought with
such intensity for so long. Within months they had almost run out of
munitions. The lengthening casualty lists were also far more severe
than anticipated. Instead of a decisive battle, the Western Front settled down to trench warfare. Attempted breakthroughs through artillery barrages followed by infantry dashes across 'no-man's land'
became synonymous with futile slaughter.

The consequence of a frustrating stalemate was a build-up of social and political pressures, which over time led to mutinies, revolutions, and civil wars. There were unpleasant innovations, such as
poisoned gas, bombing from the air and attacks on merchant shipping. These all made their appearance in the spring of 1915 as a result of German frustration with the impasse and a sense that their
enemies were better able to cope with a long war.[27] The limits of the
'cult of the offensive', which was more of a rhetorical than practical
feature of pre-war military plans, had become apparent.[28] The naval
blockade helped sap German strength and resources. Its attempt to
gain some initiative at sea through unrestricted submarine warfare
provided another example of bold military moves having larger political consequences, as this was the issue that brought the United
States into the war. Yet the classical model of war remained intact.
The war concluded with two large offensives, the first by the Germans in the spring of 1918 which left them exhausted and the second
that autumn by the Allies which was successful and led to a formal
German surrender. In addition, possibilities for new forms of warfare
had been opened up, notably involving tanks and aircraft. These kept
alive hopes for future wars ending quickly with knockout blows.

[5]

Failures of Peace

The passionate desire to prevent war determined the whole initial course and direction of the study. Like other infant sciences, the science of international politics has been markedly and frankly utopian.

E. H. CARR,
The Twenty Years Crisis, 1939[1]

In a book first published privately in 1909 as *Europe's Optical Illusion* and then the next year across the world as *The Great Illusion*, Norman Angell, Paris editor of the *Daily Mail*, sought to demolish the idea that war made any sense at all. He noted the widespread assumption that 'a nation's relative prosperity is broadly determined by its political power; that nations being competing units, advantage in the last resort goes to the possessor of preponderant military force, the weaker goes to the wall, as in the other forms of the struggle for life.' He then went to challenge 'this whole doctrine', arguing that:

> [war] belongs to a stage of development out of which we have passed; that the commerce and industry of a people no longer depend upon the expansion of its political frontiers; that a nation's political and economic frontiers do not now necessarily coincide; that military power is socially and economically futile, and can have no relation to the prosperity of the people exercising it; that it is impossible for one nation to seize by force the wealth or trade of another—to enrich itself by subjugating, or imposing its

will by force on another; that in short, war, even when victorious, can no longer achieve those aims for which people strive...

He insisted later that the illusion in the title referred to the idea that war could be beneficial, not that it could occur at all. Economic interdependence made such a war unwise but not impossible.[2] Nonetheless the pre-war popularity of the book and its confident message meant that Angell was thereafter doomed to be cited as an example of a false prophet, one who assumed that economic rationality could triumph in the face of narrow concepts of national interest and the harsh logic of geopolitics.[3] He could claim vindication in that the economic consequences of the war were indeed dire, and possibly if bankers, industrialists, and traders had been actively consulted in the summer of 1914 their views would have caused governments to pause before risking so much. But they were not consulted.

The problem was that governments in the summer of 1914 paid no attention to the economic consequences of war and were instead caught up in a series of misapprehensions, misjudgements, and miscalculations that served to turn a potentially manageable crisis, at most a localised conflict, into all-out war. The war was far from inevitable as the crisis began. It was the outcome of some spectacularly poor decision-making. Those in government were hampered by having no idea what a war between these powers at this time would mean in practice. Margaret MacMillan described a 'failure of imagination in not seeing how destructive such a conflict would be'. Clark called those responsible 'sleepwalkers', because they were 'watchful but unseeing, haunted by dreams, yet blind to the reality of the horror they were about to bring to the world'.[4]

ANOTHER PROPHECY THAT HAS NOT STOOD THE TEST OF TIME was one made by H. G. Wells early on in the war. Keeping in mind his conviction that only a great conflagration would persuade the nations of the world to eliminate war, this appeared to be the moment. Once Germany, a 'nest of evil ideas,' was defeated, good sense would reign. This would be, he wrote, 'the war that will end war.'

It is a war not of nations, but of mankind. It is a war to exorcise a world-madness and end an age. . . . For this is now a war for peace. It aims straight at disarmament. It aims at a settlement that shall stop this sort of thing for ever. Every soldier who fights against Germany now is a crusader against war. This, the greatest of all wars, is not just another war—it is the last war![5]

The most pernicious of the evil ideas for which Germany was then held responsible was that of 'realpolitik', characterised as an amoral approach to international affairs, concerned solely with power and the narrowest definition of the national interest. The original view of realpolitik was no more than a hard-headed and unsentimental approach to international affairs, but still potentially constructive. Over time it became associated with a cynical disregard for all norms and laws and a reliance on force. In a book on *Germany and the Next War*, published in 1911, a veteran Prussian general, Friedrich von Bernhardi, took realpolitik into social darwinism. Notions of arbitrating disputes were not simply dismissed as naïve in their idealism but actually 'immoral'. War was presented as a 'biological necessity'.[6] In his influential study of imperialism, Hobson described realpolitik as having 'remodelled the whole art of diplomacy and erected national aggrandisement without pity or scruple as the conscious motive force of foreign policy.'[7]

In 1919, with this supposedly poisonous ideology now discredited and its sponsors defeated, there was an opportunity for an alternative, more enlightened and civilised approach. This alternative approach, long nurtured by high-minded liberals in Britain and the United States, was ready with its own analysis and prescriptions. It was an approach associated in the previous century with former Prime Minister William Gladstone, who had campaigned vigorously on behalf of the persecuted of Europe, and now with President Woodrow Wilson. It was highly judgemental, offering a view of war as not so much an unfortunate consequence of an unresolved conflict of interests as of culpable aggression, less the result of miscalculation or mischief and more of criminality. Any military action must therefore be motivated by conscience, undertaken in a spirit of selflessness and without expectation of material advantage. This was a 'liberal vision', animated by a 'fundamental optimism about intervention in foreign conflicts, in strategies of redemption that could put right the wrongs that had been done.'[8]

The liberal project for the aftermath of the Great War involved a new international order, edging towards world government, promoting democracy, and replacing arms races with disarmament.[9] Pushing hard on this agenda until his stroke in 1919, was American President Woodrow Wilson. He sought to guide the world away from the bad old ways, with his Fourteen Points announced to Congress as his agenda for peace in January 1918. The key principles were that:

First, that each part of the final settlement must be based upon the essential justice of that particular case and upon such adjustments as are most likely to bring a peace that will be permanent;

Second, that peoples and provinces are not to be bartered about from sovereignty to sovereignty as if they were mere chattels and pawns in a game, even the great game, now forever discredited, of the balance of power; but that

Third, every territorial settlement involved in this war must be made in the interest and for the benefit of the populations concerned, and not as a part of any mere adjustment or compromise of claims amongst rival states; and

Fourth, that all well defined national aspirations shall be accorded the utmost satisfaction that can be accorded them without introducing new or perpetuating old elements of discord and antagonism that would be likely in time to break the peace of Europe and consequently of the world.[10]

In addition to open diplomacy, freedom of the seas, reduced barriers to trade, disarmament, and 'autonomous development', he urged an association of nations that would guarantee the political independence and territorial integrity of nations. This was to be under 'specific covenants', meaning that these guarantees must of necessity be enforced through economic and military sanctions.[11] Although his fellow leaders were wary (French Prime Minister George Clemenceau quipped that compared with Wilson's Fourteen Points, 'the Good Lord only had ten') it set allied war aims and became the basis of the German surrender.

Wilson's language captured a mood, a rejection of power politics in favour of strong global institutions that could introduce the civilising influence of the rule of law. Underlying this rejection was a positive view of human nature and potential, but one that had been denied through the determination of elites to manage international affairs in a secretive way. Just as the 'rule of law' had proved to be the method for combining order with justice within states it was natural that international law, enforced through a collective security system, was presented as the answer to international insecurity. Disarmament would allow an escape from the logic of arms races, as one state built up its military strength in response to the moves of another, aggravating suspicions and in the end provoking an unwanted war. Sir Edward Grey, Foreign Secretary when the war began, looked back to the naval rivalry between Britain and Germany with which the century had started. 'Great armaments', he observed mournfully, 'lead inevitably to war'.[12]

THE NEW ARRANGEMENTS THAT EMERGED OUT OF THE 1919 Treaty of Versailles, far from calming the international order, ended up disrupting it further. Realpolitik turned out not to be the preserve of Imperial Germany but was embraced by the victorious powers; the punitive terms imposed on Germany meant they could never be accepted as legitimate; while the League of Nations, denied American participation, struggled to impose its authority. It was not that Versailles made another great war inevitable, for there were many fateful choices still to be made by political leaders, but that too much was attempted in the face of too many contradictory pressures and competing demands.[13]

Of particular importance was the demand by many nations for self-determination, the support given to this demand by Wilson, and the disarray within the imperial European states that made this the moment to realise these demands. The struggles of national groups for independence in the Austro-Hungarian and Ottoman empires during the nineteenth century had excited liberal opinion in Europe and North America. They then contributed to the tensions which had led to the war, and even provided the trigger. There was an inherent tension between liberalism and nationalism, although this was at first hidden by their shared opposition to the conservatism and oppression embodied in the 1815 Congress of Vienna and their shared demands for freedom. The liberals believed in an order based on universal rights and the growing irrelevance of national barriers; the nationalists wanted most of all freedom for their own nations.[14]

During the second half of the nineteenth century as Germany and Italy were unified, the United States held together, and great empires were constructed in the name of some national destiny, nationalism appeared as an expansionist ideology. Yet within states attempting to impose uniformity on groups which had quite distinct cultures, nationalism was also a potential source of fragmentation. Groups took on identities quite distinct from the rest of their countries. For liberals this began to pose something of a dilemma. They were arguing that states need not resort to war to resolve disputes but found it difficult to extend that argument to national-minorities demanding self-determination, lest they gave a carte blanche to the oppressors.

Self-determination was according to Wilson more than a 'mere phrase' but 'an imperative principle of action'. He explained that 'national aspirations must be respected; people may now be dominated and governed only by their own consent'.[15] It was never easy to establish what Wilson actually meant. He largely had in mind those whose nationality was already 'well-defined' and had a reasonable demand for self-government. It was therefore most applicable to those who lacked democratic means to express themselves (which is why he had little sympathy for Irish demands for independence). Yet once it was raised as a core principle the application potentially went much wider. His Secretary of State, Robert Lansing, had deep misgivings about where this could lead. There were problems of defining the self to be determined—was Wilson referring to 'a race, a territorial area, or a community'? Because the concept was so vague, Lansing feared, it would 'raise hopes which can never be realised' and would 'cost thousands of lives', before eventually being discredited.

Wilson did not create the demand for self-determination, but he offered an extension without limits. Once the principle was asserted many claimants stepped forward, without there being any obvious ways of evaluating one claim as against another. Half the people of central Europe could describe themselves as a member of a national minority and the president had implied that anyone who wanted their own state should have one.[16] Nationalism turned out to be a much more formidable ideology, precisely because it could be fashioned to local needs, than the liberal democracy Wilson had sought to promote. When the great multinational empires of the defeated powers came apart after the war the process was disorderly. What one group needed for its emancipation had an unhappy tendency to cut across what was demanded with equal conviction and historical precedent by another.

The armistice which concluded the Great War on 11 November 1918, a moment still marked with solemnity, allowed the victors to demobilise and tend to their wounds. But it was combined with extraordinary upheavals around the rest of Europe. Republics replaced emperors, territories either broke away or were taken away as new states were forged from the wreckage, and new ideologies offered a promise of a better world. Between 1917 and 1920 Europe experienced some twenty-seven violent transfers of political power.[17] In addition to the economic blockade of the defeated powers, maintained until peace terms were agreed and which led to misery and starvation, and the devastating impact of the Spanish flu on a weakened population, some four million people died in Europe as a direct result of the wars that followed the armistice.

In principle self-determination should have reduced the pressures for future war. If nations had their own states there would be less to fight about in the future. But what came about was insufficiently neat. New states were created out of the wreckage of the old, such as Ukraine (briefly), Poland, and Czechoslovakia, but they were not homogenous and contained their own ethnic mix, with old hierarchies upended, so previously oppressed groups were now on top. The Kingdom of Serbs, Croats, and Slovenes, which eventually became Yugoslavia, had a name which warned of an inherent lack of unity. Numerous Germans, Magyars, and Bulgarians were stranded in new states in which they were minorities. Cutting across questions of nationality, defined using various permutations of territory, language, and religion, were those of class and ideology. There were wars between Russia and Poland, Greece and Turkey, Romania and Hungary, as well as civil wars in Russia, Finland, Hungary, Germany, and Ireland. With boundaries uncertain and loyalties open to question, the distinction between what was an interstate war and what was civil was invariably blurred, as militias took on national armies. These wars encouraged the idea that whole populations were the enemy, for reason of class or ethnicity.

In all of this were harbingers of conflicts to come—when after the Second World War the great maritime empires also fell apart and then again when the Cold War ended with the implosion of European communism. There were clear links between these sets of wars. They took place over the same lands, and concerned the same issues of national identity and sovereignty. These were also wars which blurred the boundaries between the civil and the military, and were often fought by paramilitaries and with civilians as targets, not just because they were caught up in a battle, but also because categories of people had been dehumanised as representing evil and danger. Such views made possible massacres and expulsions. Those in the 1920s who wanted to understand future war would therefore have done well to pay more attention. But when it came to understanding future wars these were ignored. The focus remained on the great powers and what needed to be done to prevent another great war.

It took until 1923 before most of these conflicts were sorted out, either as a result of exhaustion of one side or, on occasion, international mediation. There was then a brief period when it appeared that previous promises designed to make the world a safer place were being implemented. Gradually the major powers accepted the need for a new way of doing business. Initiatives were taken to institutionalise peaceful practices. There were pledges to disarm, in line with the first substantive article of the League of Nations' Charter. Military capabilities must be sufficient for self-defence and no more. The 1925 Locarno Treaties, which confirmed Europe's new borders, were said to generate a special 'spirit'. German Foreign Minister Gustav Streseman proclaimed that they signified 'that the states of Europe at last realize that they cannot go on making war upon each other without being involved in common ruin.'[18] Under the 1928 Kellogg-Briand Pact, the brainchild of the US secretary of state and the French foreign minister, the sixty-three signatory states pledged that they would not employ war to resolve 'disputes or conflicts of whatever nature or of whatever origin they may be, which may arise among them'. In the end this was not enough.

SALVADOR DE MADARIAGA Y ROJO TRAINED AS AN ENGINEER, worked as a journalist, and then moved into the new League of Nations in 1921, first as a press secretary and then as Head of the League's Disarmament Section. He left the job in 1928 in order to become professor of Spanish at Oxford University, and wrote a book to explain why progress towards disarmament had been so slow. He was in no doubt about the need for disarmament, and his supporting argument was one that would still be widely accepted by its proponents. Military expenditure was wasteful. Vast sums were spent on preparing for war while only a minuscule provision was made for peace. Weaponry absorbed tax revenues, scarce resources, and the finest appliances yet had no productive or enduring value. They encouraged 'a spirit of distrust', with fear of dependence on others and competition for raw materials and territory. Armament firms encouraged conflict to increase demands for their products, while general staffs looked for credible adversaries to justify their existence.[19]

Yet de Madariaga stopped well short of the clinching argument that armaments were the sole cause of war. If this was the case and all weapons were abolished there would only be peace, but some weapons were needed, for both national and international policing purposes. War could never be truly outlawed, as no state would ever admit to be acting for any reason other than self-defence. The Kellogg-Briand Pact just led to wars being started without being declared, as when Japan invaded Manchuria in 1931 and Italy invaded Abyssinia in 1935.

When it came to even modest disarmament proposals the security concerns of individual states left them watered down or meaningless. Setting numbers for force levels was complicated not only by the need for measures for counting tanks or aircraft, when the same system performed different roles in their nations' strategies, but also methods for taking into account the size of countries and the nature of their rivalries, the ability to turn resources from peace to war, as well as the logistical capabilities that could ensure a supply of materiel to the front. All nations claimed to be at their minimum levels of provisions because of the threats they faced. All would estimate their own requirements in 'the most extravagant manner'. De Madariaga anticipated an approach that was followed in the 1932 Geneva disarmament conference, which was to distinguish armed forces on the basis of whether they were suitable for aggressive or defensive purposes. Unfortunately, he noted, it was intention that turned a weapon into an instrument of aggression.

As a result of these practical and political problems, disarmament conferences became yet another arena in the struggle for relative advantage, and so had fomented rather than reduced mistrust. De Madriaga's analysis did not, however, lead him to abandon the peace project but to emphasise the demanding nature of the challenge. He kept on returning to the need for a well-organised 'World Community' to settle disputes and protect smaller states. Rivalry must be replaced by cooperation: 'The world is one. It must be thought of as one, governed as one, kept in peace as one.' His was a robustly realistic analysis leading to an idealistic conclusion.

SO DESPITE THE SETBACKS UNTIL THE 1930S THE IDEALISM that had underpinned the League of Nations was still in place. During the 1930s it became increasingly hard to sustain. This can be seen in a book published in 1933. In *The Intelligent Man's Way to Prevent War*, a collection of authors committed to the peace project made the attempt. The editor, Leonard Woolf, compared war to other social phenomena 'like cannibalism, witch-burning, murder, drunkenness' that might be prevented if only it was possible to discover the conditions which caused it and those that would then make it 'extremely unlikely or impossible'.[20] The framework was set in a chapter by Norman Angell, the author of *The Great Illusion*. After 1918 Angell had continued to seek to demonstrate the folly of war. He won the Nobel Prize for Peace in 1933, as much for effort as for achievement. Like many peace campaigners he was a philosophical rationalist and so devoted himself to addressing the potential sources of irrationality. Post-war Angell veered between isolationist and internationalist positions, between believing that the best way to stay out of war was to avoid getting too entangled in the affairs of other states and then that only engagement with other states could create a new system in which war became impossible. By the time of his 1933 essay, entitled 'The International Anarchy', he was in internationalist mode. The problem was neither human nature nor capitalism. He rejected 'the guilty nation theory of war' as suggesting that some states were naturally wickeder than others. All nations going to war thought that their enemy was frightful and their own cause was just. Though nations fought for their 'rights' the meaning of such rights was often properly disputed and should not be decided by the disputant. The real problem was that 'we have made of national sovereignty a god; and of nationalism a religion', which led to the impulsive rejection of international cooperation. The best alternative, in order to achieve the 'gradual elimination of force' was a pledge that it should only be used to defend the law.

By the time the book was published, this proposal faced the formidable barrier of Adolf Hitler, who had become German Chancellor in January 1933. All the contributors to Woolf's book did what they could to sustain their convictions. They were prepared to make some allowances for Germany because of the unreasonable pressures resulting from the Versailles Peace Conference. This had created a fertile ground for Nazi propaganda. One contributor found reassurance in a speech Hitler had made in the Reichstag making the case against war: 'neither politically nor economically could the use of any kind of force in Europe create a more favourable situation than exists today.' Another hoped that responsibility 'might teach prudence to these men' while 'economic necessity may compel them to pursue a policy of great patience and moderation'. Yet the words of Hitler's manifesto, *Mein Kampf,* were hard to ignore:

> Oppressed territories are not restored to the bosom of the mother country by flaming protest but by a sword that is able to strike. To forge this sword is the task of the leaders of domestic policy; to secure that it be forged undisturbed and to seek comrades in arms is the task of foreign policy.

Training was already underway for war and children were being taught hatred and revenge. Germany must therefore be viewed as 'a peril to the world's peace.' Woolf concluded his introduction by referring to 'the turn to Fascism and Hitlerism'. Since the book had been first planned there had been a 'tremendous acceleration of the movement towards nationalism and violence and dictatorship and away from the idea of internationalism and the League'. Those with these retrograde views could make war inevitable, but they could also choose another path. There was, he insisted, 'nothing to be ashamed of in refusing to hurrah with the barbarians'.[21]

Within a few years one hope that Hitler would learn moderation gave way to another that his ambition would be satiated if only some limited demands were met.[22] The man who embraced appeasement most enthusiastically, British Prime Minister Neville Chamberlain, became a byword for feckless naiveté. After he had met with Hitler in Munich and accepted the German move into Czechoslovakia's Sudetenland, Chamberlain spoke of 'peace in our time', observing: 'How horrible, fantastic, incredible it is that we should be digging trenches and trying on gas-masks here because of a quarrel in a faraway country between people of whom we know nothing.'[23] At the start of September 1939, the Nazis marched into Poland. Just over two decades after the end of one catastrophic war Europe was embroiled in a second. Unlike the never-ending debate about the origins of the First World War, there was little controversy surrounding the origins of the Second.

AS THE WAR BEGAN, EDWARD HALLETT CARR, A FORMER DIPLOMAT, published *The Twenty Years' Crisis,* a trenchant critique of the interwar peace project. Carr was the fourth incumbent of the first chair of International Relations, named in honour of Woodrow Wilson, at the University of Aberystwyth. The donor, Liberal MP David Davies, an active and enthusiastic supporter of the League of Nations, had hoped that with a sufficiently rigorous understanding of how the international system worked measures might be identified to prevent a new slide to war. Hence his consternation with Carr's developing critique of his most cherished beliefs. *The Twenty Years' Crisis* did not so much argue for a 'realist' alternative to 'utopianism' as for a synthesis between the two, although the tenor was definitely realist. This he described as placing 'emphasis on the acceptance of facts and on the analysis of their causes and consequences' and 'to maintain, explicitly or implicitly, that the function of thinking is to study a sequence of events which it is powerless to influence or to alter.' It was only in this rejection of purpose that Carr parted company with realism.

His critique pointed to three basic problems with the utopianism of the previous two decades: first, an unwarranted belief in progress, as if humankind was bound to improve its forms of government; second, a disregard of factors of power; and third, the attempt to 'base international morality on an alleged harmony of interests which identifies the interest of the whole community of nations with the interest of each individual member of it.' When governments talked of principles, justice, and rights, he warned, they were all, perhaps subconsciously, actually talking about their national interests.[24] Given the timing, the argument that the utopian project had collapsed was hardly contentious. It was painfully evident that efforts to manage the problem of war through new international arrangements had failed.

[6]

Total War

"What will the next war be like?" "Will it be anything like the last?" These are the questions that in the present state of apprehension or resigned curiosity, are almost daily hurled at anyone who is a student of the grim branch of knowledge which is sometimes called the science of war.

BASIL LIDDELL HART,
Europe in Arms, 1937[1]

Unlike the period leading up to the First World War there was no wishful thinking about the nature of war in the years leading up to the Second. Memories of shuddering casualties mocked ideas of war as ennobling and character-forming. War had broken away from prior physical and normative constraints. The victors of 1918 had been left bruised and exhausted along with the vanquished. A future war would be more of the same, except even worse because there were new ways of killing and no evident protections for civilians. No longer appearing as the 'non-combatant' deserving of protection, civilians entered the strategic lexicon as a distinct category. They were central to the industrialised war machine and therefore targets, both 'weak and critically important'. In 1923, in the context of concerns about aerial warfare, jurists began to replace the old combatant/non-combatant distinction with that between the military and the civilian.[2]

The prospectus shaped the expectations for future war, assuming that the worst innovations of the previous one, especially air raids, would dominate the fighting from the start. After the attacks on Britain by airships in 1915 and aircraft over the summer of 1917, and despite the absence of panic, the government started to worry about popular reactions to future attacks. In the summer of 1918, the South African General Jan Christiaan Smuts wrote a report for the British cabinet that envisaged a day, not too far off,

> when aerial operations with their devastation of enemy lands, and destruction of industrial and populous centres on a vast scale may become the principal operations of war, to which the older forms of military and naval operations may become secondary and subordinate.[3]

WELLS'S VISION OF AIR POWER IN USE AGAINST DEFENCELESS populations had been challenged before the war. One reviewer observed that 'we can be sure that although the air raid will have its uses in the strategy of the future, it will remain subsidiary to other methods.' Others worried that civilised nations would be less likely to resort to such terrible methods, worrying more about what anarchists might do with such weapons.[4] After 1918 concerns about air warfare crystallised ideas about the importance of civilians in a national war effort and the possibilities of a knockout blow if directed against them specifically. So while Wells doubted that war could be won from the air and warned of a crazed competition in destruction, until world government was embraced out of desperation, a more common view was that this could be a route to victory. As early as 1909 the journalist R. P. Hearne described a war starting with a 'smashing blow' against cities that would be sufficient for national morale to collapse.[5] Others worried about the 'paralysis' that would result from a 'single well-directed blow' against what would now be described as the 'critical infrastructure'. A growing awareness of the complex interdependence of modern societies raised the possibility that the disruption of one part of the system would lead to a wider collapse. During the First World War the Zeppelin raids encouraged the thought that a war conducted against the 'very nerve centres and vital arteries of any opponent who is ill-prepared' could be decisive. This suggested an answer to the conundrum posed by a long attritional struggle. If wars could no longer be 'won on points' using traditional means, then air raids might be one way to bring a future conflict to a quick conclusion.⁶

After the war military planners evaluated the various forms of munitions that might be dropped, from incendiaries to poisoned gas, not so much according to their material effects and more by reference to the psychological. The most enthusiastic advocates of air power, such as Billy Mitchell in the United States and Giulio Douhet in Italy, sought to show how they could win wars with vigorous offensives that would bring the nation's enemies to their knees. They dismissed alternatives to mass raids against the enemy homelands just as earlier proponents of sea power had insisted that worrying about coastal defences or supporting land operations distracted from efforts best devoted to gaining command of the sea. Their claims were popularised by Douhet, whose book *The Command of the Air*, published in 1921, demonstrated how aircraft would render irrelevant the fighting underway on the ground by taking the battle straight to the heartland of the enemy, where stricken civilians would soon demand that their government capitulated.⁷

The likely impact on the popular mood of such attacks was based on little more than observation of the wartime raids on Britain, class prejudice, and the prevailing theories of crowd psychology, such as le Bon's, that stressed susceptibility to raw emotion. A close examination of the evidence would have encouraged a more nuanced view of popular reactions and provided little encouragement to the idea that people would be unable to cope. Absent such an analysis the idea that social chaos would be the inevitable result of a pounding from the air took hold. In 1926 for example the military strategist Basil Liddell Hart, who had observed the impact of Zeppelin raids in Hull, contemplated the potential destruction of a number of great cities, including London with 'the business localities and Fleet Street wrecked, Whitehall a heap of ruins, the slum districts maddened into the impulse to break loose and maraud, the railways cut, the factories destroyed.' In such circumstances, he asked: 'Would not the general will to resist vanish and what use would be the still determined fraction of the nation, without organization and central direction?'⁸

Holman has described how the 'theory of the knock-out blow solidified into a near-consensus among military intellectuals during the 1920s and by the 1930s had become an orthodoxy, accepted and promoted by pacifists and militarists alike.' The theory depended on the assumption that civilians were essential to the wartime economy but also its most vulnerable element, and also on a stereotyped script. This postulated a war starting with a surprise attack by Germany with a huge air raid leading to massive civilian casualties, certainly into thousands and possibly into the millions. In addition to the damage to the urban environment would be the disruption or loss of essential services and rural areas, which would provide little sanctuary because of the spread of famine and disease. 'With its ability to wage war severely compromised the government would have little choice but to surrender after only weeks, days, or even hours.'[9]

In this way pre-war complacency about the impact of war was replaced by post-war alarmism. What had appeared as fantasies of air fleets pounding the hapless multitudes now appeared as inescapable reality, to be added to the memories of trenches and infantry being slaughtered on an industrial scale. No great leaps of either imagination or logic were required. If civilians kept the war going by providing fresh reserves for the front and workers for the factories then they were legitimate targets, and probably more worth attacking because they would be less able to cope than soldiers. Instead of war becoming more contained and limited, the opposite appeared more likely.

The man who oversaw Germany's defeat in 1918, General Erich Ludendorff, concluded that the problem lay in a failure to understand that war must be recognised as a 'total' undertaking. In 1935 Ludendorff urged that in the next war the whole nation must be mobilised against the enemy nation. War was total, he observed, because it involved the entire territory and population of the state and not just its armed forces. This required early preparation, from before the start of hostilities, and the need to strengthen the morale of the population. In addition, total war was to be guided by one figure with supreme authority over all military actions, a role exemplified by Hitler. The pre-1914 concepts of offensive action in a war of annihilation were still present, only now it had to take in the enemy nation, because if it did not then the result would surely be the annihilation of one's own; the requirements went well beyond military strength. 'Victory is created by the spirit'.[10]

The prospect of a future war dominated by massive air raids, especially when combined with poisoned gas, provided the backdrop for the literature of the period. Clarke lists some of the titles, giving an idea of the bleakness of the theme and its ubiquity: *The Poison War*, *The Black Death*, *Menace*, *Empty Victory*, *Invasion from the Air*, *War upon Women*, *Chaos*, and *Air Reprisal*.[11] Little support was given to the idea of quick and easy victories; the scenarios pointed instead to the need for disarmament.

In 1922 Cicely Hamilton, a British feminist activist and writer, published *Theodore Savage*, later republished in the US as *Lest Ye Die*, in which a crisis in the Balkans led to an utterly destructive war. After London was struck 'a wave of vagrant destitution rushed suddenly and blindly northward—anywhere away from the ruin of explosive, the flames and death by suffocation; while authority strove vainly to control and direct the torrent of overpowering misery.' *The Gas War of 1940*, written in 1933 by Stephen Southwold, under the pseudonym Miles, was the reminiscence of a dictator who sent his son into orbit to spare him from an unsafe world. In Nevil Shute's *What Happened to the Corbetts* the story was one of a world brought low by war and subsequent disease, and the need to survive and escape, although the political message was that civilisation was not doomed, as the barbarity of the air attack turned the world against the aggressor.[12] The best known was H. G. Wells's 1933 novel *The Shape of Things to Come*, not least because a few years later it was made into a shocking movie of the same name, opening with a 'war scare' set in the Christmas of 1940. Wells stuck with his familiar message. Although at first brute force appeared to triumph, the war continued for decades, and eventually the world was saved by the intervention of the United Airmen who stood for law and sanity, and ushered in a new age of science and enlightenment.[13]

In the tradition of the war fiction of thirty years earlier, in June 1935 the London *Evening News* serialised as a 'duty' S. Fowler Wright's *The War of 1938*.[14] This eventually became a trilogy of books, in which complex romances and adventures took place against a grim backdrop of war. Wright was deeply conservative, fearful of the impact of science and contemptuous of H. G. Wells's view of progress. He had been to Nazi Germany in 1934, and his books reflected his dismay at what he had seen. His first novel opened with Germany making demands of Czechoslovakia in 1938. Prague was destroyed in an air raid, and the Czechs were warned that there was worse to come unless they acceded to German demands. Germany, they were told, had become 'fit to enforce her will, as her great destiny required that she should be able to do.' Among the noxious inventions was a gas to freeze blood, and induce blindness and imbecility. The British did not become engaged until the second novel, although there had been a warning in the first of the country's failure to prepare for gas warfare, because of its stubborn and impatient resentment with 'the depredations with which military science was active to scourge mankind.' When Germany demanded that Britain handed over the Suez Canal, it refused only to discover how ill-disciplined and ill-prepared it was now that Germany had become 'an evil pitiless sword to subdue the world'. The Americans were even worse, hobbled by the 'deep-eating cancer of communism' and persuaded by propaganda that war must be avoided at all costs. By the third novel, Germany and Russia were in combination while the United States was totally preoccupied by the Pacific. The point about these novels, which were to warn of Germany and to encourage air-mindedness, was how intimidating the prospect of air raids had become. The Germans did not need to press forward with armoured columns because they had destructive weapons against which their enemies had no answer.

ON 26 APRIL 1937 GERMAN AND ITALIAN AIRCRAFT, ACTING on behalf of the rebel Spanish nationalists, bombed the Basque town of Guernica. Figures circulating afterwards suggested that over 1,600 people had been killed in the attack, out of a town with a population of some 7,000. Those were the numbers that informed the public debate on the meaning of Guernica, although the actual number was probably closer to 300. In retrospect the episode illustrates the murkiness of the distinction between attempts to terrorise the populace and to support military operations. The objective was to trap Republican forces and stop them retreating to support the defence of Bilbao. Republican resistance did crumble in the aftermath of the attack, thereby reinforcing the view that air raids were an efficient way of breaking the popular will. The most immediate effect, however, was outrage at an atrocity. George Steer, a reporter for the London *Times* had a full and vivid account published within a couple of days:

> In the form of its execution and the scale of the destruction it wrought, no less than in the selection of its objective, the raid on Guernica is unparalleled in military history. Guernica was not a military objective. A factory producing war material lay outside the town and was untouched. So were two barracks some distance from the town. The town lay far behind the lines. The object of the bombardment was seemingly the demoralization of the civil population and the destruction of the cradle of the Basque race.

Every fact bears out this appreciation, beginning with the day when the deed was done.[15]

The artist Picasso used the event to inform a painting that had been commissioned for the Spanish pavilion at the Paris International Exposition. This conveyed the calamity in a dramatic, striking and original image that remains a powerful depiction of the horror of any war.

Not long after, a simmering conflict between China and Japan suddenly turned into a total war. The Chinese struggled against a Japanese advance, and were unable to protect their capital Nanking. In late December 1937 the Japanese entered the city. As they did so, all constraints were immediately abandoned. For some six weeks Japanese troops murdered, plundered, and raped. They claimed to be seeking out Chinese military personnel, but that could not explain, let alone justify, the atrocities. This time it was a *New York Times* reporter, F. Tillman Durdin, who described the horrors he had seen. He described the intense violence as strategic: 'The Japanese appear to want the horrors to remain as long as possible to impress on the Chinese the terrible results of resisting Japan.' The result was that Nanking was now 'housing a terrorized population who, under alien domination, lie, in fear of death, torture, and robbery. The graveyards of tens of thousands of Chinese soldiers may also be the graveyard of all Chinese hopes of resisting conquest by Japan.'[16] If that was the objective it only worked to a degree. Japanese forces continued to make progress, but China was so vast and the population so large that they could never quite finish the conquest.

THOUGH EXPECTATIONS HAD BEEN CREATED FOR A SECOND World War, when it came initially the war was fought cautiously. In his *The Shape of Things to Come*, Wells had seen the war starting between Germany and Poland in 1940, and to last between the two ten years. That is how it began in September 1939 but then it was all over in six weeks. The French and British hoped that a way might be found to break German will without major offensives. The French army waited behind its defensive 'Maginot Line' while the Royal Navy prepared once again to impose a blockade that would over time cripple the German war economy. After Poland's occupation there was relative calm, even talk of a 'phoney war'. In the spring of 1940, which saw the fall of Holland and Belgium, and eventually France's capitulation, warfare seemed to revert to the type anticipated in 1914. Germany conquered countries one-by-one through quick and efficient offensives in a matter of weeks. This was accomplished along classical lines, with regular armies fighting battles, and the political fate of nations decided accordingly.

The potential role of the tank in future warfare had been discussed avidly since the weapons first made their appearance during the First World War. All the major powers developed armoured vehicles while debating how they could best be used—for fast moves into enemy territory on their own, or to reinforce infantry in more orderly offensive, or to act as mobile firepower in a defence. The tank was always favoured by those who wrestled with the challenge of how to return to the classical ideal of war between professional armies. Instead of the pointless frontal assaults of the First World War they argued for fast-moving and enveloping manoeuvres. Now these had materialised with devastating effectiveness. Unlike the air power enthusiasts who were convinced that aircraft should only be used for a 'strategic', war-winning role, the Germans had seen how aircraft could support land operations.

The successful German offensives of 1939–40 had been made possible by a pact between Hitler and Josef Stalin, leader of the Communist Soviet Union. At the time this was seen as extraordinarily cynical. Both countries had been losers in the previous war and had become radicalised as a result. Both were totalitarian, with the ruling elite controlling every aspect of life. Ideologically they were polar opposites and wholly antagonistic. The cartoonist David Low captured the cynicism of the pact as it was announced. The two dictators met in a setting of desolation. 'The Scum of the Earth, I Believe', says Hitler. 'The Bloody Assassin of the Masses, I Presume', says Stalin. If Hitler had been content to let Stalin have his own conquests the two men could have divided Europe between them, but he could never share the continent with an ideology he deplored and a people he despised. Hitler had always assumed that at some point he would move to the East to acquire 'Lebensraum' for the German people. In late 1940, with Britain stuck in a defensive mode and the United States not yet a belligerent, he concluded that the time was ripe. A Soviet defeat would convince the British of the hopelessness of their position, while achieving what had always been the driving objective of his whole ideology. On 18 December 1940 he set down his view: 'The German Wehrmacht must be prepared to crush Soviet Russia in a quick campaign even before the end of the war against England.'[17]

As for method, Hitler intended to rely on the blitzkrieg that had served him so well in 1940. He did not believe that Soviet forces were in a fit state to cope with a sudden onslaught and expected them to crumble quickly. His was a strong nation, with an iron will, against a weak one. His generals were not so sure, but they had not been so sure prior to the invasion of France either and had been proved wrong. They understood that everything depended on speed. If Moscow managed to resist then the whole enterprise was probably doomed. A vast German army of four million was assembled, but should the Soviet army get a chance to regroup and recover it could draw on far greater numbers. As serious, if the war was not over quickly then German forces lacked the clothing and the kit for the harsh Russian winters.

When the moment came on 22 June 1941 to launch Operation Barbarossa the surprise was almost complete.[18] Stalin had been warned, but had chosen to ignore the warnings, seeing in them an attempt to disrupt a relationship that was proving to be satisfactory to both parties, allowing both to establish their own domineering sphere of influence. Initially he floundered but then regained his composure and the defence began. This became the Great Patriotic War, and for the defence of the motherland rather than for communism. Evidence of German brutality meant that those with little love for their own regime fought hard against the invaders. The Germans got close to Moscow and Leningrad, where they instituted a terrible siege, but they did not get close enough.

The important feature of Hitler's strategy lay not in the supposed originality of his military concepts and tactics. Hitler had in fact not fully appreciated the improvised quality of the blitzkrieg in Western Europe and his good fortune in facing a France that was still geared to a defensive campaign along the lines of the trench warfare of the previous war. The strategy was far less suitable to the Russian steppes. His originality lay in war aims that involved not just conquering other people but seeking to enslave and annihilate them. The damage to the enemy's society was not a means to an end: it was what the war was all about. The persecution of Jews was an established part of Nazi ideology and practice in the territories it had occupied, but a policy of indiscriminate killing and then organised extermination was formally adopted as German forces moved into the Soviet Union. After top Nazis met in January 1942 at the Berlin suburb of Wannsee, the 'Final Solution to the Jewish Problem' was assumed to require not only the systematic elimination of those Jews to the East but also those already caught by the occupation of Western Europe.[19] It was a commitment that gave meaning to the war in the East but also ensured its failure. The determination to invade the Soviet Union was 'buried so deep within the Nazi DNA that it could not be stopped'. But the diversion of resources for purposes of extermination and a brutal occupation that alienated nationalities who might have been won over to an anti-Soviet fight served to further 'retard' any chance Hitler had of winning the war.[20]

IF THE GERMAN DECISION TO ATTACK THE SOVIET UNION represented a massive misjudgement then the Japanese attack on the American Pacific fleet at its Pearl Harbor base was if anything an even greater one. One explanation for this is that—as with Hitler's Barbarossa—the Japanese were confident in their ability to pull off a surprise attack. This had worked for them in the past in the first Sino-Japanese war of 1894, and then in February 1904 when they attacked the Russian Far East fleet anchored in Port Arthur having decided that war was the only way to resolve a dispute over the status of Korea. This latter attack left Russian ships destroyed or stranded, unable to get out of port, and Japanese forces moved unopposed into Korea. To recover the situation the Tsar sent ships drawn from the Baltic fleet, but by the time they arrived Port Arthur had fallen and the Japanese Navy was ready for them. Their route through the Straits of Tsushima had been anticipated, and they were caught by surprise. In one of those rare battles that could truly be described as 'decisive', the Russian fleet lost two thirds of its ships and to avoid further catastrophe surrendered to the Japanese. Not long afterwards Russia agreed peace terms. The victory left the Japanese emboldened and other maritime powers looking to learn the lessons. Japan's success had been the result of the speed of its warships and their powerful guns, and its grasp of the potential of telegraphy.

One observer saw from early on how this success might tempt the Japanese into an attack on the US fleet. Hector Bywater combined naval journalism with occasional espionage for the UK Admiralty. After first setting out his thoughts in a 1921 book, *Sea-power in the Pacific: A Study of the American-Japanese Naval Problem*, in 1925 he expanded on his ideas with a novel, *The Great Pacific War*, which explored how a future US-Japanese war might occur and develop.[21] He noted, correctly, the importance of Japan's paucity of raw materials and the need to gain access to the Asian mainland to satisfy her needs, and that the 'enslavement' of the Chinese would be resisted by the United States. Bywater imagined that the US Navy would be caught off Manila Bay by a Japanese surprise attack, just as the Russians had been caught in the Straits of Tsushima. The greatest damage was done by naval gunnery.

On 7 December 1941, waves of Japanese aircraft from six aircraft carriers attacked the US Pacific fleet at Pearl Harbor, damaging or destroying eighteen ships, including five battleships, and destroying or damaging most American aircraft in Hawaii. Bywater, who had died the previous year, was rediscovered as something of a prophet.[22] The Japanese were certainly aware of him, as his books were translated into Japanese. But the key factor in developing plans for Pearl Harbor was the Japanese Navy's growing awareness of the possibilities of naval air power.[23] Bywater had seen a role for carrier-based aircraft, but he did not fully appreciate their possible impact. As important, however, as Bywater's forecast that a war might start with a surprise attack was his view that Japan would still eventually lose this war. He anticipated the island hopping strategy across the Pacific that the Americans eventually adopted to push the Japanese back. In the novel, Japan surrendered after a 'demonstration' American air raid on Tokyo with 'bombs' containing leaflets urging surrender rather than 'waste more lives.' Japanese failure was essential to his purpose. He had chosen the 'medium of fiction', Bywater explained, to demonstrate that 'war is never a paying proposition from any national point of view'.

While the Japanese saw merit in Bywater's description of the first stages of the war, they were less impressed by his description of their ultimate failure (which an officer in his introduction to the book described as a 'slander'). Yet the reasons why an attack might fail were fully appreciated in Tokyo, even by the war faction. The earlier invasion of China might have served as warning enough of the dangers of aggressive action. This was why relations with the United States had deteriorated leading to Washington imposing economic sanctions. During the course of 1941 intermittent diplomatic conversations failed to resolve the impasse, even though Japan was struggling to pacify China. Should sanctions continue, their economy would eventually be crippled. But Japan refused to admit they had got it wrong in China, as that would mean dishonour and probably yet more unreasonable demands from Washington.

The logic of this position was to accept the inevitability of war without an obvious route to victory. No invasion or occupation of the continental United States was contemplated. The objective was to remove American opposition to Japanese hegemony over East Asia. The plot to attack Pearl Harbor was therefore hatched knowing that however successful there could be no military defeat of the United States and that if the United States did not decide to cut their losses and negotiate a peace on Japanese terms, superior American resources should lead to their victory. The Americans never had any doubt that they would win an eventual war and had explained clearly to the Japanese why this was so. This is why they kept on pushing the Japanese, and it was why they got caught by surprise when the Japanese decided they could take it no more.

A revealing conversation between the Emperor and the Chiefs of Imperial Japanese Army and Navy (General Hajime Sugiyama and Admiral Nagano Osami respectively) took place at a crucial September 1941 conference about the probability of victory. The Emperor observed that the Army had told him when China was invaded 'that we could achieve peace immediately after dealing them one blow with three divisions'. When Sugiyama made excuses ('China is a continent with a vast hinterland with many ways in and many ways out, and we unexpectedly met big difficulties'), the Emperor was angry. 'Didn't I caution you each time about those matters? Sugiyama, are you lying to me? If you call the Chinese hinterland vast, would you not describe the Pacific as even more immense?' With a stunned Sugiyama unable to reply, Osami stepped in. He acknowledged that there was no 100 per cent probability of victory. He then offered a metaphor:

Assume, however, there is a sick person and we leave him alone; he will definitely die. But if the doctor's diagnosis offers a seventy percent chance of survival, provided the patient is operated on, then don't you think we should try surgery? And, if after the surgery, the patient dies, one must say that was meant to be. This is indeed the situation we face today ... If we waste time, let the days pass, and we are forced to fight after it is too late to fight, then we won't be able to do a thing about it.

This satisfied the Emperor: 'All right, I understand. . . . There is no need to change anything.'[24]

Admiral Yamamoto, responsible for planning the attack, believed that 'Japan's Navy must decide the fate of the war on the very first day'. The method was to 'fiercely attack and destroy the US main fleet at the outset of the war, so that the morale of the US Navy and her people [will] sink to the extent that it cannot be recovered.' The difficulty was that it was easier to sink ships than morale. Yamamoto considered the risks, including the 'possibility that the enemy would dare to launch an attack upon our homeland to burn down our capital and other cities,' but could see no other way out of Japan's current strategic predicament. This was a bold plan, but 'conceived in desperation'. In practice the best Japan could hope for was a resumption of negotiations and better terms than those available beforehand, but there was no reason to suppose that the Americans would have any interest. Prime Minister Tojo admitted that this was speculative: 'With war, if you don't try it, you can't know how it will turn out.'[25]

BARBAROSSA AND PEARL HARBOR REFLECTED THE SIMPLE logic that a state determined on war with another would seek to maximise the military impact of the first move. Aggression and surprise attack went hand in hand. In both cases the aggressions reflected a sense of inevitability. War was bound to come, and therefore it should be started on the best possible terms. For Hitler a showdown with the Bolsheviks was historic destiny; for Tojo there was a fundamental incompatibility between the United States and Japan. Without this sense of inevitability the case for war was poor in both instances because it meant taking on countries with formidable resources. Hitler believed that the Soviet Union could be defeated; Tojo was not so sure about the United States. Also in both cases, the idea that a bold first move could ensure a quick victory, a legacy of earlier wars, had been contradicted by recent experience. Germany and Japan were adding new enemies before the established enemies had been defeated.

When it came to the attacks, one over the land and one over the sea, both were helped by the complacency of the victims. Stalin distrusted those warning that Hitler was about to attack more than he distrusted Hitler. The Americans, who knew that an early attack was quite probable, were looking to the Philippines as a target and had underestimated Japanese capabilities. They had assumed that the strength of the Pacific fleet would serve as a deterrent. Moscow and Washington miscalculated in their assessments of the risks they faced because they did not appreciate that others might miscalculate so badly in the risks they were prepared to take.[26] Lastly, in both cases the military momentum gained was insufficient to bring the war to a swift conclusion, and the greater strengths of the Soviet Union and the United States were asserted, and eventually proved to be overwhelming.

The Second World War, like the First, confirmed the classical model in that its conclusion depended on a clear military victory. The European and Pacific Wars ended with the formal surrenders of the defeated armed forces. Still, the classical model was being stretched to the breaking point. What made the difference was the enormous advantage of the Allies in their combined air and sea power as this enabled them to deplete the war-making power of the enemy, eroding their ability to fight on land.[27] The blurred lines between the military and civilian spheres of war particularly challenged the classical model. The Germans took a merciless view when facing any partisan resistance in the occupied territories of Europe. This could still be accommodated within the classical model in terms of the risk that non-combatants had to accept when they took up arms or directly aided enemy forces. Once the Nazis decided to move against whole populations the model was abandoned. Attacks on civilians were not just a matter of maintaining law and order, or unfortunate consequential damage resulting from attacks on the main military-related objective, or desperate efforts to weaken the enemy will when all else had failed, but part of the whole rationale for the war, a means of asserting superiority over inferior races or of eliminating them altogether.

For the Nazis in Germany and the militarists in Japan, total war was not so much a matter of strategy as of world-view. The logic was totalitarian, not only in terms of the state controlling all aspects of the economy and social relationships but also in the presumption that all individuals must act in its service. When France folded in 1940 the right-wingers who took control under the Vichy regime saw the defeat as a consequence of the country having becoming 'pluralist, materialistic, and soft'. War was a test of a nation's health and France had failed. This logic, as it manifested itself in the Second World War, was the most 'insidious legacy' of the First.[28] Though the war had not begun as brutally as expected, at least in Europe, by its end it had become brutal in ways that few at the start could have imagined, with the attempted murder of a whole people, reckless violence against occupied populations, and single bombs able to destroy entire cities.

[7]

The Balance of Terror

Such was the crowning triumph of military science, the ultimate explosive that was to give the "decisive touch" to war...

H. G. WELLS,
The World Set Free, 1914[1]

At the start of the First World War H. G. Wells had seen the need to defeat Germany because its embrace of *realpolitik* challenged his vision of world government. His line in the Second World War was not so different. George Orwell observed that this was the 'same gospel' Wells had been 'preaching almost without interruption for the past forty years, always with an air of angry surprise at the human beings who can fail to grasp anything so obvious.' There was always the 'supposed antithesis between the man of science who is working towards a planned World State and the reactionary who is trying to restore a disorderly past.' This, Orwell warned, left Wells unable to grasp the nature of the threat and the task ahead, 'quite incapable of understanding that nationalism, religious bigotry and feudal loyalty are far more powerful forces than what he himself would describe as sanity. Creatures out of the Dark Ages have come marching into the present, and if they are ghosts they are at any rate ghosts which need a strong magic to lay them.'[2] This was not a war that could be comprehended in terms of the calculations of statesmen or narrow judgements of national self-interest.

When it came to a possible Third World War, however, Wells turned out to be more prophetic. One of his most impressive predictions was even more remarkable because he was instrumental in it coming true. Always on the lookout for scientific innovations to help the cause of political progress, he seized upon reports in the early 1900s of breakthroughs in the understanding of atomic structures. His guide was Frederick Soddy, a pioneering student of radioactivity who had gained his reputation while working with physicist Ernest Rutherford at McGill University in Canada. The two had shown that there were circumstances in which atoms might break up, in the process releasing large amounts of energy. Rutherford and Soddy understood how much potential energy might be stored in small amounts of material but could not see how this might be unleashed. Normally radioactivity was released over centuries or even millennia. If a weapon was to be developed using this knowledge, the process would have to be compressed into hours, perhaps less. Rutherford doubted that it would be possible, but Soddy was not so sure. Although later he played this down, he recognised immediately the hypothetical significance of such explosive power for warfare. In a 1904 lecture to the Corps of Royal Engineers, Soddy speculated that if the energy—'latent and bound up with the structure of the atom'—found in heavy matter could be unlocked then 'what an agent it would be in shaping the world's destiny'. The 'man who put his hand on the lever' to gain access to this vast store of energy 'would possess a weapon whereby he could destroy the world if he chose'. By way of reassurance, however, he trusted nature to guard its secret.[3]

He largely put aside this unpleasant prospect in a popular guide to the new science, *The Interpretation of Radium*, published in 1909.[4] Such a bountiful source of energy would mean the human race need not 'earn its bread by the sweat of its brow'. The happier prospect was of being able to 'transform a desert continent, thaw the frozen poles, and make the whole world one smiling Garden of Eden'.[5] Soddy did not mention any weapons, but the implication was there in an early paragraph comparing atoms as the building blocks of matter to bricks as the building blocks of houses. Imagine, Soddy asked, if one were to demonstrate to an architect that the bricks used for housing were 'capable of entirely different uses—let us say, for illustration, that they could with effect be employed as an explosive incomparably more powerful in its activities than dynamite'.[6]

Wells was one of Soddy's most attentive readers. In 1914 he acknowledged the scientist as the inspiration for a new novel, *The*

World Set Free. This was yet another homily on the merits of world government, and how these would come to be universally accepted as a result of an awesomely destructive weapon, named 'The Atomic Bomb'. He had a scientist named Professor Rufus giving lectures in Edinburgh in 1910, using Soddy's words. Wells then looked forward twenty years to 1933 when another scientist, Holsten, discovered how to master atomic energy through a combination of 'induction, intuition and luck'. It then took a further two decades before atomic weapons were used in a war between an alliance of Britain, France, and the US against Germany and Austria and almost spun out of control after an air attack destroyed the Paris headquarters of the Allied High Command. Rather than put an end to the fighting, it liberated a 'rather brutish young aviator' in charge of the French special scientific corps. No longer under control, he enthused how 'there's nothing on earth to stop us going to Berlin and giving them tit-for-tat. . . . Strategy and reasons of state—they're over. . . . Come along, my boy, and we'll just show these old women what we can do when they let us have our heads.' When they dropped their atomic bombs, large black spheres containing a heavy element 'carolinum', there was a volcanic effect—'a shuddering star of evil splendour spurted and poured up smoke and flame towards them like an accusation.'[7]

In Wells's account, two hundred major cities were lost in this way, with the residual radiation rendering them uninhabitable. He has his narrating historian observing that 'nothing could have been more obvious to the people of the early twentieth century than the rapidity with which war was becoming impossible. And as certainly they did not see it. They did not see it until the atomic bombs burst in their fumbling hands.' Thankfully, however, this dreadful experience shook men out of 'old-established habits of thought' and so led to the 'world set free.'

RUTHERFORD, SODDY'S COLLABORATOR FROM 1902, REMAINED sceptical. When Wells's novel was first published, he described the likelihood of mastering nuclear energy as not 'at all promising'.[8] By 1933 his view had not changed. In September of that year, speaking to the British Association, he restated his position: transforming atoms would be a very 'poor and inefficient' way to release energy. The idea that it could be a source of power was dismissed as 'moonshine'.

His remarks were duly reported in *The Times*, where Leo Szilard read them. Szilard, a brilliantly inventive Hungarian scientist who had moved to London from Germany because of the Nazis, was a fan of Wells, whom he had met. He had only recently read *The World Set Free*. With the book still in his mind, Szilard was bothered by Rutherford's sceptical remarks. By his own account, the explanation of how the energy might be released came to him as he crossed a London square. As he reached the curb, according to historian Richard Rhodes, 'time cracked open before him and he saw a way to the future, death into the world and all our woes, the shape of things to come'.[9] His insight was to recognise that there could be a chain reaction capable of releasing extraordinary amounts of energy if an element could be found that when bombarded with one neutron released two. Szilard, as with Wells's Holsten, the fictional and the real in 1933, were both suddenly seized with an insight that could result in both terrible and wonderful developments. In 1934 Szilard filed a patent which described a self-sustaining chain reaction but decided that the responsible thing to do was to keep it secret.

In December 1938 nuclear scientists Lise Meitner and her nephew Otto Frisch were together in Sweden. They realised that they could show that a uranium atom could split into two, a process they called fission. The community of nuclear scientists who heard the news could see at once that this could mean a new form of explosive. Whereas before Szilard might have hoped that the secret of an atomic bomb might be suppressed, now he began to fear that Nazi Germany might exploit it first. He persuaded his friend Albert Einstein to write to President Roosevelt urging him to authorise an exploration of the possibility of 'extremely powerful bombs'. It was some time before the United States joined the European war. By then Frisch was in Britain and with another émigré scientist, Rudolf Peierls, had demonstrated for the British government that an atomic bomb was feasible. In 1942 the British and American projects merged to form the Manhattan Project.

Atomic bombs were used for the first and only time in a military campaign in August 1945 when they were dropped on the Japanese cities of Hiroshima and Nagasaki, obliterating both and most of their residents. This was immediately recognised to be a step change in warfare. It was not, however, necessarily seen to be a transformation. The flattening of these two cities could also be presented as the natural continuation of the merciless air raids of the Second World War when great centres of population had been attacked regularly and remorselessly, even though social structures and even productive capacity had proved to be remarkably resilient in the face of constant pounding. The levels of damage suffered by Japan in August 1945 could have been inflicted by other means—the March 1945 air raid on Tokyo had led to more deaths. Yet the means were spectacular and the consequences were immediate. The bombs' use was followed by Japan's surrender.

It took time before the full implications of what had taken place were appreciated. In 1946 the *New Yorker* devoted a whole issue to the journalist John Hersey's stark account of the impact of the atomic bombs, including the harrowing accounts of survivors.[10] He quoted a report written to the Holy See in Rome by one of the German Jesuit priests present on the moral dilemmas raised by the new weapons:

> Some of us consider the bomb in the same category as poison gas and were against its use on a civilian population. Others were of the opinion that in total war, as carried on in Japan, there was no difference between civilians and soldiers, and that the bomb itself was an effective force tending to end the bloodshed, warning Japan to surrender and thus to avoid total destruction. It seems logical that he who supports total war in principle cannot complain of a war against civilians. The crux of the matter is whether total war in its present form is justifiable, even when it serves a just purpose. Does it not have material and spiritual evil as its consequences which far exceed whatever good might result? When will our moralists give us a clear answer to this question?

Over the next decade, with tests of new and even more powerful weapons, the likely character of a nuclear war became clear. Human beings within a large radius of an explosion would be killed by blast and fire. Those that were not would suffer severe burns, radiation sickness, and psychological trauma. The effects of radiation might be felt far away, depending on the nature of the detonation and the weather. Over time this would result in higher incidence of leukaemia and cancer. Charting the longer-term social consequences was harder. Evidently health services would be left in a terrible condition and be hard-pressed to treat even a small proportion of the victims. Help from outside would be hampered by the damage to infrastructure. Agriculture and manufacturing would be set back and cultural heritage lost forever. If significant numbers of weapons were used then distant lands would be contaminated. There were soon speculations about whether human life could be sustained.

In August 1949, much earlier than the Americans and British expected, the Soviet Union tested an atomic device. In response, the Americans moved to the next stage of nuclear technology, from atomic weapons based on nuclear fission to hydrogen or thermonuclear weapons based on fusion. These threatened almost unlimited destructive capacity. In the 1940s there had been very few atomic bombs available for American use. Over the 1950s scarcity gave way to plenitude, with many weapons available to both superpowers. The assumption that the next war would start with devastating exchanges of city-busting weapons took hold. Even more alarming was the realisation that the consequences would not be confined to the belligerents. Anyone who happened to be in the path of nuclear fallout, the radioactive dust and ash taken by the wind away from the site of a detonation, could be caught. Fallout would not respect national boundaries, let alone personal culpability. To be released it was not even necessary for there to be a war, as radioactive fallout made an unwelcome appearance in the 1950s as a by-product of atmospheric nuclear tests by the United States, Britain, and the Soviet Union.[11] Its impact was brought home in March 1954 when the US detonated a bomb combining fusion with fission on Bikini Island (one of the Marshall Islands) equivalent to 15 million tons of TNT (megatons). This was some thousand times the yield of the bomb that had destroyed Hiroshima, which had a yield equivalent to some 15 thousand tons (kilotons). Because it was greater than anticipated, a Japanese fishing boat, the *Lucky Dragon*, though ninety miles away from Bikini, was caught in the path of the fallout as a result of which the crew developed radiation sickness, and one member died. The furore this created in Japan pushed awareness of fallout to the front pages.

AFTER THE MOVE FROM THE ATOMIC TO THE HYDROGEN BOMB the fear was that the scientists might next come up with something worse—the cobalt bomb. The key feature of the cobalt bomb was that its use would actually be truly suicidal. Leo Szilard had first mooted the idea in 1950 when he spoke during a radio discussion of how governments might deliberately construct weapons to maximise fallout by 'salting' them with cobalt. Whereas people might return after a couple of months to areas hit by fallout from most planned weapons, a cobalt bomb's radiation would have a much longer half-life and so anywhere contaminated would be uninhabitable for up to a century. That was why it could be a doomsday device.

Szilard raised the idea not as an advocate but to warn about the possible consequences of an unrestricted arms race. In 1956 presidential candidate Adlai Stevenson spoke of 'the millions who tremble on the sidelines of this mad arms race in terror' and demanded that President Eisenhower reveal the government's plans for the cobalt bomb. Officials pointed to its suicidal quality as refutation of the rumours that it was close to being designed, let alone constructed. They had little success. There was a growing presumption that whatever could be built would be built. In practice there were no plans, and cobalt bombs were never built. Even if they had been and then used this would not necessarily have led to a completely depopulated planet, although the life remaining would undoubtedly have been utterly miserable.[12]

Cobalt bombs were a gift to writers of doomsday fiction, and soon became a feature of the invariably dystopian literature that grew up around the possibility of a nuclear Armageddon. The drama often lay largely in exploring how people might cope with catastrophe as opposed to how they got there. As a result descriptions of the origins of the catastrophe tended to be sketchy, combining barely plausible conflicts with some stunning misunderstandings. This was the case with the apocalyptical bestseller *On the Beach* by Nevil Shute, a British engineer who had emigrated to Australia, and who had contributed to the pre-war literature about bombing campaigns with *What Happened to the Corbetts*.[13] The new novel was one of the bleakest stories ever told, for not only do the book's main characters all die but so does all humanity, leaving behind a lifeless irradiated planet. Shute had seen the potential of the topic when he read in December 1954 a report in *Time* magazine on 'The Cumulative Effects of Thermonuclear Explosions on the Surface of the Globe', which noted that the neutrons and atmospheric debris from bomb tests 'may upset the natural conditions to which life has become adapted'.[14] The narrative power of the book came from the modest, low-key way ordinary people faced the terrifying prospect of their certain death, from which there was no escape and against which there could be no resistance. Shute's people lapsed neither into panic nor barbarity. Shute prefaced the book with a line from the poet T. S. Eliot, somewhat ironic in the light of images of massive explosions, 'This is the way the world ends/ Not with a bang but a whimper'.

The setting was Melbourne, the only place yet to be affected by fallout after a 'short, bewildering war' of thirty-seven days. The book began in Christmas 1962, already some fourteen months after the war. Shute did not explain the origins of the catastrophe by reference to a madman but instead to a combination of deliberate strategic malevolence compounded by miscalculation which led to a war in which 47,000 weapons were used. The first chapter referred to a 'Russian-Chinese war that had flared up out of the Russian-NATO war, that had in turn been born of the Israeli-Arab war, initiated by Albania.' Also cobalt bombs had been used by the Russians and the Chinese. In a later chapter some of the key figures tried to piece together what had happened, wondering whether it was worth writing a history of these events that no one would ever read. They are sitting on an American submarine tasked by the Australian prime minister to find out what happened around the country's coast. Challenging the general assumption at the time that China and the Soviet Union should be considered together as one giant Communist bloc, Shute had his original conflict as being between these two. Russia was after a warm water port, preferably Shanghai, and sought to cut down China's population by means of radiological warfare. For their part the Chinese wanted to use radiation to eliminate the industrial regions of Russia. As the discussion progressed on the submarine, the greatest revelation was that contrary to what had been supposed, the Russians had not attacked Washington and London, although Russia had received retaliation. This led to a thought so 'horrible' as to be 'incredible', that Russia had been bombed 'by mistake'. The real culprits turned out to be Egypt (Shute was writing at the time of the 1956 Suez crisis), using long-range aircraft sold to them by Russia. Meanwhile a bomb that hit Naples came from Albania, and nobody was now sure who had launched the one that struck Tel Aviv.

What was remarkable about Shute's political scenario was not its realism any more than his technical scenario, but his refusal to suggest that the predicament was the result of insane or even wholly unreasonable decisions. The participants in the discussion looked back at decisions that were rushed and taken blindly. ('It's mighty difficult to stop a war when all the statesmen have been killed.') Sympathy was expressed for someone with 'a war on his hands and plenty of weapons left to fight it with.' When it was suggested to the American

captain of the submarine that he would have tried to find a negotiated solution he demurred: 'With an enemy knocking hell out of the
United States and killing all our people? When I still had weapons in
my hands? Just stop fighting and give in? I'd like to think that I was
so high-minded but—well, I don't know.' The real blame was directed
towards the small countries that had initiated the war. That they
could do so was the result of the weapons becoming too cheap and
too freely available. The scientist on board the submarine explained:
'The original uranium bomb only cost about fifty thousand quid towards the end. Every little pipsqueak country like Albania could have
a stockpile of them, and every little country that had that, thought it
could defeat the major countries in a surprise attack. That was the
real trouble.' The scenario thus reflected a continuing belief in the
possibility of a knockout blow. Its main effect was as a warning about
fallout, which Shute helped to make a hot topic in 1957. But it was
also a warning about the consequences of the spread of nuclear
weapons.[15]

Two years later when the film of the book was made by Stanley
Kramer, there was a greater readiness to blame human stupidity. Fred
Astaire, as the scientist Julian Osborne, denied that there was a 'simple answer' to how the war started. It was the result of people accepting 'the idiotic principle that peace can be maintained by arranging
to defend themselves with weapons they couldn't possibly use without committing suicide.' The problem was still proliferation—'Every-
body had an atomic bomb and counter-bombs and counter-counter
bombs'—but this was combined with loss of control as 'the devices
outgrew us'.

'Somewhere some poor bloke...

Probably looked at a radar screen and thought he saw
something.

He knew that if he hesitated one thousandth of a second . . .

His own country would be wiped off the map, so—

So he pushed a button . . .

And . . . And . . .

The world went... Crazy...'[16]

BY THIS TIME THE POSSIBILITY OF ACCIDENTAL WAR WAS
becoming prominent. The idea that great tragedy could be the result
of a human error or mechanical malfunction was bound to make an

impression on a creative imagination.[17] In a 1958 novel, *Red Alert*,[18] a delusional Air Force general launched an attack, using a war plan which assumed that the government was no longer functioning. Once this was discovered, the president was determined to work with the Soviet Union to prevent catastrophe, but the US aircraft countermeasures were too good for Soviet defences. The general killed himself before he could be forced to reveal the recall code for the bombers, but the code was found on a desktop pad. All aircraft were recalled, save one which had been damaged by air defences. Fearing the worst, the president offered up Atlantic City, New Jersey, by way of compensation, but this turned out to be unnecessary when just one hydrogen bomb partly detonated and fortunately only in open countryside.

Another novel, *Fail-Safe*, had a similar theme, so much so that *Red Alert*'s author sued for plagiarism. In this case a civilian airliner off-course triggered an alert as the intrusion into American air space of an unidentified aircraft. The alert was cancelled but a 'go-code' was sent in error to a group of bombers, an error exacerbated by a new Russian system successfully preventing communications between the aircraft and their headquarters. Even when the jamming ended, the aircraft crew decided that their protocols required them to continue with the mission. As in *Red Alert*, the president offered to trade one city for another, in this case New York for Moscow.[19] Somewhat chillingly the novel appeared as a three-part serial in the *Saturday Evening Post* in October 1962, coinciding with the Cuban Missile Crisis, before being published the next year as a book. The authors introduced the book saying: 'Men, machines, and mathematics being what they are, this is, unfortunately, a "true" story. The accident may not occur in the way we describe but the laws of probability assure us that ultimately it will occur.' The implication was that a simple, apparently minor, mechanical failure could have unthinkable, catastrophic effects.[20]

Both novels were turned into well-regarded movies. The first and most memorable was *Red Alert*, except that director Stanley Kubrick turned it into a black comedy and renamed it *Dr. Strangelove*.[21] The deranged general responsible for the disaster became Jack D. Ripper, convinced that Russia was seeking to pollute the 'precious bodily fluids' of Americans. He was in command of a wing of nuclear-armed B-52 bombers, which he ordered to attack Russia. As the president brought in the Soviet ambassador to warn him of the danger to his country, and to help the Russians shoot down the planes if they could, it transpired that the Soviet Union had created a doomsday device consisting of many buried bombs, laced with cobalt, to be detonated automatically should any nuclear attack strike the country. As in *On the Beach*, the result would be to wipe out all human and animal life. The doomsday system might have had a deterrent effect had it been public knowledge. Unfortunately its existence was to have been revealed the next week. As with George's ending in *Red Alert*, the recall code was seized from Ripper's base, and most planes were successfully recalled, though one continued on its mission, damaged by Russian defences and without communications. This time, however, when the bomb was released it detonated and the Doomsday device was triggered.

Kubrick introduced Dr Strangelove, a civilian strategist with a Nazi past. There was no such character in *Red Alert*, although there was an equally sinister Professor Groeteschele in *Fail-Safe*. Both Groeteschele and Strangelove were modelled on Herman Kahn, who had written the bestselling account of nuclear strategy, *On Thermonuclear War*, published in 1960, and had become something of a celebrity as a result of his provocative analyses and an apparent tendency to playfulness when talking about mass death. Kahn was a favourite target of critics, and his humanity had been questioned—'no one could write like this; no one could think like this.'[22] He had written his book at the RAND Corporation, the most famous of the 'think-tanks' where the mysteries of nuclear strategy were explored, although he left soon after its publication to set up his own Hudson Institute, in part because his colleagues at RAND objected to his showmanship and because he felt they were becoming too bureaucratic.[23]

In both movies the Kahn character allows nuclear war to be discussed in terms of a cold rationality, detached from any human emotion. The role is to illuminate the perverse logic behind plans for mass murder and the continuing dilemma of extracting strategic benefit from these plans by demonstrating how they just might be implemented. Groeteschele explains coolly the reasoning behind a first strike, pointing out that from 'their point of view' the Japanese were 'right' to attack Pearl Harbor in December 1941 because the United States was their 'mortal enemy'. 'As long as we existed, we were a deadly threat to them. Their only mistake was that they failed to finish us at the start. And they paid for that mistake at Hiroshima.' This is the importance of the knockout blow. If there was one thing worse than failing to take your chance, it was taking your chance and then failing. Groeteschele assumed that the risk of an American doomsday machine would persuade the Russians to stay their hand even if the unauthorised aircraft were allowed to continue with their mission. There would only be more loss if they retaliated. He saw the communists as mortal enemies and wanted to bring the Soviet Union down. 'They are not motivated by human emotions, such as rage and pity. They are calculating machines; they will look at the balance sheet and they will see they cannot win.'

Kahn had explored the idea of a doomsday machine in *On Thermonuclear War*, describing it as being

> protected from enemy action (perhaps by being put thousands of feet underground) and then connected to a computer which is in turn connected, by a reliable communications system, to hundreds of sensory devices all over the United States. The computer would then be programmed so that if, say, five nuclear bombs exploded over the United States, the device would be triggered and the earth destroyed.

He did explain that such a device was never likely to be adopted by a government, although this appears to be for reasons of expense as much as operational considerations.[24] In the movie, Dr Strangelove reported on a study he had commissioned from the 'Bland Corporation' on 'a doomsday machine' that would reinforce deterrence, which was the 'art of producing in the mind of the enemy the fear to attack'. The credibility of the doomsday machine derived from automaticity that 'rules out human meddling'. The trigger conditions would be programmed into a deep computer memory bank.[25]

The nuclear age was still young. A strategy of deterrence had been adopted as demonstrating resolve without provocation, a way to be firm but not suicidal. The weapons would not be allowed to support aggression, but they were there, available and on alert, to respond to aggression. So long as both sides understood the risks, and by the end of the 1950s they clearly did, then there could be an awkward but durable stalemate. The concerns raised by *Red Alert*, of a pre-programmed nuclear holocaust resulting from combinations of human and mechanical errors, independent of any political crisis, not only touched deep popular concerns but also pointed to a real weakness in the deterrent strategy. Kahn himself was well aware of George's novel, having used it for training courses, and praised 'the clever way the general negates the elaborate system set up to prevent unauthorized behaviour'.[26]

Thomas Schelling, who had also spent some time at RAND and eventually got a Nobel Prize for Economics, took the scenario seriously and advised Kubrick on the screenplay of *Dr. Strangelove*. After reading the novel he developed his ideas for a communications link between Moscow and Washington to reduce the dangers the book described.[27] In a 1960 article, which he passed on to Kubrick, Schelling observed that what might appear as accidents reflected past choices that then made possible the loss of control. 'The point is that accidents do not cause war. Decisions cause war.' He was urging people to think about the structure of a nuclear relationship to make these decisions less dangerous.[28] This was the point of nuclear strategy. We need deterrence, he explained, not only to get at the 'rational calculator in full control of his faculties' but also the 'nervous, hotheaded, frightened desperate decision that might be precipitated at the peak of a crisis, that might be the result of an accident or false alarm, that might be engineered by an act of mischief'. To do that it was necessary to make it self-evident that starting war would be unattractive in all circumstances, even if an enemy attack was feared. In practice, policymakers were becoming all too aware of the dangers of escalation into nuclear war and were becoming more inhibited than reckless as a result. In 1961, at the height of the Berlin crisis, Schelling set up a crisis game that involved members of the government to see how matters might unfold. The 'single most striking result', according to one of his colleagues, was 'our inability to get a fight started'.[29]

[8]

Stuck in the Nuclear Age

If the picture of the world I have drawn is rather bleak, it could nonetheless be cataclysmically worse.

ALBERT WOHLSTETTER,
'The Delicate Balance of Terror', 1959[1]

Over six futile weeks spent at the end of 1958, a number of representatives from five NATO and five Warsaw Pact states met in Geneva. This was the 'Conference of Experts for the Study of Possible Measures Which Might Be Helpful in Preventing Surprise Attack and for the Preparation of a Report thereon to Governments.' A sense of futility was there from the start as it became apparent that two sides were working on completely different agendas, reflecting their distinctive views about the likely source of a surprise attack. So different were the agendas, noted one observer, that it was 'difficult to understand how they could have been drafted for the same conference.'[2]

President Eisenhower had proposed the conference to promote an inspection regime that would reveal any preparations for a surprise attack. This was a time when the US was relying on covert U-2 spy plane flights to try to work out what the Soviet Union was up to amid fears that it was pushing ahead in the arms race. There were three problems with this approach. The first was that the sort of inspections the president had in mind might pick up dangers from long-range bombers but were less likely to do so with solid-fuelled rockets that could be prepared quickly for launch and reach their targets in minutes rather than hours. The second was that, in the secretive Soviet system, inspections were seen as just another form of espionage, perhaps preparatory to a surprise attack, and for that reason were bound to be rejected.

The third and most crucial problem was that the American and Soviet leaderships feared completely different sorts of attack. Both had been caught by surprise in 1941 and were nervous about being so again. The Americans were worried about a nuclear Pearl Harbor, a bolt from the blue that would take out its most vital nuclear assets and leave them without any means of retaliation. By contrast, Soviet thinking went back to Operation Barbarossa. The danger they saw lay in West German membership of NATO and its rearmament, just then getting underway. Even as the conference was starting Nikita Khrushchev was challenging the special status of West Berlin, threatening to give East Germany 'its sovereignty on land, water, and in the air'. Having already been attacked twice by Germany over the previous half century the aim was to prevent it happening a third time with an even deadlier form of blitzkrieg. The Soviet focus was not on missile deployments, an area of presumed advantage (albeit illusory as it turned out), but on preventing troop concentrations on the border, and German access to nuclear weapons of any sort. 'Fundamentally', noted Jeremi Suri, 'the salient ideological differences between the East and the West at the Surprise Attack Conference had little to do with capitalism and communism, and much more to do with geography and memories of the preceding wars.'[3]

So both sides focused on fears of what the other side might get up to while insisting that their own preparations were purely defensive in intent. This raised again the security dilemma, 'deriving from mutual suspicion and mutual fear', as states were compelled 'to compete for ever more power in order to find more security', even though the effort was doomed to be self-defeating and potentially tragic.[4] Misunderstandings and even accidents might play a role, so that a Third World War might start inadvertently. With all these weapons in existence and new countries starting their own nuclear programmes, how could there be confidence that somewhere down the line something would not go terribly wrong? In 1960 the British scientist and novelist C. P. Snow warned of the ease with which plutonium could be made and the number of states that could therefore build bombs. 'We know', he continued, 'with the certainty of statistical truth, that if enough of these weapons are made—by enough different states—some of them are going to blow up. Through accident, or folly, or madness—but the motives don't matter. . . . We genuinely know the risks. We are faced with an "either/or," and we haven't much time.'[5]

THIS CONVICTION THAT THE WORLD'S LEADERS FACED A STARK choice—between international action to control the bomb and complete tragedy—was present from the start of the nuclear age. The scientists who built the bomb had rationalised their enterprise as ensuring that Nazi Germany did not get this terrible weapon first and then as a way of shocking the international community into accepting the imperatives of world government. Once the war was over they took up the case forcefully. The objective was captured in a 1946 book with a title straight out of Wells—*One World or None*.[6]

But the world was now hopelessly divided. In June 1946 the United States did put forward a plan to the United Nations to develop nuclear energy solely for civilian purposes while prohibiting military use. But with relations deteriorating the Soviet Union detected a plot. Moscow saw that it might be denied the opportunity to build its own capabilities only to find that the United States had found a loophole to maintain its monopoly. For their part the Americans worried that without strong enforcement mechanisms the Soviet Union would cheat, allowing it to disclose a covert arsenal after everyone else had disarmed. Whether or not better-constructed proposals might have prevented a nuclear arms race at this stage, this effort soon petered out. The recent experience of another terrible war and the sudden revelation of a terrible new weapon had not enabled governments to bridge their differences and cooperate for the collective good. So if the choice was really one world or none the gloomy alternative to world government and serious disarmament started to loom large.

For firm believers in disarmament the case appeared more compelling than ever. This was no longer a matter of reducing armaments to reduce wasteful expenditure or levels of mistrust but an urgent need to save the human race from annihilation. Philip Noel-Baker, for example, had long been a vigorous proponent of general and complete disarmament. He had been involved with the founding of the League of Nations and then, as a member of the British government, in founding the United Nations. Nothing, not even the dismal experience of the interwar years, diminished his conviction in the supreme rationality of his cause. The only problem was that it had not been pursued vigorously enough. In 1958 Noel-Baker set out his beliefs in a book called *The Arms Race: A Programme for World Disarmament*. The next year he was awarded the Nobel Peace Prize for his efforts. In his Nobel lecture he reasserted his long-standing principles: '[I]t makes no sense to talk about disarming,' he asserted, 'unless you believe that war, *all* war, can be abolished.' This was the heart of his beliefs. War was a terrible way to settle disputes: there were far better forms of settlement, and they now needed to be applied. 'Unless there is an iron resolution to make it the supreme object of international policy and to realize it now,' he insisted, 'I believe all talks about disarmament will fail.' With this iron will then there could be success. Disarmament could come in stages, and an eventual treaty of general and complete disarmament would be 'a long and complex document,' but he was not of the view that the devil would be in the detail. Here he quoted Salvador de Madariaga: 'Technical difficulties are political objections in uniform.'[7]

When preparing his book, Noel-Baker recruited a bright young Australian to help him out. The partnership did not last. Hedley Bull soon became convinced that Noel-Baker's approach was both dated and mistaken. It could never prosper. This might be just as well, as otherwise it would make a bad situation worse. In 1959 he published a trenchant review of *The Arms Race*. At its heart was an analysis of the relationship between disarmament and peace. Bull offered a succinct explanation of why general and comprehensive disarmament was probably impossible:

> In an international society in which war is a possible outcome between politically competing states, and there is no supreme coercive authority, a state can provide for its security and protect its interests only by its own armed strength and that of its allies: this is the context in which states have armaments and maintain their own control over the level of these armaments.

Bull dismissed Noel-Baker's goal of substituting a system based on states taking responsibility for their own security with an alternative system based on collective security. This would require that 'any act of aggression, anywhere, by anyone, against anyone, will be resisted by all the members of the system collectively; faced with this threat of overwhelming power, no state will resort to aggression.' This, Bull described as a quite abstract and unhistorical conception of international relations, in which states are bloodless, passionless units, having no natural sympathies or antipathies, loyalties, or hostilities and, like the citizens of Victorian tracts on representative government, are moved only by the rational contemplation of right or interest.

The desirability question Bull answered by noting the growing view in the West 'that the nuclear stalemate is a preservative of peace, and should therefore be left well alone.'

This explained why Noel-Baker seemed such a lone voice. The focus was now on second-order questions such as nuclear testing. Contrary to Noel-Baker's view that it was possible to dispense with armaments because war was an anachronism, Bull insisted that war between the nuclear powers was only anachronistic because of the terrible armaments. In this respect, therefore, the 'function of nuclear armaments in the international system at the present time is to limit the incidence of war.' This situation might not be satisfactory, but it was unlikely to be abandoned without confidence in some replacement. Bull concluded: 'In the present world, states are not only unlikely to conclude a general and comprehensive disarmament agreement, but are behaving rationally in refusing to do so.'[8]

Bull here was capturing a shift in thinking that had been underway since the middle of the decade. The international system was already starting to look surprisingly stable. One reason for this was its stark clarity. The complications of a system with a number of competing great powers and fluid alliances had been replaced by one dominated by two 'superpowers' (a term introduced in 1944 to cover the United States and the Soviet Union, and then also the British Empire[9]), each developing an arsenal of awesome destructiveness. Europe had been divided quite neatly into two, with the fracture passing through Germany, and each side sharing critical features in its political and economic arrangements with its presiding superpower. Only in Berlin, also divided but stuck in the middle of East Germany, was the position still uncertain, which is why it was the main area of contention. The starkness of the divide meant that no easy reconciliation was available, but also that an act of aggression would be unambiguous, and would trigger fighting almost immediately. Because of nuclear weapons it was taken for granted that this was would soon lead to a catastrophic war.

On the NATO side the conventional forces facing the Warsaw Pact were described as having a 'trip-wire' rather than a purely defensive function. The need was to warn that a wider war would be triggered by any move across the inner-German border. This prospect introduced a degree of caution into international affairs. This was not a time to try out radical approaches. The aim instead was to encourage respect for the status quo. If the First World War had dashed confidence in the possibility of a stable balance of power, the nuclear age helped revive it. In one of his last speeches as prime minister, Winston Churchill commented on the 'sublime irony' that a stage had been reached 'where safety will be the sturdy child of terror, and survival the twin brother of annihilation.'[10]

In 1961 the new European order was put under its most severe challenge with a crisis over West Berlin. The Soviet leader Nikita Khrushchev challenged its special position, not least because it was providing an outlet for tens of thousands of East Germans who wished to escape communism. The tension grew as President Kennedy took a tough stance. In August of that year the Communists solved their problem by building a wall across the city to stop people leaving the East. The tension eased. But in October the next year there was an even greater crisis when it became apparent that the Soviet Union was seeking to install nuclear missiles in Cuba. Again the Soviet Union backed down, helped by a promise from Kennedy not to invade Cuba.[11] In both cases the logic of deterrence appeared to have worked itself through.

THE ONLY WAY THAT A NUCLEAR WAR COULD BE WON CONCLUSIVELY would be by means of a first strike that precluded enemy retaliation. The way to prevent this was to develop a second-strike capability. This would demand sufficient forces to survive an attempted first strike to be able to retaliate in kind, so the risks of attack would be too great. But if both sides were seeking a first-strike capability a dangerous edginess might develop at times of crisis that could lead to war through miscalculation. It was therefore vital to demonstrate without ambiguity that there was no premium in a first strike. This should encourage both sides to be more cautious and concentrate on diplomacy in a crisis. This was the aspect of the nuclear relationship that Schelling had identified as the key to avoiding war through miscalculation.

Whether or not a first strike option could be developed was the pressing issue of the moment. In 1954 a team at the RAND Corporation, led by Albert Wohlstetter, was asked to consider the optimum basing configurations for the US strategic bomber force. They introduced as a key criterion vulnerability to a surprise attack and in so doing demonstrated how the United States might be caught out by a calculating Soviet Union with a pre-emptive strike.[12] This was the modern-day version of war fiction, except that there was no character development or narrative tension. The approach was rigorously analytical based on the best available data (accepting that what was known about Soviet capabilities was sketchy). The plotline, however, remained focused on how an unscrupulous foreign enemy might catch the United States unawares, piling assumption on assumption to show why a country that appeared secure in its great strength was far more vulnerable than realised.

The idea that the US might just be caught out in this way gained credence from notable Soviet successes in testing the first intercontinental ballistic missile and then the first artificial earth satellite (Sputnik 1) in 1957. In an influential article, based on his study, called the 'Delicate Balance of Terror', Wohlstetter warned against assuming a nuclear stalemate just because both sides were acquiring a capacity to destroy the other. The danger would come if one saw a realistic route to victory. A nuclear first strike would have hideous consequences for the perpetrator if it failed, but it could also be an unequivocal success; any country so disarmed of its means of retaliation would have no choice but surrender. For those contemplating such an attack the difference between suicidal aggression and world domination could rest on fine calculations. Whether the system was truly stable therefore would depend on many factors, such as the range, yield, and accuracy of weapons and the hardness and mobility of targets, along with issues of warning and sequencing.[13]

This analysis was not geared to a mass audience but to policymakers. As with Kahn's *On Thermonuclear War*, the idea that a nuclear war could be imagined and discussed in this way was found by many to be chilling, normalising the idea of mass destruction. Yet this analytical framework shaped the way issues of nuclear war and deterrence were discussed in the professional community over the coming decades. It demanded a degree of technical competence while leaving questions of political motive and consequence unexplored. It influenced the way many policy issues outside the nuclear arena came to be discussed with terms like 'worst-case scenario' and 'damage limitation' entering the vernacular, as well more obvious terms such as 'assured destruction'.

While the origins of this form of analytical literature were not dissimilar to those of *The Battle of Dorking*, being a way of challenging official complacency, in this case the framework set up by the analysts meant that as new information came in, the degree of danger could be measured. Initially, long-range bombers had to be kept on continual alert to prevent them from being eliminated in a surprise attack. When intercontinental ballistic missiles (ICBMs) moved into full production in the early 1960s they were placed in hardened underground silos so that it would require an unlikely direct hit to destroy them. Even less vulnerable were submarine-launched ballistic missiles (SLBMs) which could take full advantage of the ocean expanses to hide from enemy attack and so provide a second-strike capability. Meanwhile, attempts to develop effective defences against nuclear attack proved futile. The standards for anti-aircraft defence in the nuclear age had to be much higher than for conventional air raids, since any penetration of the defensive screen would threaten the defender with catastrophe. Progress was made, using surface-to-air missiles (SAMs) in developing defences against bombers, but the move to ICBMs, with their minimal warning time before impact, appeared to render the defensive task hopeless. Measures of civil defence, which could offer little protection to the civilian populace against nuclear explosions and, at best, only some chance of avoiding exposure to nuclear fallout, also appeared pathetic in the face of the overwhelming destructive power being accumulated by both sides.

WHILE THESE ANALYSES WERE BEING DEVELOPED DURING THE 1950s and into the 1960s the expectations were of regular and destabilising technological breakthroughs. Kahn, who had been inspired by science fiction, filled the last section of *On Thermonuclear War* with predictions for the future, in the form of coming revolutions in military affairs, with four expected over the next thirteen years. Those that stand out as accurate—a man on the moon from 1969—have to be set against the others that were off mark. The problem was an exaggeration of the financial and engineering effort required, as if major breakthroughs would materialise without exceptional effort. A typical observation for 1965 was that though he had not seen any figures, 'I surmise that relatively thin margins of cost prevent us from doing such extraordinary projects as melting ice caps and diverting ocean currents.'[14] In the nuclear field he sought more defensive systems, believing these could make the difference between a recoverable society and one that was completely lost.

The assumption that the Cold War would move into outer space was widely shared, with orbiting bombs and space stations directing fire to the earth, as if this was the high ground always beloved of strategists. Perhaps because this was the new frontier that fascinated writers of science fiction it seemed only natural to make military preparations. At least one writer hoped that if the superpowers could be persuaded to fight out their battles in space then they might spare the earth.[15] In 1959 army researchers explained the vital importance of establishing a lunar outpost before the Soviet Union had a chance to do so, even though they were not yet quite sure of its military potential. By 1965 the US Army Weapons Command's Future Weapons Office was writing that:

> Because of the entirely new and different environment and conditions facing man in space, we cannot wait until the eleventh hour to "crash" a weapon program through with any hope of success, for we may even now be standing on the edge of the battleground of Armageddon.[16]

In the end there was a strong disposition to keep space free of weapons, not least because in practice there was little point sending weapons out into orbit in order to bring them back to hit targets on earth. Where space came to be of vital importance to military operations was not for weapons but for reconnaissance, navigational and communications satellites.

DESPITE THE VISIONS OF ARMAGEDDON, BY THE MID-1960S fears had eased of a technological arms race that might encourage either side to unleash a surprise attack. For the foreseeable future each side could eliminate the other as a modern industrial state. Robert McNamara, the US secretary of defense for much of that decade, argued that the two superpowers could impose 'unacceptable damage,' put at 25 per cent of population and 50 per cent of industry, on each other. Mutual Assured Destruction (MAD) conveyed exactly what it was supposed to convey—destruction would be assured and mutual and certainly unacceptable. Contrary to what had been assumed, therefore, the system tended towards stability. This was not so much a deliberate policy choice but recognition of a condition which confirmed the risks involved in any attempt to achieve a decisive victory through a knockout blow.

Yet the idea that a daring and an accomplished enemy might exploit a critical vulnerability did not go away. Albert Wohlstetter's wife, Roberta, made her name in 1962 with the publication of an original critique of how the Americans were caught out by Pearl Harbor. She understood that when designing their policies both the United States and Japan had assumed that the other would react as they would wish them to react without asking carefully whether they might react completely differently. Her answer to the question of how 'honest, dedicated and intelligent men' could get so badly caught out was the 'noise' of misleading signals that prevented them from appreciating the real clues. As a result they concentrated on the signals that supported what they already thought. There was nothing unique, she argued, about Pearl Harbor. The United States had been surprised by the North Korean invasion of the South in 1950 and then again when China entered the war months later on the North's behalf after the possibility had been dismissed by General MacArthur. As the book was published the US was surprised again by the discovery of Soviet missile sites in Cuba. The development of thermonuclear weapons had raised the stakes. If anything 'the balance of advantage seems clearly to have shifted since Pearl Harbor in favor of a surprise attacker.' Her lesson was that whatever improvements might be made to warning systems, the safest course was to ensure that the country's defences could cope even if caught out again.[17]

This was the gravamen of her husband's position during the 1950s. His warnings had been taken seriously in the design of US strategic forces during the 1960s, but then MAD suggested a stage had been reached when there was no premium on a surprise attack. By the end of the decade, however, Albert Wohlstetter was back to the fore challenging the complacency this implied. He promoted a scenario that was presented as technical discourse yet had elements of fantasy. After a slow start the Soviet ICBM programme had been through a growth spurt. According to Wohlstetter's scenario, the numbers could soon reach a point where a surprise attack by Soviet ICBMs might effectively eliminate the American ICBM force. The US would be able to retaliate but, assuming long-range bombers bases were also hit, could only do so with submarine-launched missiles. Unfortunately these were inaccurate, so while the Soviets would have attacked military targets the US retaliation would be against cities. This in turn would invite a Soviet response against American cities, thereby making the situation far worse. This scenario was first set out in making a case for a new anti-ballistic missile (ABM) system that could protect the US missile silos. This was a complex calculation, requiring assumptions about missile and warhead numbers, their accuracy, and the hardness of the missile silos. If the threat could not be confirmed then the ABM would be unnecessary. On the other hand, if the threat was even greater than claimed, the ABM would be unable to cope.

These scenarios lacked a basic credibility. Such a strike would require confidence that weapons would perform exactly as promised in an attack that had never previously been attempted; that it would not be detected in time for missiles to be launched before they were destroyed; and that, even successful, the victim would show restraint, because the attack would somehow be experienced as one solely directed against the nuclear force and not against society as a whole, despite mass casualties. Perhaps in the face of such carnage an American president might hold back in a shocked paralysis. But the Soviet leader could not rely upon such restraint, and would know that if the remaining US arsenal was used then his country would no longer exist as a modern industrial society.

Almost as soon as this idea was introduced the proposed remedy became unavailable as the United States and Soviet Union agreed to limit deployments of defences under the 1972 ABM Treaty. The schemes then designed to make land-based ICBMs less vulnerable became ever more complex. One involved a large track with many spurs so Soviet targeteers could never be sure where the missiles were hiding. The easiest place to hide long-range missiles remained underwater on submarines, which were becoming more accurate. After years of anxiety and expense addressing what was essentially a non-problem, an official commission decided that this was not an issue worth worrying about. The concern soon faded away.[18]

Contrary to the laments of those who could not imagine anything worse than a situation in which two huge, ideologically opposed and nuclear-armed alliances opposed each other, theorists of international relations continued to follow Bull and insist that this was almost the best of the possible worlds. The bipolarity produced a clarity and focus, without the complications produced by shifting alliances, while nuclear weapons were just the trick needed to hold the two behemoths back from war. There could be no doubt that war would be joint suicide. Kenneth Waltz observed in 1981 that the international system had developed a high ability 'to absorb changes and to contain conflicts and hostility'. He was in no doubt of the contribution of nuclear weapons to this happy state of affairs. They had made 'the cost of war seem frighteningly high and thus discourage states from starting any wars that might lead to the use of such weapons'. So confident was he of this effect that he welcomed the spread of nuclear weapons to other conflicts as a source of peace.[19]

The top British nuclear strategist Michael Quinlan emphasised how nuclear weapons carried war's potential 'past a boundary at which many previous concepts and categories of appraisal—both military and political—ceased to apply, or even to have meaning.' They had made 'achievable what is for practical purposes infinite destructive power, unstoppable and inexhaustible at any humanly-relevant levels.' There was a spectrum of force, with nuclear war at one end. It was tempting to divide this up to establish thresholds. But such a division would be unreliable: 'no conceptual boundary could be wholly dependable amid the stresses of major war.' Hence the restraining effect on all war: 'non-nuclear war is not just appalling in itself. It is also the likeliest route to nuclear war—in practice indeed the only likely route, since scenarios of the holocaust being launched by accident or through technical malfunction are absurdly far-fetched.'[20]

In 1983 six top Harvard scholars explained the international community's adaption to the nuclear age as a result of the 'crystal ball effect'—foreknowledge of the probable effects of a nuclear war. As a result of this knowledge there was a wise propensity to avoid war.[21] On further contemplation the Harvard team were not wholly convinced that they wished to rely on this. In a project connected to their programme on avoiding nuclear war, they considered the alternatives to deterrence, with ten scenarios for a lessened threat. These went from reducing the vulnerability of populations, less dependence upon nuclear weapons or else their abolition, to a variety of political possibilities, including accommodation with the Soviet Union and even world federalism.[22] In looking at the workings of the 'crystal ball effect' during the 1962 Cuban Missile Crisis, James Blight argued that the effect worked when combined with a 'visceral fear' that this might actually come to pass. Without the emotion that made the dangers seem so real and immediate, the knowledge would just fall into the 'trash heap of received wisdom', accepted 'by rote and not from conviction'. To get governments to behave responsibly they needed not only the crystal ball but also the fear that it might be shattered.[23] Then, as the book was published, the Cold War came to an end and the fear evaporated.

[9]

A Surprise Peace

I really do inhabit a system in which words are capable of shaking
the entire structure of government, where words can prove might-
ier than ten military divisions.

VÁCLAV HAVEL,
speech accepting peace prize, 15 October 1989[1]

The major powers avoided catastrophe by scaring themselves into
caution. But if, thankfully, wars were unlikely to be fought that
left those designing, constructing, and sustaining conventional armed
forces with a perplexing task. The word 'conventional' suggested
some link with the past 'conventions' of classical warfare, but it was
hard to see their point when there was no obvious route to a decisive
battlefield victory against a nuclear-armed opponent. The residual
role of conventional force could only be one of reinforcing deterrence, holding a defensive line against an enemy offensive, or ensuring that the enemy's advance was costly and painful. At best this
would allow sufficient time for second thoughts and active negotiations; at worst it would create the powder trail that would take the
war to its explosive climax.

During the Cold War it was assumed that the Warsaw Pact had
numbers and geography on its side, so that if it chose it could expand
into Western Europe without resort to nuclear weapons. The fateful
choice would be up to NATO: to surrender or accept nuclear suicide.
The Americans, from the other side of the Atlantic, were deeply

uncomfortable with the thought that war in Europe could put their homeland so directly at risk. While in private they doubted whether a president would ever actually take the nuclear initiative, in public they played down their anxieties lest they undermine the credibility of the deterrent. The obvious way out of the dilemma was to improve conventional forces so that at least they had alternative responses to aggression. The Americans worked to separate the nuclear from the conventional, with a firebreak between the two, and to encourage NATO to build up its regular forces. Eventually in 1967 a compromise doctrine of 'flexible response' was adopted, whereby the Europeans recognised the US requirement for an extended conventional stage, so that the first shots across the Iron Curtain would not lead automatically to a nuclear holocaust. In return, the US accepted the need for a clear link between a land war in Europe and its own strategic nuclear arsenal.[2]

It was impossible to know how well flexible response would work in practice, but the introduction of flexibility into the response meant that it was at least possible that a major war would not turn to nuclear exchanges as automatically as had been supposed. Nightmarish images of a Third World War had dominated the literature. As the risk of a superpower war appeared to subside, the harder it was to conjure up any scenario in which a moderately sane leader would risk a major war let alone authorise nuclear use. That did not prevent occasional war scares. From the mid-1970s hawkish commentators began to conjure up scenarios involving Soviet invasions. In turn this led to fears, captured by well-supported anti-nuclear movements, that an exaggerated response to this alarmism might lead to a nuclear apocalypse.[3]

IN LATE 1976 GENERAL SIR JOHN HACKETT, A FORMER NATO commander, brought together a group of retired senior colleagues from the British military, bolstered by the deputy editor of *The Economist*, to see whether they could describe how a Third World War might come about.[4] Their aim, in the tradition of *The Battle of Dorking*, was to use fiction to make a case for greater military preparedness. *The Third World War: A Future History* was a surprising bestseller (over 3 million copies worldwide), read by British prime ministers and American presidents.[5] Hackett's team stuck to what was already in the public domain about weapons and doctrines, using maps and illustrations. They envisaged a war starting in 1985, which was quite soon. There were still so many unanticipated events that a new version had to be brought out in 1982, now only looking a couple of years ahead.[6] One reason for the short timescale, according to Hackett, was that he was not trying to write science fiction, and he did not want to give away any secrets about future weapons.

'Without much in the way of characters or plot', Brians observed, 'the books are almost unreadable; but they provide a fascinating glimpse into the mind of one of the military strategists associated with NATO.'[7] There had been a forerunner, written in 1977 by Belgian Brigadier General Robert Close. This reflected concerns about the improvements in Soviet conventional capabilities. The most alarming scenario was that the alliance could be caught out by a 'bolt from the blue' standing start by the Warsaw Pact, with a minimum of mobilisation, leading to Europe being overrun in a couple of days.[8] This message was captured in the stark title of Close's book, *Europe Without Defence?*[9] Another, potentially rival, book also published in 1978, with a similar title to Hackett's, had an equally bleak message, this time with the alliance only managing to hold off for four days before the nuclear exchanges began.[10]

After thirty years of cold war it was unlikely that the Soviet Union was itching to mount an attack on the West or that Moscow had a convincing plan for a knockout blow. Hackett's view was that war between the two alliances was more likely to come 'not by design but by coincidence of miscalculation and mischance'. The danger would come if a number of crises developed together and then some spark turned them into a conflagration, comparable to the assassination of the Archduke Ferdinand in 1914. If this happened, NATO would be in trouble because its forces had been run down while those of the Warsaw Pact had continued to be built up. NATO could not sustain a high intensity war for long. The scenario envisaged a quick takeover of West Germany. All would not quite be lost because eventually, after a couple of years, the United States would gain command of the sea, sort out the Middle East and then launch a liberating offensive from France. Hackett was told by 'responsible people' that, however credible, this prospect was too dismal and harmful to the alliance. Close's book had undermined morale rather than strengthened resolve. He accepted the point, acknowledging that 'a cautionary tale that makes children pee in their beds, instead of frightening them into a sense of doing better, has failed in its object'.[11] So Hackett started again, this time assuming that the West did something right and made serious efforts to improve defences, while the Warsaw Pact did little more. Now the war could all be over within a few weeks. Instead of the rush to a cataclysm which had been the hallmark of nuclear age fiction, the book envisaged only tentative nuclear employment, somewhat late in the day. Having a limited nuclear exchange showed that it was still hard to write these weapons completely out of the script, but now also hard to develop a convincing scenario for war when they were present. The purpose of the Soviet Union's limited strike was to hit Birmingham to get Britain out of the war. This failed when Minsk was hit in retaliation and triggered the break-up of the Soviet Union. Just as Chesney piled up negative assumptions with the result that Britain was narrowly defeated at Dorking, Hackett piled up the positive assumptions so that NATO just won in 1985. The message was that without extra defence spending NATO risked failure. Another message was to keep alliances in good repair.

By contrast to Hackett, with his substantial military experience, Tom Clancy was an insurance agent who wrote in his spare time. This was until he got his breakthrough in 1984 with a thriller, *The Hunt for Red October*. Much of this book's appeal lay in the technical detail which Clancy had obtained from a voracious reading of naval literature. The story involved the defection of a Typhoon class Soviet submarine, with a Lithuanian captain who loathed the Soviet system. The drama resulted from the efforts of the Soviet fleet to prevent the boat, containing the most advanced sonar technology, falling into American hands.

His next book, *Red Storm Rising*, was more in line with Hackett's.[12] Like Hackett, Clancy did not go too far into the future and drew on the politics and technology of the time. He had help on the military side from a former naval officer and material in the public domain. The possibility of a new aircraft (which turned out to be the F-117) employing stealth technology so that it would be missed by radar was long discussed in the specialist technical press before its existence was admitted in 1988, two years after Clancy's book appeared. The plot was complex. It included Islamic terrorists from Azerbaijan creating an energy crisis by destroying vital Soviet oil facilities, leading to Soviet seizure of Gulf oil fields; a direct Warsaw Pact attack against West Germany, justified after framing West German activists for a deadly attack on a Moscow school; and the NATO air station at Keflavik, Iceland, seized (again using deception) allowing Soviet submarines to get into the Atlantic to disrupt resupply convoys. The fight back involved stealth bombers, cruise missiles, and the Marines retaking Iceland, before Soviet forces ran out of fuel, giving NATO an opportunity to turn things around with a bold move. A split in the Soviet leadership allowed for a swift and negotiated end to the fighting. No nuclear weapons were used and, in the end, no territory changed hands.

President Reagan was a fan of Clancy's. He described *The Hunt for Red October* as a 'perfect yarn'. He was even more enthusiastic about *Red Storm Rising* for it vindicated his own prejudices.[13] The president suspected the Soviet leadership to be fully capable of the sort of deception Clancy described, which included planning a war while offering the Americans arms reductions. Yet at the same time he was appalled by the prospect of nuclear war. In 1983 he launched what he called a 'strategic defence initiative' to develop layered defences against a Soviet missile attack. Better, he said, to save American lives from a nuclear attack than to avenge them after one.[14] This was why Clancy's other message, that NATO could defend itself without resort to nuclear threats, appealed to him. In 1986 he discussed the book with advisers en route to Reykjavik, Iceland's capital, for a summit meeting with Mikhail Gorbachev, the Soviet leader. There over two extraordinary days the two men almost agreed on drastic reductions in their nuclear arsenals. Reagan's refusal to concede his strategic defence initiative resulted in failure. British Prime Minister Margaret Thatcher, a convinced advocate of nuclear deterrence, was alarmed at how far Reagan had been prepared to go down the non-nuclear route. When they met in October 1986 he urged her to read Clancy's book to calm her fears. A British official recorded: 'It gave an excellent picture of the Soviet Union's intentions and strategy. He had clearly been much impressed by the book.'[15]

Both books picked up on the unease surrounding nuclear weapons and the possibility that a major war could be won without mutual destruction. Hackett relied on a growing defence budget: Clancy saw more clearly how the qualitative edge in conventional forces was shifting to the United States and that this might reduce the need to depend on nuclear threats. Both also were sensitive to the crisis in the Soviet system, although neither anticipated that the system would implode at the end of the decade, let alone that this would be triggered by a loss of legitimacy rather than failure in war. Clancy was still imagining a war between the United States and the Soviet Union in 1991, even after the Warsaw Pact had fallen apart.[16] Hackett assumed, as did almost all commentators at this time, that Moscow would take a hard line against dissidence. Yet it was essential to his plot that the old guard in the Kremlin knew that 'time was running out'. In the event, instead of a war launched to hold the Soviet bloc together, 1985 saw Mikhail Gorbachev become president and the start of a process that would soon lead to the peaceful break-up of the Soviet bloc.

JUST AS THE BOLSHEVIK REVOLUTION WAS A RESPONSE TO the inability of the old regime to cope with war it was not unreasonable to assume that it would take a war to create the crisis that would break the Soviet system. There was always a possibility that a regime that saw a deep threat to its position would take risks that in other circumstances would be rejected as foolhardy. This was why much Cold War diplomacy accepted that it was best not to push the Soviet leadership to a point where it might be provoked into recklessness. It was one thing, however to follow this principle when considering geopolitical spheres of influence but quite another when addressing the ideological contest at the core of the East-West divide. Western countries were not going to stop promoting a liberal political philosophy for fear of upsetting the Soviet leadership. This is why scenarios for war by the 1980s tended to involve a crisis of legitimacy within the Soviet system, probably involving one of the satellite states. This developing instability on the one hand promised a way to bring the Cold War to a satisfactory conclusion but on the other hand might prompt precisely those conditions which might trigger war.

Communist rule depended on the twin assumptions that any challenge would be dealt with ruthlessly and that the West would do nothing about it. These assumptions had been validated by experience. In 1956 after a rebellion threw out the communists, a new Hungarian government announced its intention to leave the Warsaw Pact. The Soviet Union sent in tanks to crush the rebellion. Although the uprising was home-grown, it had been actively encouraged by the Voice of America.[17] Yet American military action, warned US Secretary of State John Foster Dulles, 'would . . . precipitate a full-scale world war and probably the result of that would be all these people wiped out.'[18] The brutal logic of a divided Europe was underlined again in 1968. This time the Czech Communist Party moved to liberalise the system, though they were careful not to threaten to leave the Warsaw Pact. It made no difference. On 20 August 1968 the tanks went in again. Following this sad episode, NATO countries concluded that the political divide in Europe was permanent and began to develop policies of détente to manage the relationship between the continent's two halves. The implications of this were spelt out in a document signed by Presidents Richard Nixon of the United States and Leonid Brezhnev of the Soviet Union on the basic principles that could underpin a new superpower relationship: 'Differences in ideology and in the social systems of the USA and USSR are not obstacles to the bilateral development of normal relations based on the principles of sovereignty, equality, non-interference in internal affairs and mutual advantage.'[19]

Yet as this statement was made a shift was taking place that encouraged the subversion of the official Marxism-Leninism of the Warsaw Pact. Late in 1972 negotiations began on a Conference on Security and Cooperation in Europe (CSCE). For three years intense discussions took place (it took four months to agree an agenda) over a declaration that had no legal force. On 1 August 1975 the leaders of thirty-four states (plus the Vatican) met in Helsinki to sign what was described as its Final Act. This involved four 'baskets'. The first covered political and military issues, territorial integrity, the definition of borders, peaceful settlement of disputes, and the implementation of confidence-building measures between opposing militaries. The second focused on economic issues like trade and scientific cooperation. The third basket emphasised human rights, including freedom of emigration and reunification of families divided by international borders, cultural exchanges, and freedom of the press. The fourth and final basket was about further meetings and implementation.

Most of what Moscow wanted was in the first two baskets. It was the third that proved the most controversial. In one respect it appeared pointless because of deep Soviet opposition to any serious liberalisation. This is why the Nixon Administration was reluctant to expend valuable political capital on 'gestures' that would have no effect. West European governments wanted to keep up the pressure on the issue. The Soviet bloc resisted, pushing instead promises to refrain from the use of force, respect for territorial integrity, the peaceful settlement of disputes, and especially 'non-interference in internal affairs'. In the end, Moscow wanted the first two baskets too much to let their problems with the third be an obstacle. They chose to accept the language with the intention of then ignoring it. This meant signing up to a statement about human rights as 'deriving from the inherent dignity of the human person' and a requirement that they be not only respected but also promoted as a means to achieve peace and friendly relations between states. Moscow just noted that none of this would be binding under international law and there would be no legislative changes in the socialist states.[20]

US Secretary of State Henry Kissinger's views had been shaped by his own experiences of war and disorder, leaving him with little confidence in proposals for pooling sovereignty or sharing values as means of reducing international conflict. His view was that if peace was the ideal then that meant holding in check other ideals, and being prepared for the hard and often bitter grind of compromise and accommodation, requiring patience, discretion, and occasional guile. This was not a foreign policy for which there was a natural constituency in the United States. It offended liberal idealism by its hard-headed, amoral focus on national interests, and perturbed them by bringing results of which they approved, including détente, without a complementary stress on the judicial settlement of disputes or disarmament. It offended conservatives by shrinking away from a key principle that separated the Western bloc from the Eastern. To play down human rights was to allow the Soviets the conceit that one great power was as good as another, deserving of equal respect, despite the fact that the communist system was oppressing whole nations, as well as denying basic political rights.[21]

In a speech on the 'Moral Foundations of Foreign Policy' in 1975 Kissinger reminded his audience of the disastrous consequences of a major war and the obligation this created 'to seek a more productive and stable relationship despite the basic antagonism of our values.' The US was now in a position common to most other nations in history, unable either to escape from the world or to dominate it. It was not that it was impossible to use influence to promote human rights, but it was best done 'quietly, keeping in mind the delicacy of the problem and stressing results rather than public confrontation.'[22]

By contrast, President Jimmy Carter, who won the 1976 election, made human rights one of the themes of his inaugural address. He denied the tension between the moral and the pragmatic. The United States had a special obligation: 'to take on those moral duties which, when assumed, seem invariably to be in our own best interests'. He described an 'absolute' commitment to human rights, a need to demonstrate to others that 'our democratic system is worthy of emulation'. This led to a promise for a new foreign policy: 'We will not behave in foreign places so as to violate our rules and standards here at home, for we know that the trust which our Nation earns is essential to our strength.' The times were changing:

> The world itself is now dominated by a new spirit. Peoples more numerous and more politically aware are craving, and now demanding, their place in the sun—not just for the benefit of their own physical condition, but for basic human rights.[23]

By this time the 1975 Final Act was already providing dissidents in communist countries with a new tactic. They could assume their governments' sincerity and then challenge them to uphold the Helsinki provisions and ask Western governments to provide support when they did so. This was the case with the Czechoslovak movement, Charter 77. The Charter was a four-page document with 242 signatures offering to help the government meet its various constitutional and international obligations, drawing particular attention to the Helsinki Final Act.[24] The regime sought to discredit the document as 'anti-state, anti-socialist, and demagogic'. As signatories were denounced and thrown out of their jobs, international indignation grew. Helsinki now gave Western governments a reason to comment, replacing caution about interference in internal affairs with references to violations of the Final Act. For a while at least, this gave the regime pause, although they could never acknowledge much of a choice between being shown up as hypocrites and allowing a popular movement to develop that could see them overthrown.

One of the most eloquent exponents of this 'new spirit' was Václav Havel, a successful playwright, and one of the leaders of the movement behind Charter 77.[25] He asked whether human rights could be sacrificed for the sake of peace. His starting point was that life under totalitarianism was a form of death. It was not true, he wrote, that Czechoslovakia was 'free of warfare and murder'. They had just taken different forms, and had 'been shifted from the daylight of observable public events, to the twilight of unobservable inner destruction', presenting as 'the slow, secretive, bloodless, never quite-absolute, yet horrifyingly ever-present death of non-action, non-story, non-life, and non-time.' Thus to argue that it would be better to accept communism for the sake of peace, better 'red than dead', was only to offer 'an infallible sign that the speaker has given up his humanity', by being ready to sacrifice what makes life meaningful and accept impersonal power. He recalled, as an example, 'West German colleagues and friends' avoiding him in the early 1970s for fear that contact with someone out of favour with the government 'would needlessly provoke that government and thereby jeopardize the fragile foundations of nascent détente.' Havel cited this voluntary renunciation of freedom as an example of how easy it was 'for a well-meant cause to betray its good intentions'.[26]

WHEN MIKHAIL GORBACHEV BECAME SOVIET LEADER IN 1985 his aim was not to push human rights but to reform the sclerotic system which he could see to be failing by every measure.[27] Unlike those he replaced, his world-view had not been shaped by the war with Germany, and he had not worked closely with the military-industrial complex that dominated the economy. The more he discovered about the baleful, distorting influence of this complex, depriving all other sectors of resources and talent, the more he was convinced that it had to be cut back. If this was to be achieved then somehow relations with the West had to be calmed and put on to a new and more cooperative path.

From the start Gorbachev was keen to meet with Western leaders and try to chart a new way forward. A succession of summits encouraged commentators to believe that a healthy dialogue was underway and East-West relations should be calmer in the future. Gorbachev's problem was that he was still presiding over a continental empire. This included not only the satellite states of Eastern Europe, each with their own Communist Party, but also those Soviet Socialist Republics who had been acquired by Russia in the past and, in the case of the Baltic States, recently against their will.

For the empire to hold together required local party bosses to follow the path of reform he had set out for the Soviet Union. Yet many were unwilling or unable to follow him. In practice the choice was to accept dependence upon the security apparatus to maintain party control or to allow the empire to fragment. It took until 1989 before this choice became stark. With a number of Warsaw Pact countries already departing from the old ways and showing their independence, Gorbachev could not bring himself to side with the hardliners, especially those in East Germany who were demanding resistance to the West's 'human rights demagogy'. Those reformers who were in power, as in Hungary, were confident that their displays of independence would not result in military action.[28]

In a landmark speech to the United Nations in December 1988 Gorbachev effectively renounced the use of force and asserted a 'credo' that 'political problems should only be solved by political means'.[29] If Gorbachev really thought that the countries that had been coerced into adopting a Stalinist system could move as one along the path of reform he was mistaken. Without force to hold the system in place not only the Warsaw Pact but also the Soviet Union itself fragmented. The system turned out to be rotten. The ideological glue which generations of Soviet leaders had tried to spread so thickly failed to hold.[30] Anatoly Dobrynin, Gorbachev's former ambassador to the US, reported that the Soviet leader 'never foresaw that the whole of Eastern Europe would fly out of the Soviet orbit within months or that the Warsaw Pact would crumble so soon. He became the helpless witness to the consequences of his own policy'.[31]

Why did this rush of developments, viewed with a mixture of astonishment, suspicion, relief, and gratitude, catch the Western intelligence and foreign policy communities so much by surprise? The question was asked with the same intensity as if they had been caught out by a surprise military attack. The same problems of prediction were evident: deciding how to interpret the public pronouncements of the leadership (whose predecessors had been habitually deceptive), picking up real indicators of change amid the noise of conflicting signals, addressing the logic of the situation, and so appreciating the choices to be faced. Not only could there be no certainty about how Gorbachev would actually choose, it was only late in the day that he saw with any clarity the nature of the choice. In reviewing these events it is always important to keep in mind that during that same summer of 1989, as dramatic events were unfolding in Europe, the Chinese Communist Party was facing its own crisis, with mass demonstrations in Beijing's Tiananmen Square demanding reform. In this case the party leadership decided not to take the risk of liberalising the system and instead clamped down ruthlessly.

Military strength had always been assumed to be the Soviet Union's greatest asset, available in extremis to get the regime out of trouble. Whatever contrary evidence might be produced, the mindset was one in which the Soviet Union had enormous capabilities and would do whatever was necessary for the sake of its security. It was unimaginable that when the moment came that Moscow would not deploy its armed forces, emphasised by the West for so long, to prevent a catastrophic upheaval that would reduce forever its international standing. There had been decades of talking up Soviet military power. The 1980s had begun with the Reagan Administration issuing a series of alarming and lavishly illustrated publications with projections on how it was going to get even stronger. The 1985 version spoke of an 'unceasing introduction of new nuclear and conventional Soviet military capabilities'. The secretary of defense's preface opened with a quote from a NATO document referring to the Warsaw Pact's emphasis on 'the element of surprise and the necessity of rapid offensive operations'.[32] The September 1990 edition published after the fall of the Berlin Wall acknowledged the changes underway and the greater openness shown in Moscow when discussing the problems posed by its excessively large military establishment. Yet it still insisted that it would be wrong to conclude, 'no matter how much we might wish it', that this was 'an eviscerated force structure and an evaporating threat'.[33] It was hard to accept that the USSR might one day do what 'other declining powers have been impelled to do in history: that is, retreat from an empire it could neither afford to support nor hope to control over the longer term'.[34]

A National Intelligence Estimate of May 1988 noted how Gorbachev's policies had 'increased the potential for instability in Eastern Europe,' but offered comparatively mild scenarios as its outliers, certainly compared with what was to come. Though the estimate noted that Gorbachev faced 'greater constraints than did his predecessors against intervening militarily in Eastern Europe', it still assumed that 'in extremis' he would 'intervene to preserve party rule and decisive Soviet influence in the region.' Even as the real drama was about to begin in 1989 the CIA saw change coming but was still thinking in terms of years rather than weeks. As the instability took hold the intelligence community was still debating how far this might go.[35]

The problem in part was one of failing to appreciate the deep structural weaknesses of the system, despite evidence of poor economic performance, awful demographic projections, and a progressive loss of legitimacy. The failings were well known, and they had led to a number of predictions that the system could not sustain itself. One of the most famous was dissident Andrei Amalrik's 1970 pamphlet, *Will the Soviet Union Survive Until 1984?* The date had no significance other than the link with George Orwell. No state that devoted 'so much of its energies to physically and psychologically controlling millions of its own subjects', Amalrik argued, could survive indefinitely. Eventually the 'Soviet Union will have to pay up in full for the territorial annexations of Stalin and for the isolation in which the neo-Stalinists have placed the country.'[36] More significantly Ronald Reagan had asserted strongly at the start of his presidency that in the ideological competition with the United States, the Soviet Union was bound to lose.

> What we see here is a political structure that no longer corresponds to its economic base, a society where productive forces are hampered by political ones . . . the march of freedom and democracy which will leave Marxism-Leninism on the ash heap of history as it has left other tyrannies which stifle the freedom and muzzle the self-expression of the people.[37]

Yet the weight of the Sovietology community, in both academia and government, was much more cautious, convinced that the system was remarkably resilient and also capable of adjusting. Warnings of collapse tended to be dismissed as the wishful thinking of mavericks and right-wingers. Many asserted, almost to the last moment of the regime, that it would endure. Having spent their careers exploring how the system survived decades of tragedy, including revolution, civil war, famine, purges, and invasion, they assumed it could cope with economic trouble. The mainstream view was expressed that 'short of some unexpected catastrophe, the Soviet economy is unlikely to come close to collapse. . . . In the end, Gorbachev, like his predecessors, will probably have to settle for an economy that has to rely more on its natural riches than on its creative potential.'[38] If anything Gorbachev appeared as the man who would revive the system by reforming it. One problem here was that those economists studying the Soviet economy did not realise just how bad things were, not least because official statistics were largely fictional. The only exception to the sanguine view came from students of the 'nationalities problem' in the Soviet Union who recognised that the system was struggling to cope with its internal political tensions.[39]

The Bush Administration, which took over at the start of 1989, did not share Reagan's optimism about likely Soviet failure. Their concern was that a reformed Soviet system would simply be a more challenging opponent. This was the view of former President Nixon who when he published a forward look in 1988 saw Gorbachev as changing the Soviet image but not the substance. He considered 'a more prosperous, productive Soviet Union' likely to be 'a more formidable opponent, not less, than it is today.'[40] National Security Advisor Brent Scowcroft worried that the whole Gorbachev phenomenon might lull the West into a false sense of security. If his reforms revitalised the Soviet Union he would be 'potentially more dangerous than his predecessors, each of whom, through some aggressive move, had saved the West from the dangers of its own wishful thinking'. Secretary of State James A. Baker III recalled his belief that Gorbachev's strategy 'was premised on splitting the alliance and undercutting us in Western Europe.'[41] They soon changed their minds. In December 1989, not long after the Berlin Wall was breached, a summit meeting was conducted between Presidents George H. W. Bush and Mikhail Gorbachev on a boat moored in choppy waters off Malta. The Cold War began to be spoken of in the past tense. It had lasted, Gorbachev's spokesman quipped, 'from Yalta to Malta'.[42]

PART TWO

[10]

A Science of War

Until war has been systematically described it cannot be adequately understood, and with such understanding comes the first meaningful possibility of controlling it.

J. DAVID SINGER and **MELVIN SMALL**,
The Wages of War, 1972[1]

The speed with which this new situation had come about was remarkable. Almost as soon as the possibility of its demise was raised the Soviet system had passed away. The change was abrupt, and there was very little time to adjust. A whole literature on future wars, with contributions from fiction and non-fiction, was rendered obsolete with nothing much available to take its place. The greatest upheaval for decades had caught out the academic community along with everyone else. There were questions about whether the most fundamental preoccupation of the discipline of international relations—the risk of a great-power war—remained relevant while it appeared to have virtually nothing to say about the civil wars which soon came to dominate the agenda. The view that the behaviour of states could largely be explained by reference to the strategic imperatives resulting from the structure of the international system, so that the nature of regimes was at most of secondary importance, had been discredited by the Soviet experience and was soon shown to be inadequate when coming to terms with ethnic conflict and democracy promotion as a route to peace.

The challenge was greatest for the realists, who had dominated the theory and practice of international affairs since 1945, stressing the factors of power and interest when explaining the twists and turns of international affairs. Their boast was that they were not distracted by idealistic and sentimental notions of how they would like the world to be but instead considered the world as it was. Realism might be described largely as an intellectual temper, which is what E. H. Carr had in mind, but it had been turned into a strong theory under the influence of such figures as Hans Morgenthau at the University of Chicago, schooled in the harsh and uncompromising interwar German debates about politics and the state. For him international politics was 'like all politics . . . a struggle for power'.[2] The prevailing metaphor saw states as self-contained units with thick skins, like so many billiard balls, not so much directed by any inner agency but more by the impact of the other balls, ricocheting and colliding round the table. In this way the system created its own motivations for war. It was also about great powers. It would be as 'ridiculous' to construct a theory of international relations based on 'Malaysia or Costa Rica', Kenneth Waltz had observed, as it would be 'to construct an economic theory of oligopolistic competition based on minor firms in a sector of the economy. The fates of all states and firms in the system are affected much more by the acts and interactions of the major ones than of the minor ones.'[3] The promise of theory was that it could move beyond reflections on international history or commentary on current affairs to propositions about the future. These would not necessarily be predictive but could at least make claims about cause and effect. For example, the theory might explain why deterrence might work better when dealing with threats to the homeland than when an ally was in danger, or suggest how to respond to another state's military build-up. But without a great power conflict at the heart of the system realists were at something of a loss.

By 1990 realism was already subject to a number of criticisms: disinterest in economics and ideology, in the practice of decision-making, and in supranational organisations.[4] It was accused of attaching far too much weight to military power and coercive measures, while dismissing the capacity of the international system to adapt to new circumstances.[5] The realist theorists had done no better than anyone else in anticipating the end of the Cold War,[6] and even then found it difficult to accept that any sort of reappraisal was required. Even as the old order collapsed, one leading realist theorist dismissed the idea that ideological or civilisational factors were as important as the insecurities inherent in an anarchic international system, warning instead that with the end of the Cold War one form of great-power conflict would simply be replaced by another. The new multipolarity was likely to be as violent as the old East-West bipolarity.[7] It was not clear, however, why this prognosis should be any more accurate than the earlier ones that had been overtaken by events—or what might be said in a world in which conflicts within lesser powers attracted more attention than relations between great powers. Realism therefore struggled because it had little to say about the impact of major ideological shifts within great powers or the drivers of instability within minor states, or why any serious major power, secure within its own borders, would bother to try to sort out this instability.

One response to this might have been to go easy on the theory, concentrating on observing carefully what was going on in the world, and only offering propositions on causal relationships as and when they seemed appropriate and always with regard for context. Yet the dominant trend in the field was not to abandon theory but to make it even stronger. Only then could it become more predictive. For some time there had been an endeavour to move the science up a notch by developing theory along econometric lines, with a firm empirical base and high-quality statistical analysis. This approach was no more suited to predicting discontinuities than the realist approach being challenged. But the claims were larger, promising theories that would provide policymakers a much better idea of the levers to pull if they wanted to influence situations for the better.

THE AMBITION TO PUT THE DISCIPLINE OF INTERNATIONAL relations on a more scientific footing was not new. Quincy Wright's major work, *A Study of War*, begun in 1927 but not published until 1942, gathered information on everything that could be known about war and presented it systematically. The key factors relevant to the origins of war identified by Wright were technology, law, form of political organisation, and key values. A change in any of these factors could cause the system to lose equilibrium. Each could, in principle, be measured, for example by looking at the properties of weaponry, demographics, opinion polling, the number of states, and their adherence to international law. From these measurements inferences could be drawn. Because he did not wish to exclude any relevant information, his analysis did not rely wholly on what was measurable and nor did it lead to any elegant mathematics, but it offered encouragement to those intrigued by the possibilities of giving the study of war a more scientific foundation.[8]

Wright was among the first to appreciate the work of Lewis Fry Richardson, a pioneer in the statistics of war. Richardson was a prize-winning meteorologist and also a Quaker. Horrified by the First World War, in which he served as an ambulance driver, he sought to explore the nature of war as one might a disease. He did not devote himself full-time to the topic until 1940, and then as a private scholar, alone in Scotland, with little contact with others. His research reflected his scientific training. He kept his prejudices in check when seeking the best possible information, found ways to express it quantitatively, and then engaged in statistical analysis. Although his modelling had provided a foundation for weather forecasting, Richardson was sceptical about whether wars could be predicted in the same way, but he hoped that clear patterns and relationships might be identified. His book *The Statistics of Deadly Quarrels*, published posthumously in 1960, contained information on more than 300 wars between 1820 and 1949. Setting the terms for later efforts in this area, Richardson highlighted casualties in distinguishing one war from another. He was also the first to try to describe disruptive international processes, such as arms races, using differential equations. The outcomes of his equations were, he explained, descriptions of what would happen if people 'did not stop to think', if 'instinct and tradition were allowed to act uncontrolled'.[9] This clarified his aim: to identify the dangerous tendencies that a controlling mind would address to prevent war.[10]

Even with Wright's help it took time before Richardson's ideas were picked up and taken seriously. A key figure in this effort was the economist Kenneth Boulding, also a pacifist by conviction, and a Professor at Michigan. He was concerned that

> the intellectual chassis of the broad movement for the abolition of war has not been adequate to support the powerful moral engine which drives it and that the frequent breakdowns which interrupt the progress of the movement are due essentially to a deficiency in its social theory.[11]

In 1955 he became involved with a group based at Michigan, influenced by Richardson (whose writings had just become available although not yet published). They concluded that quantitative methods could generate a new field of peace research. In a 'race between knowledge and disaster', the 'longer disaster is staved off, the better chance we have of acquiring the knowledge to prevent it altogether.' A new *Journal of Conflict Resolution* was established to devise, as Boulding put it in an editorial, 'an intellectual engine of sufficient power to move the greatest problem of our time—the prevention of war.' The second major centre of peace research was set up in Oslo in 1959 by Johan Galtung. Its *Journal of Peace Research* was first published in 1964.[12]

This scientific approach was by no means confined to those with a peace agenda. It was already evident in the new think tanks, such as RAND, established to guide military policy through the Nuclear Age, and responsible for the analytical foundations of deterrence theory. The importance of meticulous gathering of data and careful analysis had been underlined by the experience of the Second World War, and it was becoming easier to undertake as a result of the development of computers capable of storing large amounts of information and supporting advanced statistical techniques. As lone scholars in the library began to be displaced by teams of researchers, funding had to be found for their projects, which were extremely expensive. To get access to funds, social scientists sought to demonstrate that they could provide research that was comparable to natural scientists in their objectivity and ability to develop systematic laws.[13]

If such laws could be developed then in principle they would allow the future of war to be controlled. Policymakers could recognise the symptoms, make a diagnosis, and then identify forms of treatment that could head off disaster. Writing in 1950 Harold Guetzkow claimed that:

> the surest and quickest way to world peace is an indirect one— the patient construction over many years of a basic theory of international relations. From this theory may come new and un-thought-of solutions to end wars and to guide international relations.[14]

In a book published in 2012 the political scientist John Vasquez cited Guetzkow as an inspiration in a collection of essays that sought to assess how far researchers had got with the application of 'the scientific method to identify those factors that promote the outbreak of interstate war and those factors that promote peace'. Even after sixty years there was still some way to go, Vasquez conceded, but there was now some core knowledge for theories of peace and war to explain.[15] In the introduction he explained how the scholarly movement to apply the scientific method was 'one of the best hopes of humanity for solving the intellectual puzzle of war.' This was because it replaced 'the solitary efforts of past great thinkers,' and here he mentioned Thucydides and Freud, with a 'large number of researchers committed to using the best method of inquiry humanity has invented.'[16] Better than mere 'speculation or intellectual argument' was to develop hypotheses that could be tested by a rigorous examination of evidence.

But when Vasquez came to report on the main conclusions of the scientific school there was not a lot that went beyond what would be obvious to any serious observer of international affairs. He noted the importance of the 'the issue at stake', how alliance formation and military build-ups could be mutually reinforcing, and that 'rivals have a much higher probability of going to war than other types of states'.[17] In seventy-six general propositions offered elsewhere he underscored the extent to which the challenge the scientific school posed to the realist school followed the lines of the earlier idealists: 'Realist norms and the practices of power politics are more associated with war than with peace'. In addition the work pointed to internationalist remedies, in the 'global institutional context'. A more orderly system in which states felt obliged to follow rules of the game would restrict unilateral action and facilitate the resolution of disputes.[18] Much of this analysis, therefore, was a continuation of old debates about the dangers of power politics. That rivalry could lead to military build-ups, alliance formation, and eventually war, depending on the issue at stake, hardly represented a unique insight. The general proposition that peace was more likely if all states avoided the crude logic of power politics and followed international rules was compelling but it offered little to states trying to play by the rules when confronted by states that were not.

With interstate war there were too few cases and too many factors in play for the scientific approach to produce more than a general sense of what issues might lead to crises and what behaviour might aggravate them. Historians, whose observations had been dismissed as being too intuitive or speculative, could retort that the yield from the effort that went into refining the methodologies and interrogating the data turned out to be meagre. There was also a cost. The scientific ambition depended on reliable, objective evidence on war. Collecting and interpreting this evidence was by no means straightforward. Just because numbers were involved did not make a statement more correct than one expressed in a more literary form, and there was a danger that spurious statistics could gain currency and even influence policy. This approach insisted on the potential importance of every incident that could be recorded but at the cost of simplifying the record of each incident. It sought to disaggregate conflicts into time-limited two-sided violent relationships, disregarding factors that could not be quantified while relying on flawed data sets. At a critical juncture in international affairs, with a shift in focus from great power conflict to internal wars, involving a number of sub-groups, the academic community was ill equipped to rise to the challenge.

AN EXAMPLE OF THE DANGEROUS ALLURE OF NUMBERS, EVEN when baseless, could be found in a piece of mischief perpetrated by Norman Cousins, the editor of the *Saturday Review* and a leading campaigner for nuclear disarmament. In 1953 he wrote a hoax newspaper article which included a purported observation from 'a former president of the Norwegian Academy of Sciences' that since 3600 BC the world had known 'only 292 years of peace'. This figure was said to reflect work done on the history of war by an international team of researchers using an 'electronic computer'. This was not the only finding. Other equally dramatic and suspiciously precise numbers were on offer. Apparently 3.64 billion people had been killed in a total of 14,531 wars during that period. Since 650 BC there had been 1,656 arms races. Of these only 16 had not ended in war.[19] Cousins repeated these numbers in an editorial in the *Saturday Review* and lastly in a 1960 book entitled *In Place of Folly*.[20] The research to which Cousins referred was 'imaginary', a 'fantasy'. He had not expected the numbers to be taken seriously. Yet they were not wholly plucked out of thin air. 'Some', Cousins explained, 'were general, some were the result of extrapolation, some were estimates, some were fanciful. No fully documented figures exist anywhere on the total casualties or total cost of all wars since the beginning of recorded history'.[21]

Curiously there was another version of the 'only 292 years of peace' claim. In 1968, in *The Lessons of History*, Will and Ariel Durant asserted that in 3,421 years of recorded history there had only been 268 without war.[22] The Durants were cited when Donald Kagan used the same statistic in his book *On the Origins of War* published in 1995.[23] It was then picked up by such diverse people as left-wing polemicist Noam Chomsky and the hawkish former Secretary of Defense and soon-to-be Vice President Richard Cheney.[24]

The Durants gave no reference. Two Dutch scholars identified the most likely source for this as well as Cousins' number of 292 years.[25] Tucked away in Bloch's massive study on *The Future of War* was the observation that 'from 1496 B.C. up to 1861 A.D., a period of 3,357 years, there were only 227 years of peace on a total of 3,130 years of war, or thirteen years of war to every year of peace'. The figures used by both Cousins and the Durants could easily be extrapolations from this source. This calculation, however, was not Bloch's. He had got the number, via a Russian military encyclopaedia, from a French philosopher Odysse Barot. In his 1864 *Lettres sur la Philosophie de l'Histoire*, Barot had undertaken some 'brutal arithmetic' that led him to conclude that in the 3,357 years up to 1861 there had been 227 years of peace and 3,130 of war.

Barot had not actually counted wars but treaties of peace and also of alliance and friendship. His assumption was that alliance formation was tantamount to the start of war and that all wars ended with peace treaties. Leaving aside whether Barot's own sources on treaties were reliable let alone comprehensive, his use of treaties as proxies for the start and conclusions of war was patently unreliable.[26] Even if the numbers were right the meaning was hard to unpack. Did it mean that an otherwise unblemished year was lost to the peace column as a result of one short, localised and relatively minor conflict? Here was a serious but misguided effort to make sense of the history of war that produced the only figures available on the incidence of conflict through the ages. For want of anything better, they were picked up 100 years later, slightly updated, and used to make a profound statement about war—either a realist point that it never goes away or an idealist point that it should.

To prevent this sort of misapprehension a major programme was begun in 1963 at the University of Michigan known as the Correlates of War (COW) Project with a grant from the Carnegie Foundation under the leadership of a political scientist, J. David Singer. When some of the first results were published in 1972, Singer and his associate, Melvin Small, observed that this represented the first 'intellectual assault of promise' launched against 'tribal slaughter'.[27] He was determined to be as careful as possible when gathering and ordering material. By stressing correlation in the title, no claims were being made about causation. The research would point to statistically significant relationships from which theories might then be constructed.

THE CONSTRUCTION OF THE RESEARCH, HOWEVER, WAS SHAPED by Singer's determination to address the claims of the then-dominant realists that everything was about an international struggle for power. His priority was war between states rather than within them. His interest lay in whether statistically interesting relationships might be established between inputs, such as capabilities and alliances, and outputs, such as the length of the conflict and casualties, rather than the actual choices made by states and the context in which they were made.

The focus on major war was reflected in the high threshold for inclusion. War was defined, somewhat arbitrarily, as 'sustained combat, involving organized armed forces, resulting in a minimum of 1,000 battle-related fatalities'. This was later modified to be 1,000 battle-related fatalities within a twelve-month period, so that as a conflict built up or petered out it would not necessarily be included. To be identified as a participant in one of these wars a state must have a population of 500,000 and suffer at least 100 fatalities or contribute at least 1,000 armed personnel to active combat. The intention was to preclude skirmishes or border clashes that did not trigger a wider conflict.[28] But once the threshold was reached there were no further distinctions. Thus the 1982 Falklands war between Argentina and the UK, which just passed the threshold in a conflict that lasted less than three months, was there at the same time as the Iran-Iraq War, which involved hundreds of thousands of casualties over eight years. Another important feature of this schema was its focus on battle. Unless civilians died directly as a result of battle their deaths were considered irrelevant.

The data set began in 1816, after the conclusion of the Napoleonic Wars. This meant excluding the most intense period of fighting in the nineteenth century, and one that set terms for conflict thereafter. In addition, COW discouraged interest in colonial or civil wars. A category of 'extra-systemic' (later 'extra-state') wars included conflicts between major states and non-state groups outside their own territory, and so included colonial wars. But only casualties of the colonising states were collected because it was hard to collect those of the colonised.

The material for the nineteenth century was heavily geared to the Western Hemisphere because much of the rest of the world was then colonised. There were only three independent states in Africa, the Middle East, and Oceania in the first half of that century, rising to ten in the second half. The efforts by the European powers to acquire and hold overseas territories explained the frequency of extra-systemic or extra-state wars. As these empires were dismantled during the twentieth century, wars in this category went into decline. They were picked up in the COW database in the first decade of the twenty-first century because of Afghanistan and Iraq, although whether these interventions were comparable to past colonial wars raised important political and moral issues as well as those of appropriate coding.

COW distinguished between civil wars fought within the 'metropole' of a state, areas integrated under governmental control, and those between the metropole and the peripheral areas which were not so integrated.[29] At issue was the working of the state system rather than totting up the costs of conflict. The focus on interstate wars meant that it took a long time before those working on COW, and like-minded researchers, took civil wars seriously.

The inadequate treatment of civil wars was one of the main criticisms of the COW, especially as they began to become a major preoccupation during the 1990s. New databases were developed to meet this need. The Uppsala Conflict Data Program (UCDP) was one of the first to collect material on civil wars, although they still focused on battle-deaths, with twenty-five a year being the threshold for inclusion. This was despite civilian casualties being one of the most salient and troubling features of most contemporary civil wars.[30] Initially this only recorded conflicts since 1989, but in 2001 in collaboration with the International Peace Research Institute in Oslo (PRIO) a data set was developed for the whole of the period since 1946. In 1993, also at Maryland, a *Minorities at Risk* data set was published with information of a range of factors contributing to sub-state violence.[31] The growing enthusiasm for interrogating data collection aggravated rather than resolved key issues. There were debates between the leading databases on the best indicators of armed conflict and on the quality of the evidence. For want of anything better were guesses admissible? Should government statistics known to be falsified be used? Whose account of inherently confusing events could be trusted? The only safe assumption was that 'knowledge' of civil wars was 'incomplete and contested'.[32]

Statistical analysis required that complex conflicts be disaggregated into what might be considered elemental units of war that could be compared and contrasted with each other. These units were distinguished by having a clear beginning, middle, and end, and were dyadic, that is they had only two belligerents, and could be classified as being interstate, extra-systemic, or civil. Factors which were ambiguous or could not be measured were excluded. This was problematic enough with interstate wars but risked a wholly skewed analysis with civil wars. In these conflicts 'battle deaths' was often a meaningless measure, as there were few battles and many causes of violent deaths. Individuals would often participate on an occasional and informal basis, military and criminal activity were intertwined, and neighbouring states were often closely involved.[33]

THIS METHODOLOGY DIVERGED SHARPLY FROM THAT OF HISTORIANS, who tended to look for particular explanations rather than the general, and be less interested in how events were coded than their conflicts across time and space. An approach based on disaggregation could not, for example, view the period 1914–1945 as a European civil war dominated by the interaction between liberal democracy, communism, and fascism/Nazism that cut across state boundaries.[34] Nor could it consider great conflicts as a whole. Until December 1941 the wars in Asia, which had begun on 7 July 1937 when Japan invaded China, and in Europe, which began on 1 September 1939 when Germany invaded Poland, were separate. They merged after Pearl Harbor. When Adolf Hitler declared war on the United States on 11 December it was easier for President Roosevelt to persuade his people that for the time being Europe had to take precedence over the Pacific. Up to this point the US was not a formal participant in the war, but it was hardly a true neutral as Roosevelt had described it as the 'arsenal of democracy' and was closely engaged with Britain on its war strategy. It might then be assumed that all these wars ended together: German forces surrendered on 8 May 1945 and Japan on 14 August that year, although it took until September before Japanese forces in China surrendered. President Truman did not, however, declare a formal cessation of hostilities in Japan until the end of 1946, noting that 'a state of war still exists'. It remained an occupying power. A peace treaty was not signed until April 1952. The state of war with Germany had been ended the previous summer. This was partly because a state of war gave the US government legal powers that it must otherwise relinquish but also because post-war situations tend to be chaotic and an early claim that it was all over could have been premature. For COW it all ended together in 1945, because that was when the battle deaths moved below 1,000.

The problem with the focus on dyads can also be illustrated by the case of Iraq. Over four decades Iraq invaded neighbours and was invaded, suffered from civil wars and insurgencies, and then became part of a conflict with the Islamist militants of ISIS who also controlled chunks of Syria. This could be disaggregated into a series of dyads. The most prominent but by no means only were: Iraq v. Iran, Iraq v. Kuwait, Iraq v. the United States (and allies), Iraq v. ISIS. Three American presidents announced the end of combat in Iraq—George H. W. Bush at the start of March 1991, his son George W. Bush on 1 May 2003 and then Barack Obama on 31 August 2010. Each time it turned out that the announcement was premature. Disaggregation might enable all these different strands to be coded and analysed as a series of separate conflicts, and avoid double counting, but in practice they were intertwined as part of a stream of conflict. Similarly, from the mid-1970s Afghanistan experienced constant war, under various configurations but with external forces heavily involved. In the 1980s there was an external intervention (Soviet Union), which then turned into a civil war (Taliban v. Northern Alliance), but began to turn into something else as the Taliban-backed al-Qaeda looked for ways to attack the United States. After they succeeded in September 2001, the established civil war and this extra-state war (United States v. al-Qaeda) became an interstate war (United States v. Taliban regime). Attempting to disaggregate to code the individual parts, count casualties, and allocate them did not in the end help understanding, for it made it difficult to appreciate how conflicts with common sources transformed and developed over time, becoming messier and more complex.

A FURTHER PROBLEM WITH WARS ONLY COMING INTO VIEW as they passed a certain casualty threshold was that this missed out on the simmering conflicts from which they emerged. To facilitate analysis of when wars were or were not avoided, during the 1990s the COW team developed a Militarized Interstates Disputes (MID) database. It contained information about all disputes since 1816 'in which the threat, display or use of military force short of war by one member state is explicitly directed towards the government, official representatives, official forces, property or territory of another state.'[35] Potentially numerous incidents fitted into MID; the data set expanded from under 1,000 for the 1816–1976 period in the first version to over 2,000 in the second.[36] So while the threshold for inclusion in COW was quite high, the one for the MID was quite low. As it was geared only to interstate conflict it could not help with analyses into the origins of colonial and civil wars.

Much of the MID was put together before the availability of modern search engines, and so used whatever material was then available in libraries. In the 2010s, a team of researchers going through the individual cases meticulously found the MID database to be unreliable, although that was not a word they used. They praised the effort and the utility of the database, insisted that they found no evidence of systematic bias, and offered detailed proposals to rectify the problems they encountered.[37] Nonetheless, their investigations identified problems with almost 70 per cent of the MID cases, leading to proposals to drop 240, merge another 72 with similar cases, revise substantially a further 234, and make minor changes to another 1009.

Many incidents discussed took place on the edges of ongoing and substantial wars, for example attacks on shipping of countries perceived by one belligerent to be supporting another. During the Iran-Iraq war in the 1980s one or other of the belligerents attacked numerous tankers. These were coded in MID as separate incidents though these make no sense when considered as individual events. At the other extreme essentially trivial matters were included. Over 300 disputes (over 13 per cent of the total) were coded as a 'seizure' of boats at sea. There were some famous incidents, such as the North Korean seizure of the USS *Pueblo* and its 83 crew members in 1968, an action that could well have escalated into something quite serious. Mostly, however, boats were seized by authorities for reasons that had little to do with interstate relations, but because their owners failed to register them properly or engaged in criminal activities. In principle such cases should not be included, and in the study cited above it was proposed that 53 should be dropped.

A separate study considered how disputes over fishing in contested areas of the ocean were considered in the MID.[38] Disputes of this type tended to involve mature democracies but not militarised responses, and rarely escalated. By and large actions were taken by a state against the private citizens (owners of fishing vessels) of another. But these were hardly major incidents. In one incident a Canadian destroyer chased an American scallop-fishing boat out of Canadian waters after firing warning shots. This was coded as an act of war, but there was no evidence that the US viewed it as such. Such incidents did not carry the 'implication of war'. The authors of this critique noted that 69 out of the 567 disputes between democracies in the MID database involved fishing. Their probable irrelevance somewhat distorted any conclusions to be made from this database about the relationship between democracy and war. When it came to the Cold War, however, a whole stage of international relations that could be described as one large militarised interstate dispute, MID only included the most visible manifestations of East-West tension, such as the standoff in Berlin in 1961, when for a while actual military units faced each other and when the risk of escalation to major war was high.

Two cases from 1969 illustrate the difficulty of categorising conflicts. One passed the casualty threshold and so reached the COW database and one stayed in the MID. El Salvador and Honduras fought what came to be known as the 'Football War', though that description trivialised the dispute. The origins lay in the treatment of Salvadoran immigrants in Honduras who were seeking to escape from repression at home. The tension exploded into violence as the two countries played each other in qualifying matches for the 1970 World Cup, in which El Salvador came out on top. The violence led El Salvador to sever diplomatic relations with Honduras, followed in mid-July with air raids and a ground offensive, and then Honduran counterstrikes. A ceasefire was soon arranged, though relations between the two remained tense. The impact was not minor but was largely confined to Central America.

Also in 1969 there was a period of deep conflict between China and the Soviet Union. Tensions between the two had been building up since the start of the decade, and burst out into the open in 1963 with some bitter polemics. The dispute was about the soul and leadership of the world communist movement but also involved old-fashioned geopolitical considerations, including a Chinese conviction that at times of previous weakness the Russians had stolen its territory and it was time to get it back. At the start of 1968 Soviet armoured vehicles attacked Chinese working on Qiliqin Island in the Ussuri River, causing four deaths. After that the border was quiet until the end of the year. Then came the first of a series of incidents on Zhenbao

Island, largely instigated by the Soviet side. In early March Chinese leader Mao Zedong decided to take the initiative with what was in effect an ambush of Russian soldiers. He moved the rhetoric to a higher gear, though refrained from further action. Mao saw the tension as a helpful contribution to the radicalising process of the Cultural Revolution. By this point, however, the Soviet leadership was seriously alarmed and preparing for a major war against China. Hardliners even argued for a pre-emptive nuclear strike before China's nuclear programme had become operational. This in turn alarmed the leadership in Beijing. They considered evacuating the capital as the Soviet foreign ministry wondered whether Russian nationals should be advised to return home. In the event an opportunity arose for talks at a senior level, and the immediate crisis was defused.

Although many died during these clashes, the COW threshold was not reached. This episode therefore appears only as 'incident 349' in the Militarised Interstate Disputes database, which has it lasting from March to December, with very few fatalities. The source materials were books published up to 1983. By this time it was known that thirty-one Russians had died in the first main clash on 2 March, and that the Chinese had probably instigated this encounter.[39] Prior to this there had been no consensus on attribution.[40]

This incident did not result in a war, although it might have done, but it did have an enormous impact on military planning and the development of international affairs. The mutual suspicions remained and led to a major build-up of forces on both sides during the 1970s. The split between the two communist giants created opportunities for the United States, which began to explore the possibilities of a rapprochement with Beijing. The Chinese, left feeling isolated and vulnerable by the Soviet Union, responded positively to the American overtures. A rich study of the events of 1969 therefore offered much of interest to those concerned with the origins of war, from domestic issues encouraging a rise in tensions to concerns about nuclear war encouraging a decline in those tensions, and how balances of power could shift quite abruptly.[41] COW was not designed to support this sort of approach but was instead a methodology that relied on extracting incidents from their historical and geographical context.

IT WAS NOT UNREASONABLE TO ASK FOR A BETTER WAY OF understanding the past in order to be better able to anticipate the future. But instead of understanding war as part of the stream of history, so that particular instances could be understood in context, past conflicts were itemised and categorised in an artificial manner in order to facilitate comparisons that only had any validity at a high and often banal level of generality. For those who were trying to make sense of what was to come there were limits to what could be learnt from any number of methodologically sound observations based on comparing bits and pieces of disparate evidence of notionally similar occurrences. As Hannah Arendt observed when writing about violence:

> Predictions of the future are never anything but projections of present automatic processes and procedures, that is, of occurrences that are likely to come to pass if men do not act and if nothing unexpected happens; every action, for better or worse, and every accident necessarily destroys the whole pattern in whose frame the prediction moves and where it finds its evidence.[42]

For students of international relations who accepted that they were always exploring a world of contingency and uncertainty, attempting to anticipate choices yet to be made, this was not a great concern. But for those convinced that it was possible to establish a true science, for whom some capacity for prediction was essential, it pointed to the problems in identifying compelling causal relationships that would hold in a significant number of cases or not be upended altogether should there be some great discontinuity in the wider international system. However sophisticated the methodology and meticulous the data gathering, the future would still be full of surprises.

[11]

Counting the Dead

History counts its skeletons in round numbers.
A thousand and one remains a thousand,
as though the one had never existed:
an imaginary embryo, an empty cradle,
an ABC never read,
air that laughs, cries, grows,
emptiness running down steps toward the garden,
nobody's place in the line.

WISLAWA SZYMBORSKA,
'Hunger Camp at Jaslo', 1993[1]

Death tolls are the simplest measure of the scale of wars, the purest description of cost and the strongest indicator of sacrifice. Their detail allows martyrs to be mourned, monuments to be erected, history books written and national myths sustained. The symbolic nature of the death toll means that it can easily acquire political baggage. Casualties can be minimised to sustain morale or exaggerated to arouse anger, used to highlight the bravery of those prepared to die for a noble cause or the burden of a foolish military adventure. Those inflicting casualties may play the numbers up, to depress the enemy, yet might also want to play them down to show that they care about the Geneva conventions. The death tolls of the past are thrown back at former enemies to recall their crimes and as a demand for contrition. The Chinese government still regularly reminds their people of the atrocities committed by the

Japanese after the 1937 invasion; the Russian government invokes the hardships of the early 1940s when explaining how harsh international conditions can be endured again; more positively, the German government atones for past Nazi atrocities. The importance of these memories and myths means that there can be anger against those who try to disturb them, suggesting that the sacrifices were pointless or that they have been exaggerated to sway popular consciousness.[2]

During the First World War the Turkish government wished to rid themselves of Christian Armenians living in the Ottoman Empire, believing them to be supporters of Russia. Their effort to do so lasted until after the war's conclusion. It left, according to some estimates, up to 1.5 million Armenians dead and others expelled. Other estimates put the number much lower, around half that amount. The question of how many died depends on what is believed to have been the Armenian population prior to the massacre, those still living in the country at its conclusion, and the numbers that escaped. The most contentious issue, however, is whether this constituted genocide, a term not in use at the time. Turkey complains bitterly whenever any reference is made to these events as genocide. They accept many Armenians died, if not in the numbers claimed, but do deny that this was deliberate and systematic, and point to Muslims killed by Armenians at the same time. One consequence of the determination with which Turkey pursues this issue is that attempts to sort out the evidence soon get caught in the crossfire.[3]

Many of the problems of counting were explored in a book published in 1923 by the Carnegie Endowment for International Peace, an organisation established in 1910 to promote the abolition of war. 'Perhaps', observed one of its authors, 'when people come to appreciate what glory, pillage, and the desire for conquest really cost they will find the price too high: and then peace will reign forever.'[4] This book consisted of a rather sketchy, 'preliminary' account of the losses incurred during the recent war, preceded by a substantial analysis of all available sources on the human cost of war up to that point, including, unlike COW, both the Seven Years' War and the Napoleonic Wars. The estimate of up to 11 million military deaths for the Napoleonic Wars remains close to numbers in current use. Samuel Dumas, a French professor, in discussing these previous wars acknowledged the problems of scanty and often unreliable evidence, and the extent to which the numbers were often subject to deliberate deception. He also stressed just how much greater the military losses were from disease than from battle. This was also true with civilians. One measure used in the analysis was declining birth rates.

Death tolls, especially when confined to battle, only capture one aspect of the tragedy of war.[5] When individuals die their families are left bereaved; of the injured some will die later and others will be incapable of returning to normal life, left physically or psychologically damaged; homes are destroyed and social infrastructure collapses. War leads to disease and malnutrition or a breakdown in law and order which adds to the overall levels of violence in society. Sexual assaults follow armies as they move through populated areas. Those seeking to flee the immediate impact of war often put themselves through terrible hardships, becoming either internally displaced or full refugees. As the fortunes of war change, some of these might return home while others will be forever exiled. War may just be the worst of many bad things afflicting a country that combine to make life progressively miserable, including oppressive governments and natural disasters. It is entirely possible that deaths from indirect causes can be almost as high as those caused by deliberate killing.[6]

Ignoring the fate of civilians distorts the reality of war, even if including them results in imprecision and uncertainty. The consequences of their exclusion can be seen by noting that, while COW lists total battle deaths for Korea as 909,000 by some accounts, if civilians were included the figure could reach some 4 million. It was starvation and disease that did for most of the estimated two million people who died in Cambodia under Pol Pot in the 1970s. The 80–100,000 people killed directly was large enough by any standards, but still perhaps only 4 per cent of the total.

During the nineteenth century brutal attacks on civilians were a way of showing enemy populations how they would suffer if they resisted. In the twentieth century the elimination of whole groups of people of supposedly inferior race or dangerous belief was adopted as a war aim. In the twenty-first century, extreme Islamist groups saw the murder of apostates and unbelievers a vital political goal. Murdering civilians with no capacity to resist in large numbers is a category of killing that is war-like but involves no battle, of which the Nazi holocaust against the Jews is the prime example. One of the most gruesome of recent times was the Rwandan genocide of 1994, with estimates of those killed put at anywhere between 500,000 and 1,000,000.[7] It did not figure in either the standard COW or PRIO databases. The PRIO developed a new category of 'one-sided violence' to accommodate such events, but these cannot really be considered separate from war, as war creates the conditions that make them possible.[8] In Rwanda the lack of actual resistance indicated the speed and single-mindedness of the militia offensive. Would some serious skirmishes in a couple of villages have suddenly moved this whole episode onto a list of wars? The deaths suffered at the hands of an oppressive government have at times been comparable to casualties in wars, but kept out of the databases of war by a lack of organised resistance.[9]

All these issues created a problem for those who wished to base their studies on accurate measurements of casualties. If the aim was to compare different wars, rather than convey their full horror, then there was a case for using the narrowest and supposedly most reliable of measures, those who died in battle. This was COW's approach. But even here care is needed. Many military deaths during a war occur away from actual battle. American battle-deaths in the COW database record 116,516 for the First World War, 405,400 for the Second World War, 54,487 for the Korean War of the early 1950s, 58,153 for the Vietnam War from 1965 to 1973, 376 for the 1991 Gulf War, but only two for the 2001 invasion of Afghanistan and 140 for the 2003 invasion of Iraq. These numbers included those who were killed in combat but also those who died as a result of accidents, disease, or also as a result of being prisoners of war. COW did not distinguish these two types of causes, but they are relevant. Combat deaths were less than half of the total in the First World War and still about half in the Second, a ratio that was maintained into the 1991 Gulf War.[10]

Contrast the 22,000 French soldiers who died of yellow fever in Haiti at the start of the nineteenth century and the approximately 18,000 British and French soldiers who died of cholera during the Crimean War with zero British fatalities from 29 soldiers hospitalised because they had contracted an infectious disease in Afghanistan in 2002. By then recruits were likely to be healthier, and so able to cope better with injury. They were inoculated against what would once have been killer diseases as they moved into unfamiliar territory. Body armour provided better protection, and if troops were injured in battle they got much improved treatment on the spot and were then speedily evacuated to a field hospital. Until the middle of the last century Disease and Non-Battle Injury (DNBI) was the major cause of death for soldiers deployed to war. Instead of the evacuation of an injured soldier involving days of being carried on a litter, a soldier fighting for a modern army should be whisked away on a helicopter and get to a well-equipped facility within an hour. So, Tanisha Fazal argued, war has become 'less lethal'. Between 1946 and 2008, there was a 50 per cent decline in known battle deaths. By contrast there was only a 20 per cent decline in estimated battle casualties. Battle deaths were therefore declining more than twice as quickly as battle casualties. The same conflict that produced 1,200 casualties in 1860 was likely to have produced 800 casualties in 1980. [11]

WITH MODERN ARMED FORCES THERE ARE ESTABLISHED AND reliable means of recording death, injury, or missing in action. With less organised armies the position is much more difficult. Retrospective forms of accounting draw on whatever information comes to hand, whether field reports from fighting units, newspaper stories, benefits claims, or medical records, but these are often incomplete or ambiguous. Mortality rates over time can identify before and after effects of a war. Census data can help work out the size of a dip in a country's population. Post-war surveys might sample the losses suffered by families and the prevalence of war-related injuries. All these measures raise their own issues of comprehensiveness, representativeness, and reliability.

The difficulties can be illustrated with the American Civil War. Not long after the event the death toll was put at 620,000, of which just over 360,000 were from the North and the rest from the South. This was the number used by COW. It was the result of painstaking work by two Union Army veterans, William Fox and Thomas Livermore. As there were no procedures in place during the war to identify and count the dead, wounded, and missing in action, Fox worked through every report and record he could find. With the North there were claims for pensions and survivors' benefits, but there was no such evidence for the South. His initial, sketchy analysis on the Confederate side offered a round number of 94,000. Livermore raised this to 258,000 by assuming the same ratio of accident and disease-related deaths to combat-related on the Confederate side as on the Union side. [12] The 620,000 number was long left unchallenged. [13] In 2011 J. David Hacker, a demographer, demonstrated that the South's losses had probably been underestimated. [14] It was less urbanised, so disease was probably much higher than in the North; its young men would not have acquired the degree of immunity to infectious 'camp' diseases. This would have become even more acute during the last year of the war, as medical care and food supplies deteriorated. Using census data to measure the impact on the overall population, Hacker concluded that 'excess' male deaths from the war were between 650,000 and 850,000, with 750,000 a reasonable midpoint. That was about 20 per cent higher than the previous estimate.

With the more confused and ambiguous situations found with insurgencies, different issues arise. To illustrate the problems of counting even on a comparatively small scale, Kelly Greenhill examined a report that the terrorist group Boko Haram had massacred between 150 and 2,000 people in a village in north-eastern Nigeria in early 2015. The incident took place in a dangerous area controlled by insurgents, beyond modern connectivity, with only satellite pictures for visual information. Getting reliable information from 'morgues, hospitals, and law-enforcement entities' was hampered because they were 'internally inept, externally obstructed, structurally inadequate, or simply corrupt'. Eyewitnesses' reports also had to be treated carefully because individuals might answer in such a way as 'to protect themselves from psychological and physical harm' or to gain reward by concocting or embellishing answers. It was difficult to distinguish irregular fighters from ordinary civilians, as they would look the same in death, and even more so to distinguish direct deaths from the indirect. Was a child drowning in a river as she tried to escape a victim of war or just of an unfortunate accident?

Greenhill noted that those who took the most care in counting casualties, by cross-referencing media reports of fatalities with figures from hospitals, morgues, and NGOs, were likely to generate lower numbers than more active methods, by getting data from statistically representative selections of individuals and households that live in or have escaped from affected areas. Here the risk was likely to be one of over-counting. In the case of this particular incident, she observed that it suited both local officials, who wanted the government to take action, and Boko Haram, who wanted to show off their strength, to inflate the numbers. And then once the numbers reached the public domain, 'they take on a life of their own.'[15]

That this could be true with one incident at a particular time threw into relief the problems of developing reliable numbers for really large wars. The Second World War resulted in unprecedented levels of killing, with conflicts in Asia and Europe merging, the murder of millions of civilians on an industrial scale, and every type of warfare, from naval encounters, massive air raids, lightning offensives, dogged defending, and partisan resistance, concluding with atomic bombs.

Germans died in many ways during the war—in battle and air raids, persecuted by their own government, or in the mass expulsions at the end of the war. Adding all these up has led to a total of some 7.5 million, but each of the component parts has been questioned. A total of 4.3 million for the losses during the military campaign is based on the German High Command's wartime figures, although these figures became increasingly unreliable as the system for their compilation broke down during the later stages of the war.[16]

These uncertainties are moderate compared with those surrounding Soviet casualties. Stalin, perhaps conscious that his own poor decisions had allowed Hitler to catch his country by surprise, at first referred to 7 million total deaths. By 1961 a much higher figure of 20 million was in official use, although acknowledged as probably too low. In 1990, President Mikhail Gorbachev spoke of 'almost 27 million'. Then the military dead, based on a hitherto-secret General Staff report from the mid-1960s, was put at 8,668,400. This was made up of 6,329,600 killed in action or died of wounds, 555,500 from non-combat deaths, and 1,783,300 missing in action who were never found and prisoners of war who did not return.[17] These figures were criticised as underestimates.[18] On civilian deaths the Russian Academy of Sciences published an estimate in 1995 that put those in areas occupied by Germans at 13.7 million. This number was made up of acts of genocide and reprisals, 7.4 million; deportations for slave labour, 2.2 million; and famine and disease, 4.1 million. An additional 3 million deaths was estimated for deaths due to famine and disease in the unoccupied regions.

Although these figures moved into general use there were many subsequent efforts from within Russia and outside to refine them. Yet the margins of error in these calculations would be enormous tragedies in themselves. How many died after being taken prisoner by Germans? These numbers were complicated by those who had been captured but escaped to return to their units, who avoided returning after the war, who did return and were then incarcerated because considered tainted, or who were treated as POWs by Germans but were actually ordinary civilians or partisans. Many deaths over this period were the result of the politics and economics of the Soviet state and the pernicious ideology of Nazism, as well as the nature of the armed conflict. The war followed years of deliberate political persecution and catastrophic social and economic policies, notably the Soviet 'gulag', made up of concentration or labour camps, or the forced starvation in Ukraine in the 1930s. According to Alexander Yakovlev, as many as 35 million died because of repression.[19] The gulag did not shut down over the war. Perhaps as many as 1 million died in prison or forced deportations while it was underway.[20] Demographic analysis suffered because the last pre-war census was falsified to play down the impact of the forced collectivisation of the 1930s.[21]

So while most estimates of the costs of war to the Soviet Union stayed close to 28 million, some reputable analysts considered it reasonable to go as high as 35 million.[22] Estimates of military deaths ranged from 5 to 14 million and of civilian deaths from 7 to more than 18 million. COW's figure of 7.5 million Soviet battle deaths, with no mention of civilian deaths, was certainly too low, and barely conveyed one aspect of the Soviet experience. In *The Better Angels of Our Nature*, Steven Pinker used 55 million total dead for the Second World War, but if numbers from the higher end of the range with Germany and the Soviet Union were taken, as well as China, where the true numbers are also hard to calculate but have been put conservatively at 14 million, then the total approached 85 million.[23]

With the more recent conflicts in Iraq and Afghanistan, the cost of occupying those countries was much less than that of dealing with the insurgencies. The analysis was complicated by COW's methodology, as the counter-insurgency operations appeared separately under extra-state rather than intrastate wars, with local resistance in Afghanistan and Iraq leading to 552 and 3,985 casualties respectively. All these could be identified by their names and the circumstances in which they died. The same was generally true of civilian contractors and members of international organisations.

On the Iraqi side the position was more complex. The number of civilians killed directly in the 1991 war as a result of coalition bombing was reported by the Iraqis to be 2,278. There were no precise estimates for military casualties. As the fighting ended, US commanders were puzzled by the large discrepancy between the estimated size of the Iraqi army and the numbers taken prisoner. The gap, they assumed, must be Iraqi dead, perhaps as many as 100,000 killed, 300,000 wounded, and 150,000 desertions.[24] But they had overestimated the size of the Iraqi Army prior to the war by presuming Iraqi units to be at full strength, when large numbers had failed to report for duty and many more had deserted at the first opportunity, so that once coalition air strikes started, there were perhaps only 200,000–300,000 troops to fight. This led one analyst to put Iraqi combat deaths from the air campaign at 750–1,500 and a maximum of 6,500 dead from the ground campaign.[25] Another assessment opted for 20–26,000 Iraqi troops killed.[26] Little of this was based on actual counts.[27]

The most difficult area to evaluate was that of consequential civilian deaths. One estimate put those for 1991 at some 100,000.[28] After
the 2003 war this became a controversial issue. It was complicated
by the extent to which Iraqi society had already been brutalised, its
infrastructure degraded and its resources depleted by a series of
events since the 1970s, including the war with Iran and repression of
discontent, sanctions, and purges. To this was added new strands of
occupation, insurgency, civil war, and general lawlessness that marred
the subsequent years.[29] Most of these dead were not directly at the
hands of coalition forces, though that hardly absolved them from
blame because of the impact of toppling the old regime on law and
order. One organisation, the Iraq Body Count, collated all available
evidence on Iraqi deaths since March 2003. For the period up to
December 2012, it proposed a range of 110,937 to 121,227 deaths,
accepting that this could be an underestimate.[30] Yet their estimates
were higher than those for organisations such as the Uppsala Conflict
Data Program as well as the United Nations.[31]

Another approach, published in the medical magazine *The Lancet*,
involved interviewing a number of households and asking about family deaths, from which they concluded that some 655,000 people had
died beyond what might otherwise have been the case from March
2003 until June 2006.[32] Questions were raised about the representativeness of the sample and the extent of the extrapolation into a
population of 26 million, and the accuracy of the assumptions on
pre-war death rates. It was almost certainly an overestimate.[33] A better study in 2013, using a similar but more refined methodology, at a
time when the situation in Iraq was less fraught, concluded that there
had been 461,000 excess deaths from 2003 to 2011. Of these about
60 per cent were found to be due to violence, of which about a third
were attributed to coalition forces (that is some 90,000). At the peak
of the war men faced a 2.9 per cent higher risk of death than they did
before the war and women a 0.7 per cent higher risk of death.[34] These
were not, of course, the only costs of war. Estimates from the numbers of Iraqis who have migrated abroad since 2003 range from 1.7
million (the United Nations figure) to 2.3 million.[35] Well over a million people also fled from violence to safer parts within Iraq.[36]

These mortality rates show how much worse things were for Iraqis
than they would have been had things continued as they were before
the invasion, but the tensions within Iraqi society could well have come
out in another way at another time and in an equally virulent form.

Next door, Syria, which appeared to be as stable as any Middle Eastern country, came to be consumed by a civil war which gathered pace in 2011. This became extraordinarily violent very quickly, largely as a result of the crude tactics used by the regime to defend itself, aggravated by the large number of players involved and the role of external actors. The United Nations tried to keep count of the death toll, seeking reasonable confirmation of deaths even though this produced a conservative estimate.[37] In August 2014 it reported that 191,369 had died by that date. A year later it gave only a round number, putting the death toll at 250,000 and then gave up trying to update the figures because of a lack of good information. The Syrian Observatory for Human Rights was able to document some 321,358 individuals' deaths by March 2017, but assumed that there were some 85,000 more that had not been documented. Of the documented, government forces and the various factions opposed to the government lost about 112,000 each. Some 96,000 civilians had been killed, of which over 80 percent were the result of government action. In addition, more than 2 million Syrians had been left injured and with permanent disabilities, and about 12 million had been displaced. This was out of a population of just over 20 million at the start of the conflict.[38]

DEATH TOLLS ARE COMPILATIONS OF PERSONAL TRAGEDIES. The meaning for each individual and their family soon gets lost as the toll rises and the counting becomes more difficult. As the numbers grow so too does anonymity until eventually the statistics defy human comprehension with margins of error equivalent to the populations of large cities. Analysts were bound to make use of the best numbers available, however flawed, but there was no science here, and the great uncertainties created opportunities for political manipulation and wilful distortion. It was important to attempt to quantify suffering, but only if it was understood that the figures were imprecise and usually relied on guesswork. Even when efforts were made to report accurately on casualties, as in Syria, at some point the numbers overwhelmed. It became impossible to keep count. As estimates were always involved there was no good reason for excluding the inherently less measurable aspects of suffering, especially those resulting from the collapse of infrastructure and the effects of disease, malnutrition, and poverty. Raw numbers, however carefully put together, still only told part of the story of war.

[12]

Democracy and War

[I]f the consent of the citizens is required in order to decide that war should be declared …, nothing is more natural than that they would be very cautious in commencing such a poor game, decreeing for themselves all the calamities of war.

IMMANUEL KANT,
'Perpetual Peace: A Philosophical Sketch', 1795[1]

The most important intersection of the developing number-crunching science of international relations and the post-Cold War policy agenda came with the question of whether more democracy could also mean more peace. The West's victory over communism was seen as a triumph for the democratic way of life. If others followed the same path there was a possibility of a transcendent community of shared values that would produce peace if only because there would be nothing to fight about. But the spread of democracy was bound to be contentious and would be resisted by autocrats.

As European communism imploded Francis Fukuyama of the RAND Corporation announced that this was not just 'the end of the Cold War, or the passing of a particular period of post-war history', but 'the end of history as such'. By this he meant 'the end point of mankind's ideological evolution and the universalization of Western liberal democracy as the final form of human government.'[2] Talking of the 'end of history' invited misinterpretation. He was not suggesting that there would be no more conflict, or other transformational events, only that there was now no serious ideological alternative to the political and economic model that had been embraced by the Western world, to their enormous benefit.

The collapse of the Soviet empire and its fragmentation into states that all claimed to be embracing democracy appeared as the latest stage in a benign trend. Samuel Huntington described three waves of the democratic ascendance. The first began in the nineteenth century and peaked at twenty-nine democracies, but then went into decline in the 1920s as dictators took advantage of depressed economic conditions. By 1942 there were only twelve. After the Second World War the second wave took the numbers up to thirty-six before there was a further falling away, going down to thirty until the mid-1970s. Then the third wave began with countries in Latin America and the Asia Pacific region adopting democratic forms of government.[3] Lastly, the former states of the Warsaw Pact, along with the Baltic States that had previously been annexed by the Soviet Union, embraced the Western ideology, and having so demonstrated their commitment, were able to join NATO and the European Union. Once the former communist countries were added the number of democracies went up to around eighty (and on some measures even higher).

The momentum behind democracy had international consequences. The communist experience was taken to demonstrate that regimes without basic freedoms tended to instability but spreading these freedoms reduced division and conflict. This challenged the idea that when it came to maintaining international order, systems of government were irrelevant. This idea was central to the UN Charter as drafted in San Francisco in 1945. Then the priority, above all, was to prevent yet more aggressive wars. The preamble acknowledged both state rights and human rights. It opened with a determination to 'save succeeding generations from the scourge of war' while also reaffirming 'faith in fundamental human rights, in the dignity and worth of the human person, in the equal rights of men and women and of nations large and small'. Yet, as the operating principles of the United Nations were described, the core objective became clear. 'The Organization', the charter explained, was 'based on the principle of the sovereign equality of all its Members.' Each must accept the obligations to settle disputes by peaceful means and 'refrain in their international relations from the threat or use of force against the territorial integrity or political independence of any state'. Even if states were acting against their people in an unjust or discriminatory matter, so long as they were not actually disturbing international peace and security, they should be left alone.

> Nothing contained in the present Charter shall authorize the United Nations to intervene in matters which are essentially within the domestic jurisdiction of any state or shall require the Members to submit such matters to settlement under the present Charter.[4]

So whatever was said about justice and human rights, the charter at its core was about removing all excuses for wars of conquest and a celebration of sovereignty. What states did within their own borders was up to them. No challenge was posed to this by President Bush when he spoke of a 'new world order' in April 1991. This, he explained:

> springs from hopes for a world based on a shared commitment among nations large and small to a set of principles that undergird our relations—peaceful settlement of disputes, solidarity against aggression, reduced and controlled arsenals, and just treatment of all peoples.

The vision, despite the use of the word 'new', was actually conservative. The new world as presented was rather similar to the old except that it would lack some of its disagreeable features. The president had been careful to avoid a promise of 'an era of perpetual peace'. The challenge was to keep the 'dangers of disorder at bay'.[5] Bush gave no indication that he expected the pursuit of justice to take precedence over the preservation of order and stability.

But the shift in the balance of power that had just occurred was bound to have more far-reaching effects than a cautious president was inclined to admit. The United States and its allies were now in a hegemonic position, accounting for the bulk of the world's military assets, and its strongest economies, with an enormous freedom of political manoeuvre. They were in a position to rewrite the rules for the international order. For over seven decades they had fought their internal and external battles with fascism and communism, and had now emerged triumphant. Their constitutions reflected their liberal philosophy, requiring that the 'impartial rule of law, and not simply the political power of the individual or group, should govern the outcome of state decisions'. Now there was an opportunity to work on the 'constitution of the society of states as a whole'.[6] The key shift was to put more stress on the rights of individuals and minority groups and less on the rights of states.

In November 1990 the heads of government of thirty-four European nations convened in Paris under the aegis of the Conference on Security and Cooperation in Europe, their first meeting together since Helsinki in 1975. They blessed the reunification of Germany and signed a new arms control treaty on Conventional Forces in Europe. A Charter of Paris was agreed. In this 'new era', democracy was 'the only system of government for our nations', as based on 'the will of the people, expressed regularly through free and fair elections'. It also affirmed that 'without discrimination, every individual has the right to freedom of thought, conscience, religion or belief, freedom of expression, freedom of association and peaceful assembly, freedom of movement'. In addition no one should be 'subject to arbitrary arrest or detention, subject to torture or other cruel, inhuman or degrading treatment or punishment'.[7] The challenge to the old order was fundamental. Instead of insisting that the best international practice was to respect the sovereignty of other states no matter how they managed their internal affairs, it was now considered to be not only appropriate but also necessary to encourage all states to embrace liberalism and democracy.

AT THIS CRITICAL MOMENT THE MOVE TO DEMOCRACY WAS reinforced by one of the most compelling claims to emerge out of the statistical analysis of war. The idea had been given credence by Michael Doyle in 1986.[8] It was set out clearly by Jack Levy in that transformative year, 1989: 'This absence of war between democracies comes as close as anything we have to an empirical law in international relations.'[9] This was picked up by Western leaders, buoyed by the democratic surge of the last quarter of the twentieth century, who found further comfort in the thought that democracy promotion was a route not only to better governance but also to more peace. At last, it seemed possible to realise the German philosopher Immanuel Kant's utopian vision of a Perpetual Peace, based on governments resting on reason and law rather than force.

This combination of academic respectability and political enthusiasm led to closer scrutiny. Democracies had not been as brutal to their own citizens as autocracies. Those governments that turned on sections of their own people in a systematic way—in the Soviet Union,

Nazi Germany, and Cambodia—were usually in the grip of some totalitarian ideology. But the records of the United States, the United Kingdom, and France demonstrated that they had been regularly at war, and not exactly soft touches when fighting against supposedly ruthless and undemocratic countries. This was why the argument was not that democracy made countries more peaceable: but only that they would not then go to war with each other.

Was this correct? The proposition set up a challenge to find instances where democracies had fought each other in order to check whether the findings were as statistically significant as supposed. As most of the time most states did not go to war with each other, did that mean even one instance where two democratic states fought negated the theory?[10] As the analysis used the COW data how much did the high threshold for war influence it? COW might exclude instances where democratic states intervened in the internal affairs of other democratic states, though not to the extent of passing the threshold of 1,000 battle deaths.[11] Or perhaps states with similar types of regimes, even if autocratic, also rarely went to war with each other.[12] When there was no war might this have been for reasons that had little to do with democracy, such as considerations of capacity and prudence?[13]

The debate added to the familiar problems of defining wars an even trickier question of defining democracy.[14] Democracy defined by majority rule and elected leaders did not always come with liberalism, which required openness and tolerance of minorities. The standard fear from the late nineteenth century onwards, after all, was of a belligerent public opinion, especially when aroused by demagogues, populists, and the press. The entry of the masses into politics was one of the conditions for the rise of nationalism over the nineteenth century. At what point did this rise of the masses turn into democracy? The obvious moment might be said to have been when universal suffrage was achieved, but that arrived in stages, from upper class men to working men, then women, and eventually young adults.

Most relevant, perhaps, was the ability of democratically elected civilian politicians to exercise actual control over decisions on war. This was clearly lacking in Germany at the start of the First World War.[15] Moreover, once a country had become a democracy the status could be lost, as political processes become corrupted and liberties qualified. Russia, for example, became less democratic over the 2010s as did Turkey. Nonetheless, the trappings of democracy were still present in both. Iran had highly contested elections for the president, but among a selected group of candidates, with the scope for public debate constrained and supreme power resting elsewhere. The higher the threshold for war and the more restrictive the definition of democracy, the more likely it was that the democratic peace theory would turn out to be true.

There was also the question of causation. Was it that democracy caused peace or that peace caused democracy? Peace made possible trade, investment, and economic growth, which were supportive of democratisation.[16] If democracy caused peace, what was the mechanism by which a country that might otherwise incline towards war instead turned away? One hypothesis was that democracies must address differences to work out internal conflicts and so come to appreciate the value of empathy, compromise, and reciprocation. These were then in play when they addressed international disputes.[17] Another was that democracies ensured that executives were held accountable through legislatures and could be removed from office through elections if they engaged in imprudent wars.[18] Other democracies might also be considered reliable and suitable allies.

All this raised the possibility that there were a number of factors reinforcing each other. Bruce Russett and John Oneal argued that democracies do go to war, just less often than everyone else. Using the Militarized Interstate Disputes database, and taking 1886 as a starting point, because democracy on any terms was relatively rare before that date, they looked for pairs of countries that might go to war. They evaluated each according to an index of democracy, and took account of alliances and power. The conclusion was that democracy made a difference. Taking as a base the likelihood that tension between an average pair of countries would turn into a militarised quarrel, this was doubled when a democracy faced an autocracy and halved when a democracy faced a democracy. They found, however, that the effect only kicked in after 1900. They also looked at economic dependence upon international trade and found that the greater the dependence the less risk of getting involved in a militarised dispute, whether or not there was much trade with the potential adversary. Market economies had even stronger pacifying effects than democracy. Lastly, they considered membership of intergovernmental organisations, and when the pairs had shared memberships. This also encouraged peaceful responses.[19]

The absence of war among democracies, therefore, might be for a variety for reasons. One alternative was that it was largely a 'capitalist peace'. Thus Michael Mousseau considered that peace amongst the advanced capitalist nations was about much more than the high costs of war, but also an interest in encouraging others to be like them. Their wealth created loyalty and the capacity to better non-capitalist states in war. This led to encouraging capitalism as 'the surest cause of peace and friendship among individuals, groups and states'.[20] Another, and more firmly based, alternative was a 'territorial peace'. According to Douglas Gibler, 'settled international boundaries decrease the level of threat to the territorial integrity of states'. This in turn allowed states to cut their armed forces, keep public opinion calm, while reducing the need for the centralisation of power.[21]

It was easiest to have peace when there was little substantial in dispute. These various explanations brought the problem back to the declinist thesis with which this book opened, and whether there was a single determining factor that might explain quite complex and often contradictory trends. Azar Gat identified the underlying process which made a difference to levels of violence, especially in Western societies, as 'modernisation', which had begun with the industrial revolution. This made it possible to satiate human desires without recourse to warfare.[22] The benefits of war went down as the costs went up. But that did not preclude terrible episodes of violent conflict, that expanded and escalated. At the heart of the issue was the interaction between social and economic developments with political choices, which could be egregious or quixotic, as well as perfectly rational.

THE DEMOCRATIC PEACE THEORY WAS ESSENTIALLY A GENER-alisation from the post-1945 experience of North America and Western Europe. A mutually reinforcing set of relationships developed among countries embracing liberal democracy, and open economies. The most remarkable example of this determination to break away from the bad habits of the past came when France and Germany, along with Italy, Belgium, the Netherlands, and Luxembourg formed the original Coal and Steel Community, which grew into a full-fledged customs union and eventually acquired a wide range of competencies and many more members to become the European Union. Whatever else it achieved it gradually calmed one of the most destructive relationships in European history.

But while one set of relationships among liberal democracies became warm and intimate another became hostile and frozen. The expansion of the Soviet system into Central and Eastern Europe in 1945 created a sense of threat that led the United States to accept, once again, some responsibility for European security. In 1949 the North Atlantic Treaty Organisation (NATO) was formed. In 1954 the Soviet Union established its own alliance, building on the control it had already established over its satellite states in Europe. The positive peace that developed in Western Europe was therefore dependent upon the security provided by the Atlantic Alliance. Any temptations for the West Germans to look east rather than west for their political and economic relationships were cut off by the Iron Curtain, the line across the continent that separated the two ideological and military blocs. This is why democracy was such an aggravating factor in the Cold War. This history helps explain the enthusiasm, once there was a chance to heal the fracture that had divided the continent, to do this on the basis of bringing democracy to the former communist states.

But even in Europe, where this effort was generally successful, there were reasons for caution. In the Balkans, for example, violence and instability resulted from a combination of moves to independence and democracy with nationalism and disputes over borders. There were other demonstrations of problems with a capitalist peace with transitions from closed economic systems to open systems that lacked the rule of law and so were susceptible to corruption. Jack Snyder noted how democratisation could produce nationalism 'when powerful elites within a nation need to harness popular energies to the tasks of war and economic development'.[23] A US government task force pointed to states in transition, or not quite democracies, as being prone to conflict, especially when political participation was tied to parochial interests:

> By far the worst situation in terms of risks of instability were for a political landscape that combined deeply polarized or facionalized competition with open contestation. The combination of a winner-take-all parochial approach to politics with opportunities to compete for control of central state authority represents a powder keg for political crisis.[24]

Almost as the theory of the democratic peace was propounded, states becoming democracies experienced conflicts and inner violence. In this way the question of democratisation became linked with the other great issue of the 1990s—the apparent surge in the number of civil wars.

[13]

New Wars and Failed States

A state is a human community that (successfully) claims the monopoly of the legitimate use of physical force within a given territory.

MAX WEBER,
Politics as a Vocation, December 1918[1]

We noted in Chapter 5 the aftershocks of the First World War as old states suffered upheavals and new states were created. Something similar happened after the Second World War, in some cases with the same countries. A civil war in Greece continued until 1947. Yugoslavia only held together amid severe factional fighting, which combined elements of both ideology and ethnicity.[2] The most substantial and enduring upheavals took place in the overseas empires of European powers. After 1945 there was little that they could do to hold on to their colonies. Their early military failures against Germany and Japan had robbed them of their aura of irresistible power. They lacked the energy and resources to hold back popular movements. Some tried more than others, taking and inflicting many casualties in doing so. The French fought bloody wars in their efforts to hold on to Indochina and Algeria. Eventually they gave up. It took just about thirty years to complete the decolonisation process. Portugal fought on the longest, until the strain of its colonial wars brought down its autocratic regime in 1974.

The end of empire meant that there were many more states. The United Nations grew from its 51 original members to the current

193. Of these new states, some fought with each other, but many more suffered conflict inside their borders.[3] Thus side by side with the Cold War, marked by ever-closer relations among the Western democracies, there was another process—decolonisation, of which arguably the implosion of European communism was the culmination.

A NUMBER OF THE NEW STATES SUFFERED FROM CHRONIC instability and consequential violence. By the mid-1990s this violence seemed to be unusually intense and widespread and was attracting attention. Though the risk of great-power war had eased, other types of war now dominated the news. The good news, as a retired US Marine general told Congress in 1999, was that: 'the days of armed conflict between nation-states are ending'.[4] The bad news was that this was combined with a sudden upsurge of unusually nasty and vicious conflicts. One study claimed that 92 out of 108 armed conflicts identified during the 1990s involved organised communal groups, fighting each other or the government.[5] From the 1980s on there were between 15 and 25 countries suffering from civil war at any single point in time.[6]

Mary Kaldor announced the arrival of what she prosaically described as 'New Wars' by contrasting them with the old wars that had gone before by reference to their goals and financing. The new wars arose out of 'national, clan, religious or linguistic' conflicts, made possible because of the 'disintegration or erosion of modern state structures',[7] and were fought with the methods of guerrilla warfare and insurgency. Others also noted the changes, even if they expressed it differently. Kalevi Holsti referred to 'Peoples' Wars', fought by 'loosely knit groups of regulars, irregulars, cells, and not infrequently by locally-based warlords under little or no central authority', to be contrasted with 'organised armed forces of two or more states'. Former NATO Commander Sir Rupert Smith declared that 'war no longer exists' when understood as 'battle in a field between men and machinery'; and as 'a massive deciding event in a dispute in international affairs'. Instead there had been a shift to 'war among the people', often involving non-state actors and apparently never-ending.[8] Martin van Creveld wrote of a 'new form of armed conflict developing', marked by 'much smaller, less powerful and, in many ways, more primitive political entities similar to those existing before 1648'.[9]

There were reasons to question the novelty. Many past conflicts took place largely within divided or fragile states, saw vulnerable groups set upon to the point of mass murder, created opportunities for criminals and adventurers as well as political activists, and involved unconventional military methods.[10] In addition, many that were prominent in the 1990s had their origins well before the end of the Cold War and reflected weaknesses left over from the post-1945 decolonisation.[11]

Nor was it the case, as Kaldor claimed, that these wars were unique in their viciousness. 'At the turn of the twentieth century', she reported, 'the ratio of military to civilian casualties in wars was 8:1. Today, this has been almost exactly reversed; in the wars of the 1990s, the ratio of military to civilian casualties is approximately 1:8.'[12] The claim that past wars barely touched civilians was without foundation. For current wars others made similar claims. In 1996 the United Nations Children's Fund (UNICEF) reported: 'In the later decades of this century the proportion of civilian victims has been rising steadily; in World War II it was two-thirds and by the end of the 1980s it was almost 90 percent.'[13] This was a statistic with a powerful political impact but also without sources.[14]

The claims could be traced to a 1991 paper detailing deaths and refugees in 36 major armed conflicts ongoing in 1988–89, which stated that of 'over five million people . . . killed in the major armed conflicts' about 4.4 million—or almost 90 per cent—were civilians. The analysis, however, was flawed. It added to those who had died those who had been uprooted by the conflicts. Once this item was excluded then the number of those left dead or injured as civilians was around 60 per cent.[15] A 1989 study had suggested that the proportion of civilian war-related deaths since 1700 had been consistently around 50 per cent.[16] When the International Committee of the Red Cross produced its own estimates in 1999 it reported that between 30 and 65 per cent of conflict casualties were civilian.[17] Studies of the 1992–1996 conflict in Bosnia gave figures for war-related deaths of 97,207, broken down into 39,684 (41 per cent) civilians and 57,523 (59 per cent) soldiers.[18] So while civilian deaths were at terrible levels they had not risen to an unprecedented height.

Yet there were differences between the newer civil wars and those that had gone before. Past civil wars had often been conducted as if they were interstate wars (as with the American and Spanish Civil Wars) with forces organised on regular lines.[19] Even campaigns starting with volunteer militias relying on ambushes and terrorism sought to graduate at some point to an army sufficiently disciplined and well-equipped to defeat that of a state. Only rarely was there a reluctant peace agreement between the belligerents, brokered by outsiders. Governments were reluctant to accept deals which by definition meant compromises with rebels. They preferred to crush their enemies. Rebels were equally reluctant to prop up illegitimate regimes. On one count, between 1946 and 1989 only twelve civil wars ended in a peace agreement while eighty-two ended in a military victory for either the government or the rebels. Although the shift was not abrupt between 1990 and 2005, twenty-seven wars ended in peace agreements while only twenty ended in a military victory.[20] If they ended with agreement that was not normally because of a sudden embrace of reason by the warring parties and a desire to put an end to the bloodshed, but because they were exhausted. The record of agreements holding was poor and violence was often resumed. The distinguishing feature of many of the wars highlighted during the 1990s (and which continue to this day) was their length, the inability of either side to bring them to a conclusion, and the extent to which the international community, with mixed success, tried to do so.[21]

AS INTEREST DEVELOPED QUICKLY IN THE TOPIC, IT BECAME apparent that despite the long history of civil wars, their academic study remained in its infancy. While interstate wars had been subjected to intense theorising the same could not be said about intrastate wars. The essential texts of international relations were preoccupied with great powers, and the databases were geared to interstate wars. As civil wars began to attract attention, the gap in knowledge and understanding became painfully evident. In 1993 the German commentator Hans Magnus Enzensberger observed that there was 'no useful Theory of Civil War'. Sixteen years later David Armitage reported that these conflicts, though more common than those between states, lasting longer and afflicting more people, were still an 'impoverished area of inquiry.'[22] Bill Kissane described it as 'a surprise, and an omission worthy of contemplation', that civil wars had 'been ignored by political philosophy', which he put down to the greater hold of interstate war, the importance of revolutionary theory when looking at tensions within states, and distaste for fratricide.[23] To the extent that there were theories, they went back to the classics on politics and the state, to Hobbes with his Leviathan bringing order out of the state of nature and then on to the democratic theories about how to combine order with continuing consent.

There was little written about internal order as an intractable problem. It was one that it was assumed could normally be solved, whether through coercion or consent, and that cases where it broke down were exceptional. Thus theories of economic development barely mentioned the importance of security. The awkward features of many post-colonial countries, from one-party rule to human rights abuses, were excused on grounds of immaturity or assumed to be a painful early stage on the progressive road to development. The rule was not to interfere but to let states make their own mistakes, recover from them as best they could, and mature in their own time. The American preoccupation with wars of national liberation in the 1960s had prompted some research. This was skewed by Cold War considerations, including the assumption that these wars were externally directed, and fuelled by socialist promises rather than by angry nationalism. This effort fizzled out after the departure from Vietnam in the 1970s, although there were still ongoing conflicts that were vicious in their own terms and were capable of drawing in the major powers. Those who had been sympathetic to the wars of national liberation tended to concentrate on the study of revolutions, which were more heroic though also less frequent than civil wars. Challenges to authority were understood in terms of responses to oppression.[24] The Correlates of War Project, having made little effort to gather data on civil wars, though there were five times as many as interstate wars after 1945, belatedly appreciated that this needed to be remedied.[25]

The 1990s saw 'a boom in the study of civil war'.[26] But the sudden interest and the past neglect meant that there was no dominant single, established disciplinary approach or model that could claim to encompass the causes, conduct, and consequences of all civil wars. There was nothing to compare with realist theories of the state system or idealist proposals about how to reform it. The sheer variety of ways in which internal order might break down challenged those attempting to construct a universal theory. The databases improved, but these were conflicts in which the military, civilian and criminal spheres often merged, and in which the notion of 'battle deaths' was ambiguous. Engagements were often localised and small-scale. Fighters spent much of their time as civilians. The questions of what should be measured and what could be measured were difficult, especially in volatile situations in which data gathering could be hazardous and unreliable. Though civil wars shared a number of features, there were often many distinctive aspects which limited their comparability, including the interaction with neighbouring states, which often had their own conflicts. A mass of material came through but the analytical findings were often partial and contradictory, varying according to the weight placed on structural or domestic factors. Some theorists saw the issue largely in terms of which states were more or less prone to internal violence; others wanted to dig deeper into the motivations and character of those causing the violence. Depending on the studies consulted, the degree of ethnic heterogeneity or of democratic reform could be aggravating or mitigating factors.[27]

The early post-1990 scholarship was influenced by the established state-centric approach of international relations, that is instead of looking up from the level of the state to the wider system they looked down to conflict below, and often did so with a similar conceptual framework.[28] It took time before serious investigations began on substate actors in their own right.[29] Over time the best studies were those that kept the statistical work on tap rather than put it on top, combining it with field work and archival research. As a result their conclusions were often less clear-cut, but they were more reliable.

IT WAS THE SUPERFICIAL FEATURES OF THE NEW WARS—THEIR savagery, ethnic polarisation, and links with criminal activity—that initially attracted most comment. This led to a focus on the factors that led to states falling apart. In June 1992 UN Secretary-General Boutros Boutros-Ghali produced a report, *An Agenda for Peace*, which among many issues addressed the problems of 'post-conflict peace-building', seeking 'action to identify and support structures which will tend to strengthen and solidify peace in order to avoid a relapse into conflict.'[30] The next year, in arguing for new forms of UN trusteeship to support states that clearly could not cope, Gerald Helman and Steven Ratner opened their article with a dramatic warning:

> From Haiti in the Western Hemisphere to the remnants of Yugoslavia in Europe, from Somalia, Sudan, and Liberia in Africa to Cambodia in Southeast Asia, a disturbing new phenomenon is emerging: the failed nation-state, utterly incapable of sustaining itself as a member of the international community. . . . As those states descend into violence and anarchy—imperiling their own citizens and

threatening their neighbors through refugee flows, political instability, and random warfare—it is becoming clear that something must
be done. . . . Although alleviating the developing world's suffering
has long been a major task, saving failed states will prove a new—
and in many ways different—challenge.[31]

Others came to write of 'collapsed states',[32] 'troubled states', 'fragile states', 'states-at-risk', or just 'weak states'. Fine distinctions might
be made between these conditions, but the basic idea remained that
some states were a danger to themselves and their neighbours and
needed to be put into an international equivalent of intensive care. By
2002 US National Security Strategy, in the aftermath of the terrorist
attacks of 11 September 2001, was observing that 'America is now
threatened less by conquering states than by failing ones'.[33]

What did it mean to say that a state was failing? The German
sociologist Max Weber's definition of statehood pointed to the importance of being able to monopolise violence and exercise authority over a defined territory. The monopoly of legitimate force could
be lost without a fight, as the result of a military coup or because
the army refused to suppress non-violent protests such as food riots
or strikes. Whenever a regime faced trouble because of popular unrest, an outright rebellion, an attempted coup, or a secessionist
movement, the loyalty of the armed forces could soon come to the
fore as a key issue. Should violent challenges to the state reach a
point where the main mission of government forces lay in beating
them off then it was a civil war. Either the rebellions prospered or
were suppressed.

The territorial side of the equation, and whether wars were between or within states, depended on how borders were drawn. Those
that were 'not drawn along previously existing internal or external
administrative frontiers' were particularly likely to lead to disputes,
along with 'borders that lack standing under international law'. As
Toft observed, because people identified with territory, and cared
more about their homeland than other sorts of land, 'wars over territory tend to last longer and be more difficult to resolve than wars
fought over other issues'.[34] For this reason much of the explanation
for the 'new wars' lay in the way that borders had been set and states
had been formed after 1945.

The basic principle adopted by the UN was that borders should
be fixed and the new states resulting from decolonisation should stick

with inherited colonial borders. Certainly when attempts were made to divide up countries to accommodate distinctive communities or ideologies, the results were not encouraging. For example there were two acts of decolonisation in 1947 for which Britain was responsible and which left questions of borders unresolved. The partitioning of the Indian Raj between India and Pakistan and of Palestine between Israel and the Arabs caused immediate conflict and led to a series of wars that may not yet be concluded. The ideological divisions of Germany and Korea between pro-Western and pro-Soviet regimes provided the most dangerous issue in Cold War Europe and a vicious war in East Asia, also not yet settled, well over sixty years after a ceasefire. In these cases the tensions between communities turned into interstate wars. When the tensions had to be accommodated within established borders then the risk was of a civil war.

THE INTERACTION BETWEEN STATE CAPACITY, FIXED BORDERS, and political tensions could be seen most sharply in Africa. The continent experienced rapid decolonisation from the 1950s, and a series of wars that tended to be large, enduring, and complex. From the 1960s to the end of the Cold War, while there were ten civil wars there were still eight interstate wars. Since 1960 at any time as many of a third of all African states were experiencing a degree of internal conflict. During the early 1990s the continent's conflicts were regularly counted as the most destructive of the 'new wars'. On some estimates by the end of the decade Africa accounted for as many as 80 per cent of the world's conflict deaths.

The principles that shaped decolonisation followed the UN Charter, and so stayed with established borders and deflected demands for self-determination. In 1960, as the process gathered pace with thirty-seven new states having come into existence in Asia, Africa, and the Middle East, the UN General Assembly issued its landmark declaration 'on the Granting of Independence to Colonial Countries and Peoples'. This confirmed that self-determination was about introducing self-government to colonies on the basis of existing borders and not about accepting the territorial claims of distinctive nationalities. There was to be no support for secession.

What was missing too often was state capacity. During colonial times these countries were occupied, exploited, and administered by foreigners. Until late in the day the authorities tended to suppress demands for independence rather than prepare the people for government. The leaders and bureaucrats of the newly independent states rarely had much experience, their previous careers spent in either minor roles in colonial governments or political agitation. These deficiencies might have been remedied by a longer and more careful transition to self-government, but this was rejected as patronising and an argument for delaying independence. In its 1960 declaration the General Assembly insisted that the capacity for self-government should not be a decisive criterion (although that had been the position in the UN Charter). Instead: 'inadequacy of political, economic, social or educational preparedness should never serve as a pretext for delaying independence.'[35] At any rate, once it was clear that independence was coming there was no incentive for the coloniser to stay.

Just as the great powers 'scrambled' to colonise Africa in the nineteenth century, during the 1950s they began to 'unscramble' in haste. One striking feature of the period from scrambling to unscrambling was how little the borders of Africa's fifty-five countries changed.[36] This was despite their arbitrariness. Colonial authorities had drawn them with scant respect for ethnography or geography, and an exaggerated appreciation for straight lines. In describing the process, Lord Salisbury noted:

We have been engaged in drawing lines upon maps where no white man's foot ever trod. We have been giving away mountains and rivers and lakes to each other, only hindered by the small impediment that we never knew exactly where the mountains and rivers and lakes were.[37]

Yet these borders were confirmed in the early twentieth century in order to manage the competing claims of Great Britain, France, Belgium, and Germany, and then again in 1963 by the Organization of African Unity (OAU). The members of the OAU pledged 'to respect the frontiers existing on their achievement of national independence.'

The OAU also set a clear norm that any attempt to break up these states must be discouraged. When the first serious test came—as Biafra sought to break away from Nigeria in the late 1960s—the OAU swung its weight behind the central government in Lagos. Despite the hardships caused by the war, the OAU in 1967 condemned all attempts at secession. In this way the logic of self-determination was contained. Governments resisted demands from disgruntled minorities for greater autonomy and even secession. Statehood took precedence over nationhood.

As countries kept their territorial formation, economic weaknesses and social tensions developed and struggled to find political resolution. This created what Robert Jackson described as an unparalleled situation in which states, however chaotic internally, could still assume that they would not face external aggression or even lesser forms of intervention. They were 'quasi-states', able to enjoy 'the possibility of international legal existence as a sovereign entity (juridical statehood) in the absence of internal socio-political existence as an effective state (empirical statehood)'.[38] Their statehood was not underpinned by a robust and collective sense of nationhood.

No state followed the same political path, but certain pathologies soon became evident. Because they neither inherited nor were able to construct the foundations for effective state institutions, those in leadership positions, usually those who had led the campaigns for independence, could not feel secure. In the first instance, the prestige of charismatic leaders and pride in independence allowed little space for credible opposition parties. Warnings about the dangers of factions in the face of the big challenges of development helped rationalise one-party rule. With entrenched power came the associated risks of patronage and corruption, used to enrich the elite and buy off opponents. Other obvious, and some not-so-obvious, rivals for power who could not be co-opted were taken out of local politics using exile, assassination, and imprisonment.

Many of the first generation of leaders managed this effectively and those that succeeded often had decades in power.[39] For others any sense of security produced by such measures was temporary. Africa's armed forces were largely organised on traditional European lines, at first often officered by Europeans, but small and ill-equipped. As the politicians sought to reform them and sometimes to suppress opponents, civil-military relations could become tense. With no alternative political outlets, military leaders began to take matters into their own hands. There were thirty-eight successful coups in Africa between 1963 and 1978.[40] Though these would be presented as saving the country, other motives were usually present, from personal ambition to fear of an imminent purge. Because of this risk, loyalty as opposed to competence was the key criterion when governments chose military chiefs. This did little for the operational effectiveness of the armies, as unity of command was discouraged and elite units were held back to protect the government.

Grievances were left unaddressed. Minority tribal groups could feel excluded, lacking representation in central government and experiencing discrimination in allocation of revenues. As a result regions could become disaffected and occasionally in open revolt: with their limited capacities and political distractions, armies were not always effective in putting them down and in their efforts to try could make matters worse. None of this was helpful to a country's economic development. Unaccountable power and the need to look after supporters encouraged corruption. When the Cold War ended only five sub-Saharan states were considered partially democratic.

In such unpromising settings, the demands of political survival shaped the policies of leaders. At a minimum it was necessary to keep control over the capital city. A rebellion in a distant region might be ignored, but once a government was ousted from the most iconic state buildings, and unable to broadcast directly to the population, it was lost. The next priority after the capital was revenue-generating regions even if that meant starving other areas of funds. The location of natural resources, whether oil fields, diamond mines, or other commodities, was a key factor in setting priorities for territorial control. Should all these measures prove to be insufficient then it was necessary to get external support. Rotten regimes could be kept going by external finance, supplies of military hardware, and training, and, in extremis, foreign troops. But then rebels might also get external support. Through 'transnational alliances', neighbouring leaders might see an opportunity to gain influence over an adjacent region or access to some key resources. They might support groups with whom they had some affinity while denying sanctuary to their own rebel groups. In earlier times they might have conquered relevant territory, but this was now precluded by the norms of fixed borders and non-aggression.[41] In many cases it was therefore more appropriate to talk of 'regional war zones' than of civil wars, as groups and action moved without regard for national boundaries. Borders had become progressively less relevant.[42]

[14]

Ancient Hatreds and
Mineral Curses

Nation states will remain the most powerful actors in world affairs, but the principal conflicts of global politics will occur between nations and groups of different civilizations. The clash of
civilizations will dominate global politics. The fault lines between
civilizations will be the battle lines of the future.

SAMUEL HUNTINGTON,
'The Clash of Civilizations?', 1993[1]

An early explanation of why there seemed to be an upsurge of
conflict in the 1990s was that what was being observed was
not really new but merely the resuscitation of enmities with deep
roots. In 1993 Samuel Huntington challenged the optimism of his
former student Fukuyama. As ideological divisions faded, he argued, more basic factors would come into play, reflecting distinctive
cultures and traditions which had been built up over centuries. The
origins of these divisions were of less interest than their persistence,
and their growing importance in the complex geopolitical setting of
the post-colonial age. He did not deny the strength of Western civilisation, but he assumed it had peaked.

The conflicting civilisations had religious roots, but the actual importance of religion was unclear because religiosity could take many forms. Religion was an easy tag of identity, but then assigned to groups of people who might exhibit minimal observance of any religious practices it meant little. Religion could also refer to deeply held beliefs that shaped all aspects of life. Unless one was separated from the other, the argument could easily become circular. If some sort of religious identity could be attributed to all political actors then all conflicts soon appeared to have had a religious cause.[2] A more discriminating approach tended to undermine Huntington's thesis. It certainly provided an unreliable explanation of past wars.[3]

As with Fukuyama the nuances of the argument were lost as his title, *The Clash of Civilizations*, turned into a slogan that appeared to capture the developing importance of nationalism and cultural identity in the conflicts of the 1990s. It reinforced an impression that the slaughter was nihilistic and almost instinctive, a reflection of ancient hatreds that consumed whole communities. The implications of a centuries-old conflict was that it was probably doomed to continue well into the future, and so little could sensibly be done to bring it to a close.

The wars in the former Yugoslavia seemed to fit Huntington's thesis because they indeed took place in and about the fault lines of Europe, the meeting points of the old Austro-Hungarian and Ottoman empires, and of Catholicism, the Orthodox Church, and Islam, and where national identities had been forged during the previous century with claims for self-determination. One of these claims, marked by a shot in the Bosnian capital of Sarajevo, had triggered the First World War. Early in the 1990s people were being forcibly moved from their homes because of their ethnicity—a process which came to be known as 'ethnic cleansing'. This was linked to comparable events in the region's history, notably the Croatian Ustashe's commitment to 'cleansing the terrain' during the German occupation of Yugoslavia, the euphemism employed in their assault against Serbs who were as often massacred as moved. This had been followed by equally brutal attacks by Serbs on Croats after the Germans had retreated, if not quite on the same scale.

So when comparable behaviour was observed in the 1990s there was an implication that this was such a deep-rooted process that it would not reach a conclusion until ethnically homogenous areas had been created:

With no sizable minorities left within any state and with the war-ring factions securely walled off behind "national" boundaries, the best that can be hoped for is that the motors of conflict will be disabled and the fatal cycles of violence that have marred Balkan history will finally have reached their end.[4]

Acting US Secretary of State Lawrence Eagleburger described the Yugoslav conflict as irrational. Ethnic conflict, he explained, 'is gut, it is hatred; it's not for any set of values or purposes; it just goes on.'[5] In 1993 the author Robert Kaplan published his book *Balkan Ghosts* which encouraged the view that the current conflicts emerged from a region 'full of savage hatreds, leavened by poverty and alcoholism', emerging out of 'a morass of ethnically mixed villages in the mountains.'[6] One implication was that there was really little to be done. President Clinton's reluctance to get involved in the conflict was said to be the result of reading Kaplan's book, which, it was noted, 'pointed out that these people had been killing each other in tribal and religious wars for centuries.'[7]

In an article that appeared in 1994, also read with approval by Clinton, Kaplan warned of a 'coming anarchy'. In place of nation states, he spoke of 'an epoch of themeless juxtapositions, in which the classificatory grid of nation-states is going to be replaced by a jagged-glass pattern of city-states, shanty-states, nebulous and anarchic regionalisms'. The prospect was grim:

> Future wars will be those of communal survival, aggravated or, in many cases, caused by environmental scarcity. These wars will be subnational, meaning that it will be hard for states and local governments to protect their own citizens physically. This is how many states will ultimately die.[8]

Later Clinton publicly regretted his embrace of the 'ancient hatreds thesis'. In 1999, now engaged in a campaign against the Yugoslav leader Slobodan Milošević over Kosovo, he apologised for blaming conflict on 'some Balkan disease' of endless ethnic blood feuds based on implacable hatreds. 'I, myself, have been guilty of saying that on an occasion or two,' he remarked, 'and I regret it now more than I can say.'[9]

Although the language often suggested that these conflicts were marked by neighbours killing neighbours, the numbers involved were usually only a tiny proportion of the adult male population. In addition, the victims were often moderates of the same grouping who opposed the extremists. Even when communities had a long history of mutual antagonism, it still had to be explained why violence broke out between them at a particular time.[10] In other conflicts with similar levels of tension, violence was avoided.

Thus one critique of the 'ancient hatreds' meme argued that what went on in Croatia and Bosnia was not so much about a 'frenzy of nationalism—whether ancient or newly inspired—but rather from the actions of recently empowered and unpoliced thugs.'[11] Warren Zimmerman, who had been the US Ambassador to Yugoslavia, observed how 'the dregs of society—embezzlers, thugs, even professional killers—rose from the slime to become freedom fighters and national heroes.'[12] That still begged the question of who had empowered the thugs. They were used for a purpose.[13] The more the analysis pointed to mutual loathing that welled up from within society rather than something that had been encouraged and developed at an elite level, the more it appeared insoluble 'rather than a mitigatable, deliberate atrocity carried out by an identifiable set of perpetrators.'[14] This did not mean that it was always so easy to identify the perpetrators. Each of the parties had its own narrative to explain why its fight was justified and in accord with the principles of self-determination.[15]

The antecedents of the Bosnian conflict were long and complex, but the origins of the immediate crisis lay in the instrumental use of nationalism by Slobodan Milošević as the president of Serbia. This put pressure on the unity of Yugoslavia. As the country broke up, then Serb strategy was to eliminate or expel the non-Serb population in Serb areas. The violence was not random but deliberate. The 'scale, range and consistency of the methods used', observed James Gow, 'required significant coordination and planning'.[16] Focusing on the elite without consideration of the circumstances which gave their nationalism credibility could be taken too far. It simplified the causes of the conflict and also flattered 'a deeply held conviction that people, like children, are generally good, and that as a consequence, bad behavior is best explained by bad leaders, teachers, or parents'.[17] Events in Yugoslava still needed to be understood by reference to the country's history, which provided the themes for the nationalist messages, or the social structures which conditioned the response. Yet in the end it was politics that led to the country's devastation. Those seeking to resolve the conflict had to make sense of this politics.

The conflicts in the former Yugoslavia and elsewhere developed because certain political and military leaders willed them, and not because of a popular clamour. As a civil war was essentially a contest between repression and dissent, it was perhaps not surprising that an intensification of both, and in particular repression by an insecure regime, provided one of the best guides to the onset of civil war (although this could be a bit like saying that the appearance of tumours is a guide to the arrival of cancer).[18] Notably the Yugoslav wars were predicted. A US National Intelligence Estimate of October 1990 observed, without qualification or dissent, that: 'Yugoslavia will cease to function as a federal state within one year and will probably dissolve within two. Economic reform will not stave off the breakup.' Bosnia was seen as the 'greatest threat of violence'.[19] The cohesion of a country with 'six republics, five nationalities, four languages, three languages, two alphabets, and one party' had long been of concern. Pessimism about Yugoslavia's chances for survival had grown during the 1980s, and by 1990 the belief that the country could 'muddle through' was untenable. Yet this estimate led to no action. Not all policymakers agreed, the diplomatic agenda was incredibly crowded with the end of the Cold War and the Gulf conflict, but also the message was so stark that it pointed to no levers to pull to prevent catastrophe. Unlike so many of the warnings discussed in this book, this one implied no remedies.[20]

ONCE CONFLICT WAS UNDERWAY, A SENSE OF ETHNIC IDENTITY could grow and acquire a harder meaning. There was no natural correspondence between 'nation' and 'state, which is why references to 'nation-states' were rarely accurate. A state was a legal construct, a nation, tribe, or ethnic group was a social construct, less embedded or 'primordial' than often assumed.[21] Many were of relatively recent origin, encouraged in the past by colonial governments as part of strategies of divide and rule, or nurtured by angry intellectuals and opportunistic political leaders. Yet whenever and however identities were constructed they could still become vital facts of political life and, once mobilised, less malleable than supposed. They could not be altered at will as political agendas changed, as if tensions could be intensified at one point but then played down for the sake of a later harmony.

When governments acted on the basis of identity, especially in a discriminatory or repressive fashion, then identity grew in salience.[22]

The longer conflict endured in one form or another, the more past grievances, atrocities, and betrayals became part of the cultures of groups, and prepared them for future rounds. Ethnic and religious diversity might not invariably lead to war, but once war occurred these animosities were likely to be aggravated and then linger. Moreover, those who spoke for the distinctive groups, even when they were culpable for the original violence, were hard to exclude from any peacemaking process. They could still demand to be part of the solution to a problem they had created. This is why in practice the combined logic of an ethnic focus and the self-determination principle led to proposals for partition and relatively homogenous statelets, and why ethnically polarised conflicts could be amongst the hardest to conclude, unless one side was actually comprehensively defeated in war.[23] When national groups were spread across states (for example the Kurds in the Middle East) then a neighbour might do its best to prevent a defeat of those with a shared identity. The interaction between social and political structures was therefore complex. Nonetheless, the starting point for any understanding of the prevalence of civil wars and the difficulty of resolving them lay in the weakness of states and the political exploitation of division.[24]

AFRICA WAS A PRIME EXHIBIT IN ROBERT KAPLAN'S 1994 warning of a 'coming anarchy'. 'Africa's immediate future could be very bad', he reported, to the point where 'foreign embassies are shut down, states collapse, and contact with the outside world takes place through dangerous, disease-ridden coastal trading posts'.[25] In 2000 a headline in *The Economist* spoke of 'Hopeless Africa'.[26] The continent displayed too many of the features that made civil war more likely. In addition to chronically weak states there was poverty, inequality, and not enough gainful employment for young men. Even the terrain seemed to suit guerrilla warfare, offering sanctuary and opportunities for ambushes and occasional territorial gains.[27]

At the heart of much of the worst African violence was the Congo, the second largest country in the continent and at its centre, with troubled countries all around it—including the Central African Republic and South Sudan to the north, Rwanda to the east, and Angola to the South, all of which had their own bloody wars. The area around the Congo basin was first established as almost a private venture of King Leopold of the Belgians until it was taken over by his government in 1908. After the country gained independence in 1960, a struggle developed among the different factions in the independence movement. This turned into a full civil war, which lasted for five years, drawing in the Belgium government, which regularly sent forces in to rescue expatriates, the superpowers, and the United Nations, offering an early demonstration of the problems of establishing a peacekeeping force without a peace. After a 1965 coup Mobutu Sese Seko came to power in the Congo, which he renamed Zaire. With inefficient and corrupt armed forces and massive debt, this apparently strong state became hollow inside. Mobutu's reach barely stretched beyond the capital Kinshasa. He exacerbated intercommunal violence to divide potential opponents. Gradually its own troubles became intertwined with those of its neighbours.

Angola only achieved its independence in 1974, after which the three different guerrilla groups who had been fighting the Portuguese began to fight each other. The Marxist MPLA formed a government in the capital Luanda. Fearful of a Soviet gain the United States encouraged Zaire and South Africa to intervene on behalf of the two other groups, the FNLA and UNITA. With Cuban help the MPLA kept hold of Luanda but were unable to establish control over the rest of the country. After 1990, though superpower rivalries no longer fuelled the civil war, it was sustained by the country's mineral wealth, which factions used to fund their armies. UNITA relied largely on the sale of diamonds. The conduct of the war, which lasted until 2002, was appalling on all sides, with young men forced to fight and young women raped and abducted. Nobody knows how many died. The figure of 500,000 usually cited is so round that it indicates the uncertainty.

On the other side of the Congo was Rwanda, one of the smallest countries in Africa, which, with neighbouring Burundi, had also been run by Belgium after they took over the colony from Germany following the First World War. There was tension between the Hutu, favoured by the Belgians, and the disadvantaged and disaffected Tutsi. The Hutu continued to control the country, often with brutal methods, but found it difficult to suppress the Tutsi whose militants often raided from neighbouring countries. After a military coup in 1973, Juvénal Habyarimana took power and seemed to stabilise the country, but with a fast-growing population competing for scarce land, tensions built up. A civil war began in 1990, as the result of a

Tutsi insurgency led by Paul Kagame's Rwandan Patriotic Front (RPF), fully backed by Uganda.[28] There was a tentative ceasefire in 1993, but Habyarimana was killed in a plane crash the next year. The radical Hutu regime in Kigali that replaced him unleashed the genocide that killed some 800,000 Rwandans over three terrible months.

The interaction between the existing tensions within Zaire and the Rwandan conflict produced a perfect storm of murder and mayhem.[29] Rwandans, including Hutu who had been involved in the genocide, flowed across the border into Zaire. The new Rwandan government worked with Uganda, Angola, and local Tutsi forces to take the offensive against the Mobutu regime. Mobutu was eventually deposed in May 1997. Laurent-Desire Kabila formed a government, and the country became the Democratic Republic of the Congo (DRC). Kabila lacked the strength to disarm the Hutu militias so Rwanda invaded again, joined by Burundi and Uganda with their own concerns about rebels finding sanctuary in the DRC. Zimbabwe and other members of the South African Development Community (Chad, Sudan, Lesotho, and Namibia) backed Kabila. To complicate matters further Angola switched sides because Kabila, unlike Mobutu, did not back UNITA.

This was now a hybrid conflict of extraordinary complexity, with breakaway factions, internecine disputes, and side deals. Foreign forces clashed with each other on DRC territory; UN peacekeeping forces were put together and then failed to make any difference. Eventually Kabila was assassinated, to be replaced by his son. A peace deal was signed between the DRC and Rwanda in July 2002. A transitional government was formed the next year. Neighbours, and in particular Rwanda, still worried about threats to their own stability and meddled continually. Conflict and violence remained routine.[30]

THE SOCIOLOGICAL EXPLANATIONS OF CONFLICT, ADDRESSING ethnic and religious differences, tended to be most in play with the wars in the Balkans. Though they certainly had relevance for the wars in Africa, here economic explanations had more influence. Until the 1990s economists, even those working in the development field, gave little consideration to civil wars. The textbooks contained few if any references to war and conflict. The field was about how to raise the living standards of ordinary people in the developed world. Military coups and extravagant arms purchases distorted economic priorities, and wars set back the development process, but beyond that there seemed little to add. The priority was to give sensible advice to states able to take it and the international bodies striving to help them develop. In 1994 Jack Hirshleifer, observing how little attention economists had paid to the 'dark side' of human affairs, of conflict, crime, revolution, and warfare, urged them to explore this whole 'intellectual continent'. Economists who did so, he added, 'will encounter a number of native tribes—historians, sociologists, psychologists, philosophers, etc.—who, in their various intellectually primitive ways, have preceded us in reconnoitering the dark side of human activity.' Betraying something of the imperial tendencies of economics, he confidently anticipated that these 'a-theoretical aborigines' would soon be brushed aside.[31]

As economists began to make their first forays into the field, one particular issue grabbed their attention—how unauthorised groups could take control of natural resources in weak states to enrich themselves. The backdrop was a steady rise in the number of conflicts in petroleum-rich and diamond-rich countries. Up to 1974 they occurred at a rate of about one a year, but over the next eighteen years this moved up to just less than five a year. One obvious reason was the rise in the number of petroleum-rich states following the 1974 OPEC price rises, up from fifteen to forty-two by 1980. The incidence of violence involving these states went up sharply. It then dropped down between 1985 and 1995, along with the oil price, before rising sharply again. Conflicts involving diamond producers also grew, notably after 1986. Another trend was an increase in the use of contraband by rebels, including gemstones, timber, and narcotics. Contraband funding was evident in seven of ninety-two civil wars beginning between 1945 and 1988, but then in eight of the thirty-six wars that began after 1988.[32] In the DRC, Namibia's president was alleged to be interested in protecting his family's mining interests while Chad had connections with Congolese gold mines. Zimbabwe was owed money by Kabila and also appears to have seen economic opportunities in the DRC's diamonds, gold, and copper. (Zimbabwean troops congregated around important mining towns). On the other side Rwanda and Uganda exploited territory to export diamonds.[33]

THE TRIGGER CONDITIONS FOR CIVIL WARS BECAME A MATTER of intense academic debate. An influential study of 2003 by Fearon and Laitin argued that:

> The conditions that favor insurgency—in particular, state weakness marked by poverty, a large population, and instability—are better predictors of which countries are at risk for civil war than are indicators of ethnic and religious diversity or measures of grievances such as economic inequality, lack of democracy or civil liberties, or state discrimination against minority religions or languages.

As in the past insurgencies had been marked by rural guerrilla warfare (although by this time urban fighting was becoming more important) and this could be sustained by as few as 500 to 2,000 active guerrillas then what mattered was 'whether active rebels can hide from government forces and whether economic opportunities are so poor that the life of a rebel is attractive to 500 or 2,000 young men'. According to this strand of thinking, civil wars were almost entirely opportunistic, an unsurprising response to a set of conditions rather than a deliberate political project. This approach discouraged attempts to look beneath broad indicators of a troubled society to attempt to understand the specific sources of conflict or pay any attention to sub-state actors. It played down the motives and aspirations of those doing the fighting, as if any cause would do.[34]

Even when looking at motives it was possible to argue that people did not really care what they said they cared about. Oxford economist Paul Collier led the way, working closely with the World Bank, arguing that in explaining the incidence of internal conflicts, 'greed' was more important than 'grievance' and 'loot' more so than 'justice'. The presence of natural resources, and in particular oil and diamonds, made countries particularly war prone. There might be no surprises in finding tendencies to violence in countries that were struggling to raise their per capita income and experiencing severe inequalities, or that young men with not much else to do were available for armies and gangs. What really made the difference, Collier and his colleagues argued, was the opportunity to make money. Here was the incentive for rebellion and the means by which a conflict could be sustained. The opportunity alone was sufficient. 'Our model suggests that what is actually happening is that opportunities for primary commodity predation cause conflict.'[35]

The most depressing conclusion was that even if a particular conflict could be stopped, unless ways could be found to generate a healthier pattern of economic development it would recur. Collier suggested that some 40 per cent of countries that had suffered con-

flict returned to violence again in the decade after fighting had supposedly been brought to a close. In a World Bank report he noted:

> Once a country stumbles into civil war, its risk of further conflict
> soars. Conflict weakens the economy and leaves a legacy of atroc-
> ities. It also creates leaders and organizations that have invested
> in skills and equipment that are only useful for violence. Disturb-
> ingly, while the overwhelming majority of the population in a
> country affected by civil war suffers from it, the leaders of military
> organizations that are actually perpetrating the violence often do
> well out of it.[36]

The power of greed could be overwhelming: 'neither good political institutions, nor ethnic and religious homogeneity, nor high military
spending provide significant defenses against large-scale violence'.[37]
Later Collier went further, taking an even more deterministic view.
'Where rebellion is feasible it will occur: motivation is indeterminate,
being supplied by whatever agenda happens to be adopted by the first
social entrepreneur to occupy a viable need'.[38] This line of argument
was criticised as being 'extremely reductionist, highly speculative, and
profoundly misleading'.[39] Collier himself moved away from his focus
on greed to explore a wider range of factors, including the influence
of culture.[40]

One key issue was how to explain the relationship between natural resources and conflict.[41] Diamonds were important in only a few
conflicts, which rendered attempts to generalise from them unsafe.[42]
With oil, which had the most pernicious effects, the impact depended
on whether it was found onshore (offshore reserves had little impact
on war proneness) and then in relatively poor regions with marginal-
ised ethnic groups. Oil wealth was also used by autocracies to help
them stay that way, and so encouraged corruption and repression.[43]
Depending on circumstances, the desire to take advantage of natural
resources could result in a coup, a secessionist movement, a local
rebellion, intervention by a neighbour, either directly or using proxies, forms of extortion so that rents could be collected from those in
charge of the resources, or permutations of these possibilities. In addition, what might happen when raw material prices were high would
be different to when they were low, especially in countries over-de-
pendent on a single commodity. Then grievances could develop as
people became suddenly poorer.

The implication of the economic focus was that a more balanced economy, with a decent manufacturing sector, would be more stable—with less inequality, and more commerce within a country. This related to a similar case to that made before 1914 about how the interpenetration of economies reduced incentives for war and so could be a force for peace.[44] As with the question of ethnicity the question of economic incentives was different when considering the origins of a war than how it was sustained. With all wars, between states as well as within them, a failure to achieve a quick victory meant that the ability to finance and sustain a military effort was as important as the ability to prevail in battle. With both types of war, opportunities were created for criminal activities, especially those engaged in smuggling and trafficking. With civil wars they could become more important than the notional issues at stake. In this respect rebel groups could suffer just as much of a 'resource curse' as the states they were subverting. Opportunities for loot helped in recruitment, but this was not the same as a deep ideological commitment to the cause and loyalty to the organisation. In poorer environments activists understood that there was to be a long struggle before they could expect to benefit.[45] When the resources were available, fighting groups took money from wherever they could, plundering resources, trafficking in arms, drugs, people, and diamonds, as well as seeking remittances from diasporas and siphoning off funds intended for humanitarian assistance. David Keen described how

> members of armed gangs can benefit from looting; and regimes can use violence to deflect opposition, reward supporters or maintain their access to resources. Winning may not be desirable: the point of war may be precisely the legitimacy which it confers on actions that in peacetime would be punishable as crimes.

For this reason 'civil wars that appear to have begun with political aims have mutated into conflicts in which short-term economic benefits are paramount.'[46] This was one explanation for the indecisiveness of contemporary civil wars: they were not resolved by battle and were often sustained by crime.[47]

[15]

Intervention

The most pressing foreign policy problem we face is to identify the circumstances in which we should get actively involved in other people's conflicts.

PRIME MINISTER TONY BLAIR,
Chicago, April 1999[1]

Until Western countries started to intervene in developing civil wars in 1991 there was every reason to suppose this was something they would be desperate to avoid, especially now that there were no Cold War imperatives to support beleaguered clients. Both realism and international law warned governments away from another's domestic quarrels. The principle of non-interference, embodied in the UN Charter, meant that other states could continue with annoying and provoking behaviour, causing economic costs and affronting cherished values, provided that they stayed within their own borders. Here the most vicious tyrannies enjoyed the same rights as the most harmonious democracies. If this was uncomfortable, so too could be engaging with distant and intractable disputes. These promised pain and frustration in return for very little reward. Peace between states took priority over peace within states.

The strength of the international norm meant those who did intervene were chastised. In 1971 Indian action helped turn East Pakistan, which was fighting a vicious civil war with West Pakistan, into Bangladesh. Eight years later Pol Pot's 'killing fields' in Cambodia were ended by a Vietnamese occupation. Also in 1979 Tanzania toppled Uganda's tyrannical leader Idi Amin. In all cases there was a net gain for human welfare (or more accurately a reduced net loss), though the interventions were explained largely on security grounds. Still they were all condemned internationally for breaching the non-intervention norm.[2] Although Michael Walzer had made the case for intervention as early as 1977 in cases of the most shocking crimes against humanity, arguing that individuals could be the victims of aggression and not just states, this gained little traction until after the end of the Cold War.[3] Even after 1990, Russia and China remained wary of self-determination, conscious of how it might be applied to their own minorities.

Why then did Western attitudes shift so sharply? There were self-interested reasons: to deal with risk to expatriate communities; to push back against pernicious and repressive ideologies; and to prevent war-torn states serving as sanctuaries for terrorists as well as bases for organised crime and various forms of trafficking, including drugs, arms, and people. Should the intensity of the fighting drive people out of their homes, as was normal, refugees could put an enormous burden on neighbouring states. There were, however, also ways of addressing these problems without direct intervention, including policing borders, transferring arms and funds to the government, and sometimes to the rebels, and working to absorb refugees, or help these people stay safe in their own countries. Civil wars certainly became more visible, and TV channels were now able to reach distant places and send back images of suffering to feed continuing news channels, such as CNN. Reports of atrocities and misery took the edge off the optimism of 1990 and the hopes of a coming epoch of peace and good governance. It was also a matter of capacity. The West now enjoyed a remarkable military preponderance, with the US alone spending as much on its armed forces as the rest of the world combined. It was in a position to act if it chose to do so.

The main reason for the sudden shift in gears, however, was a case in which it was hard not to intervene. It began with the firm opposition to Iraq's occupation of Kuwait in August 1990. The decision to use armed force to push Iraq out of Kuwait was remarkable in itself, but it was also wholly consistent with established international norms, confirmed by a series of UN resolutions. By March 1991 Kuwait had been liberated but Iraq was left as a unitary state within its recognised borders and with the regime that had caused all the trouble still in place. Frustrated, Shia and Kurdish areas exploded in rebellion, and this for a while rocked the regime. Western forces did not intervene. Saddam Hussein had kept enough in reserve, and the revolt was ruthlessly suppressed. This created a massive refugee crisis as Kurds tried to flee from northern Iraq into Turkey and Iran. The initial reaction from the United States and its allies was that this was not their business, and they had no obligation to get involved. For a moment the non-interference norm held. But then it broke. The media in the area which had been following the war were still around to record the plight of these displaced people and note words that might have encouraged them to expect Western support.[4] Eventually the US, UK, and France accepted responsibility and successfully created a protected safe haven in northern Iraq which allowed the Kurds to return to their homes.

This set a precedent. An intervention took place and was successful. Then almost immediately tensions became evident in Yugoslavia. Again the Western instinct was to stay clear or to confine the response to offers of mediation. But this was a significant part of Europe, from which conflicts had spread in the past. The fighting was taking place in and around popular holiday destinations. In addition, TV broadcasting meant that images of suffering populations could be transmitted directly into living rooms. British Foreign Secretary Douglas Hurd observed that 'mass rape, the shooting of civilians, in war crimes, in ethnic cleansing, in the burning of towns and villages', were not novel. What was new was that 'a selection of these tragedies is now visible within hours to people around the world. People reject and resent what is going on because they know it more visibly than before'.[5] Faced with heartbreaking depictions of tragedy there were demands that something must be done.

These demands grew as casualties mounted and the Serb-dominated Yugoslav government appeared indifferent to UN resolutions demanding restraint. Furthermore, following German unification and with the Soviet Union about to split into its component parts, there was less certainty that existing territorial boundaries must be upheld at all costs. The principle of self-determination made a return as an alternative basis for state-making to simple adherence to established borders, no matter how arbitrary. Diplomatic pronouncements combined talk of the 'territorial integrity of States' with the 'equal rights of peoples and their right to self-determination'. European governments together deplored acts of 'discrimination, hostility and violence against persons or groups on national, ethnic or religious grounds'. When awful things were going on in the neighbourhood, these were 'matters of direct and legitimate concern to all participating States and do not belong exclusively to the internal affairs of the State concerned.'[6]

After trying mediation, backed by economic sanctions and sporting bans, gradually Western countries became more forceful. From tentative beginnings, first in Croatia and then in Bosnia-Herzegovina, external involvement moved from unarmed monitors to lightly armed peacekeepers to more robust land forces backed by air power. The British and French, leading the intervention, were torn between their reluctance to get too involved and their growing awareness that the humanitarian mission was constantly being undermined by their inability to stop the fighting. After the massacre of Muslims in Srebrenica, with Dutch peacekeepers stuck in a passive role, air strikes began against Serb positions, which also came under pressure because of Croat and Muslim ground offensives. This was followed by an agreement which divided Bosnia up and curtailed local Serb ambitions. Serbian leader Slobodan Milošević's focus then shifted to Kosovo, a province of importance to Serbian national identity yet populated largely by Muslims. His intention appeared to be to push them into neighbouring territories. This time the response was much firmer. Starting in March 1999 NATO engaged in an extended air campaign against Serbia, leading eventually to Milošević climbing down.[7]

THE GUIDANCE THAT FLOWED FROM A NORM OF NON-INTER-ference was absolutely clear—it meant doing nothing everywhere. Guidance for a norm of possible-interference was much harder—it meant doing something somewhere. A whole range of possibilities was being opened up without agreed rules or helpful precedents. When, where and how to intervene would have to be worked out on a case-by-case basis. In April 1999 during the Kosovo campaign British Prime Minister Tony Blair set down some pragmatic criteria that could provide guidance: confidence in the case, exhaustion of diplomacy, plausible military options, readiness for a long haul, and relevance to the national interest.[8] Some cases might be clear-cut, with credible military operations available. At other times the case might be more ambiguous and the military options poor.

There was only limited, and generally unimpressive, experience on which to draw. There were essentially two models available, neither of which breached the non-intervention norm. The first was 'aid to the civil power'. This required the use of regular armed forces to help a government impose law and order because the police authorities were no longer up to the task. This was the basis for the attempts to defeat independence movements during the colonial period, and was the rationale for both the US in Vietnam and the Soviet Union in Afghanistan. The problem in these cases came with a civil power with little legitimacy or independent strength. Success on this model therefore meant building up the local government so that it could cope on its own, relying on its own armed forces and police. The British intervention in Malaysia during the early 1960s, conducted in extremely favourable circumstances, was an example of how such an effort might be successful.

The second model was peacekeeping. This had been developed by the UN and was largely about using contingents of foreign troops to ensure that a ceasefire line held. The UN exercise to try to bring peace to the Congo in the early 1960s had been so chaotic, including the death of Secretary-General Dag Hammarskjöld, that similar endeavours had been viewed warily thereafter. In this model impartiality was the key: the troops were present with the consent of the parties to the conflict. Unlike those aiding a civil power, when the upper limit on force was determined by the strength of the insurgency, and conflict could resemble a conventional war, the model for peacekeeping required forces that were non-provocative and therefore only lightly armed, with just enough for their own self-defence. By and large these forces were successful when marking a clear ceasefire line, although these lines tended to become fixed, which meant that the forces also became fixtures. The United Nations Peacekeeping Force in Cyprus (UNFICYP) for example was introduced in 1964 and never left, waiting for a definitive settlement between the Greek and Turkish communities. The peacekeeping model was adopted for both interstate and civil wars, and not only by the UN but also by multinational groups, as with the Sinai (after the Egypt-Israel peace agreement) and Beirut in the early 1980s.[9]

It was the peacekeeping model that was first employed in the Yugoslav conflicts, requiring impartiality and consent, and non-provocative forces. This was inadequate. There was no peace to keep, and lightly armed forces could not impose a peace. In addition, their mandate began to expand during the course of the conflict. The model was about keeping warring parties apart. The mission in Bosnia increasingly came to be about protecting civilians, including providing the sort of safe havens that had been found for the Kurds in northern Iraq in 1991. The difficulty was that this involved taking sides. There were few purely humanitarian acts in the midst of a war. An urgent need to send in a convoy of food and medical supplies to relieve people caught in a besieged town undermined the strategy of those laying siege who wanted those people to get desperate. When it came to brokering a ceasefire or better still a peace settlement the starting point was normally impartiality. But recalcitrance by one side could result in more coercive measures. The next step was to conclude that the only way to a satisfactory peace was for one side to win. By this time the intervention had moved a long way from the starting mission. As, for all these reasons, the old peace-keeping model came under increasing strain the talk was of 'second-generation peace-keeping' or 'wider peace-keeping' and then 'peace support' until eventually it was not clear that peace as such was present or obtainable, so the aim came to be 'stabilisation operations'.[10]

By the late 1990s intervention for humanitarian purposes had become not only acceptable but also almost mandatory.[11] In 1999 the UN Secretary-General reported for the first time on the Protection of Civilians in Armed Conflict.[12] The interventionist norm was captured by the assertion of a 'responsibility to protect'.[13] Soon this was being invoked with such regularity that it even had its own shorthand (R2P). The focus on individual responsibility for war crimes was reflected in a new International Criminal Court (ICC), which began its work in 2002.

In 2003 the African Union, formerly the Organization for African Unity, was constituted with a new act. This encouraged 'respect for democratic practices; good governance, rule of law, protection of human rights, and fundamental freedoms; and respect for the sanctity of life.' It established 'the right of the Union to intervene in a Member State pursuant to a decision of the Assembly in respect of grave circumstances, namely: war crimes, genocide and crimes against humanity.' The next year a UN 'High-Level Panel' endorsed the 'emerging norm' that there was a right of 'military intervention [as a] last resort'.[14] In a document agreed by the General Assembly in 2005, the international community was to take 'responsibility to protect populations from genocide, war crimes, ethnic cleansing and crimes against humanity'.[15]

As the need to protect civilians took centre stage it was evident that the protectors would need to be able to act robustly. This meant putting peacekeeping forces into dangerous and difficult situations, with all the inherent problems of funding, command structures, and multinationalism. In a mission to Sierra Leone in October 1999, UN peacekeepers were mandated 'to afford protection to civilians under imminent threat of physical violence'.[16] When describing in October 2014 yet another mission to deal with violence in the Democratic

Republic of the Congo, its head told the Security Council: 'the protection of civilians is more than a mandated task, it is our raison d'etre in the DRC and a moral imperative of the UN'.[17]

The more African countries were contributing peacekeeping forces in their own region, the more their own interests in influencing outcomes became apparent. The idea that peacekeepers should come from the region was encouraged for Africa, by both the local nations and the Security Council. The advantages in terms of cost and ease of deployment, and a readiness to get involved, were evident. But this could be a mixed blessing.

> While some may argue that this is all the better for promoting "African solutions to African problems", this can have negative consequences for African citizens, including exposing them to poorly paid and resourced troops with low levels of training and little respect for civilians; further entrenching despotic regimes; or regionalising existing conflicts.[18]

As with armies away from home through the centuries, sexual activity added to the misery of the communities that were supposedly being helped. This was especially true at a time when HIV-AIDS was spreading. Peacekeeping forces were one means by which it spread, including back to the contributing country.[19]

At times also they offered a promise of safety that they could not deliver. Thus in the DRC after 2006 the UN force appeared as an ally of the government, but this meant an association with an army that was still ill-disciplined and predatory.[20] As a threatened population moved in large numbers towards the UN camps for protection, they made themselves more rather than less vulnerable. It was not only in the DRC but also the Central African Republic and South Sudan, that when UN troops were 'thinly spread out, logistically hamstrung and devoid of reserves and critical force multipliers', the locations where the desperate people gathered 'provided attractive targets for attack.' In this respect there was a risk of the international effort aggravating rather than easing the conflict trap.

DESPITE THE EVIDENT FAILURES THERE WERE INTERVENTIONS that worked. In 2000 Britain helped stabilise Sierra Leone as a result of a somewhat opportunist but still successful intervention.[21] Despite the presence of a UN force, a rebel group was advancing on the capital Freetown. The British government sent a team to prepare to evacuate foreign citizens, which meant securing the airport. This by itself appeared to have a stabilising effect and soon the British army was working with Sierra Leone forces to push the rebels back. As this operation led to the rebels being disarmed and disbanded it was widely taken as a vindication of humanitarian interventions and a demonstration of the potential of a small number of highly professional regular soldiers when taking on less-well-organised militias.

In Liberia the bloody regime of Charles Taylor, which had supported the rebels in Sierra Leone, in part by illegal smuggling of diamonds and timber, eventually buckled as rebel groups put his forces under severe pressure. He fled to Nigeria, opening the way for a democratic government, a UN peacekeeping force to provide security, and his indictment for war crimes at the ICC. In 2011 French and UN forces worked together to ensure that the successful winner of the Ivory Coast's election was able to take power against the resistance of the defeated incumbent, although their rationale also involved protecting civilians against atrocities committed by both sides. The next year Islamist movements began to make their appearance as a serious destabilising factor in Africa. One succeeded in gaining control of northern Mali. At the start of 2013 a French intervention helped the Mali government defeat the Islamists.

Peacekeeping operations could reduce the risk of a relapse into war, but it depended on the type. Unsurprisingly, a peace was more likely to last if it had consent rather than if it was imposed. Operations with consent were more effective if they were forceful in their methods. Weak operations with limited consent were, again unsurprisingly, likely to fail.[22] Much depended on the grasp of the local situation, the ability to work with other missions on such tasks as promoting the rule of law and economic development, the degree of support given by neighbouring states, and the success in demobilising militias.[23]

The negative stories risked obscuring positive achievements. In a critique of the critics, Roland Paris argued that there was a strong case still to be made for 'liberal peace-building', included the promotion of representative governments. He warned of the consequences of conflating those efforts that had followed the occupations of Iraq and Afghanistan with those that had followed negotiated settlements, and warning of over-simplifying endeavours that were morally complex and exaggerating the imperial overtones.[24] The need was to learn from experience and adapt practices rather than abandon the enterprise altogether.

FOR EIGHT YEARS THE FRENCH DIPLOMAT JEAN-MARIE GUÉHENNO served as the head of peacekeeping for the United Nations, with a later spell working on a UN mission to Syria. In his memoir he described his first day in the office on 1 October 2000 with senior figures from the UN and those who had been involved in its most prominent operations in recent years. As they reviewed their record it was mixed. The end of the Cold War had meant that it was easier to get Security Council approval for new missions, and it had also provided an opportunity to settle some of the lingering conflicts of the past, including in Cambodia, Namibia, Mozambique, and El Salvador, in which the UN 'blue helmets' had been able to help consolidate the peace.

But then things had gone wrong within Yugoslavia, Rwanda, and Somalia where the peacekeepers had ended up as bystanders to tragedies, ineffectual when the moment came. By 1999 this had cast such a cloud over the organisation that it was assumed that the UN might have had its day. Yet UN members suddenly agreed to three new missions, which had provided a new impetus. These were in two areas that had fought to break away from central rule—Kosovo in Serbia and East Timor in Indonesia. The third was in the DRC. All had revealed problems—with lines of command from the HQ in New York that inhibited those with field responsibility and budgets that could not be stretched to include all the development work that needed to go hand in hand with keeping the peace.

Guéhenno quoted another Frenchman, Bernard Kouchner, who had been in charge of the UN effort in Kosovo, explaining how 'humanitarian interventions are political interventions'. The most humanitarian act was to fix the politics, but that could not mean forgetting the need to fix injustice.[25] Here was the core problem of peacemaking at any level. Peace required a political settlement, but was that to be based on a calculation of the balance of power at the time, or a sense of the rights and wrongs of the conflict, which might address the underlying, and probably still simmering, grievances that had led to the conflict? There was also the issue of whether the UN was now to become the effective government of these war-torn countries or was to work on restoring sovereignty as soon as possible, and get in place an effective government.

The urgency of 2000 had dissipated by the middle of the decade. The Security Council was more divided than it had been since the end of the Cold War, making life difficult for those who had to get the organisation working to support those in the field. Moreover, a controversial UN mission to Iraq after the US-led invasion came to a sad close when one of the UN's most experienced figures, Sergio Vieira de Mello, was killed along with twenty-two colleagues by an act of terrorism. The mission in the DRC had lost credibility and suffered its own scandal when peacekeepers were accused of widespread sexual abuse, yet new missions had been agreed in Haiti and Côte d'Ivoire overstretching the organisation. Duties had been added without the extra resources to enable them to be met.

Back in 2000 the senior UN official Lakhdar Brahimi had urged caution. The Security Council should contain its ambition, avoiding sending peacekeeping missions unless there was a peace to keep, and setting tasks with mandates marked by clarity, credibility, and achievability.[26] Yet soon, and against the backdrop of the 'Responsibility to Protect', twenty-one new operations were established.[27] Brahimi's guidance was largely ignored. It was too tempting to use these missions to signal resolve, appearing to take action while doing little to ensure success.[28] There was no cost in expressing ambition, only in trying to realise it. Western interventions had fared little better. Neither Iraq nor Afghanistan achieved a stable peace. Although a degree of order had been brought to both countries by 2011 in neither case was the political order stable enough to cope as Western forces withdrew. Another intervention that year in Libya, with UN backing, faltered.

In 2015, like de Madriaga over eighty years earlier, Guéhenno looked back ruefully to an international community that could never have the cohesion of a national community, and could authorise noble ends but not always the means to achieve them.

> Grand plans were elaborated and immense hopes were generated among the people we had suddenly decided to help. But hope was often dashed, and we then faced resentment if not outright hostility, while on the home front, ambition has been replaced by a pressing desire to pack up and leave.[29]

The problem was not a lack of need or value, but too many disappointing experiences.

[16]

Counter-Insurgency to Counter-Terrorism

They did not know the simple things: a sense of victory, or satisfaction, or necessary sacrifice. They did not know the feeling of taking a place and keeping it, securing a village and then raising the flag and calling it victory. No sense of order or momentum. No front, no rear, no trenches laid out in neat parallels. No Patton rushing for the Rhine. . . . They did not have targets. . . . They did not know strategies. . . .They did not know how to feel . . . they did not know which stories to believe. . . . They did not know good from evil.

TIM O'BRIEN,
Going after Cacciato,[1] 1978

W hile the British and French had embraced the interventionist role, the United States had been much more cautious. One reason for this was the shadow cast by the long war in Vietnam. The outcome troubled the collective conscience, not only about the desolation of Vietnam and the impact of a communist victory but also about American losses and the poor treatment of veterans. Those who had fought in Vietnam suffered pain and injury and yet could not even find comfort in having played some part in a heroic struggle. Too much of what had occurred was considered shameful. This traumatic experience became a vital reference point in American culture, reflected in novels and movies that shaped both memories about what this war had been about and expectations about what might happen if the US got involved in similar wars in the future.

The Vietnam War was a product of the Cold War but this aspect tended to be missing from its various fictional representations. The only movie that came out while the war was at its height, and which did attempt to offer a rationale, was *The Green Berets*, directed by and starring John Wayne. This was unabashed propaganda. Wayne had asked for government support so that 'not only the people of the United States but those all over the world should know why it is necessary for us to be [in Vietnam]'.[2] In order to arrange government help Wayne got involved in extended negotiations with the Pentagon who demanded that the war be portrayed fairly. This meant that by the time the film was eventually released in 1968 there were very few Green Berets (special forces) left in Vietnam and the war had become deeply unpopular at home. Wayne reprised his familiar role in Westerns as a decent but tough lawman, fighting outlaws. He added a 'hearts and minds' aspect, promising the Pentagon that the film would portray the professional soldier 'carrying out his duty of death but, also, his extracurricular duties—diplomats in dungarees—helping small communities, giving them medical attention, toys for their children, and little things like soap, which can become so all-important.'[3] Even with the Westerns the simple dichotomy between goodies and baddies was historically dubious. With this conflict it was even more problematic.

After the war was over, and Saigon had fallen to the communists, a number of movies appeared with a Vietnam theme which treated the actual fighting in an almost surreal fashion. The war served as a backdrop for stories that could have been set at different times and places. Michael Cimino, director of the *Deerhunter* (1978), which focused on Pennsylvanian steelworkers caught up in the war, described it as having 'little to do with the American experience in Vietnam .... It could be any war. The film is really about the nature of courage and friendship.' Francis Ford Coppola envisaged his *Apocalypse Now* (1979) as not necessarily political but 'about war and the human soul'.[4] Other movies were more realistic, but described the war at the micro-level, far from considerations of grand strategy, as tests of character more than policy. *The Boys in Company C* (1978) emphasised the dehumanising basic training and then the incompetence and callousness of the war. Its tag line was 'To keep their sanity in an insane war they had to be crazy'. *Platoon* (1986), reflecting director Oliver Stone's own experiences in Vietnam, described the experiences of an infantryman, and was tagged with the line 'The first casualty of war is innocence'. *Hamburger Hill* (1987) was about seizing a piece of ground at immense cost, only for it then to be relinquished. Its tag line was 'War at its worst. Men at their best'. The cumulative effect was to reinforce anti-war sentiment. They were not just about the discomforts and pain of combat but the lack of evident purpose. Jane Fonda, the anti-war activist, recalled crying with veterans as they watched *Platoon* together. She told an interviewer: 'A movie like this helps to insure that it [another Vietnam] will never happen again.'⁵

In 1984, reviewing a number of novels to emerge out of war experiences, C. D. B. Bryan identified a 'Generic Vietnam War Narrative'. It started with an eager and patriotic young man arriving in Vietnam and soon filling a gap in a platoon.

> In his platoon our young man meets Day-Tripper, who is stoned all the time; Rebel, the crazy white guy who loves killing; Juice, the cool black dude who can smell ambushes and booby traps; the Professor, who at some point will explain why Ho Chi Minh should never have been our enemy. And he meets Doc (or Bones), the conscientious objector medic; Bascomb, the psychotic company commander who gets fragged (that is, killed) by Day-Tripper, Rebel, or Juice; Bailey, the good sergeant whose life is saved by Day-Tripper, Rebel, or Juice; Williams, the young lieutenant who gets better with experience but is killed along with Doc (or Bones) near the end of the book. By the end of the book all the characters have been killed except the young hero (who is often the narrator) and either Day Tripper or Juice, who re-enlists.

Bryan described the iconic moments—the first patrol, with 'the seductive excitement of a fire fight', atrocities when innocent civilians are gratuitously killed, lots of helicopter moments, dope scenes, and 'R&R in Saigon with Susie the bar-girl'. When the hero arrived home he found that he had become something of an embarrassment, and unable to get or hold down a job: 'he has nightmares, smashes up a few things, misses his buddies still in 'Nam, and at the very end wonders what the hell it was all about. What did it mean? What good did it do?' The point of this narrative was to chart 'the gradual deterioration of order, the disintegration of ideal-ism, the breakdown of character, the alienation from those at home, and, finally, the loss of all sensibility save the will to survive'.[6]

This was a war without happy endings.[7] The movies and novels raised broader issues but the essential message was that the partici-pants had all in some ways been left damaged. A common complaint about the books and movies inspired by Vietnam was that the Viet-namese, whether appearing as allies or enemies, spectators or victims, rarely appeared as rounded characters.[8] Their portrayal was often as tricky and malevolent, undeserving of the effort that the United States was making on their behalf. The country appeared as the background for a variety of individual melodramas. The war was therefore re-membered less as a cause and more as a backdrop to personal strug-gles and demons, for stories of survival and coping. The theme was casualty, not only in death, but in physical and psychic wounds. When, in 1978, the Vietnam memorial was unveiled in Washington, there was nothing to indicate what it was about other than a list of 57,692 war dead, giving them a degree of honour.

IF THERE WAS A STRATEGIC LESSON IT WAS CONFLICTS SUCH as Vietnam moved in circles rather than straight lines, lacking the moral clarity and military logic of previous wars. The idea that such wars were bound to be both frustrating and deeply unpopular was further reinforced by a brief but unhappy period in Beirut when a US peace-keeping mission got too close to the Christian government and was punished for its troubles by the radical Shia group Hezbollah, with a suicide car bomb in October 1983. This caused the deaths of 241 marines and undermined the will to continue. This was reinforced as American citizens began to be kidnapped, leading to withdrawal in early 1984.[9] The US Secretary of State George Shultz and the Secretary of Defense Caspar Weinberger had been on opposite sides in the policy debate and after the US withdrawal they drew distinctive lessons. In October the pro-interventionist Shultz warned that the United States must not allow itself 'to become the Hamlet of nations, worrying end-lessly over whether and how to respond. A great nation with global responsibilities cannot afford to be hamstrung by confusion and inde-cisiveness'.[10] In his riposte, Weinberger offered his own warning, this time of the dangers of getting too involved in what he called 'gray area conflicts'. His tests for US engagement in these conflicts required that it be vital to national interests and a last resort, and that when combat troops were used this should be 'wholeheartedly, and with the clear intention of winning' and with 'some reasonable assurance of the support of the American people and their elected representatives in Congress'.[11]

An attempted humanitarian intervention in Somalia reinforced Weinberger's message. The collapse of Somalia's government in early 1991 led to political chaos. A drought meant that the population faced starvation and disease as well as violence. A small UN peacekeeping force was unable to cope. In late 1992, in part as an alternative to getting involved in the developing crisis in the former Yugoslavia, President Bush sent a substantial force to provide security for the relief effort. Although President Bill Clinton inherited the mission without enthusiasm, he presided over an escalation as US forces became engaged in conflict with one of the warlords, General Mohamed Farah Aidid. In October 1993 an operation to capture some of Aidid's aides in the capital Mogadishu went badly wrong as two helicopters were shot down by militiamen killing eighteen US soldiers, some of whose bodies were dragged through the streets of the city. Many hundreds of Somalis also lost their lives in the battle.[12] Although Clinton insisted at first that this incident would have no impact on the US commitment within a few months American troops were withdrawn.

Clinton drew the lesson that it was best to stay clear of African conflicts. Unfortunately the next test came with the vicious massacres engulfing Rwanda in 1994. Despite the evidence of genocide the US avoided any involvement. The appalling death toll later weighed heavily on the international (and Clinton's) conscience.[13] One study calculated that as few as 5,000 peacekeepers could have prevented much of the violence.[14]

Another who drew a lesson from the US withdrawal from Somalia, along with that of the Soviet Union from Afghanistan, was Osama bin Laden, the leader of the Islamist terror group, al-Qaeda, based in Afghanistan. In a 1997 interview with CNN's Peter Arnett he remarked

> After a little resistance, the American troops left after achieving nothing. They left after claiming that they were the largest power on earth. They left after some resistance from powerless, poor, unarmed people whose only weapon is the belief in Allah the

Almighty, and who do not fear the fabricated American media lies. . . . The Americans ran away from those fighters who fought and killed them, while the latter were still there. If the US still thinks and brags that it still has this kind of power even after all these successive defeats in Vietnam, Beirut, Aden, and Somalia, then let them go back to those who are awaiting its return.[15]

His basic strategy was to inflict as much pain as possible on the US until they left the Middle East. On 11 September 2001 famous symbols of US power took direct hits from aircraft hijacked by members of al-Qaeda. The twin towers of the World Trade Center in New York were brought tumbling down while the Pentagon in Washington was badly damaged. The attackers, directed from one of the poorest of the world to one of the richest, employed one of the oldest of weapons—knives—to hijack the airliners and turn them into deadly instruments of carnage.

AT THIS POINT ATTITUDES CHANGED DRAMATICALLY. IT TURNED terrorism, largely seen as an exceptional irritant and occasional inconvenience, into a cause of national trauma. A previously unimaginable attack unlocked the most vivid imaginations. What would once have been dismissed as incredible now demanded to be taken seriously. Terrorism moved from a way of pushing otherwise ignored grievances onto the international agenda, as with hijackings of aircraft by Palestinian groups or attacks on US troops abroad, to a direct threat to homeland security. Past terrorism was violent and purposive, but it was hard to think of it as war. By contrast 9/11 was experienced as an act of war. It was an odd war that pitted a small band of Islamist extremists against a superpower. The political motives of the enemy received less attention than the opportunities available in open societies for those who wished to cause maximum havoc. Everything from energy facilities to food supplies could now be seen as a critical vulnerability.

Concern about what was at first called 'Islamic Fundamentalism' had been around from the 1980s, then largely associated with Iran, because of the stormy aftermath of the 1979 revolution. The term later fell out of use because it implied that the problem was extreme piety rather than a highly politicised form of Islam; eventually terms such as 'Islamism' or 'Jihadism' were more widely used. During the Cold War those of this persuasion had been seen as more threatening to atheistic communists rather than the West, which is why they had been supported in Afghanistan. The most extreme Sunni writers were clearly very hostile to Western ways, but it was not evident how this hostility might turn into war.[16] Bernard Lewis warned in 1990 of the revival of 'ancient prejudices' leading to Muslim rage against the West.[17] In his *Clash of Civilisations* (a term initially used by Lewis), Huntington cautioned that 'this century-old military-interaction between the West and Islam' could become more 'virulent'.[18] Anthony Dennis described how the collapse of communism had given fundamentalist Islam, led by Iran, an opportunity to fill the gap. He anticipated that 'Islam in its violent, reactionary, fundamentalist form would continue to be the number one threat to world peace and the very survival of the human species'.[19] The austere Wahhabism, promoted by Saudi Arabia, was fundamentalist but was combined with pragmatic policies towards the West. The radicals were largely devoted to harassing Arab governments, including the Saudis, as much as pursuing Western targets. Other than for the special circumstances of the Lebanese civil war, terrorism in the Middle East had largely been associated with the secular Palestinian cause.

In 1991 the plot of Tom Clancy's novel *The Sum of All Fears* depended on a Palestinian group triggering a war between the United States and the Soviet Union by detonating a nuclear weapon (actually a lost Israeli device) in the Superdome, killing senior members of the US administration. In an afterword to the paperback version the next year he observed: 'All of the material in this novel related to weapons technology and fabrication is readily available in any one of a dozen books. . . . The fact of the matter is that a sufficiently wealthy individual could, over a period of from five to ten years, produce a multistate thermonuclear device'.[20] In practice the technical difficulties were hardly trivial, even if sufficient fissionable material and capable engineers could be acquired, and there were obvious risks that would be faced by anyone trying to put a crude weapon together. Nor did it seem to fit with the strategies of most terrorist groups. Few seemed to need to cause mass casualties to make their political points.[21] Weapons of mass destruction had not been considered weapons of choice for terrorists. Their past priorities had been assumed to be getting 'a lot of people watching, not a lot of people dead'.[22]

The pattern had begun to change in the 1990s, although this only came to be fully appreciated with hindsight, looking back after 9/11.

They became integrated into the narrative of the 'war on terror' almost in the form of a *Star Wars* prequel. An earlier attack on the World Trade Center in 1993 made a limited impact because of the few casualties caused. Then al-Qaeda had attempted high casualty attacks—on the US Embassies in Kenya and Tanzania and on the USS *Cole* from Yemen—but these had been away from the United States.[23] In February 2001, CIA Director George J. Tenet reported that the threat from terrorism was his priority, noting that terrorists were becoming 'more operationally adept and more technically sophisticated', looking at softer civilian targets as military targets came to be better protected. 'Usama bin Laden and his global network of lieutenants and associates remain the most immediate and serious threat ... capable of planning multiple attacks with little or no warning'.[24]

A number of high-level reports had urged that attention be paid to the threat of weapons of mass destruction being used against unprotected American cites. The twin assumptions were that such weapons would be the best way to terrorise population centres but also that their use would most probably be organised and implemented by a capable state. Thus the Hart-Rudman Commission, which had identified 'unannounced attacks on American cities' as the gravest threat, also suggested that

> terrorism will appeal to many weak states as an attractive, asymmetric option to blunt the influence of major powers. Hence, state-sponsored terrorist attacks are at least as likely, if not more so, than attacks by independent, unaffiliated terrorist groups.[25]

North Korea and Iraq appeared as likely culprits, so that the most credible form of this threat was in fact a derivative of the standard scenarios used in defence planning.

There was all the difference between speculation about a potential threat, however plausible, from a panel of specialists and distinguished figures and a frightful reality hitting unsuspecting people out of the blue. Inevitably on 9/11 thoughts immediately turned to Pearl Harbor, the last time American territory had been attacked from overseas and the moment that came to mind every time the US was caught by surprise. In the case of the 9/11 attacks there was a sharp psychological impact and anxiety about the possibility of further attacks. There was no risk of a defeat in any meaningful sense but there was a keen awareness of a new type of vulnerability. From the president downward, the message was that this 'changes everything' and all security issues had to be addressed with fresh eyes, so that the US was never caught out in such a way again. An image of future war had been opened up that was quite different from anything that had gone before.

INEVITABLY RADICAL ISLAM NOW LOOMED LARGE IN THIS IMAGE of future war. Huntington had already pointed to Islam as the most war-prone of civilisations. As this atrocity, and others attempted or succeeded, was undertaken in the name of Islam, this appeared to vindicate at least one reading of Huntington. For others this was a dangerous conclusion and every effort had to be made to show that the terrorists were not at all representative of mainstream Islam. Either way there was a surge in interest in whether the teachings of this religion were responsible for the conflict. More books were published on Islam and war in the aftermath of 2001 than had been published in all prior human history. Some 80 per cent of scholarly articles on the topic ever published also came after 9/11. This was another example of academia trying to catch up with a phenomenon that had caught it, along with government, by surprise. By comparison there was far less interest in Christian, Jewish, or Hindu approaches to war. When Islam was mentioned it tended to be in the context of extremism and violence.[26]

Now all the issues connected with 'weak' and 'failing' states acquired a harder edge. The prompts to US action were far more profound than the humanitarian concerns of the early 1990s. Bin Laden's intent behind the 9/11 attacks might have been to persuade the US to avoid entanglements in the Middle East. Given the responses to Beirut and Mogadishu this was not a wholly unrealistic expectation. Earlier, when mass-casualty terrorism was a more abstract fear, it was noted that it might be wise to avoid further provoking the angry groups already making a nuisance of themselves in Middle Eastern politics.[27] In the aftermath of the attacks, however, with over 3,000 dead (and initial estimates much higher), the responses took the form of an unremitting display of US military capabilities. Offending regimes were toppled, first in Afghanistan and then in Iraq, after the opportunity was taken in 2003 to overthrow Saddam Hussein.

[17]

From Counter-Terrorism to Counter-Insurgency

Reports that say that something hasn't happened are always interesting to me, because as we know, there are known knowns; there are things we know we know. We also know there are known unknowns; that is to say we know there are some things we do not know. But there are also unknown unknowns—the ones we don't know we don't know. And if one looks throughout the history of our country and other free countries, it is the latter category that tend to be the difficult ones.

US SECRETARY OF DEFENSE DONALD RUMSFELD,
February 2002[1]

When the US invaded Afghanistan and Iraq it did so with equipment that had been conceptualised during the Vietnam era but with a great-power war still most in mind. The disinclination to get involved in more thankless overseas quagmires was combined with a determination to stick with the regular wars for which the armed forces were best suited. From the start of the 1970s full attention was given once again to the inner-German border and plans to hold back a Warsaw Pact invasion. Academic strategic studies could also turn with relief away from the perplexities of counter-insurgency to the more familiar terrain of preparations for conventional war in the centre of Europe.[2] The army began to rebuild its strength, now with an all-volunteer force instead of conscripts, and with new weapons that were far more capable than anything known in the past. The reconstruction effort originated in the determination to reduce dependence upon nuclear threats, but this effort was then propelled forward by the potential of these new technologies that could take information and turn it into a form that could be processed, stored, and transmitted through digital circuits, equipment, and networks. A new version of future war was opening up.

How this might develop was apparent by 1968:

> The pinpoint of targets by land-based, airborne or satellite radar, the use of infra-red to reduce the concealment obtained from darkness and overcast weather, and miniaturized battlefield computers will together allow for a centralized control of conventional fire-power; its efficiency will be further increased by the use of advanced proximity fuzes that detect their targets.[3]

A number of different strands of technological development came together. Satellites were in use for reconnaissance purposes by 1961 and for communications in 1965. Work on the development of integrated circuits, allowing complex processes to be managed in ever-smaller packages, had begun in the 1950s. In 1965 Gordon Moore promulgated his famous and remarkably prescient law that the number of transistors in a dense integrated circuit would double every two years. The first 'smart' bombs, relying on these technologies, were employed by the USAF during the closing stages of Vietnam.[4] Whereas once it might have taken numerous sorties for an important bridge to be destroyed, now this could be achieved with a single weapon. The success of air defence and anti-tank weapons during the opening stages of the October 1973 Arab-Israeli War suggested that the trend could include moving as well as fixed targets.[5] It was now becoming possible to work out where enemy forces were and what they were up to, and then they could be hit with a high probability of success.

In 1980 the futurologists Alvin and Heidi Toffler offered a schema for basic changes in society. After the familiar move from an agricultural to an industrial age had come an information age—the 'third wave'. During the second wave, of industrialisation, the focus had been on mass, standardisation, and bureaucratic organisation.[6] With the third wave, knowledge was at the centre of all decisions, and organisations would be more flexible. In the military sphere this went beyond improved weapon design but to a new way of thinking about warfare, along with all other human activities, in more systematic, holistic terms. The ability to identify enemy vulnerabilities within a complex setting and target them swiftly raised possibilities for disruption and disorientation as well as pure destruction. Later, the Tofflers took their investigations into the way the US army was adjusting to the information age as confirmation that 'the way we make war reflects the way we make wealth'. Unusually for books on future war they also explored the future of peace, or 'anti-war', showing the influence of the Balkans conflicts in urging the need to think about war as a means of preventing even greater violence.[7]

THE EXTENT OF THE CHANGE COULD BE MARKED BY A COMPARISON with Liddell Hart's *The Revolution in Warfare*, completed in 1945 just as the Pacific War concluded. He had then regretted the transformation of war 'from a fight to a process of destruction.' He judged that the rot had set in to modern warfare when it was realised that air raids could not be used to hit specific military targets but instead large civilian areas. 'Inaccuracy of bomb-aim resulted in inhumanity of war-aim'. The corollary of this was that if now bomb aim was more accurate so too could be war aim. War could become once again more of a fight.[8]

At first improved accuracy and lethality appeared to reinforce defence. Anything visible and in range, whether aircraft, tanks, or warships, would be vulnerable to accurate missiles. That put a premium on manoeuvrability as the best way to get round strong defensive positions. From their study of Warsaw Pact exercises and military literature, NATO planners concluded that their adversaries had put a lot of effort into developing armoured divisions and plans for their use geared to moving fast to outflank NATO defences.[9] This led to pressure for NATO to start preparing along the same lines, improving mobility to match that of the Warsaw Pact. Much more fluid and complex battles were envisaged, increasingly facilitated not only by precise weaponry but also improved infrastructure, so that surveillance and communications became much easier.

Even prior to 1991 there had been indications of the possibilities of the new technological generation. They were then employed in the Gulf War for the first time to fight an essentially classical conventional campaign to a swift and decisive conclusion and with limited casualties (especially on the coalition side). Helpfully Iraqi forces fought along Warsaw Pact lines (reflecting past training), only not as well. This demonstrated the advantages American commanders enjoyed as a result of improvements in sensors, data management, and communications as well as accuracy. Iraqi units were left stranded, picked off with ease, while cruise missiles arrived at individual targets in the middle of built-up areas and destroyed them with minimal damage to any other buildings in the vicinity. Desert Storm was proclaimed as the world's first 'information war'.[10] The Iraqi military were rendered blind, deaf, and dumb. Though the weapons were not quite as effective as some of the initial propaganda suggested, it did not take much imagination or leaps of technological fancy to see how this form of warfare could be taken further. A rosy future for the American armed forces was at hand, in which they might expect to be completely dominant. There was talk of a 'revolution in military affairs' (RMA).[11]

As described, the revolution would result from the interaction of systems that collected, processed, fused, and communicated information with those that applied military force.[12] As a result, military force in the future would be directed against a discombobulated enemy still working out what to do as they were rocked by incoming fire. A swift and unequivocal victory could be achieved with scant risk to troops, let alone the home population and territory. What was once the 'battlefield' was now to be known as the multi-dimensional 'battlespace'. With 'Dominant Battlespace Knowledge', information could be processed to describe the overall operational environment close to real time, making possible 'Near-Perfect Mission Assignment' and thus 'Precision Violence'. This sort of capability was well on its way to being developed by the US Navy, because at sea, as in the air, it was possible to contemplate a battlespace empty of all but combatants. The challenge of the RMA was to demonstrate that this approach could work with ground forces, where warfare had always been subject to a greater range of influences.

Historically, the infantry made up around 80 per cent of US combat deaths, even though they accounted for just 4 per cent of the total force.[13] There was therefore great interest in finding ways of prevailing on land without putting troops at excessive risk. This naturally led to greater reliance on directed firepower, especially from the air, to influence the course of battle so that ground forces need not be committed too early in an operation. The idea was that by striking with precision over great distances, time and space could become less serious constraints. Enemy units within the battlespace would be engaged from outside. The command systems could cope with attacking many targets simultaneously.[14] It would be less important for ground forces to close with the enemy, but if they needed to do so they could stay agile and manoeuvrable, carrying only the firepower required for self-defence, with anything else called in from outside. No longer would there be a need for large, cumbersome, self-contained divisions and their associated potential for high casualties. The infrastructure of war, which required the mobilisation of whole societies, could be reduced. The accuracy of weapons meant that fewer would be required, putting less strain on industry and the transport infrastructure. The 'heavy dependence upon ports, munitions depots and a large transport network' would decline.[15]

The technological optimism underlying the RMA was overdone. While information technology might still be following Moore's Law, other trends were less dramatic, for example propulsion systems and ordnance. In many respects this was not a major problem for the United States as in most contingencies it would enjoy an overwhelming advantage in firepower. This more brutal feature of American strength, however, tended to be missed in the focus on qualitative developments. The smarter the technology, the sharper the choices. As accuracy improved over time, it became possible to move the focus beyond large military formations and facilities and on to specific units, and then particular buildings, even in the middle of civilian areas, eventually reaching designated individuals, isolated from whatever protection they might have hoped for from their surroundings. Range became irrelevant as a constraint. The same accuracy that was first available with short-range and air-launched missiles was soon offered by long-range cruise missiles. Then unmanned drones, controlled from a distance, could hover over an area, identify targets, and attack them on command.

This whole trend of development pushed towards an idealised version of classical warfare, pitting regular forces against each other while barely touching the civilian population. Hackett and Clancy had envisaged wars that must involve large armies and navies on the move, fought across the world, with setbacks and close calls before combinations of raw strength, political determination, and strategic acuity would save the day. Now a vision of war was developing which would get the whole affair over quickly with few casualties. Extracting the pain from war was essential to the project. If warfare could become both high-impact and low-casualty, then it could be socially contained and retained as a political instrument.

When wars were fought on an industrial scale, suffering was both widely shared and largely anonymous. With the new systems, levels of casualties, military as well as civilian, which in the past might have been deemed to be tolerable, now appeared as excessive or disproportionate.[16] Poignant images and harrowing personal stories created a democracy of casualty. Those killed, and not only one's own personnel, acquired equality as victims because—by and large—they were not personally responsible for the violence which consumed them. With campaigns fought by smaller specialist, volunteer forces, individual deaths and injuries stood out more. Dwelling on larger strategic considerations could appear heartless.

Western sensitivity to the casualty issue created its own strategic logic. It led to a strong military presumption that popular support would drain away if significant numbers of casualties began to be taken.[17] If massive loss of life need no longer be tolerated as an unavoidable consequence of war, the focus could be on disabling an enemy's military establishment with the minimum necessary force. In 1993 the US Joint Chiefs of Staff insisted that: 'In all cases, US military forces must be able to undertake operations rapidly, with a high probability of success, and with minimal risk of US casualties.'[18] No more resources should be expended, assets ruined, or blood shed than absolutely necessary to achieve specified political goals. As a result a high premium was put on the protection of one's own force rather than the actual mission objective. This affected the US approach to the way that forces were deployed, as if they must be kept out of harm's way.[19] Even when the operations were less discretionary, as with Afghanistan and Iraq, with government insisting that military success was vital, casualty aversion encouraged a relatively small footprint on the ground and greater reliance on air power.

THE NEW TECHNOLOGIES THAT INFORMED THE REVOLUTION in Military Affairs were celebrated as promising a return to wars decided by battles between regular forces. In such wars not only would civilians be spared but also casualties on all sides would be reduced to a minimum. With accurate weapons targets could be chosen solely for their military relevance. Because they could be launched from a distance, and from places relatively invulnerable to enemy attack, the risks to those doing the launching were minimal. This was true whether the weapons were cruise missiles launched from submarines or missiles from aircraft. This supported the view that armed force could be used as a precise and not a blunt instrument, and could be directed exactly against the armed forces of the opponent, with the minimum of associated damage to civilian life and property. There would be no need to put innocents at risk either inadvertently or deliberately.

As an idealised form of warfare this fitted in entirely with American preferences. But for that reason it was unlikely to be followed by others. The technologies and concepts behind the RMA came to be applied in settings far removed from those for which it had originally been envisaged. Michael O'Hanlon observed in 2000, not long before the point became painfully apparent, that instead of situations which might show off these benefits, US forces might instead be facing foes whose forces were 'interspersed among civilian populations and in combat settings where even relatively unsophisticated enemy units will have opportunities to ambush American troops or booby-trap and mine their likely paths of advance.'[20] Instead of taking on other regular forces in some grand battle, they had to prove their worth coping with terrorism and guerrilla warfare in Afghanistan and Iraq.

Moreover, the abstract analyses about future combat surrounding the RMA had not really addressed the problem of fighting in urban areas. Until modern times, cities, with their walls and elaborate defences, had always posed a severe strategic challenge to the point where armies had to break off from their advance through a country to lay siege. As a result of urban sprawl and with armies shrinking, cities had become too large to be encircled and sealed off. The alternative prospect of fighting through streets and alleys was deeply unattractive. Buildings allowed enemy fighters opportunities for concealment, ambushes, and snipers. Attempts to dislodge them by artillery, bombs, and mortars might simply create rubble that would complicate movement and provide new opportunities for defenders.

Cities therefore challenged the aspirations of the RMA. Their structures obstructed sensors and reduced the scope for manoeuvre operations. Forces would need to fragment as they moved through streets, becoming harder to coordinate as they did so. Because urban combat tended to be greedy on ammunition, it posed extra logistical challenges. Faced with multiple players and sudden movements the environment was stressful and frustrating. Yet in modern conflict cities were hard to avoid. 'We long for gallant struggles in green fields', observed Ralph Peters, yet 'the likeliest "battlefields" are cityscapes where human waste goes undisposed, the air is appalling, and mankind is rotting'. Before it might have been jungles and mountains but now cities were the 'citadels of the dispossessed and irreconcilable'. Here warfare would be as much vertical as horizontal, 'reaching up into towers of steel and cement, and downward into sewers, subway lines, road tunnels, communications tunnels, and the like'.[21]

This was not a prospect greeted with enthusiasm. Historically big battles for cities had been painful. Stalingrad was just one example of how hard it was to defeat stubborn defenders. In Vietnam marines took heavy casualties in the struggle for control of Hue, comparable to some of the worst fighting of the Pacific War. More recently Beirut and Mogadishu had seen American forces caught out. All commentators mentioned the painful Russian experience in the Chechen capital of Grozny during the mid-1990s where they took fearful casualties while failing to defeat rebel militias. A 2001 study reported both historical cases and training exercises as suggesting that it would require a rifle company (100-200 individuals) to take a defended city block in about 12 hours. This would lead to an unsustainable level of 30-45 percent casualties. The survivors would be both physically and emotionally exhausted and modern Western armies, reliant on volunteers rather than conscripts, lacked reserves. Posen noted that the active US Army then had 'only perhaps 180 rifle companies' and the Marines another 60-70. An army or marine infantry division had 27 rifle companies; an army mechanized division, a dozen.[22] In 2016 the same point was made by observing that 'America's treasure house of close-combat soldiers is only marginally larger than the New York City Police Department.[23]

If the Americans allowed themselves to get enticed into cities, warned General Robert Scales in 1996, all its military advantages would be neutralised. He dismissed the possibility that Western forces could render a city uninhabitable by pounding it with firepower. Instead he argued for doing everything possible to avoid direct urban combat, if possible by preventing an enemy force retreating into a city but, if that were not possible, by establishing 'a loose cordon around the city and control of the surrounding countryside'. The aim would be to isolate the city from the outside world. 'All avenues, including air, sea, and land arteries, would be blocked', while the 'coalition would seek to control sources of food, power, water, and sanitation services'. Information entering the city would also be controlled. Accurate standoff missiles could attack targets inside the city. In short, he envisaged a modern version of a siege,[24] though this would be a tall order with a large metropolis and the enemy enjoying the propaganda advantage of being demonstrably in charge.

The test of the RMA came not in a conventional campaign but in the 'war on terror'. The US Secretary of Defense Donald Rumsfeld explained that Afghanistan was going to be a new type of war, 'like none other our nation has faced'.[25] He saw opportunities to demonstrate that future war could be won with only a modest force so long as it was backed by the most advanced 'transformational' capabilities. Instead the US found itself fighting with its allies in Afghan and then in Iraq wars that were drawn out, with their own similarities to Vietnam. The enemy adopted the traditional tactics of guerrilla warfare. The resultant wars were described as 'asymmetric'.[26] A symmetrical war would involve two belligerents of similar capabilities. The outcome would be determined by small differences growing in importance, whether superior training, tactical prowess, strategic imagination, technical innovation, or the capacity to mobilise national resources. In such cases the victor was likely only to emerge through attrition, when the hurt reached a point where small margins of staying power could make the difference. By contrast, in an asymmetrical war, belligerents with quite different capabilities and priorities would clash, with the outcome determined by one side's superior ability to find counters to the capabilities of the other.

AT FIRST ALL WORKED AS PLANNED. A RELATIVELY SMALL SIZED invasion force, backed by advanced air power, could overwhelm weak and outgunned adversaries. In both Afghanistan and Iraq the initial stages of the war were asymmetrical only in the sense of being completely one-sided as the Taliban and the Iraqis tried to fight like regular armies against the world's only superpower. In both cases the enemy lacked the organisation, morale, and numbers even to offer a staunch urban defence. The fighting was less fearsome than anticipated. Later as the insurgencies developed cities came to present different sorts of dangers. The environment suited forms of guerrilla war, with scope for riots, ambushes, and improvised bombs, harassing and stressing troops, at times leading to disproportionate and count-er-productive responses.

Eventually the US military realised that their scripts were for the wrong sort of war. [27] The US Government had been warned before the invasion that a force of 500,000 would be needed to maintain order once the old Iraqi regime had been toppled.[28] The warnings were dismissed. As a result the US and its allies struggled with a frac-tion of the necessary forces, until a 'surge' in 2007 when they were able to take advantage of a more favourable political situation. The lesson was that in this sort of war numbers mattered, despite all the advanced equipment now available to American forces.

Their opponents often enjoyed substantial local support, were linked to broadly based political movements, and benefitted from considerable freedom of movement. Instead of relatively civilised combat, professionally conducted by high-quality regular forces, the struggle was against murky, subversive forms of insurgency and ter-rorism. The enemy did not oblige by providing targets that could be attacked by accurate fire. Instead militias drawn from the aggrieved sections of society moved in and out of civil society, with strategies geared to maximising pain. They relied on the assassination of senior political figures or indiscriminate assaults against civilians, with or without warning, or else the sabotage of critical infrastructure and ambushes of army or police patrols. They preferred to remain hidden and, in some cases were even prepared to accept a martyr's death as human bombs. Unlike traditional armies, insurgents did not expect to hold territory, as their priority was to play for time rather than hold space, allowing them to gain in support while the enemy was drained of patience and credibility. All the clichés of guerrilla warfare, dimly remembered from the 1960s, of an enemy hiding in the shad-ows and the tactics of darting flea bites, returned. The Americans and their allies were caught in a prolonged, doleful, and disappointing form of warfare—the opposite of that idealised in the Revolution of Military Affairs and exactly the sort they hoped to avoid.

Because the US had taken the initiative to topple the regime its commitment was much greater than if it had intervened to try to calm an already fraught situation. It was, with the UK, an occupying power and then, even after Iraqi governments took over, accepted a respon-sibility to support them until they could cope on their own. The Iraqi governments were to meet political standards that made them worthy of support. Though this was a divided country that had suffered years

of brutal rule and calamity, it too was to have a representative government that would respect human rights. Success in this regard
would turn Iraq into a beacon for the rest of the region. President
George W. Bush, and Prime Minister Tony Blair in Britain, picked up
this theme. In 2004, as he was promoting democracy as a solution to
the numerous problems of the Middle East, including in Iraq, Bush
insisted that 'the reason why I'm so strong on democracy is democracies don't go to war with each other. . . . And that's why I'm such a
strong believer that the way forward in the Middle East, the broader
Middle East, is to promote democracy'.[29]

BY 2005 IT WAS EVIDENT THAT, FAR FROM IRAQ MOVING
forward, it was beset by multiple problems, with a range of conflicts
going on at once, within and between communities, with coalition
forces taking regular casualties. Somewhat sobered by this experience, the US Army and Marines decided to revise their Field Manual
on counter-insurgency (FM-3-24). Conrad Crane, a professor at the
US Army's Strategic Studies Institute, coordinated the exercise.[30]
Prior to the US engagement in Iraq he had warned that the US Army
had failed to learn lessons from Vietnam. It had instead treated
Vietnam as an aberration that must never be repeated rather than
try to prepare for anything at all similar.[31] The lack of preparedness
was evident in the run-up to the Iraq War, with little thought given
to the impact of the 'deep religious, ethnic, and tribal differences
which dominate Iraqi society'. Crane warned how 'US forces may
have to manage and adjudicate conflicts among Iraqis that they can
barely comprehend'. An exit strategy would require a degree of political stability that would be difficult to achieve given Iraq's 'fragmented population, weak political institutions, and propensity for
rule by violence'.[32]

Crane was in charge of the drafting the new manual for which he
established a substantial team of like-minded colleagues.[33] It was a
group that had gathered around General David Petraeus, who was
the main sponsor, having been frustrated by the poor management of
the situation in Iraq post-invasion. The manual eschewed a rigid
script and allowed flexibility in interpretation of the guidance offered.
The core to their message was that this was an essentially political
undertaking. The military role was to gain popular support for the
government. This required learning and adaptation.

Unusually for such an exercise it involved academics and was even eventually published by an academic press.[34] Harvard's Sarah Sewell, a specialist in human rights, argued the benefits of developing international human rights law, restraint in the use of military force and more reliance on conventional policing. More controversially the anthropologist Montgomery McFate encouraged improved cultural awareness as a means of avoiding foolish errors. Working so closely with the military did not go down well with other anthropologists, reviving the old debate as to whether mitigating the harmful effects of war simply made it more acceptable and easier to undertake.[35] Yet one group of academics was absent. Stathis Kalyvas noted that 'the manual betrays zero impact by political science research'. This, he noted, was because the political scientists had largely attended to the causes, duration, termination, and aftermath of civil wars, rather than their content. In addition, 'political scientists, including large-n practitioners, have failed so far to produce startling results.' He doubted 'that the most robust finding of the econometric literature, namely, that poor countries face a higher risk of civil war, would have impressed (or been of much use to) the manual's writers'. Nor had it picked up on the supposedly central role of natural resources, sticking firmly with the presumption of 'grievance' and playing down 'greed'.[36]

Instead the Counter Insurgency Field Manual was firmly placed within a tradition of thinking about revolutions, insurgencies, and guerrilla warfare, going back to T. E. Lawrence and Mao Zedong, with a nod in the direction of the French officer David Galula who had developed theories of counter-insurgency during the French war to hold on to Algeria in the 1950s.[37] From this tradition came a focus on separating the enemy militants from the population. The government would be rendered more attractive through reforms as the insurgent cause would be shown to be hopeless. To achieve this, violence must be controlled, away from killing as many militants as possible, which was the instinctive military approach, to concentrating on the political effects. The use of deadly firepower was now described as 'kinetic', to be distinguished from softer forms of power.[38] The 'kinetic' had its place, but if employed excessively risked driving even more people into the enemy ranks.

The authors were careful not to refer to 'hearts and minds', a phrase which now carried a lot of baggage left over from Vietnam as a failed attempt at social engineering. The aim was to change behaviour, but phrases such as 'carrots and sticks', which might be more accurate, were also eschewed as too simplistic. To capture the emphasis, the non-kinetic approach was described as 'population-centric' as opposed to 'enemy-centric'. There were to be no hard and fast rules. Action had to be sensitive to context. Officers needed to think about how they might protect their forces without making people less secure and when it was best to do nothing, even in the face of severe provocation. The document also recognised the inherent problem faced by outsiders, whose position, at least in the first instance, depended on superior military strength. 'Eventually all foreign armies are seen as interlopers or occupiers; the sooner the main effort can transition to HN [Host Nation] institutions, without unacceptable degradation, the better'. The key objective was to isolate the enemy by winning over the population, in part by rendering the government more attractive through reforms while also demonstrating the hopelessness of the insurgent cause.

THE CREDIBILITY OF THE DOCUMENT BENEFITTED FROM BEING followed by a turn for the better in Iraq in 2007, a result of disaffection with al-Qaeda among Sunnis and the additional resources deployed as a result of the 'surge', combined with Petraeus's leadership. This episode illustrated that Iraqi civil society was much more complicated than the simple elite-mass distinction on which revolutionary theorists based their analyses or the broad ethnic distinctions which Western policymakers tried to make sense of local politics. In addition to the broad groupings of Sunni, Shia, and Kurds, there were also tribal and village allegiances, and local leaders with their own connections to more senior figures. Loyalties could be fluid and flexible, groupings were prone to factionalism, and political authority was multi-layered. It was thus not necessarily a shift in attitudes by the people as a whole that led to increased Sunni support for the battle against al-Qaeda, but a decision by some local Sunni leaders to work with the US military despite the risks and distaste for the occupation.

The document was subject to a number of criticisms. The most fundamental was that while there were techniques of counter-insurgency, which, if properly applied, could address the timeless dynamics of insurgency, in practice there were formidable contingent factors at work in all these conflicts.[39] Another, to which we will return, was that it set impossible targets for political action. Critics of the approach later argued that Petraeus and his strategy were flattered by political circumstances over which they had little control and the development of misleading narratives with regard to what had gone right for the British in Malaya and wrong for the Americans in Vietnam.[40] For those who saw the enemy as implacable and fanatical the approach was simply too soft.[41] They argued that the only plausible strategy was to kill militants until their numbers were depleted and they were demoralised. But as events in Iraq later demonstrated, military successes depended on isolating the enemy politically. The apparent victory achieved over insurgents in 2007 did not produce lasting benefits because the politics was subsequently mishandled.[42]

The practical challenges revolved around the nature of the government's relationship with the people. The script pointed to putting more effort into studying and appreciating local culture and attending to grievances, so that the people could be persuaded to support a hitherto unpopular government. This was given support by an underlying optimism that this was part of an effort to 'advance those societies mired in backward customs and the slough of authoritarianism along the road of socioeconomic improvement and democratic development.'[43] The difficulty with this was that reforms could only be implemented by local elites who were often the beneficiaries of the structures that needed reforming.

There was another view. This accepted that a section of the population, if not the whole, would always be hostile to the government, but that if life was made sufficiently miserable then they could be persuaded not to support a rebellion. On this basis the most effective strategy for dealing with insurgents was not to win the people over but by 'out-terrorising them'.[44] Those making this observation were not advocating this for the US and its allies. Their point was that because the Americans could not adopt such a strategy their efforts were doomed to failure, not least because their alternative, of achieving popular consent, could not succeed.

[18]

The Role of Barbarism

Be stirring as the time: be fire with fire;
Threaten the threatener and outface the brow
Of bragging horror.

SHAKESPEARE,
King John, Act V, Scene I

There was an interesting contrast between film-making during the course of the Iraq War and that during Vietnam. Whereas the main film that was made during the Vietnam era, *The Green Berets*, was propagandistic, no comparable film was made on Iraq, although there were regular rumours about the possibility of one being made about the 2004 battle for Fallujah. Unlike Vietnam many other films were made about how the war was being fought while it was still under-way—Martin Barker identifies twenty-three Iraq war films. Some, like *The Hurt Locker* (2008), about a bomb disposal specialist, gained critical acclaim and Oscar success, though that was largely apolitical. Most were barely noticed and often lost money. They were caught up in the contradictory emotions prompted by Iraq. The 9/11 aftermath stimulated patriotic feelings but these were coupled with deep misgivings about the necessity for and likely outcome of the war. The reaction to Vietnam had been to challenge the legitimacy of US motives and the role of the military. With Iraq doubts about the government's strategy were unavoidable but it was more problematic to challenge the competence and motives of the military. This meant that discussion of brutal behaviours towards Iraqis were rationalised as responses to the stress of combat. 'The crisis over America's role in Iraq is being played out', observed Barker, 'more than anything, through cracks in the image of the American "soldier".' The soldiers might appear 'crude, misogynistic and racist' when off-duty, but 'the moment they step out onto the streets of Iraq they become innocent, bewildered and desperate'. The net effect, as with Vietnam, was to emphasise the damage that war did to individuals as much as countries, however much veterans might complain about being habitually portrayed as 'drugged out, burned out, stressed out.'[1]

The more positive accounts of both the Iraq and Afghanistan campaigns tended to reflect the accomplishments of individuals and small units, acting against specific targets, often at the edges of a larger battle or on some special mission, accepting personal risk while using superior skill and technology to best a vicious enemy. This literature began with CIA operatives working with anti-Taliban forces in Afghanistan in late 2001 and peaked with memoirs of the killing of Osama bin Laden in his hideaway in Pakistan by a Navy SEAL unit a decade later. It provided an opportunity to highlight confrontations that had clarity and personal meaning against the backdrop of campaigns that otherwise had so many uncertain and confusing elements. It also demonstrated how the need to avoid harming the wider population was encouraging efforts to identify and track the deadlier individuals, using biometrics (iris recognition, DNA, as well as fingerprints). In one of the best books of the genre, Brian Castner's *All the Ways We Kill and Die*, this material becomes part of an effort to humanise an enemy that has helped design and plant so many bombs resulting in the deaths of a particular comrade. The man responsible, something of a composite figure, he described as 'The Engineer'.[2]

These more personalised operations made it possible in principle if not always in practice to avoid actions that hurt innocents. Given a counter-insurgency strategy that precluded punishing the wider population for allowing militants to live in their midst, the trend was bound to be one of increasingly identifying and taking out militants. This approach emphasised the break from the past. In earlier wars it was understood, if regretted, that they had to be won by whatever means necessary, and sometimes that might mean inflicting harm on civilian populations. Now that approach was as unnecessary as it was unacceptable.

TERRORISING POPULATIONS INTO SUBMISSION HAD LONG been part of the logic both of conquest and of maintaining order. Twentieth-century air power allowed civilians to be attacked independently of campaigns of conquest, motivated by an urge for revenge or a determination to intimidate. This led to nuclear weapons with their complete detachment of destruction from conquest. Their use supposed the destruction of that which might be conquered. They were kept as a form of intimidating reserve, rationalised by deterrence theory, available to inflict terrible destruction on other societies, but there was no evident strategic value other than deterrence. The deliberate slaughter of civilians was discredited as serving no military purpose. Analysis of the effects of the great air raids of the Second World War, confirming that bombing urban centres had achieved little, reinforced this judgement.[3] The key lessons were that societies absorbed pain in preference to surrendering, and if innocents were killed then populations would be turned against the perpetrators. In this way the moral dilemmas were eased. A vicious and uncontained approach to war would not only be reprehensible but also counterproductive.

A similar line of thought developed with civil wars. Although there were many precedents from earlier centuries, the view that at times populations must be treated cruelly developed in the context of nineteenth-century colonial campaigns and the American Civil War.[4] The coercive properties of air power were first explored in dealing with colonial rebellions (the first bombs were dropped from aircraft during an Italian struggle with the Ottoman Empire for control of Libya in 1911). When facing an uprising in Iraq in 1920 the British lacked sufficient troops to quell it so they opted for air power instead. The strategy was described as one of 'identifying the most inaccessible village of the most prominent tribe which it is desired to punish'. That a 'relentless and unremitting' attack on people, houses, crops, and cattle was brutal was acknowledged, but this was the way to ensure that a lesson was learnt. The draft manual for *The Use of the Air Arm in Iraq* observed that in 45 minutes 'a full-sized village ... can be practically wiped out, and a third of its inhabitants killed or injured, by four or five machines which offer them no real target and no opportunity for glory or avarice'. Sir Aylmer Haldane, the Commanding Officer, took the conventional view that only harsh punishment would impress Arabs. His favoured method was burning villages. The best way to do this was discussed in an appendix to his memoir of the campaign, advising on the need for separate parties to fire houses and dig up and burn grain and loot, and noting that it could take as much as an hour to do the job properly.[5] Even after the Second World War, Western powers could be quite severe when countering insurgencies, whether the French in Algeria, the British in Kenya, or the Americans in Vietnam.

Counter-insurgency doctrine shifted over time. 'Population-centric' strategies came into vogue, abjuring arbitrary killing and collective punishment. Yet the circumstances often challenged the doctrine. Whatever the intentions, civilians got caught up in fire-fights or struck as a result of poor intelligence or stray bombs. To allow for this possibility the concept of 'collateral damage' began to be employed during Vietnam. It recognised that there was such a thing as 'non-combatant immunity' that meant that civilians should be spared but also that even weapons directed at purely military targets could affect people with no combat role. If civilians were killed unintentionally it was somehow more acceptable than if there had been an intention, and so was 'literally beside the point'.[6] But over time, the excuse that 'this is what happens in war' became less acceptable because of the expectation that in contemporary conventional warfare the fortuitous discrimination made possible by new weapons meant that commanders were expected to exercise an extraordinary amount of control. Any civilian deaths therefore were likely to be castigated as premeditated choices rather than inadvertent accidents.[7]

International humanitarian law was focusing increasingly on the rights of individuals over those of states. Whereas the laws of war were largely utilitarian, and bowed in the direction of military necessity, human rights law was much more rigorous on behalf of individuals.[8] It took their side even if the actions that were threatening them were legal under the customary laws of war. For Western armies the shift was problematic. In 2001 Air Force Colonel Charles Dunlap introduced the term 'lawfare' to capture the way which he believed that strict rules on targeting and the need to avoid civilian hurt were being used to hamper Western military operations. He evolved the definition into a 'strategy of using—or misusing—law as a substitute for traditional military means to achieve an operational objective.' This would be done by creating an impression, even if unwarranted, that the distinction between combatants and non-combatants was being violated. In this respect it appeared as a form of asymmetric warfare, allowing militants to exploit the values—and courts—of their

Western opponents while taking no notice of the same normative framework in their own operations. As an example Dunlap cited a 2007 NATO statement in Afghanistan that promised that its forces would not 'fire on position if they knew that civilians were nearby'. This, he argued, gave the Taliban comfort that if they chose their positions carefully they could continue with their operations without interference.[9]

If Western countries were shown to be responsible for civilian suffering then that risked undermining claims that their campaigns were animated by a desire to protect innocents. The reasons for Western intervention during the 1990s was the harsh treatment meted out by the Iraqi government to Shiites and Kurds, and then the 'ethnic cleansing' in the former Yugoslavia. This humanitarian focus had strategic consequences. Addressing the problem of war in terms of the suffering caused, and justifying any intervention as protecting the vulnerable, shifted the focus from causes to consequences, from the politics to the violence. The rights and wrongs of a conflict were reduced to the question of whose behaviour was the most outrageous. The judgement could shift with the latest atrocity and become totally confused when yesterday's victims turned into today's villains. Ending the fighting might be the vital objective of the detached but caring observer, with no stakes in the fight, but to other states, with their own stakes in the conflict, what mattered was who won rather than who had the most brutal methods.[10] The focus also inevitably encouraged the warring parties to stress their own vulnerability and victimhood.

If the prime rationale for intervention was civilian suffering, this created its own perverse incentives for those who wanted outside help. With little choice but to fight alone, the aim would be to persuade the enemy that it was not a soft touch, that it would fight fiercely and inflict blows upon those who wished it harm. But a party with a chance of external support could make known weakness, especially if a key factor would be perceptions of suffering shaped by media reports. This tendency was evident with the 1991 defence of the Croat city of Vukovar when there were suggestions that it was not properly defended against Serb attack as it served the government's strategic purpose more to use it to gain international sympathy. In the former Yugoslavia, the need to demonstrate victimhood meant that, in Gow's words, 'media manipulation became not so much a complement for military engagement as a substitute for it.'[11] Evident massacres, such as those in 1995 in the Bosnian city of Srebrenica, meant that the West was more ready to escalate. When NATO went to war against Serbia in 1999 because of its actions in Kosovo, much of the controversy surrounded just how bad the authorities had been in their persecution of the Muslim population.

THUS DESPITE THEIR OWN HISTORY OF PUNITIVE STRATEGIES Western countries had come to assume that such strategies were as inhumane as they were ineffectual and deserved to be opposed. The consensus position, supported by academic research and embraced by the senior US military leadership, was that 'if the desired objective is long-term political control, barbarism inevitably backfires'.[12] In the debate over Field Manual 3-24 critics charged that this was naïve. Given the difficulties of winning a disaffected population over by political reforms, which they were unlikely to find credible, the optimum way to deal with a rebellious population was to make lives as miserable as possible until there was a return to docility. When the West had taken this view, in colonial campaigns and with unrestricted air raids, the rationale was that this was a way to get wars over quickly. Even if this involved a few massacres that might still be better—in some disturbing accounting—than a prolonged war that never quite came to a conclusion. The critics acknowledged that democracies would 'find it extremely difficult to escalate the level of violence and brutality to that which can secure victory',[13] and also that such a strategy was contrary to international humanitarian law. But was it really so clear that it was bound to fail?

The strategic rationale, going back to the classics of revolutionary warfare, started with the dependence of guerrilla groups on the local population. The most famous formulation was that of the Chinese leader Mao Zedong, who spoke of the people as being the 'water' and the troops 'the fish who inhabit it'.[14] For those struggling with a rebellion, especially one moving beyond the point where it was possible to appeal to the loyalties of the people, the idea of 'draining the sea' had some appeal. The civilian population were fixed while the militants were mobile. If only the civilians could be moved the militants would be exposed. Such a strategy risked international condemnation and stored up trouble for the future. But for desperate governments, with a greater capacity for massacre than their opponents, and bereft of better alternatives, it could still make strategic sense.

Most governments facing substantial insurgencies over the 1945–2000 period did not go down this route, but about a third (24 out of 75) did. In Chapter 14 we noted the role of population attacks in the former Yugoslavia. Another example was Guatemala, in a war that began in the late 1970s, when the wide civilian support for guerrillas left the army floundering. Eventually the government vowed to 'dry up the human sea in which the guerrilla fish swim.'[15] The result was civilians were treated as though they were combatants. The killings were not 'accidental "abuses" or "excesses"; rather, they represented a scientifically precise, sustained orchestration of a systematic, intentional massive campaign of extermination'.[16] In some areas about a third of the local population was slaughtered, with about 750,000 killed in total. In another example, which underscored the instrumentality of the approach, in Eritrea's war with Ethiopia for independence the civilian population was targeted by the government, essentially forcing it into starvation.[17] After Eritrea gained independence in 1991 there was in 1998 another war with Ethiopia, which, though bloody, was largely between competing armies.[18] Valentino et al considered the efforts by guerrilla groups who terrorised civilians in Algeria during the 1990s. The violence was not driven by a radical 'ideology that justifies the extermination of a category of people' or by senseless bloodlust, as many observers had suggested. Instead, it was calculated to push people away from supporting the government.[19] The instrumentality of mass killings lay in their role as a way of removing political opponents, as in the purges undertaken by communist countries, or in removing hostile populations, especially when it was difficult to expel them in sufficient numbers, or as a means of intimidating civilian sources of support.[20]

THE EXAMPLE THAT GAINED MOST ATTENTION DURING THE 2000S, and which was used to show that a harsh approach could be successful, was the Sri Lankan Civil War. Its origins went back to British colonial rule and the early days of independence which saw discrimination against the minority, and increasingly resentful, Tamils. Fighting began in 1983 with demands for an independent Tamil state, led by the Liberation Tigers of Tamil Eelam, or the Tamil Tigers. The tactics of the Tamil Tigers were vicious while Sri Lankan forces were hardly restrained. In the late 1980s India sought to keep the peace, but disengaged after a Tamil assassinated Prime Minister Rajiv

Gandhi in 1991. The Tigers were ruthless against non-Tamils in their areas, and even against alternative militias, using suicide bombing as a regular tactic. A ceasefire agreement was brokered in 2001, but hostilities soon resumed. In the end the government launched a re-morseless offensive in 2006. The Tigers were pushed out of the east of the country and then the north until they accepted defeat in 2009 with a deal which granted Tamils more autonomy but not secession.

After the conclusion of what were described as 'humanitarian operations' in 2009 a Sri Lankan model was identified, under the name of President Rajapaksa. Its basic premise was that 'terrorism has to be wiped out militarily and cannot be tackled politically'. Among the 'eight fundamentals of victory' were 'political will' to eliminate the enemy, a readiness to tell the international community to 'go to hell' when negotiations were proposed as an alternative, a refusal to negotiate because ceasefires had been used in the past by the enemy to get time to refresh and recuperate, and then a readiness to shut the world out by maintaining silence about operations and regulating the media to make sure they did not provide the reports of civilian casualties that might lead to more international pressure.[21] The Sri Lankan government's determination to resist pressure to negotiate may well have allowed the campaign to proceed unimpeded, but the LTTE collapsed as much because it was already weak as because of the ruthlessness of the onslaught. The area the LTTE dominated was impoverished and the organisation was now 'a shadow of its former self, bankrupt, isolated, illegitimate, divided, and unable to meet an invigorated government offensive of any kind.'[22]

ANOTHER INFLUENTIAL CAMPAIGN WAS THAT WAGED BY RUSSIA in the province of Chechnya against secessionist rebels. From 1994 to 1996 Russian forces fought a hard and ultimately futile battle against secessionists. A settlement left the Chechen capital, Grozny, in secessionist hands, although with an agreement on any new constitutional settlement delayed. In August 1999, with a new prime minister, Vladimir Putin, at the helm, the Russians decided that firm action needed to be taken. There was a risk of contagion as a band of Chechen rebels moved into neighbouring Dagestan. There were also exploding apartment buildings in Moscow blamed on Chechens (although there were deep suspicions that this was an operation by Russian security forces).[23] This time the Russian methods were unrelenting: air raids followed by armoured columns. After a series of defeats in battle the insurgents resorted to guerrilla tactics, but they suffered from internal divisions, largely between Islamist and Nationalist factions. Gradually the resistance subsided, with the occasional acts of terrorism.

There were a number of reasons for the success of Russia the second time round. One was turning the conflict into more of an intra-Chechen war, engaging a local leadership who understood the country and were also able to take control and deal ruthlessly with any residual opposition.[24] A second factor was an uncompromising use of firepower. In the first war the Russians tried to take the city with tanks and infantry, and then got caught up in urban warfare for which they were poorly prepared. In the second war Grozny was battered with artillery and air power, against which the defenders had no response.[25]

In 2011 Bashar al Assad had refused to compromise with a reform movement in Syria and civil war began to take root. The West did little more than provide tentative support for some rebel groups. The regime showed no compunction in seeking to blast away civilian resistance, especially once it was apparent that there was little chance that with more restrained tactics they could regain popular support. In September 2015 Russian forces intervened in Syria to keep Bashar al-Assad in power. Mark Galeotti described their tactics as implementing a lesson learnt in Gozny: 'All war is terrible; sometimes the art is to be the most terrible.'[26] In late 2016 after a ceasefire quickly broke down, Russian aircraft attacked an aid convoy bringing relief to the besieged city of Aleppo. As they moved to force the rebels out of the city they worked to make life as difficult for all inhabitants, including systematically bombing hospitals. Eventually both the residents and rebel fighters evacuated the city. The Russian air campaign underlined a point often neglected in the discussions of the impact of the development of weapons of improved precision. This not only meant that civilian sites could be easier avoided: it also meant that if so desired they could be targeted more effectively.

There was no law which insisted that casualties would encourage people to continue with a tough fight just as there was no law that suffering would cause them to give up. Individuals who otherwise may have kept their heads down or given passive support to the government might be turned into militants because of the loss of relatives. On the other hand, communities giving insurgents vital support might feel that they had little choice but to flee. Micro-studies on attacks on civilian populations tended to confirm that they could be successful. In one meticulous piece of research Jason Lyall demonstrated that when the Russians employed indiscriminate violence in Chechnya, by shelling villages, the effect was to suppress the insurgency. It weakened their local organisation and ability to deploy forces, showed that the insurgents could not protect their people, and caused division among their ranks. Lyall found that in the aftermath of artillery strikes there was a decrease in insurgent attacks when compared with nearly identical villages that had not been struck.[27] Building on this, Souleimanov and Siroky undertook further research on those caught up in the Chechen War. They distinguished between random violence which hardened popular attitudes against the Russians, while 'retributive' violence in response to actions by the insurgents was more instrumental and effective, although the effects were largely short-term and often had the effect of displacing the retaliatory violence to other areas.[28]

Other studies showed that it made a difference to popular attitudes when foreigners perpetrated violence against civilians, even when it was not intended.[29] There appeared to be a less forgiving attitude towards casualties caused by foreigners than those caused by local forces. One study in Afghanistan showed that when Western forces inflicted harm then their support went down and that of the Taliban went up. The reverse, however, was not the case. Taliban violence made little difference either way. The Taliban had a 'home team discount' and were more likely to be forgiven.[30]

The question of the effectiveness of the strategy was in some respects beside the point. By and large, to the extent that it was even considered, the conclusions followed the general view in Western political and military circles that a strategy involving deliberate attacks on civilians was likely to stiffen the resolve of the victim population. Any short-term benefits would be contradicted by a bitter legacy and a popular desire for revenge.[31] It was normally chosen for want of anything better by beleaguered governments rather than because they were sure that it was effective. Once they started they had little choice but to see the strategy through, given the bitterness generated, and if they could see it through then at one level the strategy could be said to work. A regime prepared to use terror to sustain its position could do so, providing they had no compunctions about being utterly ruthless and there was no foreign interference.

In a rare study of why insurgencies often succeeded Seth Jones stressed the importance of external support, in the form of intelligence and air power but not conventional forces. He found no benefit from tactics 'that inordinately punish the local population'.[32] Barbarism caused anger and bitterness, so once it failed to shut down a rebellion then the government would be in even deeper trouble. A 2010 RAND study considered thirty cases of counter-insurgency since 1978 of which only eight were unequivocal victories for the government, with others producing more mixed results, for example significant concessions to the insurgents. The study showed that repression and collective punishment on occasion produced temporary benefits for the government but they tended not to last. What made a real difference was tangible support, such as from neighbouring countries, whether personnel, materiel, financing, intelligence, or sanctuary. Ideally this would be coupled with popular support, but on its own tangible support would trump popular support.

As this study came at the end of a decade in which the US had been involved in two thankless operations, there was a big lesson for the US government. A lot depended on the 'host-nation government'; that is the one that would go under if the insurgency succeeded. The study described 'democracy, government legitimacy, [and] strategic communication' depending on this host-nation government. Without them there would be no guarantee of victory. 'The United States should think twice before choosing to help governments that will not help themselves.'[33] Most students of the problem came back to the limits of what a foreign power could do in a country when the regime they supported lacked legitimacy. One scholar, who had been developing hypotheses about the importance of organisational cultures in armies tackling insurgencies, got the opportunity to serve in Afghanistan. After working with Afghan local police and US special forces, he concluded that getting the command structures, doctrine, and training right made little difference without effective local allies: 'time and again the program ran up against the local reality that the government was unpopular and intransigent'.[34]

[19]

Cure Not Prevention

I have often thought that you need a ... kind of layered map to understand Sudan's civil war. A surface map of political conflict, for example—the northern government versus the southern rebels; and under that a layer of religious conflict—Muslim versus Christian and pagan; and under that a map of all the sectarian divisions within those categories; and under that a layer of ethnic divisions—Arab and Arabized versus Nilotic and Equatorian—all of them containing a multitude of clan and tribal subdivisions; and under that a layer of linguistic conflicts; and under that a layer of economic divisions—the more developed north with fewer natural resources versus the poorer south with its rich mineral and fossil fuel deposits; and under that a layer of colonial divisions; and under that a layer of racial divisions related to slavery. And so on and so on until it would become clear that the war, like the country, was not one but many: a violent ecosystem capable of generating endless new things to fight about without ever shedding any of the old ones.

DEBORAH SCROGGINS,
Emma's War, 2004[1]

Weber's definition pointed to the essential feature of statehood in monopolising force within borders, and set a clear if limited marker for state failure. This was essentially the one adopted by the US government's State Failure Task Force, which identified 136 occurrences of state-failure in the period between 1955 and 1998. It considered four kinds of internal crisis—revolutionary war, ethnic war, adverse regime change, and genocide—and the task force found that between 20 and 30 per cent of countries were in 'failure' during the 1990s.[2]

The modern state, however, was expected to perform against many other criteria. States need administrative capacity and revenues (if only to wage wars). Over time their functions expanded to include provision of health, education, and welfare. Their governance moved from monarchs to political leaders more or less accountable to legislative assemblies and to public opinion. After 1990, as Central and Eastern Europe embraced democracy and enjoyed economic growth, the idea took hold that this experience could be replicated throughout the world in a benign process of globalisation, generating virtuous cycles of prosperity, democracy, and peace. Further support was found in the fact that the most successful new states, especially those in Asia, had gravitated towards the liberal capitalist model, and so there was greater confidence that this was the best route for all who wished to raise their sights to a more stable future.

A modern state could therefore be declared a failure against a range of criteria. As more sophisticated indices of failure or fragility were developed by international organisations as a form of early warning, it became apparent that the concept was broad enough to cover many disparate states with a range of problems. States such as North Korea, a dictatorship which failed to meet the needs of its people, still effectively monopolised force within their borders. The concept of a successful state, derived from the Western experience, was one which many states would struggle to meet. States might fail their people in many ways yet still function. As states were assessed by criteria well away from Weber's basic definition involving monopolised violence and borders, the more could be judged to have failed.[3]

If a state was failing it was not sufficient to bring an end to violence. Success meant strengthened institutions, ensuring that no minority was excluded and all enjoyed opportunities for political and cultural expression, competent economic management, an absence of corruption, and responsive administration. Thus the high-level international Carnegie Commission on Preventing Deadly Conflict, reporting in 1997, provided the headline answer to the challenge posed by its title:

> This is done by creating capable states with representative governance based on the rule of law, with widely available economic opportunity, social safety nets, protection of fundamental human rights, and robust civil societies.

This was not so much an answer to the question as reframing it. The same could be said for the recommendation that it was important when there were signs of trouble to react quickly and have a comprehensive, balanced approach to alleviate the pressures that trigger violent conflict and 'an extended effort to resolve the underlying root causes of conflict', which went back again to 'fundamental security, well-being, and justice for all citizens'.[4] The basic requirement was to strengthen the state sufficiently enough to deal with violence and then, with security, to collect taxes and rebuild infrastructure. The consensus was captured by Francis Fukuyama's observation that state-building, defined in terms of the creation or strengthening of government institutions, was the major foreign policy challenge, because weak or failed states were 'the source of many of the world's most serious problems.'[5] An article urging a much more systematic global effort to promote better governance as 'the only real way to create lasting peace' observed that: 'These elements of state weakness constitute structural threats akin to dead leaves that accumulate in a forest. No one knows what spark will ignite them, or when.'[6]

It was easy to set standards to which states might aspire and reasonable to note that when they were unable to do so that trouble might ensue. As a preventative measure shoring up the quality of governance and on that basis pushing forward with economic and social reforms would also make sense, although it could be noted that Western advice on these matters did not always have the desired effects. The problem, however, when considering the question of state failure in the context of counter-insurgency and peacekeeping was a backdrop of violence and degradation. The consequences of constant fighting could be seen in the infrastructure left damaged and never repaired, economic activity subdued, law enforcement minimal and corruption rampant, displaced people unable to return, health and education services stretched, grievances festering without satisfaction, and distrust dominating all political activity. The challenge here was one of cure rather than prevention. Wendy Brown expressed the unreality of the expectations this could create in her critique of The Counter-Insurgency Field Manual 3-24:

> In short, it requires—from the US military no less—a degree of political intelligence and foresight worthy of Rousseau's Lawgiver, a degree of provision for human needs worthy of the farthest reach of the communist imaginary, a degree of stabilization through governance worthy of Thomas Hobbes or perhaps Immanuel Kant, an ability to "decipher cultural narratives" (the manual's words) worthy of a trained ethnographer, and an ability to manipulate these narratives worthy of Plato. It also entails the paradox of fostering the strength and legitimacy of what are often puppet regimes, and doing so while the occupiers are still on site. And all of this in a milieu of upheaval, violence, and complexly riven societies with weak or nonexistent states.[7]

It was always ambitious to expect that a state reconstructed in such unpromising circumstances would be other than disappointing when set against the highest standards. At best it would be led by a strong man sufficient to function to a degree but well short of liberal democracy. Once the new regime was strong enough to have agency it would likely begin to clash with its external patron, for example to pursue sectarian interests or engage in corrupt practices. While documents such as FM 3-24 assumed that the American interest and that of the host government could be brought into close alignment that was usually overoptimistic, as was the case in both Iraq and Afghanistan. An intention to change a client state's behaviour, so that it could be shown to be deserving of the support it was getting, required attaching conditions to any assistance. Unfortunately once considerable resources had already been invested in protecting and building up the client, the patron dare not let it relapse back into failure even if its state practice remained lamentable.[8]

THERE WAS NO FORMULA TO SATISFY ALL CASES. DIFFERENT countries started at different places in terms of their economic and political capacity and the legacies of past conflicts. In some cases there were political leaders who could reach out across communities, or commodities that could ensure revenues. Some states had a history of centralisation, which tended to be the case with oil-producing states, whereas in others demands from the capital were generally ignored and more attention paid to local leaders. There were those who argued that the first priority was to get the state functioning, so that violence could be contained and economic activity organised. Others put more stress on nation building, so that divisions could be healed and a sense of common purpose instilled. And then there was the question of democracy. Could regular votes for parliaments create legitimacy and a sense of political access that had previously been lacking, or might it instead accentuate divisions, as parties were organised on religious or ethnic lines, and just provide the new political class with opportunities to indulge their greed?

As we noted earlier, although stable democracies had many advantages introducing democratic practices at times of political turbulence did not always help the cause of order and stability. Democracy was associated with elections, for that meant that all citizens could participate and that there was a choice. But there were problems with elections. Political parties were likely to reflect national divisions and their campaigns could aggravate a sense of grievance. Without strong institutions, including an independent judiciary, winning an election could be seen as an opportunity for patronage and corruption. It was to the good if one election took place, but the challenge in these circumstances was always to get the second.[9] Although establishing democracy helped to stabilise a country this was only if it could be reinforced and sustained, lest the country drift back into authoritarianism and so become vulnerable once again to civil war and military coups.[10]

Demanding that more attention be paid to popular views meant that less regard was placed on state sovereignty and established borders while encouraging the principle of self-determination as an expression of the rights of a free people. Once this principle was asserted it was hard to know when to stop. It was one thing to assert the need for self-government against rule from a distant and oppressive capital, but another to insist that any minority should be allowed to govern itself. A new state, detached from its parent, could soon face the same issue as some even smaller minority began to assert its rights and so challenge the new borders. This became painfully evident as

Croatia and Bosnia peeled away from the Yugoslav Federation and then became subject to forms of partition.

A WHOLE NEW CADRE OF SPECIALISTS DEVELOPED AROUND all these questions, some working for governments and other for the international organisations, including the various UN agencies, the IMF, and the World Bank. There were the large NGOs, such as the International Committee of the Red Cross and Oxfam, and smaller charities, perhaps with a focus on education or getting relief to the victims of sexual abuse. They did what they could with projects and contracts, offering advice on best practice and training, and developing theories on what should be done. And there were also those addressing security issues, provided by the UN, friendly governments, and private contractors. Others sought to get militias demobilised and disarmed and reintegrated into a national army, weaning underpaid police forces away from corrupt practices so that they could fight crime, working with local forces to deal with signs of reviving rebellions or insurgencies as quickly as possible.

There was a degree of irony in all of this. Many of the states now being consumed by their own weakness had emerged out of colonialism. By definition, a country that could only be stabilised by outside intervention was no longer fully self-governing, and was likely to be somewhat distant from a long-term settlement based on harmony, justice, and consensus. Was the logic to take them back, to create a new form of trusteeship that would give authority to the international forces and administrators that came into a country to provide order and start reconstruction once the fighting had subsided? Jennifer Welsh, reporting on an Oxford seminar, noted a 'recurring theme' that 'humanitarian interventions contain within them imperialist implications'. What might be necessary to create 'lasting stability' would also raise 'thorny questions not only about self-determination but also about the accountability of western-sponsored transitional authorities.'[11]

An imperial role, however, carried the implications of control, whereas the reality was often getting caught up in situations that were hard to control, leaving those with good intentions compromised. Deborah Scroggins used the story of Emma McCune as a vehicle for exploring the confused motives and mixed effects of Western aid efforts. McCune was a British aid worker, full of enthusiasm for human rights and initially engaged setting up schools, who went to Sudan in 1988 and died in a car crash in Kenya in 1993.

Sudan had gained independence in 1956, and then come to exhibit all the symptoms of persistent conflict: division between the Muslim northern and non-Muslim southern parts of the country (which had been administered separately until 1946 by the British); successive coups in the capital Khartoum, resulting in Marxist, non-Marxist, and eventually Islamist regimes; oil fields in the South the North wished to control; peace agreements of variable duration; casualties that defied calculation (normally put at some two million); meddling external powers with Eritrea, Ethiopia, and Uganda supporting the Sudan People's Liberation Army (SPLA) who led the fight against the north.[12]

When McCune died she was married to Riek Machar, an SPLA commander. Riek had tried to overthrow SPLA leader John Garang, ostensibly in the name of a 'secular, democratic Sudan', which led to vicious fighting. In late 1991 his forces killed some 2,000 civilians in Bor and wounded several thousand, looting villages and raiding cattle. Some 25,000 died in the ensuing famine and another 100,000 left the area. Yet the idealistic Emma became a committed partisan on her husband's behalf, to the dismay of the rest of the expatriate aid community.

In 2011 South Sudan eventually gained its independence from Sudan, but it remained poor, with limited economic prospects, and full of weapons and fighters. It was divided from the start between factions based on the Dinka and Nuer tribes, with little having been done to bring them together after independence. The UN arranged a power sharing agreement and sent in a force of 12,000 peacekeepers. Riek's role in this ongoing tragedy continued. He became vice president of South Sudan when it became independent. In 2016 he was dismissed from office by the president and fled to Britain, vowing to return.[13] As the fighting flared up again a UN base was attacked along with foreign aid workers, who were beaten and raped.

Scroggins's conclusion, reflecting her own disillusion, was that the wider expatriate community had become compromised in their own way, caught up in a vicious multifaceted conflict that they barely understood. Their 'salvation fantasies' combined a conviction that they were doing something worthwhile and effective though their actions, which they often were, though a consequence of the assistance they dispensed was to perpetuate rather than ease the violence. She questioned whether external assistance did much good at all while providing no reasons to believe that left alone matters would improve on their own accord.

There was certainly no shortage of assistance coming into South Sudan after independence—with consultants pouring in to sort out the country's administration, along with its education and health services. *The Economist* explained the problem:

> But it was all carrot and no stick. With no conditions attached, the money rarely found its way to infrastructure projects and public services. The consultants' advice, especially when it was about boosting governance and reforming the army, was ignored. Chiefly focused on state-building, Western aid also failed to bring together estranged communities. All this left plenty of leeway for factional chiefs to whip up tensions and consolidate power, their rivalries culminating in a full-blown civil war in 2013.[14]

This fitted in with a general argument developed by Monica Toft, that a successful resolution of a civil war required not only the effective delivery of benefits, and withdrawal of financial and other support from the warring parties, but also 'a credible threat of harm or punishment to those who defect from the treaty.'[15]

THERE WAS THEREFORE AN ARGUMENT THAT FOREIGN INTER-vention simply made bad situations worse and undermined natural forms of recovery. According to this argument the focus on the vice of war, and especially its dire humanitarian impact, missed its virtue as a means of resolving political conflicts which could lead to a lasting peace. The historian Ian Morris answered the question 'What is war good for?' with peace. 'What has made the world so much safer is war itself.'[16] War led to the development of strong states capable of keeping internal violence in check, bringing an end to the more localised, unregulated, commonplace violence of more 'primitive' times. After wars the winners were often able to incorporate the losers into even larger states. 'In retrospect', observed Charles Tilly, 'the pacification, cooptation, or elimination of fractious rivals to the sovereign seems an awesome, noble, prescient enterprise, destined to bring peace to a people'.[17] There was evidence in more recent times that strong states did emerge out of prolonged wars, having had to improve their abilities to raise funds, maintain discipline, and manage complex operations. Arguably, therefore, if wars kept on being inter-rupted and prevented from reaching a definitive conclusion, strong states would never be given a chance to develop.

Edward Luttwak urged that wars must be allowed to run their natural course until a resolution was reached. International interven-tion, of whatever sort, from demanding ceasefires to interfering with the fighting, interrupted this process and so prevented lasting settle-ments. Often they achieved no more than a pause in the fighting, as belligerents took the opportunity to recuperate and revive their forces. The weaker side, which might have made the compromises necessary for peace, was provided cover for intransigence. In Bosnia the factions had been left with incentives to prepare for future war rather than reconstruct their societies. 'Uninterrupted war would cer-tainly have caused further suffering and led to an unjust outcome from one perspective or another, but it would also have led to a more stable situation. . . . Peace takes hold only when war is truly over'.

Moreover, peacekeepers had given endangered civilians an illusion of security, when the wise course would have been to flee, although in something of a contradiction Luttwak also complained about large refugee camps as sustaining defeated populations in their anger and providing a base for continued resistance. Luttwak's claim was that conflicts did not end because 'the transformative effects of both deci-sive victory and exhaustion are blocked by outside intervention'.[18]

There were obvious counter-examples to Luttwak's analysis, not least the scale of violence that could overwhelm societies or the inter-ventionist role played by neighbouring countries which were bound to look after their own interests. Yet research suggested that of all the outcomes to a civil war, a clean military victory was the one that was most likely to result in a stable peace. Civil wars did not recur in 85 per cent of the countries that experienced a military victory, while war resumed in 50 per cent of the conflicts settled by means of nego-tiation.[19] Toft reported similar findings and also noted that the most satisfactory aftermaths tended to be those following rebel victories.[20] The problem with negotiated settlements was that they did not resolve power struggles but instead left them in a state of suspended anima-tion, making it harder for a government to act in a unified and con-sistent way. When a single party dominated the government then it could act with more consistency and determination.[21] Strong leaders, emerging out of tough conflicts, could manage economic recovery, even without external assistance.[22]

Others pointed out that countries have capacities for economic self-generation that were often missed in the belief that they are helpless without external assistance. This became a similar argument to those about welfare-dependency, and finding the right balance between encouraging individuals—and states—to become self-reliant and providing a safety net, upon which they might become too dependent. The difficulty with this argument was that it implied the possibility of keeping conflicts geographically contained, while neighbours and the wider international community waited for them to burn themselves out or one side to win. In practice there were all sorts of reasons why they were likely to spread into neighbouring regions, because of cross-border allegiances, opportunities for plunder, and refugee flows.

Weinstein used the example of Yoweri Museveni following the victory of his National Resistance Movement (NRM) in Uganda in January 1986. This came after a succession of disasters—coups (including the calamitous rule of Idi Amin) and civil wars. Per-capita GDP had declined by 40 per cent in fifteen years. Museveni ushered in a period of political stability, with the army in control around the country, and the country prospering and poverty falling. The economic reforms followed Western guidelines but less so the political methods. His achievements came as an 'enlightened autocrat.'[23] And like most autocrats as time passed he found it harder to imagine how the country could manage without him. His view of political parties was that they exacerbated sectarian divisions, and he therefore sought to govern using a broad-based movement.

The hallmark of Western democracy was strong institutions that could manage competition, cope with transfers of power, and provide continuity of administration independent of any particular leader. In other states with more fragile structures, stability tended to come in the form of individuals whose rule might bring benefits at first until these were overtaken by the costs of personality cults. This is why rebellions and coups at times offered the only hope of refreshing government structures. So sticking narrowly to Weber's definition of states gave priority to internal order and stability, requiring backing strong leaders, even if they were doing little to address popular grievances and creating troubles for the future. After all, the violence in the Middle East was the result of the old generation of anti-colonial, and largely secular, strong men losing their grip or being overthrown. The tradition, however, remained strong. After Egypt's President Mubarak fell the elected President Morsi's Islamist policies generated dissent and he was replaced in a coup by the military chief Abdel Fattah el Sisi, adopting the 'strong man' governance model.

DESPITE OPTIMISM, EXPRESSED AS LATE AS 2014, THAT 'Africa has become dramatically more peaceful over the last 15 years',[24] this trend was already in reverse. Hopes that defeated leaders would accept democratic, peaceful power transitions were regularly dashed. From 2008 there were marked declines in freedom of expression combined with rising levels of corruption and bureaucratic incompetence. Coups remained common.[25] The lack of accountability meant that rebels returned to the fray after a period of tenuous peace so that most wars were 'repeats'. This repetition was a feature of some 90 percent of all civil wars, including in Africa.[26] The biggest cases involved the same countries that had experienced violent conflict for many years. One consequence of this was cumulative misery in terms of disease, famine, poverty, and large numbers of refugees and internally displaced people.[27] In April 2017 it was reported that 20 million people in four countries that had faced constant conflict— Nigeria, South Sudan, Yemen, and Somalia—were at risk of starvation. Rebels often deliberately denied them food while governments were either incompetent or diverted resources to regions where they exercised more control. The conflicts had limited the ability of aid workers to reach affected people, and they were too scared to move.[28]

The only new war in Africa was in Libya, one of the countries to fall under the spell of the Arab Spring. This broke out with demonstrations against authoritarian regimes, beginning in Tunisia in December 2010. In 2011 Libyan President Gaddafi was overthrown.[29] This was a small country with oil resources, and it was assumed that it could look after itself. Instead the state fell apart; civil war developed, with Islamist groups getting footholds. The Western interveners watched aghast as this country also descended into chaos. As part of the Syrian civil war, which also began in 2011, the Islamist group ISIS was able to establish a base and move into Iraq (where the overthrow of Saddam Hussein in 2003 had given the Islamists their opening) prompting intense fighting and a massive refugee crisis that had an unsettling effect on European politics as they tried to absorb an influx of desperate people. They were dislodged from cities such as Mosul only with enormous effort and great suffering, leaving ruins and rubble behind them.

Islamist groups, such as al-Shabaab in Kenya and Boko Haram in Nigeria, were becoming a more important feature in African conflicts as elsewhere. Barbara Walter wrote of the 'new new civil wars'. Not only had the number of conflicts gone up but the majority of those starting up or reviving were in Muslim-majority countries and involved rebels embracing radical Islamist goals. These different groups were linked and their goals were as much transnational as national. The ominous features of these wars were that they looked likely to last for some time, were impervious to attempts to negotiate settlements, and carried the risk of contagion into neighbouring territories.[30] The extremism of Islamism was instrumental as a powerful recruiting and fund-raising tool, potentially capable of appealing to all Sunni Muslims (some 90 per cent of total) though the majority were more moderate in their beliefs. It justified harsh measures against apostates and non-believers, adding to the intensity of the violence. Groups that had been seen in the 1990s as vicious but marginal had become major players.

The choices got starker for the major powers. Failing to address humanitarian crises meant becoming spectators to immense suffering, watching opportunities being created for extremism, and then having to come to terms with the consequences in terms of pressure to take refugees and risks of terrorism. Military interventions meant participation in frustrating and often cruel wars, from which disengagement was difficult. Limiting the contributions to advice and air power meant limiting political influence. Success came increasingly to depend on the quality of local partners. Once the problems connected with transforming other peoples' states were recognised, the partners could not be expected to share all core values. The first priority was that they were credible and competent which often meant working with old-fashioned 'strong men' as the best available bulwark against Islamist movements. The objectives were often more about preventing a bad situation deteriorating rather than easing conflict by raising societies to a new level of development. The compromises were awkward and the results rarely matched the scale of the challenge. All this was far from the liberal optimism of the early post–Cold War period.

PART THREE

[20]

Hybrid Wars

In the aftermath of the relative certainty of doctrine, training, tactics, adversary, and known terrain of the Cold War, our military today is in a sense operating without a concept of war and is searching desperately for the new "unified field theory" of conflict.

GENERAL DAVID BARNO,
'Military Adaptation in Complex Operations', 2009[1]

By early in the twenty-first century it was apparent that the inherited scripts for future war were inadequate. The US military had clung to an ideal type derived from the classical model and then faced a more unruly form of warfare for which it was poorly prepared and from which it struggled to extricate itself. Their British allies believed that they understood the requirements of Iraq based on their peacekeeping experience of Bosnia and aid to the civil power in Northern Ireland, but their scripts were also inadequate; they found themselves struggling even more than the Americans.[2]

Was there a way of thinking about war that might prepare forces better for the sort of challenges that they might meet in the future? It was evident that it was not sufficient to prepare just for the type of war which Western armies wished to fight. But did that mean that it was necessary to prepare for a great variety of contingencies, each with their own special scripts, or might something else be going on, in which different forms of warfare were being followed at the same time? In 1997 US Marine Corps Commandant General Charles C. Krulak coined the term "Three Block War" to convey the special requirements of the modern battlefield.

> In one moment in time, our service members will be feeding and clothing displaced refugees, providing humanitarian assistance. In the next moment, they will be holding two warring tribes apart— conducting peacekeeping operations—and, finally, they will be fighting a highly lethal mid-intensity battle—all on the same day . . . all within three city blocks.[3]

This idea that a number of different tasks had to be accomplished at the same time was eventually turned into a form of strategy, capable of confounding an opponent. This would stretch an adversary relying solely on conventional warfare. With problems in Iraq, this intermingling of irregular with regular forces attracted more interest. In 2005 General James Mattis and Lt. Col. Frank Hoffman described a 'four-block war', with the additional block dealing 'with the psychological or information operations aspects'. They described this as a 'hybrid war'.[4] The term was given greater prominence in 2007 by Hoffman, referring not just to how irregular forces might be used to add to the pressure on the regular but something more coordinated and melded.[5] Over time it came to refer to an approach drawing upon instruments from across the full spectrum, including terrorism, insurgency, criminality, and conventional operations, along with the extensive use of information operations.

Hoffman's prime example of the concept at work was Hezbollah's campaign against Israel in the Second Lebanon War of 2006, in which the IDF relied on air power to attack Hezbollah sanctuaries but then faced rocket attacks from Lebanon. They were then drawn into Lebanon where they struggled to deal with the militia. Hoffman described this as 'a classic example of a hybrid threat':

> The fusion of militia units, specially trained fighters and the anti-tank guided-missile teams marks this case, as does Hezbollah's employment of modern information operations, signals intelligence, operational and tactical rockets, armed UAVs and deadly anti-ship cruise missiles. Hezbollah's leaders describe their force as a cross between an army and a guerrilla force, and believe they have developed a new model.[6]

Hezbollah was an interesting case, both well embedded in its community and sponsored by Iran, which provided it with money and arms. In 2006 its tactics showed up those of Israel, which judged the demands of the war poorly, relying too much on air power without a strong ground presence. But the war was also costly for the militia, with a lot of fighters killed, and the Israeli campaign battered its urban sanctuaries.[7]

Interest in the approach was revived as it was apparently followed by Russia in its campaign against Ukraine that began in 2014. In early 2013 Valery Gerasimov, chief of Russia's general staff, had described how this might work. He noted how in Middle East conflicts there had been a progressive erosion of the distinctions between war and peace and between uniformed personnel and covert operatives. Wars were 'not declared but simply begin,' so that 'a completely well-off and stable country' could be transformed into 'an arena of the most intense armed conflict in a matter of months or even days.' In these circumstances, military means became more effective when combined with non-military means, including 'political, economic, information, humanitarian and other measures.' These could be supplemented by covert and thus deniable military measures as well as offers of peacekeeping assistance as a means to strategic ends. 'New information technologies' would play an important role. As a result, 'frontal clashes of major military formations . . . are gradually receding into the past.' At issue was how these capabilities related to the local population, whose support could swing a campaign one way or the other. Gerasimov suggested that they could be fired up as a fifth column and by 'concealed' armed forces.[8] The Russians were also looking for way to prevail in a conflict without having to rely on superior force in a classic battle.

A year later when in response to an uprising in Kiev, which saw the Ukrainian President flee and an anti-Russian government take over, Moscow moved first to annex Crimea while launching an incursion into parts of Eastern Ukraine, all while claiming that these were indigenous, spontaneous, popular movements managing without Russian military personnel. The Russian claims did not survive scrutiny. There were professional soldiers in uniforms without markings playing key roles. The role of the separatists had some similarities with Hezbollah. They also had a state sponsor, which ensured that they had resources and modern weaponry, though they were more of a proxy for Russian interests. Unlike Hezbollah they did not have deep roots among local people, at least not in Eastern Ukraine.[9]

The experience demonstrated the limits of hybrid warfare as well as the possibilities.[10] Complex command arrangements complicated Russian attempts to control the situation on the ground, while efforts at deception were by and large ineffectual, as they became progressively transparent. The aim was more to avoid accepting the political and legal implications of what outside observers assumed to be true. Admitting the role Russian forces were actually playing in Ukraine would have required admitting aggression. The pretence was therefore that the individuals concerned were volunteers or on holiday. When one of their anti-aircraft missiles shot down a Malaysian Airlines aircraft in July 2014, with the loss of 298 lives, instead of accepting responsibility they sought to implicate the Ukrainians, with explanations of the shoot-down becoming ever more fanciful. One possible success with this approach was in projecting a more menacing image than Russia's actual strength warranted, which served to deter the West from escalating the conflict.

By and large, however, the result was that Russian officials were not believed about anything, even when telling the truth. Russian propaganda played extremely well in Russia but badly everywhere else, which had the effect of increasing Russia's sense of isolation but not of its influence. 'Russia may have a megaphone', observed Mark Galeotti, 'but this just means that when its message is laughable or offensive it can alienate more people at once'.[11] In terms of the campaign on the ground, the Russian operation got stuck in September 2014 and despite a peace process there was little movement to bring the conflict to a close either militarily or diplomatically. On the ground the fighting was reminiscent of so many wars, old and new, with exchanges of mortar and small arms fire.

In this respect 'hybrid war' emerged as a lesser form of warfare, coming to the fore because of problems with regular warfare, and an appreciation of the possibilities of popular resistance. It gave coherence to what was often no more than a set of ad hoc and improvised arrangements. As with many similar concepts, such as asymmetric warfare, once adopted as a term of art 'hybrid war' tended towards a wider definition. As the term came to be adopted by the US armed forces, the theory became more elaborate, exploring the social and cultural links between the disparate elements.[12] If pushed it could encompass almost everything. It could describe the mingling of types of operations and forces evident in many contemporary conflicts but it lacked specificity. No conflicts could be considered in some sense 'pure'. All tended to include regular and irregular elements, and there were many precedents.[13] Commanders had long faced the challenges of combining classical forms of conventional warfare with partisan campaigns on the one hand and forms of civilian destruction (such as air raids) on the other.

As a deliberate strategy it generated its own demands. A competent and extensive command structure was needed to pull together the different strands of activity so that they reinforced rather than contradicted each other. More seriously, there was a distinction between capabilities that were necessary to achieve the objectives of war, which normally meant reasonably disciplined and substantial forces able to take and hold contested territory, and supporting capabilities that could help to disorient and demoralise an opponent and erode the ability to sustain a conflict over time (such as economic measures) but did not by themselves provide for political control.

NATO nonetheless became sufficiently alarmed that this was a new type of warfare for which it was unprepared that it issued its own report on how to counter the challenge in the future. Thus in 2015 NATO's Secretary General reported that:

> Russia has used proxy soldiers, unmarked Special Forces, intimidation and propaganda, all to lay a thick fog of confusion; to obscure its true purpose in Ukraine; and to attempt deniability. So NATO must be ready to deal with every aspect of this new reality from wherever it comes. And that means we must look closely at how we prepare for; deter; and if necessary defend against hybrid warfare.

He described hybrid warfare as 'a probe, a test of our resolve to resist and to defend ourselves' but also as a possible 'prelude to a more serious attack; because behind every hybrid strategy, there are conventional forces, increasing the pressure and ready to exploit any opening.'[14]

One part of the mix—information operations—was assumed to be the most original and required the most attention.[15]

Russia had a long history of controlling media, but was also sensitive to the role played by uncontrollable and subversive foreign media in stimulating the Soviet Union's crisis of legitimacy and then how a number of governments in post-Soviet states had been overthrown in 'colour revolutions' backed by the west.[16] Although Marxism was no longer the official ideology, it left an intellectual legacy in which issues of mass consciousness and how it could be shaped were to the fore. In addition, the possibilities of disinformation as war-fighting had been part of Soviet military doctrine.[17] Russian efforts used social media to spread false messages and create misleading impressions to weaken opponents, especially with their own public opinion. The EU spoke of 'hybrid threats' because it saw this as a form of activity that could help undermine security even at times of comparative peace. Evidence was found in the role, confirmed by the US intelligence community, played by Russia during the 2016 presidential election, employing disinformation and leaks of hacked emails, in undermining Democrat Party candidate Hillary Clinton.

THE TERM 'INFORMATION WAR' HAD BEEN AROUND SINCE THE early 1990s with two different but easily confused meanings. The first referred to measures designed to disable systems dependent upon flows of information; the second referred to attempts to influence perceptions by affecting the content of information. The first was about engineering, the second about cognition. Information war as propaganda was a continuation of practices that had developed along with the development of newspapers with mass circulation, then radio and TV. Each had in their own way set new opportunities and limits on the ability of elites to shape popular attitudes to war, both in anticipation and once the fighting was underway, and for enemies to subvert their messages.

The two big changes made possible by the digital age were the ease of access to multiple sources of information, international as well as national, and the ability to share thoughts and plans with others. Communication with informal networks, without any commanding organisation, could be achieved through numerous outlets, some protected and some open. RAND analysts John Arquilla and David Ronfeldt saw how this created an opportunity for what they called 'netwars', described as 'an emerging mode of conflict (and crime) at societal levels, short of traditional military warfare, in which the protagonists use network forms of organization and related doctrines, strategies, and technologies attuned to the information age'. The stress was on the features normally associated with insurgencies such as dispersal and limited central control, coming at opponents from various and often unexpected directions. According to Arquilla and Ronfeldt:

> The most potent netwarriors will not only be highly networked and have a capacity to swarm, they will also be held together by strong social ties, have secure communications technologies, and project a common "story" about why they are together and what they need to do. These will be the most serious adversaries.[18]

These were features generally associated with radical social movements, as well as terrorist or insurgent groups.

The importance of the common 'story' or 'narrative' in this analysis was to provide not only an ideological rationale for political struggle but also an account of the struggle's likely course, explaining why one side was likely to prevail. The narrative therefore gave meaning to events and so shaped responses. For those engaged in counter-insurgency operations this was a very big issue as they needed communities on-side as they could offer the enemy sanctuaries, recruits, and supplies. They appreciated that this was difficult to achieve whilst ordinary people were suspicious if not downright hostile. David Kilcullen observed how the insurgents' 'pernicious influence' drew on a 'single narrative', that was simple, unified, easily expressed, and could organise experience and provide a framework for understanding events. He understood that it was best to be able to 'tap into an existing narrative that excludes the insurgents' involving stories that people naturally appreciate. Otherwise it was necessary to develop an alternative narrative, which would be more challenging.[19]

This fitted in with longer-standing concerns about the need to win over disaffected populations as part of a counter-insurgency campaign, demonstrating that by backing the government side they could expect protection from the insurgents and that life would generally get better. Yet even an appreciation of the importance of popular perceptions and how they might be influenced by social media, as well as by print and broadcasting, did not mean that they could readily be reshaped. Attempts to encourage different thoughts might benefit from sophisticated forms of propaganda but would still fail if the messages did not make sense in terms of local culture or accord with everyday experiences. It required considerable discipline to sustain a set of messages, not only in what was said but also in ensuring that behaviour in the field conformed to what was being claimed. It was especially difficult for those connected with a foreign force to construct a credible narrative that would appeal to the indigenous population.[20] Whatever was said would have to stay close to public opinion back home as well as address local concerns. The greatest difficulty lay in addressing popular grievances effectively, promising reform and military success, when it was often the failures of the host government to achieve any of this that was the reason for the insurgency in the first place.

With all military operations there was a constant and uneasy relationship with the media. At the very least armies had to be aware of the impact of images of retreat, casual cruelty, or just the regular miseries of war. Once smartphones became available in 2007, incidents could be videoed and transmitted worldwide within seconds. Military operations became transparent. The sort of secrecy that commanders would have demanded in the past was no longer possible. The only hope for surprise would be that with so much noise cluttering the Internet, bits and pieces of crucial information could easily be missed. Because there was no longer any control over what could be posted on the Internet, opportunities also grew for manipulating opinion. Information campaigns could put out misleading evidence to create completely false impressions in order to construct or break allegiances and sympathies. The causal relationships were much harder to grasp when it came to the information aspects of war, as opposed to those that were more crudely kinetic. It was not possible to reshape belief systems with the same care and precision that could now be put into lethal attacks. Distant messages from unfamiliar sources competed for attention with the direct experience of war and its human consequences. The most telling messages were often unintended as people observed the actions of troops in their neighbourhood, or heard garbled reports of what politicians had said, or picked up lurid stories from the Internet that reinforced their prejudices.

The concept of 'hybrid war' implied the possibility of disparate activities having a controlling mastermind, ensuring that they were mutually reinforcing. In practice the activities were likely to remain disparate, each with their own dynamic, thwarting attempts by governments and military commanders to assert control.

[21]

Cyberwar

Cyberspace. A consensual hallucination experienced daily by billions of legitimate operators, in every nation, by children being taught mathematical concepts. . . A graphic representation of data abstracted from the banks of every computer in the human system. Unthinkable complexity. Lines of light ranged in the nonspace of the mind, clusters and constellations of data. Like city lights, receding.

WILLIAM GIBSON,
Neuromancer, 1984[1]

The other form of information warfare was to interfere with the information flows necessary to keep modern military and civilian systems working. In this respect it was as much an aspect of 'cyber war' as 'hybrid war'. The idea of cyberwar was a natural inference from the digital revolution. If all military activity depended on the rapid collection, processing, and transmission of data then should not that be as important a focus of attention as launching strikes or blunting enemy attacks? What if one side suddenly found itself in the dark, with screens either blank or full of misleading information, and was unable to send out orders to local commanders or else had these orders substituted by false instructions? In such circumstances even the strongest military machine would be left helpless and hapless. Take the analysis a step further and look beyond military activity and then an even more alarming thought developed. If all key functions of a modern society—energy, transport, banking, health, and education services—depended on these flows of information, might it be possible to bring a country to its knees without firing a shot? Stopping the flow would be like pulling out a gigantic plug. Everything would go dark, screech to a halt, or clatter and bang, leaving an economy in tatters and a society struggling to meet its most basic needs.

Unlike other visions of future war this was only in part a question of imagining how technologies might develop. The vulnerabilities created by the digital age were evident in everyday stories of viruses and worms infecting computers, of foreign agents, disgruntled employees, would-be extortionists, or just curious youngsters hacking into supposedly secure systems, undertaking acts of malicious interference, sometimes no more than an irritating nuisance, sometimes causing serious damage and disruption. There were reports from past conflicts of enemy air defences caught napping, command systems confused, and propaganda opportunities exploited. From the start the question was not one of whether or not there was an issue here but how the risks and opportunities were to be measured, and how the relationship between this new arena of conflict and the nature of warfare as a whole was to be conceptualised. The problem appeared as being somewhere on a spectrum from the equivalent of a nuclear war to a minor inconvenience.[2]

There was a link to the post-Second World War thoughts about a coming 'push button war', in which guided missiles would rule and armies might become redundant.[3] As we saw in Chapter 7, once nuclear warheads were added to these missiles and they acquired intercontinental ranges, two types of fears began to dominate the debate on future war. The first was whether one side might be able to configure its nuclear forces so as to launch a disarming first strike, transforming an apparent balance of power into one-sided dominance. The other, even if there was no premium in striking first, was the potential interaction of human failings and technical malfunctions that would turn an otherwise manageable situation into a global cataclysm. Norbert Wiener, who had developed his ideas on cybernetics from his work on anti-aircraft weapons during the Second World War, had become increasingly alarmed at the implications of developing air defence systems which had to work so quickly that there was barely a chance for human intervention.[4] The theme of lost control over a situation hurtling towards tragedy was the basis of the movies *Dr. Strangelove* and *Fail-Safe*.

IN 1979 TWO SCREENWRITERS, LARRY LASKER AND WALTER
Parkes, developed an idea for a movie based on the interaction between a dying old scientist and a smart, rebellious teenager, which
soon revolved around their shared understanding of computing.
Aware of stories about how the North American Aerospace Defense
Command (NORAD) could mistake innocent signals for an incoming
Soviet attack, they toured NORAD. There they met with the commander who, on their telling, shared his concerns about the risk of
over-automated decision-making. They also learnt about simulated
war games. Out of this came the core plot of the movie *WarGames*,
released in 1983. A teenager, David Lightman (played by Matthew
Broderick), hacked into a supercomputer designed to predict outcomes of nuclear war known as War Operation Plan Response
(WOPR). Lightman noted a number of familiar games but then saw
one called 'Global Thermonuclear War' which he decided to play.
This turned out to be a programme that could convince the systems
operating nuclear missiles that this was the real thing. When he realised what he had done, and after arrest by the FBI for the hack,
Lightman reached the embittered, dying scientist who had invented
the programme to persuade him to give him the clue to turning it off.
This was done seconds away from catastrophe. As WOPR was a
learning machine it could realise that some games led to futility,
which became a metaphor for mutual assured destruction. After this
point was reached through a drawn game of tic-tac-toe the computer
had the last line: 'A strange game. The only winning move is not to
play. How about a nice game of chess?'[5]

As with the doomsday machine in the earlier movies, the plot depended on a prior decision to give deterrence a form of automaticity
that prevented human beings interrupting the launch sequence. The
movie opened with a surprise drill in which, when confronted with an
incoming nuclear attack, the USAF personnel supposed to turn the
keys to launch retaliatory strikes failed to do so. Instead of a Ger-
manic think tanker the villain now was an all-American systems engineer who, against the advice of the NORAD commander, insisted that
the launch process must be automated, which is why WOPR had this
crucial role. When the movie was released the Pentagon was at pains
to point out that it was misleading about NORAD's role and also the
possibility of the nuclear arsenal being out of human control. Whether
or not the intent was to make a film in the spirit of *Fail-Safe* or *Dr.
Strangelove*, alerting the audience to the risks of an inadvertent

nuclear catastrophe, the main thought left by *WarGames* was the ease with which an outsider might hack his way into the most vital computer networks, highlighting the risks posed by remote access and simple passwords. This was the message taken away by President Reagan, a friend of Lasker's parents, who was invited to an early showing and was sufficiently disturbed to ask officials whether this movie had a basis in any conceivable reality. As the issue was investigated it turned out to be more serious than had been realised, leading to a set of studies into what was then described as 'Telecommunications and Automated Information Systems Security'.[6]

This was a time of exploration into this developing networked world of information, a disembodied place where real things could be made to happen by anyone who could gain access. *WarGames* had pointed to the possibility of a war starting from within cyberspace. Yet not only was the term itself still unfamiliar, but the prefix also already had connotations of cyborgs, man-machine combinations with extended powers.[7] The prospect of computers gaining the upper hand in some future conflict was linked naturally to the idea of robotic warriors, a standard feature of science fiction.

Robots were introduced in a 1921 play by Czech writer Karel Čapek about a company that sold machines that looked like people as forms of slaves. He got the term from 'robotniks' or surfs. As he was aware that these robotniks had rebelled against their masters in 1848, Čapek had his robots also turning on their human masters, introducing a regular theme into science fiction.[8] As mechanical devices increasingly performed simple but demanding household tasks during the twentieth century it was natural to consider how they might take over as soldiers. In 1968 a professor of Mechanical Engineering described how it would not be long before radars would be able to propel themselves forward, seek out enemies and kill them. 'A line of such robots spaced twenty metres apart might be deployed to move at fifteen kilometres per hour through a jungle and destroy all men encountered there'. Within 'a few years' men would 'cease to be valued in battle'. They would complicate matters because they would lack comparable 'information storage, decision-making, sensory input and pattern-recognition'. The human role was likely to be to 'stand helplessly by as a struggle rages between robot armies and navies, and air and rocket forces'.[9]

In the first article to talk of 'cyberwars', published in 1987, robots dominated the scene. They were fearless and irresistible, pushing away any poor humans sent to confront them. If everything was automated then future wars would be between machines with artificial brains, with their controllers hidden away in command bunkers.[10] Cyberwar dominated by robots that 'do much of the killing and destroying without direct instructions from human operators' was also the theme of an article in the *Bulletin of Atomic Scientists* in 1992. The idea of a network was still missing. What was alarming about these systems, whether crewless tanks or anti-missile satellites, was their autonomy.[11]

The team of Lasker and Parkes released another movie in 1992 called *Sneakers*. It had been conceived while *WarGames* was being made, and took on a similar theme, this time involving a device stolen from the National Security Agency (NSA) that could decode all encrypted data. It did not make the same impact, except for the fact that it was watched by the NSA's head, Admiral Mike McConnell, who was taken by a line in the script:

> The world isn't run by weapons anymore, or energy, or money. It's run by ones and zeroes, little bits of data. It's all just electrons ... there's a war out there, old friend, a world war. And it's not about who's got the most bullets. It's about who controls the information: what we see and hear, how we work, what we think. It's all about the information.[12]

This vulnerability had already been identified in a 1991 report by the National Research Council:

> We are at risk. Increasingly, America depends on computers. They control power delivery, communications, aviation, and financial services. They are used to store vital information, from medical records to business plans to criminal records. Although we trust them, they are vulnerable—to the effects of poor design and insufficient quality control, to accident, and perhaps more alarmingly, to deliberate attack. The modern thief can steal more with a computer than with a gun. Tomorrow's terrorist may be able to do more damage with a keyboard than with a bomb.[13]

An IT entrepreneur from Tennessee, Winn Schwartau, first in a journal article, then in Congressional testimony, and eventually in a self-published novel, *Terminal Compromise*, highlighted the danger. He told Congress: 'Government and commercial computer systems are so poorly protected today that they can essentially be considered defenceless'. Drawing on the unavoidable analogy, he spoke of 'an electronic Pearl Harbor waiting to occur'.[14] The plot of his novel had at its centre a Japanese survivor of Hiroshima, seeking revenge against the United States, and involved 'Arab zealots, German intelligence agents and a host of technical mercenaries' identifying 'the weaknesses in our techno-economic infrastructure' to land blows that hurt the US economy, taking in Wall Street as well as the carmakers Ford and Chrysler.[15] In their 1993 book *War and Anti-War*, the Tofflers quoted Schwartau warning of an electronic Pearl Harbor and others alarmed about the possibility of 'info-terrorists'.[16]

The idea of the electronic Pearl Harbor gained more traction in policy circles following a 1995 crisis simulation led by RAND analysts Roger Molander and Peter Wilson who had been engaged in a series of exercises on nuclear warfare. They put to decision-makers a developing crisis and asked them to consider issues of escalation. Now they envisaged a series of attacks that disabled a Saudi Arabian refinery, derailed a high-speed train, crashed an airliner, took down power grids, and put CNN offline. An 'electronic Pearl Harbor' meant 'that some country or terrorist might attack US computers in one sudden, bolt-out-of-the-blue strike, causing death, destruction, and mayhem.'[17] Policymakers appeared to be at a loss to know how to respond, yet could not deny the problem. 'The electron', explained CIA Director John Deutch, 'is the ultimate precision guided weapon'.[18] In his confirmation hearings as Secretary of Defense in 2011, Leon Panetta deployed the analogy yet again to warn of a 'digital Pearl Harbor'. A former chairman of the Joint Chiefs of Staff warned the same year: 'The single biggest existential threat that's out there, I think, is cyber.'[19]

The persistent use of the most searing experience in recent American military history to frame future attacks pointed very deliberately to the potential for surprise. But Pearl Harbor, of course, was not a knockout blow. The US recovered and defeated the perpetrator. This hypothetical case, therefore, raised exactly the same questions of why an enemy would do this, how they would follow up any achievements in the initial strike, and what political purpose might be served. There was also the question of how confident the attacker could be that all would work as planned. A lot would need to be known not only about the target's vulnerabilities, and whether defences had been improved, but also the degree to which the target was dependent upon the systems being attacked. As Wilson, one of the designers of the

RAND simulation, observed, these were more weapons of mass disruption than mass destruction, and that 'by painting doomsday scenarios, government officials lose credibility and, over time, their ability to influence the public.'[20] The issue was also perplexing because while some attacks might cause loss of life most would not.

As one group worried about how the United States might take advantage of the vulnerabilities of information systems to mess with enemies, others worried about how the same vulnerabilities in their systems might allow the enemy to mess with them. Given the resources allocated to this issue it could be assumed that the Americans were well able to interfere with the systems of others. Small but significant acts illustrated the possibilities. First Iraqi and then Serb air defences were degraded by messing with their software. The Israelis did something similar with Syrian air defences when they took out a nuclear reactor under construction in 2007. The Stuxnet virus, probably a joint US-Israeli project, was designed to set back uranium enrichment in Iran by disabling centrifuges.[21] This had some effect but also showed how hard it was to stop these attacks spreading away from the original target. The virus was noticed when non-Iranian systems were hit.

Every time national systems were tested to see how well they could defend against interference from others, they were found to be wanting, and for all types of networks, malevolent hacking became regular. In 2014 there were almost 80,000 security breaches in the US, more than 2,000 of which resulted in lost data. Hackers stayed inside the networks they had breached for an average of 205 days.[22] Behind the attacks were criminal groups and political activists as much as governments, although the line between them could get blurred. They normally appeared as 'bolts from the blue', but they tended to be damaging more than crippling, and usually had far more to do with the theft of business secrets, or malicious attacks on individuals or companies, than with international affairs. Sometimes it was difficult to work out what was deliberate interference and what was a consequence of the fragility of some of the connections. Internet services regularly went down because of accident or error. In one incident a 75-year-old Georgian grandmother cut off the Internet to Armenia with a shovel, almost leading to an international incident as Russia was at first blamed.[23]

The assumption that it would be impossible to attribute attacks was challenged as the forensics improved.[24] The US became more ready to assign blame, whether it was a North Korean attack on Sony Corporation for a movie which considered the possibility of the assassination of its leader, or, more seriously, Russian attempts to swing the 2016 presidential election. In these cases the US government also spoke openly of retaliation. The US became explicit about the deterrence aspects of its cyber-strategy in the military sphere as well, threatening to 'use cyber operations to disrupt an adversary's command-and-control networks, military-related critical infrastructure, and weapons capabilities.'[25]

As with all new developments the question was whether this was a way to get a decisive result in a conflict or just another means of engaging in a dispute without necessarily being able to bring it to a conclusion. In earlier debates about the impact of first air power and then nuclear weapons a distinction had been drawn between strategic and tactical effects, with the former making possible a decisive victory and the latter only having their effects as a result of working with other types of forces and in particular armies. Arquilla and Ronfeldt sought to redefine cyberwar in a 1993 article away from automated forms of physical forces to the centres of knowledge and communication at the heart of modern military and social systems.[26] This fitted in with a wider trend in thinking about warfare, represented as a shift from mindless attrition, which relied on physical destruction, to more intelligent manoeuvrist strategies, which depended on getting inside the enemy's head to confuse and demoralise.[27] The next shift was from interference with the information processes that kept military systems working to those that did the same for a whole country.

According to Arquilla the purpose of this article had been to stress tactical effects, showing how disruption of networks might interfere with one side's ability to fight a conventional war, while they were sceptical about the 'strategic attack paradigm' which saw the attacks being directed against national information infrastructures. Yet, he observed, the academic and policy debate soon got drawn to 'a kind of information analog to strategic bombing'.[28] This was not to deny the evident tactical value in exploring the weaknesses in enemy forces. One general reporting on his experience in Afghanistan described how he 'was able to use my cyber operations against my adversary with great impact. . . . I was able to get inside his nets, infect his command-and-control, and in fact defend myself against his almost constant incursions to get inside my wire, to affect my operations.'[29] The challenge lay in showing how cyberwar should be viewed strategically. The issue was not one of how hurt might be caused but of linking the hurt to a political purpose, especially if that was the sole form of attack.

To do major harm would require substantial preparation, including considerable research into the system being targeted to identify its vulnerabilities, in the hope that this would not be detected, and then customising a package to implement the required sabotage. Whatever the options developed during prior reconnaissance there were likely to be major uncertainties about their effectiveness until an attack was actually launched, including whether the target had noticed that its systems had been penetrated. These attempts therefore could not be spur of the moment decisions but must be prepared well in advance of any attack, and the options might degrade quite quickly. The adversary might have been doing its own probing and found evidence of a planned offensive. A state picking up on an adversary's preparation might decide to make a fuss or simply make any attack harder to execute and wait to see what happened. None of this might be visible other than to those directly involved.[30] These uncertainties would all make cyberweapons an uncertain foundation for aggression.

An imagined cyberwar was the natural culmination of a yearning for non-kinetic wars, forms of engagement that would disarm and disable a whole society without mass slaughter. This is why there was continuing anxiety about the worst case of 'an electronic Pearl Harbor', with a sudden attack leading to social and economic breakdown. The everyday reality, however, was more of a level of threat that was routine and ubiquitous. Not only was it the case that any conflict, even one that was largely non-violent, exhibited cyber elements, but also that this had become almost a preferred form of engagement, precisely because it was relatively minor. It provided opportunities for soft forms of coercion, signalling concern, or hinting at some future escalation. This is one way to interpret Russia's electronic bombardment of Estonia in 2007 and Georgia the next year.[31] In neither case was the effect of the denial of service attacks lasting, but both served as warnings of what might be done in the future. In this way states behaved 'more and more like individual hackers, carrying out crimes of petty vandalism, theft, disruption, destruction, and even cyber-bullying.' It was an unrestricted form of conflict without obvious limits, probing while avoiding excessive provocation, but still undertaken at a level inconsistent with responsible state behaviour.[32] In this respect, cyber-attacks became more analogous to irregular war than strategic bombing, another way to harass and subvert, to confuse and annoy, but not a way to win a war.

[22]

Robots and Drones

The Three Laws of Robotics, from the "Handbook of Robotics, 56th Edition, 2058 A.D.":

1. A robot may not injure a human being or, through inaction, allow a human being to come to harm.
2. A robot must obey the orders given it by human beings except where such orders would conflict with the First Law.
3. A robot must protect its own existence as long as such protection does not conflict with the First or Second Laws.

ISAAC ASIMOV,
'Runaround', 1942[1]

In the Star Wars series the most formidable of all weapons was the Death Star, a moon-sized battle station constructed by the Galactic Empire. It had one weapon—a superlaser capable of destroying planets. The aim was to suppress the rebels by confronting them with an irresistible force, demonstrated when the planet Alderaan was destroyed. But the rebels got hold of the Death Star's plans and noticed that it had one vulnerability, a small thermal exhaust port linked to the main reactor. Leading a desperate attack the young Jedi Luke Skywalker managed to fire a torpedo through the port and destroy the whole system[2]. The Galactic Empire then went on to construct a second, and even larger, Death Star but the programme was subject to severe delays, prompting great anger from the evil Darth Vader.[3] This was also taken out by the rebels and this time before it had a chance to fire its weapon. In 2012 a petition was placed on the White House's website urging that a real Death Star be built in order to stimulate the economy and defend the nation. The Obama Administration offered three reasons for rejecting the petition. First, the cost would be $850,000,000,000,000,000. Second, it was not policy to blow up planets. Third, why 'spend countless taxpayer dollars on a Death Star with a fundamental flaw that can be exploited by a one-man starship?'

Dan Ward, a specialist in defence acquisition, saw the Death Star as a metaphor for what had gone wrong with weapons design in the Pentagon. It would always be a challenge to build such a large and complex system without overlooking some critical vulnerability.[4] Only one of these could be built at a time so that if the vulnerability proved fatal there was no benefit at all from the investment. By contrast, he noted, the simple, inexpensive and small droid—R2D2—was constantly showing its value. Whereas Death Stars were about brute force, droids were about finesse.[5]

The charge that the fixation with mighty and intimidating platforms would lead to unnecessarily complicated and unaffordable weapons was familiar. As the digital revolution progressed there were constant warnings that far too much attention was still being paid to expensive platforms, which were vulnerable to relatively cheap missiles, and not the long-range weapons systems that they were supposed to carry and which would enable them to operate at some distance from danger. The military attachment to its big-ticket items was hard to shake off. In 1984 Norm Augustine plotted the exponential growth of unit costs for fighter aircraft since 1910 and then pointed to an absurd conclusion:

> In the year 2054, the entire defense budget will purchase just one tactical aircraft. This aircraft will have to be shared by the Air Force and the Navy 3½ days each per week except for leap year, when it will be made available to the marines for the extra day.[6]

The $1.5 trillion F-35 programme, leading to unit costs of $100 million per aircraft, suggested that the problem was a real one, and that eventually the qualitative edge that might be provided by the most advanced platforms and missiles would be lost by reduced quantity. While the US Navy and Air Force budgets grew in real terms at 22 per cent and 27 per cent respectively from 2001 to 2008 the number of combat ships declined by 10 per cent and combat aircraft by 20 per cent. Eventually, when faced with numerous targets, the military would run out of weapons. One response was to look to droids equivalents. 'Uninhabited systems' could 'help bring mass back to the fight' by expanding 'the number of sensors and shooters in the fight' at relatively low cost. With a lower premium on survivability a greater emphasis could be put into having large numbers of systems in action at any time.[7]

EARLY IN THE TWENTY-FIRST CENTURY THE FIRST UNINHABITED systems to attract wide notice were unmanned aerial vehicles, or drones, carrying deadly missiles. They could hover above targets, re-laying information back to a distant operator who could then decide whether to unleash a missile. Rudimentary drones had existed since the First World War, used for example for target practice as well as intelligence gathering. The modern concept of drones could be traced back to an Israeli designer Abraham Karem who was convinced that they could be used to provide real-time intelligence. After the *Gnat*, which was deployed in the Balkans, came the *Predator*.[8] After 9/11 *Predator* was armed with *Hellfire* air-to-ground missiles and deployed to Afghanistan. At the same time, the Bush Administration adopted legal guidelines that gave the CIA wide powers to kill al-Qaeda ter-rorists anywhere in the world. Places where the US had little to work with on the ground, such as Yemen, Somalia, and parts of Pakistan, attracted particular attention. In November 2002, a drone struck a suspected al-Qaeda leader and five of his associates in Yemen, signal-ling that the United States was prepared to take out its enemies be-yond a recognised combat zone. In 2007 the *Reaper*—described as a 'true hunter-killer'—came into service.

Drones brought together many critical technologies: highly effi-cient engines, advanced sensors, the global positioning systems, and instantaneous communications. Their operators could identify, mon-itor, and then strike a target thousands of miles away, without putting American lives in direct danger. Because they hovered over their tar-gets for hours there was greater confidence than there could be with manned aircraft that appropriate targets were chosen, with innocent civilians hopefully out of the way. They were nonetheless criticized on two grounds. First, they created situations of complete asymmetry.

The drone pilots faced no dangers and could live a relatively normal life in their free time, picking up their kids from school after killing someone on the other side of the planet: their victims knew nothing about their impending doom and could not challenge their covert death sentences, let alone fight back. Second, targeted killing was ethically and legally dubious, and of uncertain strategic value.

The first issue had been raised from the start of air power. It was thrown into relief once Western air power enjoyed freedom of the skies. Michael Ignatieff described the 1999 Kosovo War as a 'virtual' conflict, at least for citizens in the NATO countries. Such one-sided fighting he complained was too much like a 'spectacle,' which aroused 'emotions in the intense but shallow way that sports do.'[9] Yet, if anything, drone pilots knew their human targets better than most, as they watched them before striking and then, after the strike, were able to see what was left of the victim and whoever else stepped into the frame at the last minute. Though the stress might be less than that experienced in actual combat, the drone pilots were not just playing glorified computer games. Yet on the second issue there was a question of impunity and moral hazard. Was it too easy to mount attacks without worrying much about the ethical implications?

The practice of targeted killing was developed by the Israelis after they had withdrawn from the Gaza Strip and were trying to find ways of coping with the threat posed by Hamas. The Bush and then Obama Administrations picked up on the idea as a way of dealing with radical Islamist groups, especially those operating in territories where it was difficult to reach them on the ground. This reflected a sharp focus on hostile groups prepared to attack the US homeland as well as its citizens and assets abroad. The numbers involved were small and the casualties caused by terrorism were not in themselves large, but their randomness and viciousness meant that the danger could not be ignored. The most important responses involved good intelligence, domestic policing, and addressing the social position of Muslim communities in Western countries. But even those militants living in the West gained their inspiration, and sometime recruitment and training, from countries in which there were active Islamist groups. The objective was to degrade them by taking out identified individuals, either because they were leaders or had specific skills, such as bomb-making. Here drones seemed to be the perfect weapon for personalised killing.[10]

There was evidence that decapitating an insurgent group could reduce its effectiveness, while relentless attacks on key cadres would leave them weakened.[11] Occasional attacks, however, risked creating gaps that would quickly be filled, possibly with leaders who might be even more ruthless.[12] In addition, finding the right people to kill was not always straightforward. There were, therefore, significant civilian casualties, resulting from haphazard intelligence, local tipsters providing false information to help eliminate rivals, or excessive confidence in 'signature' strikes, in which individuals were killed because their behavior suggested that they were up to no good, even though there was no definite proof.[13]

While the number being killed was comparatively low, at least compared with what else was going on in these conflicts, individual incidents (such as wedding parties being struck) caused anger. The 'blowback' from killing civilians was said to be counterproductive, risking a loss of local support and inspiring more recruits to join insurgent groups, thereby outweighing any gains from killing particular militants. The temptation to use drones to gain tactical victories even though they provide scant strategic benefit was described as addictive.[14] There was little evidence of addiction. Perhaps because the benefits were hard to confirm, while profound ethical and legal issues were being raised, the Obama Administration cut back on their use in Pakistan in 2012, and then worked to develop guidelines on targeting. As the number of drone strikes in Pakistan and Yemen fell, so, too, did civilian casualties.[15]

Unmanned systems had other roles in counter-insurgency, for example in dealing with Improvised Explosive Devices (IEDs). All this harked back to the early expectations of robot war, with all the anticipated advantages: 'They don't get hungry. They're not afraid. They don't forget their orders. They don't care if the guy next to them has been shot. Will they do a better job than humans? Yes.'[16] Yet while they might allow their operators to stay out of harm's way they still needed to be controlled. So-called unmanned systems appeared to require large numbers of people to operate them effectively. Moreover these systems were flattered when dealing with insurgencies. Against more capable opponents, drones, with their slow speed, low altitude, and vulnerability to air defences and electronic countermeasures, would be more restricted in their use. In conventional war the effectiveness of existing systems would be limited because of the the speed with which an automated system might process and act upon evidence of danger or a vulnerable target, and the risks of malfunction and enemy interference.

Under the Obama Administration, the US adopted a strategy (described as the 'Third Offset' to capture the idea that it must use technological strengths to compensate for the advantages of its opponents) based on 'collaborative human-machine battle networks that synchronize simultaneous operations in space, air, sea, undersea, ground, and cyber domains'.[17] To the fore was artificial intelligence allowing decision-making authority to be delegated to machines. This strategy looked forward to systems capable of managing big data, supporting human decisions so that they were better and faster, and also humans in combat, for example with wearable electronics and apps, and getting better cooperation between manned and unmanned systems. Defensive systems might work 'at the speed of light' to respond to attack while offensives would be more efficient, so that the lead rocket in a salvo could ensure that those following were sent to the best targets.

How far could this go? Nanotechnology, the manipulation of individual atoms and molecules, particularly important in biomedicine, offered the prospect of extraordinary miniaturisation. It was possible to imagine insect-like drones taking pictures at will and even injecting individuals with poisons, perhaps after checking their DNA, or else uniforms that could sense danger nearby, alert medics of injury, and even begin treatments of their own. In one particularly alarming account a physicist described how nanoweapons might destabilise the balance of power, with dramatic scenarios of 'nano-electronics guiding hypersonic intercontinental ballistic missiles or millions of insect-sized nanobots [nano-scale robots] capable of assassinating the population of a nation', leading mankind to extinction. Louis Del Monte envisaged a line of development from computers designing nanoweapons, within parameters set by humans, to a 'singularity computer', one more intelligent than the whole human race, in place by 2050.[18] All this required enormous technical problems to be solved in miniature—including the furnishing of these tiny robots with a power source, antennae, communication, and steering.[19]

Well before such issues arose there were still troubling matters to be addressed. Artificial intelligence referred to computer systems capable of performing tasks normally requiring human intelligence, such as visual perception, speech recognition, and decision-making.[20]

This could involve quite mundane tasks. At issue therefore was the level of complexity that could be achieved. In war this would require selecting and engaging targets without meaningful human control, so that their behaviour would vary according to circumstances even in the same broad operating environment. The levels moved from systems that were human operated, to those where humans delegated and then supervised, to full autonomy. The system's reasoning ability and choices would depend upon the quality of its sensors and the algorithms through which information was processed. It would not be following a standard script but would make up its own scripts as situations developed. The 'Terminator Conundrum', referring to the robotic assassin played by Arnold Schwarzenegger in a series of movies, described the issues raised by an independent machine able to decide whom to kill. The choices would require not only good information but also an ethical sensibility. 'Should a drone fire on a house where a target is known to be hiding, which may also be sheltering civilians?'[21]

In practice it was likely that machines would remain 'teamed' with humans, who would remain 'in the loop', able to countermand the notionally autonomous systems if they made poor choices. As with any soldiers the problems were likely to result not so much from formal command arrangements as from the contingencies of battle. Ideal subordinates in any military command chain were sufficiently obedient to follow orders as given but also capable when necessary of taking decisions on their own, perhaps because communications were down or senior commanders had been killed. In such circumstances soldiers might run away or fight on their own initiative. So might robots, except they would turn off rather than run away. Control might also break down when distant human controllers could no longer cope with the speed and fluidity of a battle so that decisions on targets had to be delegated to the machines. This could escalate a confused situation, so that fire from a friendly source could rapidly lead to a fratricidal fight.

IT WAS ONE THING TO HAVE FAR BETTER SITUATIONAL AWARE-ness or logistics, and even a degree of automatic protection when a unit or individual might be caught by surprise. It was quite another to have systems leading themselves with the humans playing supporting roles. And then there were the obvious nightmares about rogue systems turning on their supposed masters or just deciding against a critical mission. One way to interfere with drones (especially the simpler, commercial models) was to develop means of interfering with their electronics. Given the concerns about hacking, how much reliance could be placed on systems that might be 'turned' if penetrated by a foreign power? There was a logical interaction with the developing debate on cyber-war, which was all about a constant struggle between the offence and defence over the security and integrity of information, and this debate which often presumed that great trust could be put in the programmed decision-making of autonomous systems.

The future may not arrive so quickly. There were always obstacles to technological advances. The introduction of new capabilities, especially without the urgency of an ongoing war, was usually far slower than futurists supposed or enthusiasts found acceptable. Military organisations had been known to resist anything which threatened human redundancy, for example in the 1950s Strategic Air Command resisted ICBMs as alternatives to manned bombers. In addition the record of turning exciting new technologies into actual systems was less impressive than often supposed, with funding, bureaucratic, and engineering issues often causing severe delays.[22]

Another factor affecting the introduction of autonomous vehicles was that the lead with the new technologies was taken by the private sector. The most developed example was a driverless car, a much more challenging machine than a drone and one expected to have much more autonomy. As it moved forward on the ground it had to be aware of numerous potential obstacles and other vehicles with their own dynamics. The challenge grew the more urban and dynamic the operating environment. Driverless cars were first developed as a Pentagon programme in 2004 but resources were only poured into it as a commercial venture, which not only meant that the advances were out of state control but also that the state took second place in competition for the skilled engineers and software developers needed to take the work forward. Competition for a mass market and vast R&D expenditures moved driverless cars to viable products while military programmes for autonomous vehicles lagged behind.

A key feature of many of the vital systems introduced for the digital age, including Internet providers, search engines, hardware manufacturers, and software developers, was that they were owned and operated by private companies with global interests. Smartphones carried capabilities such as satellite imaging, navigations, data stores, and instant, encrypted communications of a quality once available to only the most advanced military organisations. Even drones were mass-produced, for aerial surveillance of local neighbourhoods and carrying items over distances, and so opened up the possibility of also delivering crude explosives.

These readily accessible systems made it possible for individuals and small groups to hurt others. They also showed how individuals and communities, living in apparent safety, were becoming exposed to new risks. Attacks could come without reason and notice, from across hemispheres yet with extraordinary speed, taking in the innocent as well as intended victims.[23] Here the fears about new technology became linked with developing concerns about terrorism. With many examples of extreme Islamist groups, or just 'lone wolf' supporters, ready to attack random civilian targets in Western countries, it was natural enough to worry about what might be done with access to the most lethal technologies. This had been high on the security agenda since 9/11. Yet for extremist groups the most obvious advantages of the Internet were found in their smartphone apps: the ability to disseminate messages to vast audiences around the world without interference, harass opponents, post videos of their victims and martyrs, while they took advantage of encrypted communications. When it came to killing one feature of many terrorist atrocities was the simplicity of their methods—knives, bombs and guns, or driving trucks into crowds. These weapons were crude but effective, well understood by those using them and with proven capabilities, demanding no special expertise to make them work.

So while the new technologies were developed with large wars in mind their applications were found in the context of insurgencies and social disorder. The team of Arquilla and Ronfeldt offered a conceptual way forward that might link the two types of warfare. They described an approach to battle based on 'swarming', distinguished from 'the chaotic melee, brute-force massing, and nimble maneuver' of the past. This required a progressive improvement in the ability to coordinate and command individual units. With swarming targets were attacked from all directions by 'myriad, small, dispersed, networked maneuver units'. It was relevant, they argued, to anything from social activism to high-intensity warfare yet to gain the greatest advantage (so that action did not degenerate into a melee) there would need to be some central strategic control.[24] At a basic level this could be observed with guerrilla warfare. At a higher level, technological developments might make it possible to synchronise attacks undertaken by devolved robots to ensure maximum effectiveness. It was a natural approach for a networked organisation because it could gain the maximum advantage from the ability of a number of separate units to communicate with each other and execute complex movements and patterns of fire.

As attention moved to robotic systems, Paul Scharre noted how well they were suited to swarming. This would require moving from having individual units each with their own operators to a central command being able to manage many at a time, although at some point it was possible to imagine the individual units being self-coordinating while seeking to disrupt the capacity of an incoming enemy swarm.[25] Conceptually the idea of swarming, and its potential applications in war-fighting, was not difficult to grasp. It offered new ways to defeat an opponent. As with much of the military thinking of the digital age, it was easier to imagine swarming in the air or at sea (as in fighter aircraft or submarine wolf packs of the Second World War) where there would be fewer obstacles or sources of confusion than there would be on land. What it could not do was provide an answer to the problem of holding territory and especially cities in the face of a hostile population.

It was territory that still mattered most. The most serious danger posed by Islamist groups, for example, came in 2014 from their control of chunks of Syria and then Iraq, to the point of proclaiming their own state.[26] The Islamic State of Iraq and Syria (ISIS) attracted activists from around the world to join its ranks and potentially offered a base which would allow them to train these activists and send them around the world to cause trouble. Drones had a role to play in the campaigns to dislodge them, not least in streaming real-time intelligence, but little could be done without ground forces provided by local powers. Though the technology would improve, the basic limitation of air power still applied. Territory could not be won or controlled from the air, whether by drones, helicopters, or jets, without the benefit of supporting ground forces. The idea of robot armies had a certain appeal, but they would struggle with counter-insurgency when the enemy mingled with the local population, or if the militants learnt how to confuse the sensors of the systems coming after them.[27] It was a constant temptation to believe that there were technical fixes for what were essentially political problems, but they often turned out to be sub-optimal in their effects. In her history of the Defense

Advanced Research Projects Agency (DARPA), Sharon Weinberger noted that 'press releases tout devices that can help soldiers scale glass skyscrapers, while American forces fight in a country dominated by mud houses'.[28]

Thus while the weapons demonstrated the possibility of attacks of ever-greater complexity, precision, and speed over ever-greater distances, with reduced risks to the operators, they did not answer the question of exactly what was being achieved. Numbers were still needed to take and control territory, and it was the effort this required that put a strain on Western countries. After 9/11 President Bush accepted that if the United States neglected unstable parts of the world it could get caught out. 'We will fight them over there so we do not have to face them in the United States of America.'[29] By 2014 President Obama, after being faced with a decision on Syria in 2013, decided that the public's tolerance for expeditionary warfare of the sort seen in Iraq and Afghanistan had been exhausted: 'the time of deploying large ground forces with big military footprints to engage in nation-building overseas, that's coming to an end.'[30] The reliance on drones to engage in targeted killings was part of that determination. It was also possible to note that defences in the form of intelligence and police work had not done a bad job in preventing another 9/11. Indeed, for all the talk about developing vulnerabilities and the erosion of distance, defensive measures along with natural barriers— such as oceans and mountain ranges—could still make a difference. Even a country as potentially exposed as Israel put as much effort into improving its means of defence, from security walls to anti-missile systems, as it did perfecting new means of attack. Despite the common assumption about globalised war, geography still made a difference. Technology did not necessarily 'trump terrain'.[31]

From Israel came proposals for another way of approaching threats emanating from territories that would be difficult to control directly. Instead of re-occupation of territory which had been relinquished because past occupations had resulted in substantial harm and upset over the years, an alternative was to rely on raiding. This had traditionally been a transient strategy, knocking back an opponent, while lacking both the benefits and costs of taking full control.[32] Looking back at the Lebanon War of 2006, which been judged a failure at the time, it seemed that enough had been done to dissuade Hezbollah from further provocations (although it could also be noted that Hezbollah were stretched in Syria trying to preserve the Assad regime). The point of a raiding strategy was to make it hard for hostile groups to assume that they had sanctuaries from which to mount their attacks:

> Raids offer a valid way to curb the threat and contain it at minimum risk and cost. In addition to continuous small raids from the air and by special operations forces, larger raids with heavy ground forces are needed periodically to "mow the grass", that is, to inflict heavy losses and impair the opponents' capabilities.[33]

At the heart of the exploration of this alternative was the search for a way of avoiding the grief and cost of prolonged occupation. Arguably if US forces had left Iraq soon after Saddam Hussein had been toppled in 2003, then most of the US goals would have been accomplished. To be sure there could have been mayhem in Iraq as a consequence, but that was hardly absent with the occupation.[34] But leaving behind disorder and chaos without any effort to set the society on a more stable path would have just stored up trouble for the future. In 2011 Western countries helped defeat President Gaddafi in Libya but refrained from getting involved on the ground to help stabilise the situation in the aftermath.[35] The result was vicious faction fighting, opportunities for Islamists, and refugees desperate to get to the West by any means available.

Raiding could wear down an opponent's resitance and remove some capability, but it was unlikely to do more than contain a problem, as Israel's own history demonstrated. It was one thing when used against a relatively stable opponent (Hamas in Gaza) but another when the consequences could only be chaotic. H. R. McMaster saw raids as being of short duration and limited purpose, unable 'to effect the human and political drivers of armed conflict or make progress toward achieving sustainable outcomes consistent with vital interests'.[36]

AS RESEARCH PROJECTS MOVED INTO CYBER WARFARE, artificial intelligence, and robotics, science fiction was a natural place to go for insights.[37] In 2015 journalist August Cole combined with policy analyst Peter Singer in *Ghost Fleet*, a novel that combined concerns about China with energy scarcity with the developing technologies of war. Their inspiration was Tom Clancy's *Red Storm Rising*.[38] Their aim with this 'useful fiction', based on extensive research (the book had 400 endnotes), was to wrestle with the issues surrounding a future great-power conflict in order to 'help prevent such a confrontation from straying from the novel to the actual battlefield.'

Ghost Fleet described an old-fashioned geopolitical war with China. It opened with a surprise attack designed by the Chinese leadership, and so in the tradition of attempted knockout blows. The trigger was an energy crisis, resulting from the aftermath of an Iran-Saudi war, a combination of crashed global markets and a vastly inflated oil price. The Chinese leadership, a military-industrial elite, were irritated at the way that the US, secure in its own energy supplies, interfered with China's ambitions, and threatened economic sanctions to get its way. A large gas field, which only China could reach and exploit, promised economic security but needed protection. The theme of the admiral who drove the war policy, as with his Japanese counterpart in 1941, was that there was no choice. The Americans must be made to come to terms with China's rise. This was not the time to 'grow meek on the brink of the next great step.' It was 'a simple question of the arc of history: If now is not the time, then when?'

The surprise attack plan was complex. It involved taking out supporting infrastructure (including space-based elements), and neutralising the most advanced components of the US Navy and Air Force. This included disabling the software packages on the US F-35s (which unfortunately for the Americans included a Chinese microchip) and tracking nuclear submarines. The plan also depended on an alliance with Russia, which was otherwise assumed to be on the brink of war with China. This all required skillful orchestration, reliance on untried methods, and also a massive failure of American intelligence. It was also a gamble because it was assumed that nuclear weapons would not be used. American ballistic-missile carrying submarines were not attacked although they might have been. Sparing them signalled to Washington that there was to be no escalation to the highest level. According to one of the key characters, by the time the government worked out what was going on, there was no point: 'going nuclear would just be revenge to the point of suicide'. They could not even be sure that the orders would get through.

The Chinese were still left with the problem that the United States was not actually defeated. The three classic problems with a surprise attack that fell short of a knockout blow manifested themselves. First, popular resistance developed on Hawaii, which had been occupied by the Chinese. Second, not all American forces were destroyed. The situation was saved by the 'ghost fleet' of the title, referring to mothballed ships kept in reserve, which could now be revived and refitted for duty, just as old aircraft were found to replace the sadly ineffectual F-35s. Third, while most allies had been pathetic and no help at all to the Americans, the Anglosphere of Britain and Australia were still supportive. The country still functioned and was able to work out how to retrieve the situation. Manufacturing resumed, in part due to 3-D printing. In the end the US fought back sufficiently to regain something of the old order. The conclusion was a messy stalemate, both sides having 'shown they could pound each other into a weakened equilibrium' with 'most of each other's fleets' now sunk.

Ghost Fleet warned of the over-reliance on advanced technologies and a failure to think through their software vulnerabilities, and reminded of the importance of patriotism, heroism, and individual initiative. The preference of Singer and Cole was simpler and more agile systems, with quick impact, such as drones, rail guns, and lasers. They also show how personalised war could become, including individual aids to fighting whether in the form of stimulants that make it possible to cope with fatigue and strain, or a version of Google glasses which enabled immediate access to information. In its core scenario for the surprise attack, *Ghost Fleet* fitted in with what *The Economist* described as a distinctive feature of the genre that began with *The Battle of Dorking*, by presenting 'new technologies as decisive, both a thrilling idea and a necessary device if ... dominant nations were to be portrayed, initially at least, as victims,' and as a means of imparting a stark message 'of the wrongheadedness of politicians or senior officers, of national decline, of geopolitical change'.[39]

Cole was to the fore in an Atlantic Council project encouraging authors to generate insights in its 'Art of Future Warfare Project'.[40] One early product was a slim volume of short stories to demonstrate how fiction might alert policymakers to future possibilities. The themes varied from an American senator making an effective political pitch by encouraging crowdsourced cyber-attacks on Russian and Chinese systems to British intelligence analysts attempting to profile the population to pick out likely terrorists (in this case missing the brother of one of the analysts), to drone operators who could see distant battles better than those fighting them and so advise constantly on coming dangers and vulnerable targets. The heroes, male or female, achieved their goals because of their mental rather than physical toughness. They tended to be super-smart graduates of the best universities, grasping the powerful technologies at their command. Following the long traditions of military literature they were often mavericks, unimpressed by authority yet patriotic to the core.

The origins of their wars were often traced back to previous wars, the details of which were dimly remembered though they had left the world unstable and prone to yet more conflict. Despite this wretched history of chaos and mayhem, somehow the science of war had progressed and even more ingenious methods found for taking out the enemy. The drama came from the tactical and operational, as these super-smart people made their complex systems do whatever they needed them to do. The strategic picture remained murky. They were fighting the evil and malign because they could not let them win. Behind all this lay some great political failure, but that was not where the story was to be found.

[23]

Mega-Cities and
Climate Change

In our world there are still people who run around risking their lives
in bloody battles over a name or a flag or a piece of clothing but
they tend to belong to gangs with names like the Bloods and the
Crips and they make their living dealing drugs.

FRANCIS FUKUYAMA,
The End of History, 1992[1]

As Fukuyama looked with optimism at the West's liberal triumph
in the early 1990s, there was also anxiety about whether a lack
of anything serious to fight about would lead it into a soft decadence. The Bloods and the Crips were two famous Los Angeles street
gangs. The Bloods were formed at first to resist the influence of the
Crips in their neighbourhoods. They later came to be known for a
'take-no-prisoners' attitude and violence. During the 1980s they had
divided up into smaller sets and began to compete for control of
different neighbourhoods. Their involvement in narcotics led them
to grow in size and take their rivalry across the United States, often
in alliance with other city gangs.[2] Gang warfare pointed to an important feature of contemporary violence that would grow in salience, although it was normally discussed as if it had little to do
with actual war.

Edward Newman, writing when analyses suggested a definite decline in the numbers of civil wars, argued that this focused on a 'classical' model of civil war which essentially involved major forces in competition, those of the government versus those challenging it for anti-colonial, ideological, or secessionist reasons. What was neglected and excluded, he warned, were 'a broad phenomenon of political and social violence characteristic of low-intensity conflict, low-level insurgencies, and state weakness.'[3] The statistics of war only acknowledged deaths that occurred in battle, but battle accounted only for a moderate percentage of the annual tally of violent deaths—some 17 per cent of the total between 2010 and 2015. By contrast intentional homicides counted for 69 per cent. While it was the case that countries racked by civil war were dangerous places to live, even more so were many Latin American and Caribbean countries that, strictly speaking, were not at war. This was the only region in the world where rates of lethal violence increased after 2000. It was also the most urbanised part of the world, with 80 per cent of the population living in cities. Some forty-five of the fifty most dangerous metropolises in the world were in Latin America. In general internationally, while rural violence had been in decline, urban violence was rising.[4]

A focus on cities developed as the international organisations concerned with development found the concept of 'fragile state' more useful than the loaded concept of 'failed state'. If the problem was seen largely as one of disorder and violence then military coups and repression could be presented as solutions, not least by those responsible, even though this was rarely peaceful or durable. A fragility framework, by contrast, could take in a range of issues, keeping a sharp focus on issues of governance. A fragile state was one lacking representation and accountability, stable legal standards, and checks to coercive action by the state, combined with an inability to control territory and borders.[5] It also took in economic management and social cohesion. As states were examined for signs of fragility, and by these standards most states had some, it became apparent that in many cases the fragility was concentrated in particular spaces, especially cities. The growth of cities was a striking trend that was set to continue. According to the United Nations in 2016, there were 512 cities around the world with at least 1 million inhabitants, and 31 megacities with at least 10 million inhabitants. By 2030 these numbers were projected to grow to 662 and 41 respectively.[6] More than half of the world's population lived in cities. As the bulk of population growth took place in cities this number would grow.

By and large urbanisation was a positive development, promoting economic growth and bringing people out of poverty. There were reasons why people gravitated to cities as places to find work and enjoy life. Much of the urban growth was in medium-sized cities that coped well. Yet there were places where this rapid urbanisation resulted in a miserable, stressed environment damaging the inhabitants. Tensions were generated as people became compressed into relatively confined urban areas, competing for scarce resources in ramshackle housing, amidst poverty and poor sanitation, without effective governance and ineffectual policing. Violence was an unsurprising result. Robert Muggah described cities as 'the new frontier of warfare.'[7] Cities have long been the setting for insurrections, mob violence, and crime, but this was reaching a new level. Christopher Coker noted how the fate of their inhabitants was compared with junkyards and waste-disposal, and, with extreme wealth often being found not far away, of being 'supersaturated with Darwinian competition'.[8] In 2003 Richard Norton wrote of 'feral cities', defined as 'metropolises with population of more than a million people in a state the government of which has lost the ability to maintain the rule of law within the city's boundaries yet remains a functioning actor in the greater international system.' In many cases not only was effective policing absent but also the police force had 'become merely another armed group seeking power and wealth. Citizens must provide for their own protection, perhaps by hiring independent security personnel or paying protection to criminals.'[9] In such settings gangs controlled the slums and shanty towns, whether in the form of structured criminal organisations, groups that just hung about together, watching over their territory, or vigilante groups put together by local communities who had given up on the police.[10]

Most had little interest in directly challenging the state, so long as they were left alone, but those with both muscle and wealth, often because of drug trafficking, could challenge governments. When insurgencies did develop they were suited to urban areas. Battles have tended to be rural affairs. As we have noted already cities had always been seen as trouble by advancing military forces, which is why they went out of their way to bypass them or else relied on frustrating sieges. The equipment and tactics of sophisticated armies usually worked better in the open.[11] Yet the issue of cities could not be avoided. In any war with North Korea one of the South's greatest vulnerabilities was the location of its capital and mega-city Seoul close to the border, within artillery range. Even if the urban fights in the invasions of Afghanistan and Iraq had proved to be less demanding than anticipated this was not the case with the subsequent insurgencies. When it came to terrorism, prosperous cities offered many targets, with an outrage likely to shut down city centres, close down transportation networks, and gain early media commentary as those on the spot distributed details almost immediately. This was far more than could ever be achieved in a rural outpost. Refugees, especially if they had been forced out of city homes, tended to pour into other cities when possible, putting a strain on public services and potentially creating new tensions. This could be seen in the impact of the Syrian War on Jordan and the Lebanon. The latter hosted 1.1 million registered refugees, compared with a total population of 4.4 million, and the influx threatened the balance of sectarian power within the country.

A US Army study described megacities as 'becoming the epicenters of human activity on the planet and, as such, they will generate most of the friction which compels future military intervention'. The study looked, inter alia, at two Brazilian cities: São Paulo in May 2006 when over 1,300 attacks were launched by individuals associated with First Command of the Capital (PCC) drug gang and, at the same time, riots occurred in seventy-three prisons. The government found itself negotiating with the prison drug gang in Rio in November 2010 when over 3,000 police officers and military personnel were required to end city-wide violence emanating from a single favela (slum community) out of the city's 600.[12] San Pedro Sula in Honduras regularly appeared as one the most violent cities in the world. The reason for this was that so much economic activity was channelled through the city, offering rich opportunities for extortion, and so it became a place where criminal gangs fought each other for the privilege. It was also vital to trafficking in cocaine, and so engaged other gangs, including from neighbouring countries. In Mexico, which could never be considered in any way a failed state, there was horrific violence resulting in well over 120,000 deaths, connected with government attempts to crack down on drug trafficking syndicates, responsible for the bulk of the cocaine reaching the United States. The potential interaction with political violence could be seen in Colombia. There had been a full-blooded civil war from 1948 into the early 1950s, followed by fighting between left-wing guerrilla groups and right-wing paramilitaries that lasted until the 1990s, and then, after subsiding, picked up again, as the government decided it was time to crack down on the main militia, FARC, which subsidised its insurgency with drug-trafficking, and was also able to use neighbouring Ecuador and Venezuela for sanctuaries.[13]

One view was that fighting for profit came under a different heading to fighting for ideology or power. Yet, as FARC demonstrated, the categories could not easily be distinguished. Those criminal groups that moved beyond the level of street gangs to organised business with their own distribution systems, political and financial networks, and coercive means could challenge states and undermine their authority, or else become part of their power structures.[14] In an examination of the situation in Rio de Janeiro in early 2017 Robert Muggah asked whether the violence in the city had reached a stage where it deserved to be considered as 'armed conflict'. Over 6,000 people had been assassinated in 2016, a rate of 41 homicides per 100,000 residents. The military police were involved in killing 920 residents, while the casualty rate among the city's security forces was described as being higher than combatants in recent wars. As they moved into communities with armoured vehicles and assault rifles they faced well-armed groups, often fortified by former policemen who had swapped protection for extortion, and on occasion with access to heavy machine guns and rocket-propelled grenades. Stray bullets penetrate the walls of hospitals and schools. The norms of international humanitarian law, intended to protect civilians, needed to be applied as much in Rio as in any armed conflict.[15] Phil Williams observed that violence in Mexico, also comparable to civil wars elsewhere, was multi-layered. Some was personal and careless, but much related to the rivalry between criminal organisations engaged in the drug trade as well as factionalism within them. It resembled, he noted, 'Mafia clan violence in Sicily, blood feuds among criminal organizations in Albania, and the upsurge in contract killings in Russia during the 1990s.'[16] While terrorism was readily included in analyses of contemporary conflict this was less so with criminal organisations. Yet while the state might be functioning unimpaired the society was still being damaged.

WHAT WAS DISCUSSED MUCH MORE WAS 'RESOURCE WARS'. One feature of many war scenarios involved a struggle to control energy supplies. These often assumed that oil reserves had peaked and that expanding economies (with China an important addition) were going to struggle to find what they needed. For some analysts this, as much as any other geopolitical factor, was likely to drive future conflict.[17] Countries such as Russia, with its vast energy resources, could well find itself in a pivotal position, able to dictate terms, and influence European foreign policies because it could turn gas supplies on and off. From the moment he took power, Vladimir Putin of Russia saw the country as a potential 'energy superpower' and the means by which it could be restored to its rightful place in the international hierarchy.[18]

Energy resources were not only vital to the functioning of modern economies but also a great wealth generator for those fortunate enough to be sitting atop oil reserves or playing major roles in its extraction and distribution. The distribution of oil reserves had a continuing geopolitical influence over the twentieth century. It helped identify strategic parts of the world, notably the Middle East, and also shaped military campaigns in fights to seize oil assets. It was an important aggravating factor in civil wars. Those with oil wealth were able to buy off domestic opponents and fund an assertive foreign policy, from military adventures to supporting proxies in other states. Greater risks might be taken than would otherwise be the case in addressing conflicts, such as the Iraqi takeover of Kuwait in 1990, because of the implications this might have for control of the oil market (especially if Iraq had moved into Saudi Arabia as well), or fears about control of transit routes, whether pipelines or choke points such as the Straits of Hormuz. At the most extreme, the value of oil assets provided a rare economic incentive for conquest.[19] There was an easy assumption, common among international relations students as much as radical conspiracy theorists, that oil was at the heart of the strategic calculations of the great powers.

At times when energy prices were high these concerns gained currency. This was true in the 1970s after the massive increase in the price of oil, the coincident imposition of an embargo by Arab oil producers on some Western states following the 1973 Arab-Israeli War, and the later impact of events such as the Iranian revolution. Yet in the 1980s the price fell dramatically, even while two oil producers—Iraq and Iran—were at war with each other. During the 2000s the price rose again, encouraging Russia in its optimism about becoming an energy superpower, but then in 2014 prices fell dramatically. Russia was left facing budget deficits but also a loss of markets, as its past attempts to coerce countries using its market position had led the targeted countries to seek alternative suppliers.[20] Meanwhile, because of the exploitation of shale gas, the US had become once again a major energy producer.

There was a familiar pattern to future projections of energy security, which was to assume that supply was close to its peak while demand was continuing to grow. Such claims tended to ignore more sanguine market information, failed to think about the impact of prices on discovery of new reserves or the development of more efficient alternatives to fossil fuels, and assumed that consumers would be left helpless after supplies were cut off without being able to find alternative routes.[21] It was less straightforward than assumed to disrupt supply for a long period. If anything, the United States might be as well placed to take advantage of the oil weapon (as it was on economic measures more generally) than others.[22] So while there was an oil dimension to many conflicts it was rarely the sole reason why a country would go to war. Cases attributed to oil motives often turned out to be about other issues. At most they reflected concerns about security of supply rather than greed.[23]

Although the oil issue had long been a feature of discussions about future conflict, in the 1990s another issue began to gain prominence. This posed more general problems of resource scarcity, made worse by the consequences of climate change. In 1994 Thomas Homer-Dixon of the University of Toronto reported the findings of a major research programme into what he called 'environmental security'. It opened with a stark prediction:

> Within the next fifty years, the planet's human population will probably pass nine billion, and global economic output may quintuple. Largely as a result, scarcities of renewable resources will increase sharply. The total area of high-quality agricultural land will drop, as will the extent of forests and the number of species they sustain. Coming generations will also see the widespread depletion and degradation of aquifers, rivers, and other water resources; the decline of many fisheries; and perhaps significant climate change.

These scarcities, he warned, were 'already contributing to violent conflicts in many parts of the developing world'. This was just the early stages of what would probably be an 'upsurge of violence in the coming decades that will be induced or aggravated by scarcity'. This would not lead to interstate wars but instead violence that would be 'sub-national, persistent, and diffuse', evident most in poor societies. The immediate causes would be population movements and the impoverishment of already weak states, possibly leading to their fragmentation.[24] Over the following two decades this concern grew and became bound up with the wider controversies about the extent of global warming, its consequences, and how it should be tackled.[25]

In 2007 UN Secretary-General Ban Ki-moon observed that while the conflict in Sudan's Darfur region was discussed as 'an ethnic conflict pitting Arab militias against black rebels and farmers,' it was one that had begun as an 'ecological crisis, arising at least in part from climate change.' A drought lasting two decades had meant that there was insufficient food and water, and this was in part responsible for the crisis.[26] One claim from the Intergovernmental Panel on Climate Change was that glaciers in the Himalayas would melt rapidly (this was later disputed), affecting agriculture in Pakistan and potentially aggravating the dispute with India over Kashmir.[27] In 2011 it was suggested that a sudden rise in food prices, which reached record highs, was one reason for the waves of protest and a factor in the protests that toppled Tunisian president Zine al-Abidine Ben Ali and Egyptian president Hosni Mubarak. Researchers for the UN's World Food programme noted that while there was little evidence to link food insecurity to interstate war it did increase the risk of 'democratic breakdown, civil conflict, protest, rioting, and communal conflict'. The evidence linking food insecurity to interstate conflict was less strong, though there was some historical evidence linking declining agricultural yields to periods of regional conflict in Europe and Asia.[28]

By 2015 the US National Security Strategy was identifying climate change as 'an urgent and growing threat to our national security contributing to increased natural disasters, refugee flows, and conflicts over basic resources like food and water'. The next year President Obama cited national security as a major reason why climate change had to be taken seriously, pointing to the refugee flows likely to result from rising sea levels and drought. He mentioned a case study that showed how 'the droughts that happened in Syria contributed to the unrest and the Syrian civil war. Well, if you start magnifying that across a lot of states, a lot of nation states that already contain a lot of poor people who are just right at the margins of survival, this becomes a national security issue.'[29] A September 2016 presidential memorandum urged more analysis of the threat,[30] while a report from the National Intelligence Council set out the issues.

> Long-term changes in climate will produce more extreme weather events and put greater stress on critical Earth systems like oceans, freshwater, and biodiversity. These in turn will almost certainly have significant effects, both direct and indirect, across social, economic, political, and security realms during the next 20 years. These effects will be all the more pronounced as people continue to concentrate in climate-vulnerable locations, such as coastal areas, water-stressed regions, and ever-growing cities.

As examples it cited how the terrorist group al-Shabaab exploited the 2011–13 famine in Somalia to coerce and tax international aid agencies, while insurgent groups in northern Mali used deepening desertification to enlist local people in a 'food for jihad' arrangement.[31]

As with energy security there was a presumption that issues of environmental security were unavoidable and were bound to intense disputes between communities and even states. This presumption was criticised as being too deterministic, not allowing for ways by which human ingenuity and economic incentives would lead to new ways of managing resources. A definite trend would have been evident in rising raw material prices, yet these had often fallen. Gloom-laden projections of this sort were not new, and their record was unimpressive. Societies coped more effectively than anticipated. Governments were capable of recognising that in the event of shortages cooperation often made more sense than conflict. This was evident even with water shortages—an issue which was often highlighted as the most likely source of conflict. Those predicting a dark future could not point to any established causal mechanisms.[32] One study described war over water as 'neither strategically rational, hydrographically effective, nor economically viable'. Another, looking hard at the causes of African civil wars, saw no 'robust correlational link between climate variability and civil war'.[33] Studies attempting to identify direct causal links between shifts in weather patterns and conflict produced spurious results because they ignored all the highly influential contextual factors. It was not that factors such as 'deforestation, land degradation, and scarce supply of freshwater, alone and in combination with high population density' were irrelevant to future conflict. They increased the risk of it happening within states. But they were unlikely to trigger war. The evidence pointed to the importance of levels of economic development and the nature of the political regime.[34]

The need to separate factors affecting the conduct of a conflict from those causing it was evident with claims about the impact of drought on Darfur. The International Peace Research Institute in Oslo questioned the claim:

> Warlords—who foster conflict—may exploit drought, flooding, starvation, agricultural or natural disasters in their strategies, like they did in Somalia and Darfur. But what will drive their fight is not the rain, the temperature, or the sea level—they will always fight for the same goals of power, territory, money, revenge, etc.

Similarly with Syria, a broad range of factors was behind the war. Drought did play a role in the country's economic decline,[35] but this was an aggravating factor. Wars, in the end, were not responses to poor living conditions but culminations of political struggles.

The main area where there did seem to be a correlation with environmental degradation was with non-state conflict, particularly in the rural areas of Sub-Saharan Africa. Non-state conflict was between armed groups neither of which represented the state. It was not about seeking to seize control of the state apparatus or about the overall balance of political power between rival groups within a state. It was more likely to involve local groups competing for scarce resources. When governments were weak and unable to exercise control over many areas within their notional borders, then peripheral communities coped as best they could on their own. By far the largest number of these conflicts were in Africa, often in countries suffering full-blown civil wars at the same time, and most appeared to be connected with local issues, including access to 'water, land, and livestock'. Environmental changes would be likely to trigger or aggravate these conflicts.[36] There was an obvious parallel here with urban gang warfare discussed earlier in this chapter, in forms of conflict that might not normally count in the mainstream discussions of war and peace but nonetheless reflected on the inability of some states to monopolise the legitimate use of physical force within their given borders.

[24]

Coming Wars

Well, at any rate, judging from this decision of yours, you seem to us to be quite unique in your ability to consider the future as something more certain than what is before your eyes, and to see uncertainties as realities, simply because you would like them to be so.

THUCYDIDES,
the Melian Dialogue[1]

'The least successful enterprise in Washington DC', observed Major General Bob Scales, was 'the one that places bets on the nature and character of tomorrow's wars.' It was a vast enterprise, involving 'the services, defense industries, and their supporting think tanks, along with Congress, academia, and the media'. Yet the success rate was poor. 'Virtually without exception, they get it wrong'.[2]

He identified five schools: 'Scenario Development', which simulated 'excuses for going to war with one of the usual suspects with serious military capabilities—China, Iran, North Korea', with Russia as the 'nostalgic favourite'. The 'Emerging Technology School' consisted of 'frightened and well-remunerated techno-warriors who constantly scan the threat horizon anxious to alert the security community to enemies who they sense are harnessing the diabolical genius of home-grown weapon makers'. They mistakenly assumed that enemies put the same trust in technologies as did the United States. The 'Capabilities-Based Assessment' school created a 'huge military toolbox from which weapons and forces can be retrieved and tailored to meet unforeseen threats.' The 'New Concepts Masquerading as Strategy' school was after a new 'war-fighting concept'. He cited examples such as 'shock and awe',[3] 'Net-centric warfare', and 'Effects-based operations'. Lastly the 'Global Trends School' sought 'to launder politically and socially popular global concerns into future military threats. These included global water supplies, HIV epidemics, [and] urbanization' but without actually explaining why they all led to war.

Reviewing the various prospectuses for future war published since the end of the Cold War, the influence of all these schools was there to be seen. They revealed much about prevailing perceptions about international and sub-state conflict and likely sources of trouble in coming years. The scenarios tended to be based on conflicts which were active, or at least latent, but currently lacked the spark that would turn them into war. The effort to find that spark provided the impetus to the literary creativity that went into generating scenarios for future war.[4]

AFTER THE SOVIET UNION COLLAPSED, THOSE LOOKING FOR a suitable 'peer competitor' to fill the large gap left had to cast about. The struggle to find a compelling prospective enemy was exemplified by the reliance upon Japan as a candidate. At the time Japan's reputation and influence were at its post-war peak, buoyed by its spectacular recent economic performance, based on its manufacturing strength. In 1988 the historian Paul Kennedy had assumed Japan's growing importance when considering *The Rise and Fall of Great Powers*, especially when set against relative American weakness.[5] This importance could be reflected in trade and financial policy without turning into a power struggle. Japan had been at war with the United States in living memory, but that was unlikely to be an experience that it wished to repeat.

In *The Coming War with Japan*, however, George Friedman and Meredith Lebard warned that, without the Cold War framework holding the United States and Japan together, deep economic differences were developing.[6] These pointed to a trade war as Americans worked to squeeze Japanese exports, first out of the US and then elsewhere. As Europe followed this protectionist logic, Japan was bound to create its own regional market, excluding the US. The US would push against this, leading to a military confrontation. This was the same logic that led to Pearl Harbor and the disaster of the last war, as if everything could be gambled in an effort to escape from dependence upon others for vital commodities. In a sympathetic review of Friedman and LeBard's book,

James Fallows considered talk of war 'extreme' but still warned that 'there is sure to be more antagonism than we have seen in the last forty years'.[7] The expectation was reflected in fiction, with economic tension (and racist depictions of the Japanese) behind Michael Crichton's *Rising Sun*,[8] and Tom Clancy's *Debt of Honor*, which involved combined military and economic action against the United States.[9]

As so often with predictive work of this sort, the trends were turning even as the books were published. Japan was entering into a long period of stagnation, and would struggle to hold on to its market position. Instead of aggressive economic policies, which tend to lead to market collapse, the Bush Senior and Clinton Administrations promoted the benefits of open trade. The scenarios also strained credibility by suggesting that Japan would think itself to be in a position to challenge the US militarily or that if it did this would be on a better basis than 1941. By 1998 the same team of Friedman and LeBard in a book on *The Future of War* had concluded that Japan would be 'loath to challenge American power' in the Pacific, although it could—unlike the Indians and Chinese who would never be able to find the resources to create a blue-water navy. Their core conclusion now was that, largely because of 'precision-guided munitions', this was 'a dramatically new global epoch in which the United States holds, and for the foreseeable future continues to hold, center stage'.[10] A decade later Friedman was still confident that the United States would remain the dominant global superpower through the twenty-first century but, in some flights of geopolitical fancy, the possibility of a Japanese-American war was revived, inevitably involving a 'sneak attack' (on Thanksgiving Day 2050). Japan was allied with Turkey, and eventually France and Germany, while on the American side was Britain, the 'Polish Bloc', India, and China. Friedman was less impressed with China than other forecasters. He predicted it would fragment in the 2010s.[11]

The most common reason to show how the United States might be in more peril than commonly realised was to encourage a higher level of military preparedness. In 1998 the former US Secretary of Defense Caspar Weinberger warned of 'victory disease', a complaint following success that meant the victims ignored the dangers they faced and so failed to make proper preparations. He offered a collection of complex scenarios combining fact and fiction, in a form somewhat derivative of Tom Clancy. Governments had to cope with more than one crisis at a time. While a full-scale war was raging on the Korean peninsula, escalating to nuclear use, China decided to seize Taiwan.

Iran not only inspired Islamic fundamentalists to overthrow secular Arab governments but also organised terrorist attacks in the United States, and a nuclear weapon was exploded in Europe. Mexico might be invaded in 2003 to topple a corrupt regime dealing in drugs and propelling vast numbers of refugees across the border into the US. Weinberger also revisited old struggles as a resurgent Russia sought to conquer Europe using its nuclear power, while in his version of Japan picking up from 1945, 'cyberstrikes' were involved as well as chemical and nuclear weapons. The focus was still on dangerous states and classical forms of war, with the added complications of weapons of mass destruction, rather than irregular threats involving guerrilla warfare and terrorism. As the US could get into so much trouble in so many ways, the key message was that it must rebuild its conventional forces and continue its pursuit of effective missile defences.[12]

By this time China was emerging as the most serious long-term challenger to the United States. This was always a more credible prospect than Japan. China was a much larger country than the United States, with a massive population, and by the late 1990s its economic growth was staggering. Its government was authoritarian, notionally communist, and historically antagonistic to the United States, even though relations had been warmer since the early 1970s and there was considerable economic interdependence. Most importantly, China was a genuinely revisionist power. It was dissatisfied with its current borders, considering them relics from a period when it was weak and regularly humiliated. Lastly, its civil war, which had led to the Communists dominating the mainland, still left its old enemies, the Nationalists, in charge of the island of Taiwan. Much of its diplomatic activity went into denying that Taiwan had any legitimacy as an independent entity.

Jed Babbin and Edward Timperlake, a conservative commentator and a former naval officer respectively, argued with a mixture of fact and fiction that as soon as China had a capability to strike the United States it would do so. They were not tied to any specific scenario, considering not only Taiwan but also the continued division of Korea (China had fought American troops in defence of North Korea in 1950) and its various claims around the Pacific Rim.[13] They imagined a President Hillary Clinton conceding most of Asia to China rather than have a fight, but also US nuclear use against North Korea and even Iran after they had used their nuclear weapons on other countries—Japan and Israel. Nonetheless, a nuclear exchange between China and the US was not in the plot. As with other such books the key themes depend on the rise of a new superpower, which it was assumed must come at the expense of the United States, an energy crisis of some sort which provided the trigger for conflict, and a conviction in Beijing that war was inevitable.

More than any of the other prospective threats the question of the rise of China acquired importance because it provided an occasion for a major debate on the future of naval power. Most scenarios for war inevitably involved the movement of forces on land, for wars were normally about the control of chunks of prized territory. The focus on civil wars had reinforced this preoccupation with land warfare. The naval consequences of the instability they represented tended to come down to the need to deal with piracy and people trafficking, as refugees took to dangerous boats to flee from violence in the Middle East to Europe.

Yet a backdrop to all post-1945 international affairs had been US mastery of the seas, and its ability to reach distant lands and exert power around the world. It was US naval strength that had allowed it to forge alliances in both Europe and Asia, to reach out to them with military reserves and essential supplies at times of crisis, and to threaten enemies with bombardment from the sea, economic blockade, or an amphibious landing. This had been very much in evidence during the 1991 Gulf War.[14]

As China grew economically so did its navy as the most palpable manifestation of its strength, posing a short-term challenge to the US in terms of its ability to assert freedom of navigation and in the longer-term to come the aid of its allies. The capability required by the Chinese if they were to get control of the seas close to their shores was described as 'Anti-Access/Area Denial', with its own acronym 'A2/AD'.[15] This focused debate on how far the Chinese military really had to go before they could challenge American naval predominance.[16] The A2/AD concept became too vague—either 'an impenetrable "keepout zone" that forces could enter only at extreme peril to themselves', a 'family of technologies' or a 'strategy.'[17] The issue pointed to a larger issue of whether the US could expect to continue to use its naval mastery to project power close to enemy shores, reflecting the problems of quality coming at the expense of quantity, so there were fewer platforms to go round, and how each expensive unit might be vulnerable to a variety of anti-ship weapons, including small, unmanned submarines. In this way the US-China strategic relationship came to be framed as a classic form of great-power rivalry—a developing contest for control of the Western Pacific, detached from the political considerations over whether there were other ways of managing their conflicts of interests or the extent to which the key factor would remain the extent of their economic inter-dependence.

IN 2007 ANDREW KREPINEVICH, WHO HAD BEEN ONE OF THE first to talk about the revolution in military affairs, offered his scenarios for the period up to 2016.[18] His hierarchy of enemies now had North Korea and China at the top. Iran was assumed to be behind most mischief in the Middle East. His book opened with Pearl Harbor and the blitzkrieg to show how surprise might happen. His scenarios included a collapse of Pakistan and a scramble to make sure its nuclear weapons did not fall into the wrong hands, a real worry at this time, while a multifaceted Islamist 'Wall of Fire' took to an extreme every fear about the worst terrorists could do. The most interesting scenario, in that it related to an actual development, was a US withdrawal from Iraq leading to chaos. Krepinevich assumed America's loss of resolve would lead to Russia and China coming to take responsibility for stabilising the Middle East. The problems with the scenario lay in the detail: the assumption that Prime Minister Maliki in Iraq would reach out to Kurds and Sunni (which he notably failed to do), the neglect of Syria (where Russia did take responsibility), overstating Iran's role and President Obama's eventual recognition that he could not let ISIS overcome Iraq.

By 2015, following its invasion of Ukraine (including the annexation of Crimea), Russia had put itself back into the running as a threat to be taken seriously. That year, General Richard Shirreff, recently retired as Deputy SACEUR, published his account of a coming war with the explicit purpose of demonstrating the dangers of the decline in British defence spending, and the 'semi-pacifist' inclinations of the government, who had made an 'appalling gamble' that the international scene would remain benign. They had neglected the danger posed by Russian President Putin, determined to reunite 'ethnic Russian speakers under the banner of Mother Russia' and ready to grab the Baltic states that had been part of the Soviet Union up to 1991 but were now members of NATO. Shirreff did not try to invent a scenario for war. He took a contingency already being taken seriously by the alliance[19] to its most alarming conclusion. In doing so he followed the standard form of the genre. A cunning enemy, free from democratic constraints, surprises feckless Western countries that find themselves in a war for which they are unprepared.[20] The situation was only recovered because it turned out, perhaps surprisingly, that the West was better at cyberwar than the Russians.

Douglas Cohn, another retired officer, offered scenarios for World War 4 (assuming the Cold War was World War 3)[21] that also occurred because states inclined to aggression could barely help themselves when opportunities came their way. Any weakness and they would pounce, in order to revenge old defeats or achieve long-held ambitions. Compared with the scenarios from the early 1990s, Cohn's forward look was dominated by fragmentation—old NATO allies coming to blows, the collapse of the Eurozone and a Belgian civil war, Russia attempting to reverse its post-1990 losses, including a move into the Baltic states, China becoming expansionist or succumbing to its own civil war, and then conflicts developing because of a rush to colonise the polar regions or even the moon, or gain access to fresh water, as well as more familiar concerns related to nuclear terrorism, currency manipulation and cyberwar.

The theme of all these books was that the improbable could always happen and so, in effect, it was essential to be prepared for everything. This was Cohn's conclusion. National defence could not be 'predicated upon easily defined threats' and so the United States must be prepared 'for the whole gamut of possibilities'. His worry appeared to be less that the US government lacked the capabilities to deal with these challenges than, in a common lament, it would lack the will to do so.[22] But in practice governments needed to set priorities, and to accept that there were some problems that could not be addressed adequately and the national interest would not be served by trying to do so.

There were some forecasters who were not making a point about looming dangers but were attempting to develop methodologies for forward planning. A book such as *Inevitable Surprises* by Peter Schwartz, published in 2003, sought to identify 'pre-determined elements' that were bound to shape the future. In this category he mentioned refugee movements, the impact of Islam on European societies, and an aging population. He also exaggerated economic growth and productivity gains, doubted that worries about globalisation would gain much traction, and assumed that financial regulation would work. His optimism extended to a rather muddled view of strategic defences as providing 'American military dominance of the planet, in near perpetuity'. In addition 'willingly or not the US will be drawn into the role of high-tech global policeman'. He was even optimistic on Europe's behalf forecasting stability for the EU and success for the Euro. Russia might even eventually join the EU. While all this was positive, elsewhere there would be trouble. The Saudis might succumb to an Islamic rebellion, Pakistan and Egypt to coups, Indonesia to ethnic conflict, Mexico to drug wars. Much of Africa, Latin America, and the Middle East could be almost written off.[23]

These books, with their range of speculations and contingencies, were of little value to policymakers in terms of deciding how to allocate their energies and resources. If the aim was to push for policy responses then it was to keep the focus sharp. How to do this could be seen in two books by Graham Allison, the Dean of the Belfer Center at Harvard University. The first concerned the nightmare of a non-state group getting hold of some sort of nuclear device and carrying it into a city centre. This concern gained credibility after 9/11. Al-Qaeda was clearly keen on killing as many people as possible and there was evidence that it had explored the possibility of building its own weapon or buying one on the open market, perhaps taking advantage of the disarray in the former Soviet Union that created risks of pilfering of poorly secured nuclear materials or even devices—the so-called 'loose nukes'. Then there was the shock of the discovery of the A. Q. Khan network in Pakistan which had been selling relevant technologies to Iran, North Korea and Libya.[24]

In 2004 Allison explored the possible ways in which terrorist groups might be able to get hold of a nuclear device or build their own and then use it to cause carnage. He reported experts from within government who considered such an attack as being a matter of 'when not if'. This was classic 'worst case' for no other act of terrorism could compare with a nuclear explosion. Even those next in the list had a nuclear element, such as crashing aircraft into a nuclear power station or creating a 'dirty bomb' using radioactive materials, although this would be more disruptive than destructive. Though these were the worst forms of terrorism imaginable there were others, using for example chemical or biological weapons that could cause great panic. They were far easier for non-state groups to construct. Chemical weapons had been used by states and terrorists had tried biological attacks. There had been a scare after 9/11 in the US when five people died from posted anthrax spores. So there was no reason to suppose that an attack with these weapons was either less likely or needing of prevention.

Allison kept his focus on the most dire case:

Given the number of actors with serious intent, the accessibility of weapons or nuclear materials from which elementary weapons could be constructed, and the almost limitless ways in which terrorists could smuggle a weapon through American borders .... In my own considered judgment, on the current path, a nuclear terrorist attack on America in the decade ahead is more likely than not.[25]

Without determined action, largely to make sure that weapons and fissionable material were kept secure, a disaster was almost certain.

Michael Levi did not dismiss the concerns or the need for robust policies but did challenge the methodology of adding worst case upon worst case to produce the most alarming conclusion. He doubted that there was a 'nuclear black market', or that building a nuclear weapon was 'as simple as surfing the Internet', or that smuggling nuclear materials was 'the same as smuggling drugs'. The best test of defences, he suggested, would be not so much against 'an infallible ten foot tall enemy' but against a 'possible failure-averse, conservative, resource-limited five-foot tall nuclear terrorist'.[26] A decade later, with fortunately no nuclear incident, and some limited progress on defensive measures, the concerns had not gone away. One analyst expressed surprise that there had not yet been any nuclear terrorism, and took little comfort from that absence for the future.[27]

By this time Allison had moved on. In 2017 he published another book, focusing on another looming tragedy that was also preventable so long as the right measures were taken. In this case it was a war between the United States and China. The method was similar with authoritative figures being quoted to underline the gravity of the situation, and the same layering of worst case assessments, until a series of recommendations explained how to keep the peace between the two great powers. 'On the current trajectory', Allison warned, 'war between the US and China in the decades ahead is not just possible, but much more likely than currently recognized'. It was not, however, 'inevitable'. [28] China would soon overtake the United States in economic, and then potentially, military power. Huntington was invoked to explain the clash of cultures between the two. There were also the real points of tension over Taiwan, the South China Sea, North Korea, and trade, from which Allison could generate plausible scenarios for conflict.

Allison's 'big idea' was to frame this moment as part of a recurring historical pattern, when predominant powers saw their positions threatened. This he called the 'Thucydides Trap', referring to the Greek historian's famous explanation for the Peloponnesian War: 'It was the rise of Athens and the fear that it instilled in Sparta that made war inevitable'. Allison provided many examples of this trap in action over the centuries, including the rivalry between Germany and Great Britain which led to the Great War. Leaving aside the question of whether this really was a good explanation for the war between Athens and Sparta, there were other difficulties with this formulation. China's rise unsettled a whole region. There were lots of great-power interactions in play.

Until 1990 China's most likely antagonist was the Soviet Union. In 1983 Edward Luttwak had forecast a major war between the two. For two decades Soviet military power had grown spectacularly—'the product of an armament effort of entirely unprecedented dimensions'—which enabled Moscow to cope with NATO countries that in every measure other than the military were much more powerful. Now it would take down an enemy that the Soviet leadership clearly feared, despite their shared ideology, so that it did not grow into a major threat.[29] To take another example, in 2014 China's claims over the Japanese Senkaku Islands (which it knew as the Diaoyu Islands), led Japanese Prime Minister Shinzo Abe to wonder aloud about the disturbing similarities between the situation a hundred years earlier in Europe and the current position in Asia.[30]

The Chinese leadership might also look to India. This was a country with which it had gone to war in 1962, over a disputed border, which was in constant dispute with China's ally, Pakistan, and which also had a massive population and had moved into a higher economic gear.[31] The issue for China was not its struggle for power with the United States so much as its potential struggle with most of the other big players in the region. Returning to the China question in 2012, Luttwak saw the danger facing China as an almost autistic tendency for self-aggrandizement, common to great powers, that was bound to 'evoke adversarial reaction'. The real challenge for China, if it did not want its neighbours to gang up on it, was to learn humility and restraint. If it did, and managed to avoid an unnecessary war, then this suggested its rise could be irresistible.[32]

THE MOST SYSTEMATIC ATTEMPT TO ANTICIPATE HOW THE world might develop in the future and the potential security implications was the US National Intelligence Council's quadrennial assessment of global trends, published after a presidential election but before the inauguration. The series began in 1997. The first looked forward to 2010: the one after the 2012 election to 2030. The most recent, published in January 2017, did not restrict itself by a timeframe. The issues covered did not change very much, with consideration of demographic trends, the impact of climate change, developments in the world economy, the rise of Asia, the violence in Africa, and turmoil in the Middle East. There were always questions to be asked about how Russia was coping with its reduced circumstances and the meaning of China's ascent. Because this was a series it was possible to comment on what had been missed and the implications for the methodology. It was not surprising that the council was caught out by specific events that in principle might have been foreseeable (the 1998 financial crash was an early example), but each successive edition considered how they might do better in anticipating a discontinuity, something that was not a trend at the time of writing, or a 'black swan', a rare event that seemed to come from nowhere yet changed everything.[33]

When the series started, the document picked up on the key themes of the 1990s—the impact of globalisation, that most conflicts were internal to states rather than between them, that precision-guided munitions and information technologies would 'continue to be the hallmarks of the revolution in military affairs' and the likelihood that adversaries would attempt to blunt this US advantage using 'asymmetric means—ranging from the increased use of terrorism to the possible use of weapons of mass destruction'. 'Increasingly, the national security agendas of policymakers will be dominated by five questions: whether to intervene, when, with whom, with what tools, and to what end?'[34] By December 2000, the relationships of states to criminal and terrorist groups had more focus, including the observation that 'asymmetric approaches—whether undertaken by states or nonstate actors—will become the dominant characteristic of most threats to the US homeland'.[35] By December 2004, after the dramas of 9/11 and the invasion of Iraq, the authors dressed up their scenarios as works of fiction set in 2020. Thus a continuing Pax Americana was illuminated by a UN Secretary-General's diary entry noting the US still exercising leadership but in 'an increasingly diverse, complex, and fast-paced world', a letter by a grandson of Osama Bin Laden recounting an attempt to establish a 'New Caliphate', and an exchange of text messages between two arms dealers exploring a WMD deal as states intensified security measures.[36]

The 2008 document was published just as the international economy was reeling under the shock of another financial crisis, which was barely reflected in its pages. It saw considerable continuity with little expectation of a great-power war, but problems arising in an arc of instability 'spanning Middle East, Asia, Africa'. The uncertainties revolved around the possibility of 'precipitating events leading to overthrow of regimes' and the 'ability to manage flashpoints and competition for resources'. This was a 'story with no clear outcome'.[37] The 'shape and nature of international alignments' were in a 'state of flux'. The world described showed an increased tendency for internal conflict, in which some states would fail, causing more grief and disrupting neighbourhoods, while even the more prosperous and stable states were finding it difficult to control national agendas because of globalisation. It also recognised that American policies were 'an important variable in how the world is shaped, influencing the path that states and nonstate actors choose to follow'. This was both obvious yet an important insight—the world is unpredictable because it depends on choices that your country must make.

By 2012 the US role was more under question. Aware of the optimism engendered by the idea that war was in decline, the document accepted that 'the disincentives will remain strong against great-power conflict: too much would be at stake'. But it urged caution 'about the prospects for further declines in the number and intensity of intrastate conflicts', while noting how the shifts in the international system were increasing the risks of interstate conflict:

The underpinnings of the post-Cold War equilibrium are beginning to shift. During the next 15–20 years, the US will be grappling with the degree to which it can continue to play the role of systemic guardian and guarantor of the global order. A declining US unwillingness and/or slipping capacity to serve as a global security provider would be a key factor contributing to instability, particularly in Asia and the Middle East.[38]

The next document, published a few weeks after the 2016 election, was bleaker than those that had gone before. Since 2012 there had been Russian interventions in Ukraine and Syria and growing tensions over Chinese assertiveness in the South China Sea. It noted the mood of 'anti-immigrant and xenophobic sentiment' in the core Western democracies. Nationalism was being employed in countries where 'leaders seek to consolidate political control by eliminating domestic political alternatives while painting international relations in existential terms'. It warned of 'rising tensions within and between countries' over the coming five years, with 'an ever-widening range of states, organizations, and empowered individuals' shaping geopolitics.

> For better and worse, the emerging global landscape is drawing to a close an era of American dominance following the Cold War. So, too, perhaps is the rules-based international order that emerged after World War II. It will be much harder to cooperate internationally and govern in ways publics expect. Veto players will threaten to block collaboration at every turn, while information "echo chambers" will reinforce countless competing realities, undermining shared understandings of world events.

Despite temptations to 'impose order on this apparent chaos' this would 'ultimately would be too costly in the short run and would fail in the long.' The lessons of the past century were summoned to note how difficult it would be to overcome less powerful adversaries. It warned of Russia and China being emboldened, curtailed international cooperation, and a tendency towards the revival of 'spheres of influence'.[39] Donald Trump was inaugurated as 45th president of the United States on 20 January 2017.

[25]

The Future of the
Future of War

I had been at the start of something: of a new era in which conflict surges, shifts, or fades but doesn't end, in which the most you can hope for is not peace, or the arrival of a better age, but only to remain safe as long as possible.

MATTI FRIEDMAN,
Pumpkinflowers, 2016[1]

This book opened discussing a period when politicians and commentators had a shared idea about the nature of war, how it would be fought and also how it might be contained. According to the classical model of war, political struggles were decided by means of battle. In the great wars of the modern era this was the case. The belligerents threw everything into the fight, the end was marked by victory and defeat, and this was sufficient for the international system to be set on a new course with a hierarchy of powers confirmed. But these were long and arduous struggles, involving enormous sacrifices and terrible devastation. It was not what the strategists of the nineteenth century had in mind, which was to achieve their objectives as quickly as possible. This was why surprise attacks loomed so large in thinking about future war. The need for a quick victory put a premium on making the most of the very first blows directed against the enemy. Whatever the expectations about the war's likely course, it would be foolish to move only tentitively once it had begun or give an opponent a chance to prepare and defend by signalling an imminent offensive. Surprise would always gain some advantage. The aim would be to leave the enemy floundering and helpless. If the first blow was indecisive that could mean a long, hard struggle with an uncertain outcome.

The importance of the opening moves in wars is why writing on their future was always full of imaginary first blows that caused the defeat of their victims. Far less was written on second and third blows, and less still about those later years when an impasse had been reached and the fighting ticked over, with casualties but no breakthroughs. After the First World War the strategists looked to tanks and aircraft to ensure that the next war was shorter. The writers who did dwell on the possibility of even longer and deadlier wars did so not to dream up clever campaign plans but to grasp how societies might cope and adapt to such a situation. The entry into the nuclear age provided another boost to dystopian imaginations while turning strategic design into a form of abstract reasoning. Now even more than before, any war plan would have to gamble everything on the first strike, because anything less than the complete elimination of the enemy's nuclear capabilities would mean that that their own country must suffer a terrible revenge. Over time, as new forms of warfare emerged, including the use of cyber-attacks that barely involved armed force, surprise attacks still dominated the literature. This was the case even as military practice gravitated towards long, drawn-out struggles which lacked clear beginning and endings.

The prominence of knockout blows in writing about future war was the result not only of their potential strategic impact or their drama but also because they helped make a point. They warned of a country left vulnerable to cunning aggressors as a result of political negligence and popular complacency. The same theme appealed to those intending to take the military initiative with an irresistible offensive. Wars usually started with at least one side confident about the outcome. John Stoessinger argued that the origins of war lay in the persistent influence of misperceptions about adversaries and about what armed force could achieve. On the brink of war, 'each confidently expects victory after a brief and triumphant campaign'.[2] Even leaders aware of the pitfalls when making their decisions became more confident as war was seen to be virtually inevitable, reassuring themselves that victory was within reach.[3]

Both Operation Barbarossa and Pearl Harbor underlined the point. They were such shocks to those on the receiving end that they exercised remarkable holds over their strategic imaginations thereafter, although in both cases surprise was achieved but victory was not. They were not taken as warnings of the folly and futility of aggression but instead of how the unwary might get caught. And because surprise remained of the essence when starting a war, there have been a number of attempted knockout blows since 1945—North Korea's attacks against the South in the summer of 1950, Argentina's seizure of the Falkland Islands in 1982, and Iraq's occupation of Kuwait in 1990—all of which failed to achieve their objective. Even when a first blow was successful, as in Israel's demolition of the Egyptian air force on 5 June 1967, the aftermath could be frustrating, with the defeated parties refusing to accept the result and a conquered population putting up resistance.

One regular assumption was that the odds of success might be shifted decisively as a result of some new technology. Gunpowder to muskets, steam turbines to aircraft, missiles to digital networks, all changed the character of warfare, opening up new possibilities while closing off others. But the technology was rarely monopolised or else, even if one side enjoyed superiority, adversaries found ways to limit their effects. Even for modern Western forces, technology encouraged a fantasy of a war that was fast, easy, and decisive: yet they still found themselves facing 'slow, bitter and indecisive war'.[4] The conviction that 'future conflict will be fundamentally different from all historical experience' led H. R. McMaster to identify a 'vampire fallacy', so called because it was impossible to kill. 'New concepts with catchy titles' promised 'fast, cheap and efficient victories in future war'. Doubters were 'dismissed as being wedded to old thinking'. As an example he cited how 'information and communication technologies' were said to lead to the 'Quality of Firsts', by which forces would 'see first, decide first, act first and finish decisively'. The fallacy lay in neglecting 'war's political and human dimensions' and equating 'targeting to tactics, operations and strategy'. It failed to recognise the 'uncertainty of war, the trajectory of which is constantly altered by varied interactions with determined and elusive enemies.'[5]

The vampire is unlikely to be killed off soon. It has become natural to explore new developments by pushing them to their most extreme potential impacts. Should another major war start to loom larger as a serious prospect then all forms of offensive scenarios,

however improbable or difficult to execute, will demand careful attention. Colin Gray has warned against assuming that just because
we have avoided a war between great powers for some time that this
will continue indefinitely, and also of becoming so beguiled by new
types of war that we forget to think about classical war.[6] When a
Harvard group explored the parallels between the rise of Germany as
a great power at the start of the twentieth century and the current rise
of China, they considered poor diplomacy, unreasonable allies, insufficient economic interdependence, domestic upheavals, offensive doctrines, and the logic of the rise of one power inevitably coming at the
expense of another. The main conclusion drawn from the comparison, however, as a guide to how to avoid a major war with China in
the future, was to watch out for the 'little things', contingent features
of the situation, chance factors and then specific decisions, that might
have gone another way but together worked to turn a manageable
crisis into a catastrophe.[7] From this perspective any thinking about
future war geared to prevention should look to innovation in diplomacy and international communications as much as to military strategy. Problems could emerge not out of the blue with some all-or-nothing
attack but instead out of an assertion of rights in contested territory,
a principled stand that embarrassed a rival, probing actions to explore weaknesses that came up against strength, military manoeuvres
to 'send a message', or displays of resolve that turned into actual
clashes and escalated quickly.

THE INNOVATION THAT DID MOST TO TRANSFORM THINKING
about war, and why the risk factors at play during the first decades
of the twenty-first century were so much more severe than those in
the first decades of the twentieth, was the development of nuclear
weapons. These weapons were first introduced at the end of a war
that had seen the Holocaust, carpet-bombing, and attacks from long-
range missiles. Atom bombs were a logical culmination of what had
gone before, and also apparently brutally successful in bringing a
total war to an end. The simplest if depressing assumption was that
war had become progressively more murderous, with ever more sophisticated means being found to slaughter people on a large scale,
and that future wars would be even more intense and existential. This
prospect encouraged great caution, even when it came to quite minor
crises. The risks were just too great and reliable offensive strategies

were out of reach. This caution has been internalised by successive generations of world leaders—expressed in a slogan shared by Ronald Reagan and Mikhail Gorbachev: 'a nuclear war cannot be won and must never be fought'.[8] But will this last?

In the past, credibility about any war 'going nuclear' depended on the likely passions raised by the preceding conventional campaigns, in which many would already have died. In 1945 nuclear war appeared as a natural extension of what had gone before but now there is much less of a connection between the two types of war. The trend in conventional war, at least in the West, has been increasingly to adopt strategies that sought to spare civilians, not always successfully. The United States and its allies have also been confident enough in their overall strength to see nuclear weapons as a reserve, deterring extreme actions by another nuclear power. But under the strain of war, attitudes could switch, as they have switched before, into a position where the old arguments about getting at governments through their miserable populations will appear credible again. Countries lacking comparable conventional strength to the US will also continue to see nuclear weapons as a vital leveller.[9] When President Putin wished to dissuade the United States from acting on behalf of Ukraine in 2014 he observed: 'Thank God, I think no one is thinking of unleashing a large-scale conflict with Russia. I want to remind you that Russia is one of the leading nuclear powers.'[10]

There are scenarios separate from a great-power conflict which could see nuclear use, for example involving India and Pakistan. In addition, a number of the big crises of this century had a nuclear dimension. The US and its allies went to war against Iraq in order to preclude a future nuclear programme, threatened war, imposed sanctions and eventually cut a deal with Iran to prevent them acquiring enough enriched uranium for their own nuclear weapons, and began 2017 seeking to stop North Korea taking its already advanced nuclear and missile programmes further, though facing a risk of nuclear retaliation. If and when nuclear weapons are again used in anger this will affect all subsequent discussions on war, either because it was as bad as feared or alternatively because it helped one side come out on top.[11]

Chemical weapons might have been seen as a lesser form of nuclear weapon. Their human effects would undoubtedly be horrific, but their strategic effects still limited compared to what can be achieved by traditional forms of bombardment. Biological weapons are also potentially unwieldy and their use would carry an even greater stigma. Both give counter-terrorism forces cause for concern.

Another key question is whether and how much the United States will play a role in future conflicts. The literature at least as it applies to interstate wars, assumes that the United States is actively engaged in the generality of the world's problems. Americans have written the key works, not least because of the country's role as the guarantor of a certain sort of international order. It is hard to think of a single development that would transform security calculations around the world, including whether or not to build national nuclear arsenals, than a decision by the United States to disentangle itself from its alliance commitments. This is why allies spent so much time following Washington security debates and wondering how much they could continue to rely on US support in a crisis. Any discussion about the various maritime challenges posed by China to the Japanese, or by Russia to the Baltic States, takes on a completely different light should these challenges come to be seen as tests of the principle of alliance.

This in turn raises the question of whether the United States will continue to enjoy such a predominant military position. It remains the only power with a truly global reach in conventional forces, but it can no longer assume straightforward victory even in battles fought on its own terms. US forces have been blown up by hidden roadside bombs, but it is a long time since they have faced serious threats from the air (possibly Korea in 1953) or expected to lose ships in a confrontation at sea. Russia would pose a serious threat so long as it did not stray too far from home territory, but its economic weakness works against it becoming an even greater power. So long as it maintains internal stability China can expect to get stronger. This is why, when coupled with the complexity of its regional politics, Asia provides a more likely setting for a future great-power war.

WITH CIVIL WARS THE EXPERIENCE HAS BEEN EVEN MORE salutary. The category has never been clear-cut because internal conflict often prompts external intervention—by like-minded militants supporting a religious or ideological cause, neighbours with local interests, and major powers acting out of humanitarian or security concerns. At times external forces have sought to hold the ring or monitor a fragile ceasefire in the guise of a peacekeeping force. Sometimes there was no peace to keep, and external intervention effectively took sides, either by preventing one side from winning by unacceptable means—starving or massacring civilians, for instance—or ensuring that the most ideologically sympathetic party came out on top, as was attempted in both Iraq and Afghanistan. On the ground, instead of being fought by disciplined regular forces serving the purposes of either the state or its challenger, civil wars often pitted relatively disorganised militias against each other. In these cases, the conflicts tended to be driven by ground-level considerations of individual and group security, and the violence was often more personal. They broke up communities that had previously been apparently harmonious, and left legacies of bitterness, division, and impoverishment.

Whatever the higher cause they were notionally supporting, individuals and groups could develop their own agendas, geared to criminal activities, such as smuggling and trafficking in drugs, natural resources, and people. These interests could keep a conflict bubbling along, despite the efforts of peace mediators or armed peacekeepers. If state structures remain immature or contested, the situation might never improve, leading to outside powers and international organisations accepting a quasi-permanent role in the politics of the host country and some continuing responsibility for pacifying hostile elements.

After the end of the Cold War, Western countries, out of a mixture of motives, found themselves getting involved in conflicts far from home. What might have started with enemies being rolled over by the sheer weight of firepower and sophisticated equipment turned into long, complex, and messy campaigns. Their troops entered a world of shadowy militias, with accomplished bomb-makers, angry mobs, cynical warlords, and energised youngsters brandishing their AK-47s. Protest movements morphed into militias and then militias morphed into criminal gangs or into rival factions, fighting each other with the same ferocity that they once fought their shared enemy. The conflict zones were populated by altruistic volunteers for NGOs, private security contractors, offering protection for all those who were not in the military (and whose numbers often exceeded the military), conciliators and journalists, smugglers and traffickers. All had to navigate their way through broken social structures, corrupt economies, and unreliable political institutions. No one was truly safe. For those living in these countries this form of warfare could become something habitual, routine, to which it was necessary to adjust. Those intervening were able to walk away. They could decide that engagement was not such a good idea. Perhaps, they might conclude, the people were beyond help, or no longer deserved support, as they had done insufficient to help themselves. In this way they might accept outcomes that would have been characterised as defeat while the fighting was at its height but became tolerable when the alternative was persisting with what had become a futile endeavour.

This left another large political question—the answer to which will influence the future of war. The reputation of interventions suffered after Iraq, Afghanistan, and Libya, although Syria was a poor advert for holding back. What may make a difference in the future may not only be the extent of the human distress being caused by the conflict but also the desperation of fleeing refugees and the opportunities for terrorism. Humanitarian motives may not be sufficient to ensure engagement, but that may mean conflicts that do not spill out of their borders will be left alone until exhaustion sets in. Some influence could be exercised by relying largely on air power and on others to provide the land forces. That might see the major enemy pushed back or even defeated, but it would also empower those who were making the sacrifices. It would mean relinquishing control over events on the ground, and accepting the agenda of local allies, with their distinctive interests, so that the relationship between military action and political objectives became further attenuated. To side with a government could mean propping up those whose practices had created the conflict in the first place; to side with rebels was not only more problematic in terms of international law but could mean promoting a radical political project that went well beyond resisting oppression.

Over this century approaches to intervention have moved from humanitarianism with nation-building to counter-terrorism with nation-building to counter-terrorism on its own. Islamist extremism is now seen as a global challenge—networked, ruthless, and capable—and one that requires a robust response. The form this response should take has been the subject of an intense debate since the opening of the 'war on terror', including the extent it can and should be fought in line with established Western values and respect for human rights. This debate has yet to be concluded.[12] There has also been a corresponding shift from a Cold War understanding of civil wars as largely anti-colonial and ideological struggles, to what might be expected with states with weak foundations and high poverty, to a phenomenon with many different strands, but showing the increasing influence of hard-line Islamist movements.

A COMMON THEME OF THOSE REFLECTING ON THE STATE OF the military art was of the blurring of boundaries—between peace and war, the military and the civilian, the conventional and unconventional, the regular and the irregular, the domestic and the international, and the state and the non-state, the legitimate and the criminal.[13] The talk was of 'grey zone' conflicts, found somewhere between peace and war, where the action chosen was deliberately kept below the threshold that would spark a major war.[14] Another term referring to the same phenomenon, but with a double meaning, was 'Cool War':

> On the one hand, it is a little warmer than cold because it seems likely to involve almost constant offensive measures that, while falling short of actual warfare, regularly seek to damage or weaken rivals or gain an edge through violations of sovereignty and penetration of defenses. And on the other, it takes on the other definition of "cool," in that it involves the latest cutting-edge technologies in ways that are changing the paradigm of conflict to a much greater degree than any of those employed during the Cold War—which was, after all, about old-fashioned geopolitical jockeying for advantage in anticipation of potential old-school total warfare.[15]

The risks attached to major war and the reluctance to commit substantial forces to lesser conflicts have led major powers to search for ways, whether subversion of the political process, economic coercion, cyber-attacks, or brazen disinformation campaigns, to influence events while keeping their liabilities limited and risks managed. Again there was the difficulty that these methods were unlikely to bring much to a conclusion but instead encouraged niggling, persistent conflicts until at some point a way was found to sort out the underlying issues or else some spark moved them out of the grey zone and back into open warfare.

War therefore has a future. It can make an appearance wherever there is a combination of an intensive dispute and available forms of violence. The international system has its known fault lines, between and within states, and there is always a possibility of some eruption. The violence may be connected with parochial or even private issues, will often be linked with criminality and connected with simmering social tensions. At first it may bear little resemblance to our common views of war, but any continuing violence has the potential to turn into something bigger, just as wars always leave their traces when they have notionally concluded. So long as forces are maintained, weapons developed, and the plans kept up to date, there is the risk of another clash of arms that will resemble the regular wars of the past.

It would be against the spirit of this book to predict the incidence and form of future wars. A number of factors make it hard to anticipate the future. One is that prediction is often purposive, closely bound up with advocacy, and so is about the present as much as the future. In principle by following the advocated course of action the direst outcomes will be avoided while the more optimistic realised. When it comes to urging war this can lead to an almost willful underestimation of the resourcefulness of adversaries, their capacity to find reserves or acquire allies. Those lamenting national complacency, decadence and spinelessness often underestimate the resilience of their own people at times of emergency. Such underestimates help explain why the biggest surprises in war often lie in what happens after the first engagements.

Similarly, lobbyists for one branch of the armed services, new weapons systems, or even peace proposals, paint alternative pictures of the future according to whether their arguments are accepted or ignored. Even academics find it hard to look forward without offering some recommendations about how the future might be improved. The aim is to identify strategies, investments and actions to enable us to retain a degree of control over our destinies. In these ways security debates get framed and priorities set, with some issues deemed highly salient as others are pushed to the margins. When governments are caught by surprise, as with the collapse of the Soviet Union or mass-casualty terrorism, or engage in activities for which they were poorly of prepared, such as the interventions of the 1990s and 2000s, this was often not because they were unthinkable but because there had been no prior reason to push them to the top of the security agenda. As other possibilities were being illuminated they had been left unexplored.

Another tendency is to assume that the recent past can be extrapolated into the future, that trend lines will continue, as with claims that war as an institution is in inevitable decline. Another and quite different tendency is to assert that we are on the verge of a great, transformational discontinuity. The possibility that much will carry on as before is far less interesting. Yet the continuities in warfare are striking, as can be seen in those countries that have long forgotten the experience of peace, and by observing how much modern killing is achieved by relatively old-fashioned weaponry that would have been recognised by earlier generations. As much guidance on the future is provided by the unending wars of sub-Saharan Africa as by the promise of artificial intelligence.

These tendencies so evident in the history of the future of war are therefore likely to persist in its future. As in the past there will be a stream of speculative scenarios and anxious warnings, along with sudden demands for new thinking in the face of an unexpected development. Whether couched in the language of earnest academic papers, military appreciations or fictional thrillers, these will all be works of imagination.[16] They cannot be anything else because the future is not preordained. This is the main reason why prediction is so difficult. There are decisions yet to be made, even about challenges that are well understood, along with chance events that will catch us unawares and developments already in train that have been inadequately appreciated. These works of imagination will often have value in helping to clarify the choices that need to be faced and at times will even turn out to have been prescient. For that reason many will deserve to be taken seriously. They should all, however, be treated sceptically.

NOTES

INTRODUCTION

1. Margaret Atwood, *Morning in the Burned House*. (New York: Houghton Mifflin, 1995).

2. John Gaddis, *The Long Peace: Inquiries Into the History of the Cold War* (London: Oxford University Press, 1989). This first appeared as 'The Long Peace: Elements of Stability in the Postwar International System', *International Security* 10.4 (1986).

3. John Keegan, *A History of Warfare* (New York: Knopf, 1993) 59.

4. John Mueller, *Retreat from Doomsday: The Obsolescence of Major War* (New York: Basic Books, 1989) 13.

5. Steven Pinker, *The Better Angels of Our Nature: Why Violence Has Declined* (London: Penguin Books, 2011).

6. Pinker 290–1.

7. Pinker 50.

8. Human Security Report Project, *Human Security Report 2013: The Decline in Global Violence: Evidence, Explanation, and Contestation* (Vancouver: Human Security Press, 2013).

9. A British military think tank reported in 2014, citing Pinker as evidence, 'that the frequency and intensity of wars, as well as the number of violent deaths, has been declining sharply and is likely to continue to fall.' Ministry of Defence, *Strategic Trends Programme: Global Strategic Trends—Out to 2045* (Shrivenham: Doctrine, Concepts and Development Center, 2014) 96. For similar forecasts see Frank Hoffman, *Foresight into 21st Century Conflict: End of the Greatest Illusion* (Philadelphia: Foreign Policy Research Institute, 2016). Other key contributors to this debate have been Joshua Goldstein, *Winning the War: The Decline of Armed Conflict* (New York: Dutton, 2011), and Azar Gat, *War in Human Civilization* (Oxford: OUP, 2008). See also Azar Gat, 'Is War Declining and Why?', *Journal of Peace Research* 50.2 (2013). See also a collection of pre-Pinker assessments found in Raimo Väyrynen, ed., *The Waning of Major War: Theories and Debates* (London: Routledge, 2006). The post-Pinker debate is assessed in a number of contributions, including one by Pinker, to a symposium edited by Nils Petter Gleditsch, 'The Decline of War—The Main Issues', *International Studies Quarterly* 15.3 (2013). Other books with a similar thesis are Richards Jesse, *The Secret Peace: Exposing the Positive Trend of World Events* (New York: Book & Ladder, 2010), and John Horgan, *The End of War* (San Francisco: McSweeney's, 2012).

10. Pinker 361.

11. Pinker 672.

12. Pinker takes the term from Norbert Elias who wrote of a 'civilizing process' in a two-volume book published in German on the eve of the Second World War. See Norbert Elias, *The Civilizing Process: Sociogenetic and Psychogenetic Investigations*, eds. Eric Dunning et al. (Malden, MA: Blackwell, 2000).

13. Pinker 97.

14. *Human Security Report* 37. Perhaps aware of the danger of appearing to rest his case on a statistical trick, Pinker acknowledged that uncertainties in the numbers might mean this war did disrupt the trend and so should be understood as an outlier, a 'last gasp in a long slide of major war into historical obsolescence' (Pinker 107).

15. Tanisha M. Fazal, 'Dead Wrong? Battle Deaths, Military Medicine, and Exaggerated Reports of War's Demise', *International Security* 39.1 (2014) 95–125.

16. Carl Kaysen, 'Is War Obsolete?: A Review Essay', *International Security* 14.4 (1990): 42–64.

17. Pinker 291.

18. Pinker 672.

19. Therese Pettersson and Peter Wallensteen, 'Armed Conflicts, 1946–2014', *Journal of Peace Research* 52.4 (2015) 536–540.

20. Håvard Hegre et al., 'Predicting Armed Conflict, 2010–2050', *International Studies Quarterly* 57 (2013): 250–270.

21. Daniel Howden, 'The future of war is looking bleak', *Independent*, online, 22 Nov. 2012. Available: http://www.independent.co.uk/news/world/politics/the-future-of-war-is-looking-bleak-8344462.html

22. John L. Comaroff, and Paul C. Stern 'New Perspectives on Nationalism and War,' *Theory and Society*, 23:1 (1994), 35.

CHAPTER 1

1. George Chesney, 'The Battle Of Dorking: Reminiscences Of A Volunteer', *Blackwood's Magazine* (May 1871), online, Project Gutenberg Australia. Available: http://gutenberg.net.au/ebooks06/0602091h.html

2. Cited in James Q. Whitman, *The Verdict of Battle: The Law of Victory and the Making of Modern War* (Cambridge, MA: Harvard University Press, 2012) 207–8.

3. See I. F. Clarke, *Voices Prophesying War: Future Wars, 1763–3749* (Oxford: Oxford University Press, 1972), and Patrick M. Kirkwood, 'The Impact of Fiction on Public Debate in Late Victorian Britain: The Battle of Dorking and the "Lost Career" of Sir George Tomkyns Chesney', *The Graduate History Review* 4.1 (2012): 3.

4. Clarke 9.

5. Clarke 8.

6. Katherine C. Epstein, *Torpedo: Inventing the Military-Industrial Complex in the United States and Great Britain* (Cambridge, MA: Harvard University Press, 2014).

7. Brian Holden Reid, 'A Signpost That Was Missed? Reconsidering British Lessons from the American Civil War', *The Journal of Military History* 70.2 (2006): 385–414. See also Jay Luvaas *The Military Legacy of the Civil War: The European Inheritance* (Lawrence, KA: University Press of Kansas, 1959).

8. Clark 45.

9. Cited by Clarke, 34.

10. On Jomini, see John Shy, 'Jomini', *Makers of Modern Strategy from Machiavelli to the Nuclear Age*, ed. Peter Paret (Princeton: Princeton University Press, 1986) 143–185, and Michael Howard, 'Jomini and the Classical Tradition in Military Thought', *Studies in War & Peace* (London: Temple Smith, 1970) 31.

11. It was first translated into English in 1854. Baron Antoine-Henri de Jomini, *The Art of War* (London: Greenhill Books, 1992).

12. Hew Strachan, *European Armies and the Conduct of War* (London: Allen & Unwin, 1983) 71.

13. Sir Edward Creasy, *The Fifteen Decisive Battles of the World: From Marathon to Waterloo* (Boston: IndyPublish, 2002). Available: http://www.gutenberg.org/files/4061/4061-h/4061-h.htm

14. Other examples of the genre are J. F. C. Fuller, *The Decisive Battles of the Western World and Their Influence Upon History*, Vol. 1–3 (London: Eyre & Spotiswood,

1963), and Paul K. Davis, *100 Decisive Battles: From Ancient Times to the Present* (Oxford: Oxford University Press, 1999).

15. Victor Davis Hanson, *Carnage and Culture: Landmark Battles in the Rise of Western Power* (New York: Doubleday, 2001).

16. Yuval N. Harari, 'The Concept of "Decisive Battles" in World History', *Journal of World History* 18.3 (2007): 251-266.

17. Cathal J. Nolan, *The Allure of Battle: A History of How Wars Have Been Won and Lost* (Oxford: Oxford University Press, 2017).

CHAPTER 2

1. William Le Queux, *The Invasion of 1910: With A Full Account of the Siege of London* (London: Nash, 1906). Available: http://www.gutenberg.org/ebooks/36155.

2. Clarke, *Voices Prophesying War*, p. 73

3. Cited by Clarke,62–3.

4. Rear-Admiral P. Colomb et al., *The Great War of 189_: A Forecast* (London: Heinemann, 1893). Available: https://archive.org/details/greatwarof18900colorich

5. William Le Queux, *The Great War in England in 1897* (London: Tower, 1894). Available: http://www.gutenberg.org/files/37470/37470-h/37470-h.htm

6. A subsequent fiction, *Spies of the Kaiser: Plotting the Downfall of England* (London: Hurst & Blackwell, 1909), ostensibly 'based on serious facts within my own personal knowledge', encouraged a major spy scare. Philip Knightley, *The Second Oldest Profession* (New York: W. W. Norton, 1987).

7. Le Queux, (1906). The book is discussed in Clarke and also in Charles E. Gannon, *Rumors of War and Infernal Machines: Technomilitary agenda-setting in American and British Speculative Fiction* (Lanham, Rowman & Littlefield, 2005).

8. In the decade up to 1914 the arms manufacturer Vickers was supplying the War Office with under eleven machine guns per year, which was increased to about ten a week after the war started. Thereafter, thousands were produced, so in 1918 Vickers delivered almost 40,000. John Ellis, *The Social History of the Machine Gun* (London: Cresset, 1975) 39.

9. Antulio Echevarria, *Imagining Future War: The West's Technological Revolution and Visions of Wars to Come, 1880–1914* (Westport, CT: Praeger, 2007).

10. Echevarria 55. See also Brian Bond, 'Doctrine and Training in the British Cavalry 1870–1914', *The Theory and Practice of War*, ed. Michael Howard (London: Cassell, 1965).

11. Jean de Bloch, 'The Transvaal War: Its Lessons in Regard to Militarism and Army Reorganisation', *Journal of the Royal United Service Institute* 45 (1901), and T. H. E. Travers, 'Technology, Tactics, and Morale: Jean de Bloch, the Boer War, and British Military Theory, 1900–1914', *The Journal of Modern History* 51.2 (1979) 264–286.

12. I. S. Bloch, *Is War Now Impossible? Being an Abridgment of The War of the Future in Its Technical Economic and Political Relations* (London: Grant Richard, 1899). Available: https://archive.org/details/iswarnowimpossib00bloc. On Bloch's reception, see Michael Welch, 'The Centenary of the British Publication of Jean de Bloch's *Is War Now Impossible?* (1899–1999)', *War in History* 7.3 (2000): 273–294, and Christopher Bellamy, '"Civilian Experts" and Russian Defence Thinking: The Renewed Relevance of Jan Bloch', *RUSI Journal* (1992): 50–56.

13. Jean de Bloch, 'The Wars of the Future', *The Contemporary Review* 8 (1901): 305–32.

14. Chesney, 95.

15. Le Queux 269.

16. Robert Baden-Powell, *Scouting for Boys: A Handbook for Instruction in Good Citizenship* (London: H. Cox, 1908) 328. On prevailing ideas of degeneracy in western

societies, see Daniel Pick, *Faces of Degeneration: A European disorder, c.1848-c.1918* (Cambridge: Cambridge University Press, 1989), and Travers 280.

17. The term comes from a musical hall song in Britain at the time of the Russo-Turkish war of 1878 (in which the British did not get involved):

We don't want to fight but *by Jingo* if we do
We've got the ships, we've got the men, we've got the money too
We've fought the Bear before, and while we're Britons true
The Russians shall not have Constantinople.

It was soon in common use on both sides of the Atlantic to describe any enthusiasm for war.

18. Quoted by Gannon, 81.

19. H. G. Wells, *Anticipations of the Reaction of Mechanical and Scientific Progress upon Human Life and Thought* (London: Chapman & Hall, 1902). Available: http://www.gutenberg.org/files/19229/19229-h/19229-h.htm

20. T. H. E. Travers, 'Future Warfare: H. G. Wells and British Military Theory', *War and Society: A Yearbook of Military History*, eds. Brian Bond and Ian Roy (London: Croom Helm, 1975).

21. Jules Verne, *The Clipper of the Clouds*, (London, Sampson Low, 1887), 233-4. Available: https://archive.org/details/clipperclouds00verngoog,

22. Jules Verne, *Master of the World*, (London: Sampson Low, 1904). Available: http://www.gutenberg.org/cache/epub/3809/pg3809.txt

23. In *War of the Worlds* (1898) and *When the Sleeper Awakes* (1889).

24. H. G. Wells, *The War in the Air* (London: George Bell & Sons, 1908). Available: http://www.freeclassicebooks.com/H.G.%20Wells/The%20War%20in%20Twentiethe%20Air.pdf, p. 241

25. Ray Norton, *The Vanishing Fleets* (London: Forgotten Books, 2015).

26. Hollis Godfrey, *The Man Who Ended War* (New York: Little Brown & Co., 1908).

27. W. Warren Wagar, 'H. G. Wells and the Genesis of Future Studies', *World Future Society Bulletin* (1983): 25–29.

28. Wells, *War in the Air*, 84.

29. *Ibid.*, Preface to the 1921 Edition.

30. Wells, *Anticipations* 280. On the development of Wells's social and political thought, see Gordon D. Feir, *H. G. Wells at the End of His Tether: His Social and Political Adventures* (Lincoln, NE: iUniverse, 2005). Edward Mead Earle, 'H. G. Wells, British patriot in search of a world state', *World Politics*, 2:2 (1950), 181–208

31. Gustave Le Bon, *The Crowd: A Study of the Popular Mind* (New York: The Macmillan Co, 1896).

32. Max Hastings, *Catastrophe: Europe Goes to War 1914*, (London: Collins, 2013), 3

33. Bellamy 52.

34. Saki, *The Complete Saki* (London: Penguin, 1982) 821, with editor's notes. Cited in Bellamy 51.

CHAPTER 3

1. David Cortright, *Peace: A History of Movements and Ideas* (Cambridge: Cambridge University Press, 2008) 34.

2. Sandi E. Cooper, *Patriotic Pacifism: Waging War on War in Europe, 1815–1914* (Oxford: Oxford University Press, 1991).

3. Jean de Bloch, 'The Future of War', *The Contemporary Review* 80 (1901): 305–32.

4. The prize exhibit here was Boris Zaharoff, a Greek-born arms dealer and the man for whom the term 'merchant of death' was invented. In the late 1880s he managed to sell a steam-driven submarine of doubtful quality, rejected by the major powers, first to the Greeks and then to the Turks, on the grounds that they were now threatened by

this new Greek capability, and then to the Russians because they should be worried about what was going on in the Black Sea. None of these submarines ever saw service. See Anthony Alfrey, *Man of Arms: The Life and Legend of Sir Basil Zaharoff* (London: Thistle Publishing, 2013).

5. John Gittings, *The Glorious Art of Peace: From the Iliad to Iraq* (London: Oxford University Press, 2012) 145.

6. White's biography cited by Diana Preston, *A Higher Form of Killing: Six Weeks in World War One That Forever Changed the Nature of Warfare* (New York: Bloomsbury Press, 2015) 16–7.

7. Cooper, *Patriotic Pacifism*, Chapter 4.

8. Joseph Conrad, 'Autocracy and War', *Note on Life and Letters*. (Cambridge: Cambridge University Press, 2004) p. 89.

9. Stephen Neff, *War and the Law of Nations* (Cambridge: Cambridge University Press, 2005) 161, 168.

10. D. Schindler and J. Toman, *The Laws of Armed Conflicts* (Boston: Martinus Nihjoff Publisher, 1988) 102.

11. Henry Dunant, *A Memory of Solferino*, 1862, online, International Committee of the Red Cross. Available: https://www.icrc.org/eng/resources/documents/publication /p0361.htm. Michael Barnett describes this book as 'one of the first unvarnished accounts of war'. *Empire of Humanity: A History of Humanitarianism* (Ithaca: Cornell University Press, 2011) 78.

12. Neff, *War and the Law of Nations*, 189.

13. International Committee of the Red Cross, *Convention (II) with Respect to the Laws and Customs of War on Land and its annex: Regulations concerning the Laws and Customs of War on Land*, 29 July 1899.

14. On Lieber's wider views, which allow him to be identified as an early theorist of international relations, see David Clinton, 'Francis Lieber, Imperialism, and Internationalism', *Imperialism and Internationalism in the Discipline of International Relations*, eds. David C. Long and Brian Schmidt (New York: SUNY Press, 2005).

15. The Lieber Code of 1863, Article 15, General Orders No. 100. Available: http:// www.civilwarhome.com/liebercode.htm

16. John Fabian Witt, *The Laws of War in American History* (New York: The Free Press, 2012).

17. Geoffrey Best, *Humanity in Warfare: The Modern History of the International Law of Armed Conflicts* (London: Methuen, 1980) 155.

CHAPTER 4

1. Walt Whitman, 'The Million Dead, Too, Summ'd Up', in 'North Carolina's Futile Rebellion Against the United States, 1860-1869', Walt Whitman, *Complete Prose Works*, (Philadelphia, PA: David Mckay,1892), 80. Available: http://whitmanarchive .org/published/other/CompleteProse.html#leaf043r1

2. Lieber Code, Articles 20–22.

3. Bruce Vandervort, 'War and Colonial Expansion', *The Cambridge History of War*, Vol. IV, *War and the Modern World*, eds. Roger Chickering et al. (Cambridge: Cambridge University Press, 2012) 69.

4. Jean Quataert, 'War-making and restraint by law', in Chickering et al. 156.

5. Colonel Charles Callwell, *Small Wars: Their Principles and Practice* (London: HMSO, 1886).

6. Callwell 72.

7. Bloch, *Is War Now Impossible?* x.

8. J. A. Hobson, *Imperialism: A Study* (New York: James Pott & Co., 1902). Available: http://files.libertyfund.org/files/127/0052_Bk.pdf

9. Paul Daley, 'Why the number of Indigenous deaths in the frontier wars matters', *Guardian*, 15 July 2014. The article is based on paper given to the 2014 Australian

Historical Association Conference by Raymond Evans and Robert Ørsted-Jensen, '"I Cannot Say the Numbers that Were Killed": Assessing Violent Mortality on the Queensland Frontier'.

10. Wells, *The War in the Air* 278.

11. Vandervort 93.

12. Williamson Murray and Wayne Wei-Siang Hsieh, *A Savage War: A Military History of the Civil War* (Princeton: Princeton University Press, 2016), 483, and Matthew Carr, *Sherman's Ghosts: Soldiers, Civilians, and the American Way of War* (New York: New Press, 2015) 75.

13. Murray and Hsieh 483.

14. Best 209.

15. Paul Hutton, *Phil Sheridan and His Army* (Norman, OK: University of Oklahoma Press, 1999) 204–5, and Geoffrey Wawro, *The Franco-Prussian War: The German Conquest of France in 1870–1871* (Cambridge: Cambridge University Press, 2003) 279.

16. Stig Förster, 'The Prussian Triangle of Leadership in the Face of a People's War: A Reassessment of the Conflict Between Bismarck and Moltke, 1870–71', *On The Road to Total War: The American Civil War and the German Wars of Unification, 1861–1871*, eds. Stig Förster and Jorg Nagler (Cambridge: Cambridge University Press for the German Historical Institute, 1997) 115–140.

17. Colmar von der Goltz, *The Nation in Arms*, trans. Philip A. Ashworth (London: W. H. Allen, 1883). Available: https://archive.org/details/nationinarms00ashwgoog. See Robert Foley, *German Strategy and the Path to Verdun: Erich von Falkenhayn and the Development of Attrition, 1870–1916* (Cambridge: Cambridge University Press, 2005).

18. Stanley Karnow, *In Our Own Image: American Empire in the Philippines* (New York: Random House, 1989) 194.

19. Thomas Pakenham, *The Boer War* (New York: Random House, 1979) 493.

20. Isabel V. Hull, *Absolute Destruction: Military Culture and The Practices of War in Imperial Germany* (Ithaca, NY: Cornell University Press, 2005).

21. Helmut Moltke, 'On the Nature of War', Letter to Johann Kaspar Bluntschli, 11 December 1880, online, Brigham Young University, 28 May 2009. Available: https://wwi.lib.byu.edu/index.php/On_the_Nature_of_War_by_Helmut_Moltke_(the_Elder). It was in this letter that von Moltke associated himself with the 'humanitarian striving to lessen the sufferings that come with war', but went on to add: 'Eternal peace is a dream—and not even a beautiful one. War is part of God's world-order. Within it unfold the noblest virtues of men, courage and renunciation, loyalty to duty and readiness for sacrifice—at the hazard of one's life. Without war the world would sink into a swamp of materialism'.

22. Amanda Alexander, 'The Genesis of the Civilian', *Leiden Journal of International Law* 20.2 (2007) 364.

23. Neff 204–210.

24. Arthur Conan Doyle, 'Danger! Being the log of Captain John Sirius', *The Strand Magazine*, July 1914. See Clarke 91, and Tom de Castella, 'Arthur Conan Doyle's eerie vision of the future of war', online, BBC News Magazine, 28 August 2014. Available: http://www.bbc.co.uk/news/magazine-28954510

25. John N. Horne and Alan Kramer, *German Atrocities of 1914: A History of Denial* (New Haven: Yale University Press, 2001).

26. David Stevenson, 'Strategic and Military Planning, 1871–1914', *The Fog of Peace and War Planning: Military and Strategic Planning under Uncertainty*, eds. Talbot Imlay and Monica Duffy Toft (London: Routledge, 2006) 91.

27. Diana Preston, *A Higher Form of Killing: Six weeks in World War I That Forever Changed the Nature of Warfare* (New York: Bloomsbury Press, 2015).

28. Jack L. Snyder, *The Ideology of the Offensive: Military Decision Making and the Disasters of 1914* (Ithaca: Cornell University Press, 1984).

CHAPTER 5

1. E. H. Carr, *The Twenty Years' Crisis* (London: Macmillan, 1939). 16.

2. Norman Angell, *The Great Illusion: A Study of the Relation of Military Power to National Advantage* (London: G. P. Putnam's, 1910). Available: http://www.gutenberg .org/files/38535/38535-h/38535-h.htm. It was first published in 1909 under the title *Europe's Optical Illusion*. For a biography of Angell, see Martin Ceadel, *Living the Great Illusion: Sir Norman Angell, 1872–1967* (Oxford: Oxford University Press, 2009).

3. See for example Paul Krugman, 'The Great Illusion', *New York Times*, 14 Aug. 2008.

4. Christopher Clark, *The Sleepwalkers: How Europe Went to War in 1914* (New York: Harper, 2012); Margaret MacMillan, *The War That Ended Peace: The Road to 1914* (New York: Random House, 2013); and Thomas Otte, *July Crisis: The World's Descent into War, Summer 1914* (Cambridge: Cambridge University Press, 2014).

5. H. G. Wells, 'The War That Will End War', *The Daily News*, 14 Aug. 1914. This was published later in the year as a book with the same title by Frank and Cecil Parker. Available: https://archive.org/stream/warthatwillendwa00welluoft#page/n5/mode/2up

6. John Bew, *Realpolitik: A History* (New York: Oxford University Press, 2016) 96.

7. Hobson, *Imperialism*, 13.

8. Peter Clarke, *The Locomotive of War: Monet, Empire, Power, and Guilt*, (London: Bloomsbury, 2017), 22.

9. William Mulligan, *The Great War for Peace* (New Haven: Yale University Press, 2014) 233–5.

10. 'President Wilson's Address to Congress, Analyzing German and Austrian Peace Utterances', 11 Feb. 1918, online, The World War I Document Archive, 12 July 1997. Available: http://www.gwpda.org/1918/wilpeace.html

11. 'President Wilson's Fourteen Points', 8 Jan. 1918, online, Brigham Young University, 28 Feb. 2008. Available: http://wwi.lib.byu.edu/index.php/President_Wilson's _Fourteen_Points

12. Viscount Grey of Fallodon, KG, *Twenty-Five Years, 1892–1916*, Vol. 1 (London: Hodder & Stoughton, 1925) 89.

13. Margaret MacMillan, *Peacemakers Six Months that Changed The World: The Paris Peace Conference of 1919 and Its Attempt to End War* (London: John Murray, 2011), and Carole Fink, 'The search for peace in the interwar period', *The Cambridge History of War*, Vol. IV, eds. Chickering et al., 285–309.

14. Michael Howard, *The Invention of Peace* (London: Profile Books, 2000) 45. See also his *War and the Liberal Conscience* (London: Temple Smith, 1978).

15. Wilson's Address to Joint Session of Congress, 11 Feb. 1918. https://wwi.lib.byu .edu/index.php/President_Wilson's_Fourteen_Points

16. MacMillan, *Peacemakers* 19–21.

17. Robert Gerwarth, *The Vanquished: Why the First World War Failed to End* (London: Allen Lane, 2016) 7.

18. Mulligan 339.

19. Salvador de Madariaga, *Disarmament* (New York: Coward-McCann, 1929) 12.

20. Leonard Woolf, ed., *The Intelligent Man's Way to Prevent War* (London: Victor Gollancz, 1933) 10.

21. Woolf 270, 408, 18.

22. David Faber, *Munich, 1938: Appeasement and World War II* (New York: Simon & Schuster, 2009).

23. Broadcast (27 Sept. 1938), quoted in 'Prime Minister on the Issues', *The Times*, 28 Sept. 1938, p. 10.

24. The 1946 edition of Carr can be found at http://www.spa.zju.edu.cn/eclass /attachments/2015-04/01-1427863185-17726.pdf. See also Jonathan Haslam, *The Vices of Integrity: E. H. Carr, 1892–1982* (London; New York: Verso, 1999).

CHAPTER 6

1. Basil Liddell Hart, *Europe in Arms* (London: Faber & Faber, 1937) 269.

2. Amanda Alexander, 'The Genesis of the Civilian', *Leiden Journal of International Law* 20.2 (2007): 360.

3. Cited by Tami Davis Biddle, *Rhetoric and Reality in Air Warfare: The Evolution of British and American Ideas about Strategic Bombing* (Princeton: Princeton University Press, 2002) 33.

4. Michael Paris, *Winged Warfare: Literature and Theory of Aerial Warfare in Britain, 1859-1917* (Manchester: Manchester University Press,1992), 38.

5. R. P. Hearne, *Aerial Warfare* (London: John Lane, The Bodley Head, 1909).

6. Claude Grahame-White and Harry Harper, *Air Power: Naval, Military, Commercial* (London: Chapman & Hall, 1917).

7. Giulio Douhet, *The Command of the Air*, trans. Dino Ferrari (Washington DC: Office of Air Force History, 1983). Available: http://www.au.af.mil/au/awc/awcgate /readings/command_of_the_air.pdf. This is discussed in my *Strategy: A History* (New York: Oxford University Press, 2013), Chapter Ten.

8. B. H. Liddell Hart, *Paris or the Future of War* (New York: E. P. Dutton, 1925).

9. Brett Holman, *The Next War in the Air: Britain's Fear of the Bomber, 1908–1941* (London, Ashgate: 2014) 23–4.

10. Erich Ludendorff, *The Nation at War*, trans. A.S. Rapaport (London: Hutchinson, 1936) 101, and Hans Spieir, 'Ludendorff: The German Concept of Total War', *Makers of Modern Strategy: Military Thought from Machiavelli to Hitler*, ed. Edward Mead Earle (Princeton: Princeton University Press, 1943) 306–21. On total war in practice see Jeremy Black, *The Age of Total War*, 1860–1945. (Westport, Conn.: Praeger Security International, 2006).

11. Clarke, *Voices Prophesying War* 169–170.

12. These novels are discussed in Susan R. Grayzel, *At Home and under Fire: Air Raids and Culture in Britain from the Great War to the Blitz* (Cambridge: Cambridge University Press, 2012), and Holman, *The Next War in the Air*.

13. In his pre-1914 stories on air power *With The Night Mail*, (1905) and *As Easy as ABC* (1912) Rudyard Kipling had introduced the idea of the 'Aerial Board of Control' which had turned into a de facto world government. Kipling's novels are also interesting because while he suggested that the possibility of air raids had put war 'out of fashion' they might be useful for quelling riots and so serve as a form of social control. Paris suggests that British use of air power for imperial policing owes something to Kipling. *Winged Warriors*, 40–1.

14. *Evening News*, 14 March 1935, cited by Holman. It was published in book form as S. Fowler Wright, *Prelude in Prague: A Story of the War of 1938* (London: George Newnes, 1935). It was followed by *Four Days War* (1936) and *Megiddo's Ridge* (1937). For plot summaries, see Mary Weinkauf, *Sermons in Science Fiction: The Novels of S. Fowler Wright* (Rockville, MA: Wildside Press, 2006).

15. 'The Tragedy Of Guernica: Town Destroyed In Air Attack: Eye-Witness's Account', *The Times*, 26 April 1937, online. Available: http://www.thetimes.co.uk/tto/news/world/europe/article2601941.ece

16. Cited by Rana Mitter, *China's War with Japan, 1937–1945: The Struggle for Survival* (London: Allen Lane, 2013) 137.

17. Christian Hartmann, *Operation Barbarossa: Nazi Germany's War in the East, 1941–1945* (Oxford: Oxford University Press, 2015) 13.

18. Barton Whaley, *Codeword Barbarossa* (Cambridge, MA: MIT Press, 1974), and Steve Twomey, *Countdown to Pearl Harbor: The Twelve Days to the Attack* (New York: Simon & Schuster, 2016).

19. Christian Gerlach, 'The Wannsee Conference, the Fate of German Jews, and Hitler's Decision in Principle to Exterminate All European Jews', *The Journal of Modern History* 70.4 (1998): 759–812, and Richard Evans, *The Third Reich at*

War: How the Nazis Led Germany from Conquest to Disaster (London: Allen Lane, 2008).

20. Andrew Roberts, *The Storm of War: A New History of the Second World War* (London: Penguin, 2009).

21. Hector Bywater, *Great Pacific War: A History of the American-Japanese Campaign of 1931–33* (New York: Applewood Books, 2002).

22. The book was republished soon after Pearl Harbor with the subtitle 'A Historic Prophecy Now Being Fulfilled'. In an introduction, Hanson W. Baldwin, military editor of the *New York Times*, described the book as 'deeply prophetic'.

23. W. H. Honan, *Visions of Infamy: The untold story of how journalist Hector C. Bywater devised the plans that led to Pearl Harbor* (New York: St. Martin's Press, 1991).

24. Jeffrey Record, *A War It was Always Going to Lose: Why Japan Attacked America in 1941* (Washington DC: Potomac Books, 2011) 86–7.

25. Craig Nelson, *Pearl Harbor* 76–8, 166.

26. Richard Betts, *Surprise Attack: Lessons for Defense Planning* (Washington DC: Brookings Institution, 1982).

27. Phillips Payson O'Brien, *How the War Was Won: Air-Sea Power and Allied Victory in World War II* (Cambridge: Cambridge University Press, 2015).

28. Joseph Maiolo, *Cry Havoc: How the Arms Race Drove the World to War, 1931–1941* (New York: Basic Books, 2010) 337.

CHAPTER 7

1. H. G. Wells, *The World Set Free* (London: Macmillan, 1914).

2. George Orwell, 'Wells, Hitler and the World State', *Horizon*, (August 1941) 133–9, http://orwell.ru/library/reviews/wells/english/e_whws. Wells always understood that science could be employed for evil purposes. John S. Partington, 'The pen as sword: George Orwell, H. G. Wells and journalistic parricide', *Journal of Contemporary History*, 39:1 (2004); 45–56; John Stone, 'George Orwell on politics and war', *Review of International Studies*, 43:2, (2016) pp. 221–239.

3. Cited by Richard Rhodes, *The Making of the Atomic Bomb* (New York: Simon & Schuster, 1986) 44.

4. Frederick Soddy, *The interpretation of radium: being the substance of six free popular experimental lectures delivered at the University of Glasgow* (London: John Murray. 1908) 8, and Richard E. Sclove, 'From Alchemy to Atomic War: Frederick Soddy's "Technology Assessment" of Atomic Energy, 1900–1915', *Science, Technology, & Human Values* 14.2 (1989): 163–194.

5. Soddy 251.

6. Soddy 172.

7. Wells, *The World Set Free* 55–8.

8. P. D. Smith, *Doomsday Men: The Real Dr Strangelove and the Dream of the Superweapon* (London: Allen Lane, 2007).

9. Rhodes 13, and William Lanouette, *Genius in the Shadows: A Biography of Leo Szilard, the Man Behind the Bomb* (Chicago: University of Chicago Press, 1994).

10. John Hersey, 'Hiroshima', *New Yorker*, 31 August 1946. Available: http://www.newyorker.com/magazine/1946/08/31/hiroshima

11. In the event, the Soviet Union tested the biggest ever device—some 57 megatons—in 1961 on the island of Novaya Zemlya. They lacked any means of delivering a weapon of this size to a target.

12. See Smith, Chapter 18.

13. Nevil Shute, *On The Beach*, (London: Heinemann, 1957).

14. His knowledge of cobalt bombs came from Ernest Titterton, a nuclear scientist at the Australian National University who had a chapter on 'radiological warfare' in his 1956 book *Facing the Atomic Future*, (London: Macmillan, 1956) 'If some madman

decided that he wished to poison the whole of the human race with radioactivity', observed Titterton, 'it would be possible to arrange for a shell of cobalt around a fission or fusion bomb to absorb the excess neutrons and make radiocobalt'.

15. A 1953 speech at the United Nations by President Eisenhower offered 'atoms for peace'. This was an effort to enable states to harness atomic energy for peaceful purposes in return for promises not to exploit it to build weapons. This became a good example of the law of unintended consequences. The United States offered developing states research reactors, fuel, and scientific training in return for the commitment to use the technology only for civilian purposes. Among the early beneficiaries of the initiative were India, Pakistan, Iran, and Israel—all of whom went on to develop military programmes. See Leonard Weiss, 'Atoms for Peace', *Bulletin of the Atomic Scientists* 59.6 (2003): 34–44.

16. Screenplay, *On the Beach* (1959), http://www.script-o-rama.com/movie_scripts /o/on-the-beach-script-transcript.html

17. Paul Brians, *Nuclear Holocausts: Atomic War in Fiction 1895–1984* (Kent, OH: Kent State University Press, 1987). An updated electronic version is available at http:// public.wsu.edu/~brians/nuclear/.

18. Peter Bryant, *Red Alert* (Rockville, MD: Black Mask, 1958). This was a pseudonym for Peter George (who, when he wrote this book, was an RAF officer). After the movie's release he published a new version based on its script. It has been republished with an introduction by George's son and a note by George on the Strangelove character in Peter George, *Dr Strangelove or How I Learned to Stop Worrying and Love the Bomb* (Cardiff: Candy Jar Books, 2015).

19. Eugene Burdick and Harvey Wheeler, *Fail-Safe* (New York: McGraw-Hill, 1962).

20. Gannon 141.

21. Smith cites a letter from Alastair Buchan, then-Director of the Institute for Strategic Studies, claiming to have handed Kubrick a copy of George's book after trying to dissuade him from making a movie based on such a far-fetched premise. Somewhat later in his career Buchan examined my PhD.

22. The quotation comes from James Newman's eviscerating review of Kahn's *On Thermonuclear War* in *Scientific American* (March 1961). Newman published this and some other pieces in *The Rule of Folly*, with a preface by Erich Fromm (London: Allen & Unwin, 1962). Kahn had a mischievous sense of humour to the point that one biographer considers his potential as a stand-up comic. See Sharon Ghamari-Tabrizi, *The Worlds of Herman Kahn: The Intuitive Science of Thermonuclear War* (Cambridge, MA: Harvard University Press, 2005).

23. The first book on RAND was Bruce L. R. Smith, *The RAND Corporation; Case Study of a Nonprofit Advisory Corporation* (Cambridge, MA: Harvard University Press, 1966). The personal rivalries come out in Fred Kaplan's *Wizards of Armageddon* (Stanford: Stanford University Press, 1983).

24. Herman Kahn, *On Thermonuclear War* (Princeton: Princeton University Press, 1960) 144.

25. The actor who played Strangelove, Peter Sellers, modelled him on Wernher von Braun, the German rocket scientist whose skills had been put to use after the war at the Army's Redstone Arsenal. See Eric Schlosser, 'Deconstructing "Dr. Strangelove"', *New Yorker*, 18 Jan. 18 2014. Available: http://www.newyorker.com/News/News-Desk /Deconstructing-Dr-Strangelove

26. Kahn 228.

27. See Ghamari-Tabrizi.

28. Thomas Schelling, 'Meteors, Mischief, and War', *Bulletin of the Atomic Scientists* 16 (1960): 292–296, 300.

29. Alan Ferguson quoted in Freedman, *Strategy* 173.

CHAPTER 8

1. Albert Wohlstetter, 'The Delicate Balance of Terror', *Foreign Affairs* 37.2 (1959).

2. Bernhard G. Bechhoefer, *Postwar Negotiations for Arms Control* (Washington DC: Brookings Institution, 1961) 470.

3. Jeremi Suri, 'America's Search for a Technological Solution to the Arms Race: The Surprise Attack Conference of 1958', *Diplomatic History* 21.3 (1997).

4. John H. Herz, *Political Realism and Political Idealism* (Chicago: Chicago University Press, 1951).

5. C. P. Snow, 'The Moral Un-Neutrality of Science', *American Association for the Advancement of Science* (1960).

6. The Federation of American Scientists, *One World or None: A Report to the Public on the Full Meaning of the Atomic Bomb*, ed. Dexter Masters (New York: McGraw Hill, 1946). The New Press republished it in 2007.

7. Philip Noel-Baker, 'Peace and the Arms Race', Nobel Lecture, 11 Dec. 1959.

8. Hedley Bull, 'Disarmament and the International System', *Australian Journal of Politics & History* 5.1 (1959): 41–50.

9. William Fox, *The Super-Powers: The United States, Britain, and the Soviet Union—Their Responsibility for Peace* (New York: Harcourt Brace, 1944).

10. William Churchill, 'Never Despair', 1 Mar. 1955 speech to the House of Commons, online, The International Churchill Society. Available: http://www.winstonchurchill.org/resources/speeches/1946-1963-elder-statesman/never-despair

11. I deal with these episodes in Lawrence Freedman, *Kennedy's Wars: Berlin, Cuba, Laos and Vietnam* (New York: Oxford University Press, 2000).

12. Albert Wohlstetter et al., *Selection and Use of Strategic Air Bases* (Santa Monica, CA: RAND Corporation, 1954). Available: http://www.rand.org/pubs/reports/R0266.html

13. Albert Wohlstetter, 'The Delicate Balance of Terror', *Foreign Affairs* (1959): 211–234. A discussion of Wohlstetter and his writings can be found in Robert Zarate and Henry Sokolski, eds., *Nuclear Heuristics: Selected Writings of Albert and Roberta Wohlstetter* (Strategic Studies Institute: US Army War College, 2009). Also see Fred Kaplan, *Wizards of Armageddon* 108.

14. Kahn, *On Thermonuclear War* 484. This was, of course, something that eventually took place as a result of climate change. Kahn developed his career largely as a futurologist. In 1967 he published with Anthony J. Wiener *The Year 2000. A Framework for Speculation on the Next Thirty-Three Years.* (New York: Macmillan, 1967), which contains a similar mix of spot-on and off-the-wall projections.

15. M. N. Golovine, *Conflicts in Space: A Pattern of War in a New Dimension* (New York: St. Martin's Press, 1962).

16. Joseph Trevithick, 'Bizarre weapons never left the drawing board: The U.S. Army's Gun-Toting Space Soldiers', *War is Boring*, 9 Nov. 2015, online. Available: https://warisboring.com/the-u-s-army-s-gun-toting-space-soldiers-ea9f1f1d48d0#.5u0wb9fyb

17. Roberta Wohlstetter, *Pearl Harbor: Warning and Decision* (Stanford, CA: Stanford University Press, 1962) 399–401. The book had originally been published as an internal RAND document in 1958. The importance of Roberta's work and its influence on that of Albert's is brought out in Ron Robin, *The Cold War They Made: The Strategic Legacy of Roberta and Albert Wohlstetter* (Cambridge, MA: Harvard University Press, 2016).

18. David Dunn, *The Politics of Threat: Minuteman Vulnerability in American National Security Policy* (London: Palgrave, 1997).

19. Kenneth N. Waltz, *Theory of International Politics* (New York: Random House, 1979), and Kenneth N. Waltz, *The Spread of Nuclear Weapons: More May Better*, Adelphi Paper no. 171 (London: International Institute for Strategic Studies, 1981).

20. Michael Quinlan, *Thinking About Nuclear Weapons: Principles, Problems, Prospects* (London: OUP, 2009). 9–14.

21. Albert Carnesale et al., *Living with Nuclear Weapons* (Cambridge, MA: Harvard University Press, 1983).

22. Joseph S. Nye, Jr., Graham T. Allison, Jr., and Albert Carnesale, eds., *Fateful Visions: Avoiding Nuclear Catastrophe* (New York: Harper & Row, 1988).

23. James Blight, *The Shattered Crystal Ball: Fear and Learning in the Cuban Missile Crisis* (New York: Rowman & Littlefield, 1990) 172–4.

CHAPTER 9

1. The speech was published as Václav Havel, "Words on Words", *New York Review of Books*, 18 January 1990.

2. Jane Stromseth, *The Origins of Flexible Response: Nato's Debate over Strategy in the 1960s*, (London: Palgrave, 1988).

3. These various scares are discussed in Philip Sabin, *The Third World War Scare in Britain* (London: Macmillan, 1986).

4. General Sir John Hackett, 'A Third World War', Third Jubilee Lecture, Imperial College of Science and Technology, University of London, 13 Mar. 1979. For background I am indebted to Jeff Michaels, 'Revisiting General Sir John Hackett's *The Third World War*', *British Journal for Military History*, 3:1, (2016), 88–104.

5. For an enthusiastic endorsement see I. F. Clarke, *Voices Prophesying War* 198. He specifically describes it as the modern equivalent of *The Battle of Dorking*.

6. General Sir John Hackett, *The Third World War: The Untold Story* (New York: Macmillan, 1982).

7. Brians, *Nuclear Holocausts*. Available at *http://public.wsu.edu/~brians/nuclear/ index.htm*

8. A 'standing start' attack was a theme of an influential report by Senators Sam Nunn and Dewey F. Bartlett, *NATO and the New Soviet Threat*, US Senate, Armed Services Committee, 95th Congress, First Session (Washington DC: US Government Printing Office, 1977). See also Phillip A. Karber, *The Impact of New Conventional Technologies on Military Doctrine and Organization in the Warsaw Pact*, Adelphi Paper no. 144 (London: International Institute for Strategic Studies, 1978).

9. Robert Close, *Europe Without Defence?: 48 Hours That Could Change The Face of the World* (Brussels: Editions Arts and Voyages, 1976).

10. Shelford Bidwell, ed., *World War 3* (London: Hamlyn, 1978). I was a contributor to the first half of this book, which contained some scene-setting essays, but not to the fictional scenario.

11. Cited in Sabin, 29.

12. Tom Clancy, *Red Storm Rising* (New York: Putnam Publishing, 1986).

13. George Winston, 'Was Reagan Influenced By Reading Tom Clancy's "Red Storm Rising" Before A Cold War Summit with Gorbachev?' online, War History Online, Internet, 22 Feb. 2016. Available: https://www.warhistoryonline.com/war-articles/was-reagan -influenced-by-reading-tom-clancys-red-storm-rising.html

14. President Ronald Reagan, *Address to the Nation on Defense and National Security*, 23 Mar. 1983.

15. Valerie Edwards, 'How Ronald Reagan based his foreign policy on Tom Clancy books: President told Margaret Thatcher to read Red Storm Rising thriller to understand Russia', *Daily Mail* 30 Dec. 2015, online. Available: http://www.dailymail.co.uk /news/article-3378683/Ronald-Reagan-advised-Margaret-Thatcher-read-Tom-Clancy-s -thriller-Cold-War-strategy.html

16. Tom Clancy, *The Sum of all Fears* (New York: Putnam, 1991)

17. Ray Garthoff, *A Journey Through the Cold War* (Washington DC: Brookings Institution, 2001) 16. On this episode, see Jonathan Haslam, *Russia's Cold War* (New Haven: Yale University Press, 2011) 168–174.

18. John Lewis Gaddis, *The Cold War* (London: Penguin, 2007) 180.

19. Text of the "Basic Principles of Relations Between the United States of America and the Union of Soviet Socialist Republics." 29 May 1972, Available: http://www .presidency.ucsb.edu/ws/?pid=3438.

20. Daniel C. Thomas, T*he Helsinki Effect: International Norms, Human Rights and the Demise of Communism* (Princeton: Princeton University Press, 2001).

21. Kissinger describes the debates around détente in Chapter 29 of his *Diplomacy* (New York: Simon & Schuster, 1994).

22. Secretary Kissinger, 'The Moral Foundations of Foreign Policy', *Department of State Bulletin*, LXXII: 1884, 4 Aug. 1975. Available: https://www.fordlibrarymuseum.gov/library/document/dosb/1884.pdf#page=15

23. Jimmy Carter, 'Inaugural Address', *The American Presidency Project*, UCSB, 20 Jan. 1977, http://www.presidency.ucsb.edu/ws/?pid=6575

24. Thomas 179.

25. Michael Zantovsky, *Havel: A Life* (London: Atlantic Books, 2014).

26. Václav Havel, *Open Letters: Selected Prose* (London: Faber & Faber, 1992) 329, 265, 385.

27. Archie Brown, *The Gorbachev Factor* (Oxford: Oxford University Press, 1996).

28. Andrei Grachev, *Gorbachev's Gamble: Soviet Foreign Policy and the End of the Cold War* (Cambridge: Polity, 2008).

29. Mikhail Gorbachev, 'Address to the United Nations,' 7 Dec. 1988. Available: http://astro.temple.edu/~rimmerma/gorbachev_speech_to_UN.htm

30. Stephen Kotkin, *Armageddon Averted: Soviet Collapse since 1970 Updated Edition* (New York: Oxford University Press, 2009).

31. Anatoly Dobrynin, *In Confidence: Moscow's Ambassador to Six Cold War Presidents* (New York: Times Books/Random House, 1995) 632.

32. *Soviet Military Power 1985* (Washington DC: Department of Defense, 1985) 4–5. Official publication.

33. *Soviet Military Power 1990* (Washington DC: Department of Defense, 1990) 5.

34. Mick Cox, *1989 and why we got it wrong*, Working Paper Series of the Research Network 1989 1 (2008): 5.

35. Center for the Study of Intelligence, *At Cold War's End: US Intelligence on the Soviet Union and Eastern Europe, 1989–1991* (Langley: CIA, 1999).

36. Andrei Amalrik, *Will the Soviet Union Survive Until 1984?* (New York: HarperCollins, 1981)

37. President Ronald Reagan, Address to British Parliament, 8 June 1982. His substantial build-up of America's military strength at the start of the 1980s is also credited, not least by members of his administration, for persuading the Soviet leadership that it could not compete in an arms race, although that has been disputed. Richard Ned Lebow and Janice Gross Stein, 'Reagan and the Russians: The Cold War ended despite President Reagan's arms buildup, not because of it—or so former President Gorbachev told the authors', *The Atlantic Monthly* (1994). Available at http://www.theatlantic.com/past/docs/politics/foreign/reagrus.htm

38. Marshall I. Goldman, *Gorbachev's Challenge: Economic Reform in the Age of High Technology* (New York: W. W. Norton, 1978) 262. See also Cox 8–9.

39. For example Rasma Karklins, *Ethnic Relations in the USSR: The View from Below.* (Boston, MA: Unwin and Hyman. 1986)

40. Richard Nixon, *1999—Victory without War* (New York: Simon & Schuster, 1988) 26.

41. George Bush and Brent Scowcroft, *A World Transformed* (New York: Knopf, 1998) 13, and James A. Baker III, *The Politics of Diplomacy: Revolution, War, and Peace, 1989–1992* (New York: G. P. Putnam's Sons, 1995) 70.

42. Jim Hoagland, 'From Yalta To Malta', *Washington Post*, 9 Nov. 1989.

CHAPTER 10

1. J. David Singer and Melvin Small, *The Wages of War, 1816–1965: A Statistical Handbook* (New York: John Wiley, 1972) 4.

2. Hans J. Morgenthau, *Politics Among Nations: The Struggle for Power and Peace*, 5ᵗʰ ed. (New York: Alfred A. Knopf, 1978) 26. See also Christoph Frei, *Hans J Morgenthau: An Intellectual Biography* (Baton Rouge: Louisiana State University Press, 2001), and Hans Morgenthau, 'The Four Paradoxes of Nuclear Strategy', *American Political Science Review* 581 (1964): 23–35.

3. Kenneth Waltz, *Theory of International Politics* (New York: McGraw Hill, 1979) 72. Waltz was aware of the Soviet Union's weaknesses, but this was largely by way of comparison with America's strengths rather than an indicator of a coming collapse (183). See Marco Cesa, 'Realist Visions of the End of the Cold War: Morgenthau, Aron and Waltz', *The British Journal of Politics and International Relations* 11 (2009): 177–191.

4. Robert O. Keohane, ed., *Neorealism and Its Critics* (New York: Columbia University Press, 1986).

5. Richard Ned Lebow, 'The Long Peace, the End of the Cold War, and the Failure of Realism', *International Organization* 48.2 (1994): 249–277.

6. John Lewis Gaddis, 'International Relations Theory and the End of the Cold War', *International Security* 17.3 (1992/93): 5–58.

7. John Mearsheimer, 'Back to the Future: Instability in Europe after the Cold War', *International Security* 15.1 (1990): 5–56

8. Quincy Wright, *A Study of War*, 2nd ed. (Chicago: University of Chicago Press, 1965); Karl W. Deutsch, 'Quincy Wright's contribution to the study of war: a preface to the second edition', *Journal of Conflict Resolution* 14 (1970): 473; and William T. R. Fox, '"The truth shall make you free": one student's appreciation of Quincy Wright', *Journal of Conflict Resolution* 14 (1970): 449.

9. Lewis Fry Richardson, *Arms and Insecurity: A Mathematical Study of the Causes and Origins of War* (Pittsburgh, PA: Boxwood Press, 1960) 12.

10. Lewis Fry Richardson, *Statistics of Deadly Quarrels* (Pittsburgh, PA: Boxwood Press, 1960), and *Arms and Insecurity*; Oliver M. Ashford, *Prophet or Professor? The Life and Work of Lewis Fry Richardson* (Bristol: Adam Hilger, 1985); and Michael Nicholson, 'Lewis Fry Richardson and the Study of the Causes of War', *British Journal of Political Science* 29.3 (1999): 541–563.

11. Kenneth Boulding, *Conflict and Defense: A General Theory* (New York: Harper & Bros., 1962) vii.

12. Cynthia Kerman, 'Kenneth Boulding And The Peace Research Movement', *American Studies* 13.1 (1972): 149–165.

13. I discuss this in Lawrence Freedman, 'Social Science and the Cold War', *Journal of Strategic Studies* 38:4 (2015): 554-574

14. Harold Guetzkow, 'Long Range Research in International Relations', *American Perspective* 4 (1950): 421–40. Cited by John Vasquez, ed., *What Do We Know About War?*, 2ⁿᵈ ed., (Lanham, MD: Rowman & Littlefield, 2012) 329.

15. Vasquez 330.

16. Vasquez xiii.

17. Vasquez, xiv-xvi.

18. John A. Vasquez, *The War Puzzle Revisited* (Cambridge: Cambridge University Press, 2009) 405, 417.

19. For one relatively late citation, see William Hawkins, 'New Enemies for Old', *The National Review*, 42.18, (1990): 28–29. For some reason this claim still appears regularly in books on theology. According to John Gittings in *The Glorious Art of Peace* (22), the numbers appear in Edmund Osmanczyk, *Encyclopaedia of the United Nations and International Agreements*, 3ʳᵈ ed., ed. Anthony Mango (London: Routledge, 2003) 1783.

20. Norman Cousins, 'Electronic Brain on War and Peace: A report of an Imaginary Experiment', *St. Louis Post-Dispatch*, 13 Dec. 1953. In Cousins, *In Place of Folly* (New York: Harper, 1961), the number of those killed was reduced to 1.24 billion.

21. One of his statistics that attracted special attention was the claim that the value of the destruction inflicted would pay for 'a golden belt around the earth 156 kilometers in width and ten meters thick'.

22. Will and Ariel Durant, *The Lessons of History* (New York: Simon & Schuster, 1968) 81.

23. Donald Kagan, *On the Origins of War and the Preservation of Peace* (New York: Doubleday, 1995) 4.

24. For references see Barry O'Neill, 'Policy folklists and evolutionary theory', *Proceedings of the National Academy of Scientists of the United States* 111.3, (2014): 10854-10859

25. B. Jongman and H. van der Dennen, 'The Great "War Figures" Hoax: An investigation in polemomythology', *Security Dialogue* 19.2 (1988): 197–202.

26. O. Barot, *Lettres sur la Philosophie de l'Histoire* (Paris: Germer-Baillière, 1864).

27. Singer and Small, *The Wages of War, 1816–1965* 4. See also Melvin Small and J. David Singer, *Resort to Arms: International and Civil War, 1816–1980* (Beverly Hills: Sage, 1982); J. David Singer and Paul Diehl, eds., *Measuring the Correlates of War* (Ann Arbor: University of Michigan Press, 1990); and Meredith Reid Sarkees, Frank Whelon Wayman, and J. David Singer, 'Inter-State, Intra-State, and Extra-State Wars: A Comprehensive Look At Their Distribution Over Time, 1816–1997', *International Studies Quarterly* 47 (2003): 49–70.

28. By having more relaxed criteria, Kalevi J. Holsti, *Armed Conflicts and International Order: 1648–1989* (Cambridge: Cambridge University Press, 1991) identified 105 wars from 1815 of which twenty were not on the COW list.

29. Small and Singer, *Resort to Arms* 211–212. John Vasquez was amongst those who critiqued the original COW war typology in *The War Puzzle* (Cambridge: Cambridge University Press, 1993) 15–29. This artificial distinction was later abandoned, replaced by a distinction between wars for control of the central government, and those over local issues, including secession.

30. For a guide see Kristine Ecke, *A Beginner's Guide to Conflict Data: Finding and Using the Right Dataset* (Uppsala: Uppsala Conflict Data Programme, December 2005). Another database set up in 2006 is the ACLED (Armed Conflict Location and Event Data Project) 'designed for disaggregated conflict analysis and crisis mapping. This dataset codes the dates and locations of all reported political violence and protest events in over 60 developing countries in Africa and Asia.' Available: http://www.acleddata.com/

31. Bethany Lacina and Nils Petter Gleditsch, 'Monitoring Trends in Global Combat: A New Dataset of Battle Deaths', *European Journal of Population* 21.2–3 (2005): 145–166; Ted Robert Gurr, *Minorities at Risk: A Global View of Ethnopolitical Conflicts.* (Washington, DC: United States Institute of Peace Press. 1993). Another early data base was published in Roy Licklider, 'The Consequences of Negotiated Settlements in Civil Wars, 1945-1993,' *American Political Science Review*, 89: 3 (1995), 681-90.

32. Paul D Williams, 'Continuity and Change in War and Conflict in Africa', *PRISM* 6:4 (2017), 33–45.

33. Edward Newman, 'Conflict Research and the 'Decline' of Civil War', *Civil Wars*, 11:3 (September 2009), 255-278

34. For example, Donald Cameron Watt, *Too Serious a Business: European Armed Forces and the Approach to the Second World War* (Berkeley: University of California Press, 1975).

35. Daniel M. Jones, Stuart A. Bremer, and J. David Singer, 'Militarized Interstate Disputes, 1816–1992', *Conflict Management and Peace Science* 15.2 (1996): 163–213, 169.

36. Paul Hensel, 'The More Things Change', *Conflict Management and Peace Science* 19.1 (2002): 48.

37. Douglas M. Gibler, Steven V. Miller, and Erin K. Little, 'An Analysis of the Militarized Interstate Dispute (MID) Dataset, 1816–2001', *International Studies Quarterly* 60:4, (2017) 719-730.

38. Jessica Weeks and Dara Kay Cohen, 'Fishing Disputes, Regime Type, and Interstate Conflict A Research Note', Stanford University, Stanford International Relations Workshop, 7 Mar. 2006, http://citation.allacademic.com//meta/p_mla_apa_research_citation /0/9/8/1/0/pages98104/p98104-1.php. They also found that 10 per cent of cases in the set they were considering could not be verified.

39. Richard Wich, *Sino-Soviet Crisis Politics: A Study of Political Change and Communication* (London: Council on East Asian Studies, Harvard University, 1980). This was not one of the books used by MID as a source.

40. Lyle J. Goldstein, 'Return to Zhenbao Island: Who Started Shooting and Why it Matters', *The China Quarterly* 168 (2001): 985–997.

41. Y. Kuisong, 'The Sino-Soviet Border Clash of 1969: From Zhenbao Island to Sino-American Rapprochement', *Cold War History* 1.1 (2000): 21–52.

42. Hannah Arendt, *On Violence,* (New York: Harcourt, 1970), p. 6.

CHAPTER 11

1. Wislawa Szymborska, 'Hunger Camp at Jaslo', trans. Grazyna Drabik and Austin Flint, *Against Forgetting: Twentieth Century Poetry of Witness*, ed. Carolyn Forché, (New York: W. W. Norton, 1993).

2. A court in Bangladesh, for example, found a British man guilty of contempt for challenging the official death toll of 3 million from the 1971 war of independence when other researchers tend to put it closer to 500,000. See 'UK journalist guilty of querying Bangladesh death toll', BBC News, online, 2 December 2014. Available: http://www .bbc.co.uk/news/world-asia-30288785

3. See, for example, the controversy surrounding the work of Justin McCarthy who came up with a number for Armenians killed of 600,000. See *Muslims and Minorities: The Population of Ottoman Anatolia and the End of the Empire* (New York: New York University Press, 1983). Among his critics see Vahakn N. Dadrian, 'Ottoman Archives and Denial of the Armenian Genocide', *The Armenian Genocide: History, Politics, Ethics*, ed. R. G. Hovannisian (New York: St. Martin's Press, 1992) 294–7, and Raymond Kevorkian, *The Armenian Genocide: A Complete History* (London: I. B. Tauris, 2011).

4. Samuel Dumas and K. O. Vedel-Petersen, *Losses of Life Caused by War*, ed. Harald Westergaard (Oxford: Clarendon Press, 1923) 127. Available: https://archive.org /stream/lossesoflifecaus00samu#page/n4/mode/1up. Quincy Wright reviewed the book positively, pointing to the importance of accurate information in serving the cause of peace, in *American Journal of Sociology* 30.6 (1925): 722–725.

5. Milton Leitenberg, *Deaths in Wars and Conflicts in the Twentieth Century*, Cornell University Peace Studies Program, Occasional Paper #29, 3rd ed., 2006. This is an important guide to these issues.

6. Hazem Adam Ghobarah, Paul Huth, and Bruce Russett, 'Civil Wars Kill and Maim People—Long After the Shooting Stops', *American Political Science Review* 97:2 (2003): 189–202.

7. *United Nations Commission of Experts Established to Security Council Resolution 935 on Rwanda, Final Report* (Geneva: UN, 25 Nov. 1994). See also Gerard Prunier, *The Rwanda Crisis: History of a Genocide* (London: Hurst & Company, 1998). Marijke Verpoorten, 'Le coût en vies humaines du génocide rwandais : le cas de la province de Gikongoro', *Population* 60 (2005) put the Tutsi death toll at between 600,000–800,000 using a demographic analysis.

8. Kristine Eck and Lisa Hultman, 'One-Sided Violence Against Civilians in War: Insights from New Fatality Data', *Journal of Peace Research* 44.2 (2007) 233–246.

9. R.J. Rummel, *Death by Government* (New Brunswick, NJ: Transaction Publishers, 1994).

10. 'Fact Sheet: America's Wars—May 2016, revised', Department of Veterans Affairs, online, http://www.va.gov/opa/publications/factsheets/fs_americas_wars.pdf

11. Fazal, 'Dead Wrong?'

12. Thomas Livermore, *Numbers and Losses in the Civil War in America, 1861–65.* (Boston: Houghton Mifflin & Co., 1900).

13. Historians did debate how awful the war really was. See Mark E. Neely Jr., *The Civil War and the Limits of Destruction* (Cambridge: Harvard University Press, 2007), and James McPherson, 'Was It More Restrained Than You Think?' *New York Review of Books*, 14 Feb. 2008.

14. J. David Hacker, 'A Census-Based Count of the Civil War Dead', *Civil War History* 57.4 (2011): 307–348.

15. Kelly M. Greenhill, 'Nigeria's Countless Casualties, The Politics of Counting Boko Haram's Victims', *Foreign Affairs*, February 9, 2015.

16. For a full discussion of the various sources see Wikipedia entry on German Casualties in World War II, wikiwand.com/en/German_casualties_in_World_War_II

17. G. I. Krivosheev, *Soviet Casualties and Combat Losses* (London: Greenhill, 1997).

18. V. E. Korol, "The price of victory: Myths and reality", *Journal of Slavic Military Studies*, 9:2 (1996), 417-426. This cites sources that put the numbers as high as 16.2 million enlisted men and 1.2 million officers.

19. Alexander N. Yakovlev, *A Century of Violence in Soviet Russia* (New Haven: Yale University Press, 2002).

20. Maureen Perrie, *The Cambridge History of Russia: The twentieth century* (Cambridge: Cambridge University Press, 2006) 225–227; Michael Ellman and S. Maksudov, 'Soviet Deaths in the Great Patriotic War: a note—World War II', *Europe Asia Studies* 46:4 (1994): 671-80; and Boris Sokolov, 'The cost of war: Human losses for the USSR and Germany, 1939–1945', *The Journal of Slavic Military Studies* 9.1 (1996): 152–193

21. Michael Haynes, 'Counting Soviet Deaths in the Great Patriotic War: a Note', *Europe Asia Studies* 55.2, (2003): 300–309.

22. B. V. Sokolov, 'The Cost of War: Human Losses for the USSR and Germany, 1939–1945', *The Journal of Slavic Military Studies* 9.1 (1966): 151–93. Leitenberg opts for the slightly lower figure of 35 million. Other estimates go as high as 50 million.

23. Mitter, *China's War with Japan.*

24. 'Report puts Iraqi dead at 1500', *Jane's Defence Weekly*, 19:11, (1993) 5.

25. He noted that of the 71,000 Iraqi soldiers taken prisoner, only around 2,000 were wounded, while US forces buried 577 Iraqis.

26. Carl Conetta, *The Wages of War: Iraqi Combatant and Noncombatant Fatalities in the 2003 Conflict: Project on Defense Alternatives*, Research Monograph # 8, 20 Oct. 2003, Appendix 2: Iraqi Combatant and Noncombatant Fatalities in the 1991 Gulf War. Available: http://www.comw.org/pda/0310rm8ap2.html

27. The *Gulf War Air Power Survey* concluded that the ground war 'total could easily have been as high as 10,000': Thomas Keaney and Eliot Cohen, *Gulf War Air Power Survey: Summary Report* (Washington DC: Department of the Air Force, 1993), 249, and also 109–110. See also Michael Gordon and Gen. Bernard Trainor, *The General's War: The Inside Story of the Conflict in the Gulf* (Boston: Little, Brown, & Company, 1995); Maj. Lewis D. Hill, Doris Cook, and Aron Pinker, *Gulf War Air Power Survey: Statistical Compendium* (Washington DC: Department of the Air Force, 1993) 109–110; and 'Appendix: Iraqi Death Toll', *The Gulf War: An in-depth examination of the 1990–1991 Persian Gulf Crisis*, PBS Frontline, 9 Jan. 1996. Available: www.pbs.org/wgbh/pages/frontline/gulf

28. Beth Osborne Daponte, 'A Case Study in Estimating Casualties from War and Its Aftermath: The 1991 Persian Gulf War', *PSR Quarterly*, 3:2 (June 1993) 57–66.

29. COW uses numbers of 7,000 for Iraqi casualties during the actual invasion and 10,800 for those who died in an extra-state war after 2004. Nothing has yet appeared under intrastate war. Those numbers are meaningless, reflecting a devotion to coding rules while conveying very little about the meaning of the multiple conflicts that have engulfed Iraq. Carl Conetta, who did the study on the 1991 casualties, also did a study

on the initial combat deaths, from 19 March to 30 April 2003. He concluded that the combat over this period led to 'between 7,600 and 10,800 Iraqi combatant fatalities, plus some 3,200 and 4,300 noncombatants'. This relied on gathering reports of incidents and then adjusting for the regular inflation of reported deaths. Carl Conetta, 'Disappearing the Dead: Iraq, Afghanistan, and the Idea of a "New Warfare"', *Project on Defense Alternatives*, 18 Feb. 2004. See also Lawrence J. Korb and Stephen Biddle, 'Violence by the Numbers in Iraq: Sound Data or Shaky Statistics?' *Council on Foreign Relations*, 25 Sept. 2007.

30. Figures available at the Iraq Body Count website, http://www.iraqbody-count .org/database/. When official American figures reached the public domain as a result of the release of classified documents by wikileaks, they were not too far from those of the Iraq Body Count, which raised its assessment by 12,000. The US numbers were 109,032 deaths between January 2004 and December 2009, of which 66,081 were civilians, 15,196 Iraqi forces, 23,984 insurgents, and 3,771 friendly. See David Leigh, 'Iraq War Logs Reveal 15,000 Previously Unlisted Civilian Deaths', *Guardian*, 22 Oct. 2010. https://www.theguardian.com/world/2010/oct/22/true-civilian-body-count-iraq

31. Keith Krause, 'From Armed Conflict to Political Violence: Mapping and Explaining Conflict Trends', *Daedalus: Journal of the American Academy of Arts & Sciences* (2016): 117.

32. L. Roberts et al., 'Mortality before and after the 2003 invasion of Iraq: cluster sample survey', *Lancet* 364 (2004): 1857–1864.

33. Beth Osborne Daponte, "Wartime estimates of Iraqi civilian casualties", *International Review of the Red Cross*, 89:868 (Dec.2007), 943-957

34. Amy Hagopian et al., 'Mortality in Iraq Associated with the 2003–2011 War and Occupation: Findings from a National Cluster Sample Survey by the University Collaborative Iraq Mortality Study', *PLOS* 15 (2013). Available: http://journals.plos.org /plosmedicine/article?id=10.1371/journal.pmed.1001533.

35. UNHCR Statistical Online Population Database, United Nations High Commissioner for Refugees, Geneva, 2011, and SK Lischer, 'Security and displacement in Iraq: responding to the forced migration crisis', *International Security* 33.2 (2008): 95–119.

36. UNHCR Iraq fact sheet—May 2011, United Nations High Commissioner for Refugees, Geneva, 2011. http://reliefweb.int/report/iraq/unhcr-iraq-fact-sheet-may -2011

37. For best practice in casualty counting see *Standards for Casualty Recording* (London: Every Casualty Worldwide, 2016). For a discussion of the wider issues connected with counting civilian deaths see Taylor Seybolt et al, *Counting Civilian Casualties: An Introduction to recording and Estimating Nonmilitary Deaths in Conflict*, (Oxford: Oxford University Press, 2013)

38. Figures from The Syrian Observatory for Human Rights, 17 March 2017, http:// www.syriahr.com/en/?p=62760. They did not include those held and tortured by the various parties. Another Syrian policy centre estimated in February 2016 that the true number was 470,000, including 15 percent indirect deaths. 'Quantifying carnage', *The Economist*, 20 Feb. 2016. Available: http://www.economist.com/news/middle-east-and -africa/21693279-how-many-people-has-syrias-civil-war-killed-quantifying-carnage

CHAPTER 12

1. Immanuel Kant, *Political Writings*, (Cambridge, Cambridge University Press, 1991), 100.

2. Francis Fukuyama, 'The End of History', *The National Interest* (1989). The original essay was developed into a book: Francis Fukuyama, *The End of History and the Last Man* (New York: Free Press, 1992).

3. Samuel Huntington, *The Third Wave: Democratization in the Late Twentieth Century* (Norman, OK: University of Oklahoma Press, 1991). A key factor according to Huntington was not only the active promotion of democracy by the US and the

snowball effect within regions but also the growing opposition of the Catholic Church to authoritarian rule.

4. The Charter of the United Nations, signed 26 June 1945, San Francisco. http://www.un.org/en/charter-united-nations/

5. President George Bush, 'Remarks at Maxwell Air Force Base War College in Montgomery Alabama', *The American Presidency Project*, UCSB, 13 April 1991, http://www.presidency.ucsb.edu/ws/?pid=19466

6. Philip Bobbitt, *The Shield of Achilles: War, Peace and the Course of History* (New York: Knopf, 2002): 9.

7. Charter of Paris for a New Europe, *Organization for Security and Co-operation in Europe*, Paris, 19–20 Nov. 1990, http://www.osce.org/mc/39516?download=true

8. Michael Doyle. 'Liberalism and World Politics.' *American Political Science Review* 80 (1986): 1151–69.

9. Jack S. Levy, 'Domestic Politics and War', *The Origin and Prevention of Major Wars*, eds. Robert I. Rotberg and Theodore K. Rabb (Cambridge: Cambridge University Press, 1989) 88. For good surveys see Håvard Hegre, 'Democracy and armed conflict', *Journal of Peace Research* 51.2 (2014): 159–172, and Boris Barth, *The Democratic Peace Controversy: A Critical Survey* (Oslo files on Defence and Security, 2008).

10. Matthew White, 'Democracies do not make war on each other—or do they?' *Historical Atlas of the Twentieth Century*, online, 2005. Available: http://users.erols.com/mwhite28/demowar.htm. Some candidates: American Civil War (1861), as both sides had elected governments; Anglo-Boer War (1899); Spanish-American War (1898); Peru and Ecuador Border War (1995); Russia and Ukraine (2014).

11. Charles Kegley and Martin Hermann, 'Putting military intervention into the democratic peace', *Comparative Political Studies* 30.1 (1997): 78–107, and Sebastian Rosato, 'The flawed logic of democratic peace theory', *American Political Science Review* 97: 4 (2003): 585–602.

12. Suzanne Werner, 'The effects of political similarity on the onset of militarized disputes, 1816–1985', *Political Research Quarterly* 53.2 (2000): 343–374, and Mark Peceny, Caroline C, Beer, and Shannon Sanchez-Terry, 'Dictatorial peace?' *American Political Science Review* 96.1 (2002): 15–26.

13. Christopher Layne, 'Kant or Cant. The Myth of the Democratic Peace', *International Security* 19 (1994): 5–49

14. The measures are not simple—abuses of human rights, corruption, and limits on political expression can all reduce the working of a democracy, even if elections are still held regularly. Thus in 2016 the Economic Intelligence Units 'Democracy Index' judged that there were only twenty 'full democracies', with a further fifty-nine countries considered 'flawed', with another thirty-seven combining democratic and authoritarian features, and fifty-one 'authoritarian' (Economist Intelligence Unit, 'Democracy in an age of anxiety', 21 Jan. 2016). They set high standards for full democracy, so Italy and France are not actually included in this list.

15. Scott Gates, Torbjørn L. Knutsen, and Jonathan W. Moses, 'Democracy and peace: A more skeptical view', *Journal of Peace Research* 33.1 (1996): 1–10, and Carles Boix, 'Democracy, development, and the international system', *American Political Science Review* 105.4 (2011): 809–828.

16. See previous references. Quincy Wright had made this point: *Study of War* 841.

17. Michael W. Doyle, 'Kant, liberal legacies, and foreign affairs', Part II, *Philosophy & Public Affairs* 12.4 (1983): 23–353, and also Doyle, 'Liberalism and world politics', *American Political Science Review* 80.4 (1986): 1151–1169. See also Zeev Maoz and Bruce Russett, 'Alliance, contiguity, wealth, and political stability', *International Interactions* 18.3 (1992): 245–267, and Zeev Maoz and Bruce M Russett, 'Normative and structural causes of democratic peace, 1946–1986', *American Political Science Review* 87.3 (1993): 624–638.

18. Seung-Whan Choi, 'Re-evaluating capitalist and democratic peace models', *International Studies Quarterly* 55.3 (2011): 759–769, and Bruce Bueno de Mesquita et al., 'An institutional explanation of the democratic peace', *American Political Science Review* 93.4 (1999): 791–807.

19. Bruce M. Russett and John R. O'Neal, *Triangulating Peace: Democracy, Interdependence, and International Organizations* (New York: W. W. Norton, 2001).

20. Michael Mousseau, 'A Market-Capitalist or a Democratic Peace', in Vasquez (2012) 208.

21. Douglas Gibler, 'The Implications of a Territorial Peace', in Vasquez 226. See also Douglas Gibler and Jaroslav Tir, 'Settled Borders and Regime Type: Democratic Transitions as Consequences of Peaceful Territorial Transfers', *American Journal of Political Science* 54.4 (2010): 951–68.

22. Azar Gat, *Causes of War and the Spread of Peace: But Will War Rebound?* (New York: Oxford University Press, 2017).

23. Jack L. Snyder, *From Voting to Violence: Democratization and Nationalist Violence* (New York: W. W. Norton, 2000). See also Edward D. Mansfield and Jack Snyder, *Electing to Fight: Why Emerging Democracies Go to War* (Cambridge, MA: MIT Press, 2007).

24. Goldstone et al, *A Global Forecasting Model of Political Instability,* Paper prepared for the annual meeting of the American Political Science Association, Washington DC 1-4 Sept 2005, p. 20. Cited by Newman, 'conflict research', p. 272.

CHAPTER 13

1. Max Weber, *The Vocation Lectures: 'Science as a Vocation'; 'Politics as a Vocation'* (Indianapolis: Hackett, 2004).

2. Odd Arne Westad, 'The wars after the war, 1945–1954', in Chickering et al 452–471.

3. Paul Hensel, 'The More things Change…; Recognizing and responding to Trends in Armed Conflict', *Conflict Management and Peace Science* 19.1(2002): 27–53, and Kalevi Holsti, *The State, War, and the State of War* (Cambridge: Cambridge University Press, 1996).

4. General Charles Krulak, cited by Raimo Väyynen, in his introduction to Väyynen, ed., *The Waning of Major War.*

5. Peter Wallensteen and Margareta Sollenberg, 'Armed Conflict, 1989–98', *Journal of Peace Research* 36.5 (1999): 593–606.

6. James Fearon and David Laitin, 'Ethnicity, Insurgency, and Civil War', *American Political Science Review* 97.1 (2003): 75–90.

7. Mary Kaldor, *New and Old Wars: Organized Violence in a Global Era* (Cambridge: Polity Press, 1999) 78.

8. Kalevi Holsti, *The State, War, and the State of War* 27; General Sir Rupert Smith, *The Utility of Force: The Art of War in the Modern World* (London: Allen Lane, 2005); and Herfried Münkler, *The New Wars* (Cambridge: Polity, 2005).

9. Martin van Creveld, *Nuclear Proliferation and the Future of Conflict* (New York: The Free Press, 1993) 126.

10. Errol Henderson and David J. Singer, '"New Wars" and Rumors of "New Wars"', *International Interactions: Empirical and Theoretical Research in International Relations* 28.2 (2002): 165–190.

11. Mats Berdal, 'The "New Wars" Thesis Revisited', in *The Changing Character of War*, eds. Hew Strachan and Sibylle Scheipers (Oxford: Oxford University Press, 2011) 109–133. See also Stathis N. Kalyvas, '"New" and "Old" Wars: A Valid Distinction?', *World Politics* 54.1 (2001): 99–118.

12. Mary Kaldor, *New and Old Wars* 8.

13. UNICEF, 'State of the World's Children 1996: Children in War', Graça Machel, *Impact of Armed Conflict on Children*, UN doc. A/51/306, 26 Aug. 1996, para. 24.

Available: http://www.unicef.org/graca/graright.htm. Cited by Adam Roberts, 'Lives and Statistics: Are 90% of War Victims Civilians?', *Survival: Global Politics and Strategy* 52.3 (2010): 115–136.

14. Kelly M. Greenhill, 'Counting the Cost', *Sex, Drugs, and Body Counts: The Politics of Numbers in Global Crime and Conflict*, eds. Peter Andreas and Kelly M. Greenhill (Ithaca: Cornell University Press, 2010) 128–9. Although the UNICEF report referred initially to the 1986–1996 period, this point was often missed when the formulation was repeated without amendment in subsequent years.

15. Christer Ahlström, with contributions by Kjell-Åke Nordquist, *Casualties of Conflict: Report for the World Campaign for the Protection of Victims of War* (Uppsala: Department of Peace and Conflict Research, 1991) 19. See also *The Human Security Report 2005* (Oxford: Oxford University Press, 2005) 75. Available: http://www.humansecurityreport.org. Another possible source was the annual *World Military and Social Expenditures* produced by Ruth Leger Sivard with analyst Fred Buckhardt. The 1991 issue stated that 'in the decade of the 1980s, the proportion of civilian deaths jumped to 74 percent of the total and in 1990 it appears to have been close to 90 percent'. These numbers, however, were very dependent upon war-related deaths, including famine, and so were unavoidably guesses. Ruth Leger Sivard, *World Military and Social Expenditures 1991* (Washington DC: World Priorities, 1991) 20.

16. William Eckhardt, 'Civilian Deaths in Wartime', *Bulletin of Peace Proposals* 20.1 1989: 89–98. This used the 1923 Carnegie report as a source. Eckhardt's main aim appears to have been to draw attention to 'structural violence', the deaths resulting from the reduced life chances of those without money or power, which he argued far exceeded those caused by war.

17. The International Committee of the Red Cross, *Arms Availability and the Situation of Children in Armed Conflict* (Geneva: ICRC, 1999). See also Kelly Greenhill, 'Counting the Cost'.

18. The methodology used in this analysis may have exaggerated the proportion of soldiers, but not enough to get anywhere close to the 90:10 ratio. A similar 60:40 military to civilian ratio emerged from work undertaken by the Demographic Unit of the International Criminal Tribunal for the former Yugoslavia (ICTY). Jan Zwierzchowski and Ewa Tabeau, 'The 1992–95 War in Bosnia and Herzegovina: Census-based Multiple System Estimation of Casualties' Undercount', paper for International Research Workshop on 'The Global Economic Costs of Conflict', Berlin, 1–2 Feb. 2010, pp. 1 and 18–21. Available: http://www.diw.de/sixcms/detail. php?id=diw_01.c.338475.en. On 2007 report, see 'Justice Report: Bosnia's Book of the Dead', *Balkan Investigative Reporting Network*, 21 June 2007, http://www.birn.eu.com/ en/88/10/3377/.

19. Stathis N. Kalyvas, 'The Changing Character of Civil Wars', Strachan and Scheipers, 202–219.

20. Joakim Kreutz, 'How Civil Wars End (and Recur)', *Routledge Handbook of Civil Wars*, eds. Edward Newman and Karl DeRouen Jr. (London: Routledge, 2014).

21. Ann Hironaka, *Neverending Wars: The International Community, Weak States, and the Perpetuation of Civil War* (Cambridge, MA: Harvard University Press, 2005).

22. David Armitage, *Civil Wars: A History in Ideas* (New York: Knopf, 2017) 7. The Enzensberger quote comes from Hans Magnus Enzensberger, *Civil War*, trans. Piers Spence and Martin Chalmers (London: Granta Books, 1994) 12.

23. Bill Kissane, *Nations Torn Asunder: The Challenge of Civil War* (Oxford: Oxford University Press, 2016).

24. Ted Robert Gurr,. *Why Men Rebel*. (Princeton, NJ: Princeton University Press, 1970)

25. Errol A. Henderson and David J. Singer, 'Civil War in the Post-colonial world, 1946–92', *Journal of Peace Research* 37.3 (2000): 248–5. For an extended discussion of the problems with COW when extended to civil wars, see Christopher Cramer, *Civil War is Not a Stupid Thing: Accounting for Violence in Developing Countries* (London: C. Hurst & Co., 2006) 57–86.

26. Stathis Kalyvas, 'Civil Wars', *The Oxford Handbook of Comparative Politics*, eds. Carles Boix and Susan C. Stokes (Oxford: Oxford University Press, 2007) 416–34, and T. David Mason and Sara McLaughlin Mitchell, *What Do We Know About Civil Wars?* (Lanham: Rowman & Littlefield, 2016).

27. Newman, 'Conflict Research'.

28. For example Barry Posen considered developing civil wars in Europe as a problem of 'emerging anarchy' comparable to the realist view of the international system as anarchic. 'The Security Dilemma and Ethnic Conflict,' *Survival*, 35:1, (1993) 27–47.

29. This is a theme of Monica Duffy Toft, 'The Origins of Ethnic Wars: An Historical and Critical Account', in Manus Midlarsky, ed., *Handbook of War Studies III*, (Ann Arbor, MI: University of Michigan Press, 2008).

30. *An Agenda for Peace: Preventive diplomacy, peacemaking and peace-keeping*, Report of the Secretary-General pursuant to the statement adopted by the Summit Meeting of the Security Council, 31 Jan. 1992.

31. Gerald Helman and Steven Ratner, 'Saving Failed States', *Foreign Policy* [vol.]89(1992–93): 3–20.

32. William Zartman, *Collapsed States: The disintegration and restoration of legitimate authority* (Boulder, CO: Lynne Rienner, 1995).

33. *The National Security Strategy of the United States of America* (Washington DC: The White House, 2002) 1.

34. Monica Duffy Toft, 'Territory and War', *Journal of Peace Research* 51 (2014): 185–198.

35. 'Declaration on the Granting of Independence to Colonial Countries and Peoples', Adopted by General Assembly Resolution 1514 (XV), 14 Dec. 1960.

36. Jeffrey Herbst, 'The Creation and Maintenance of National Boundaries in Africa', *International Organization* 43.4 (1989): 673–692; Saadia Touval, *The Boundary Politics of Independent Africa* (Cambridge, MA: Harvard University Press, 1972); and Rene Lemarchand, 'Patterns of State Collapse and Reconstruction in Central Africa', *African Studies Quarterly* 1: 3 (1997) pp. 5–6; and Stuart J. Kaufman, 'An "International" Theory of Inter-ethnic War', *Review of International Studies* 22.2 (1996): 153.

37. Quoted in Adkunle Ajala, 'The Nature of African Boundaries', *Afrika Spectrulm* 83 (1983): 180.

38. R. H. Jackson, *The Global Covenant: Human Conduct in a World of States* (Oxford: Oxford University Press, 2000) 207. For an earlier version see Robert H. Jackson and Carl G. Rosberg, 'Why Africa's Weak States Persist: The Empirical and the Juridical in Statehood', *World Politics* 35 (1982): 21. See also Boaz Atzili, 'When Good Fences Make Bad Neighbors: Fixed Borders, State Weakness, and International Conflict', *International Security* 31.3 (2006/07): 139–173.

39. For recent examples, see Yoweri Museveni in Uganda, Paul Kagame in Rwanda, and Robert Mugabe in Zimbabwe.

40. Patrick J. McGowan, 'African Military Coups d'Etat, 1956–2001: Frequency, Trends and Distribution', *Journal of Modern African Studies* 41 (2003): 339–70. See also Samuel Decalo, *Coups and Army Rule in Africa* (New Haven: Yale University Press, 1976).

41. Henning Tamm, 'The Origins of Transnational Alliances: Rulers, Rebels, and Political Survival in the Congo Wars', *International Security* 41.1 (2016): 147-181See also the essays in Jeffrey Checkel, ed., *Transnational Dynamics of Civil War* (Cambridge: Cambridge University Press, 2013).

42. Fredrik Söderbaum and Rodrigo Tavares, 'Problematizing Regional Organizations in African Security', *African Security* 2.2–3 (2009): 69–81.

CHAPTER 14

1. Samuel Huntington, 'The Clash of Civilizations?', *Foreign Affairs* 72: 3 (1993), 22–49. As with Fukuyama, the original essay was later turned into a book: Samuel

Huntington, *The Clash of Civilizations and the Remaking of World Order* (New York: Simon & Schuster, 1996).

2. Ron Hassner, *Religion on the Battlefield* (Ithaca: Cornell University Press, 2016). Hassner sees this as one reason for the contradictory and disappointing findings arising out of research into religion and war.

3. Errol Henderson and Richard Tucker, 'Clear and Present Strangers: The Clash of Civilizations and International Conflict', *International Studies Quarterly* 45 (2001): 317–338, and William Cavanaugh, *The Myth of Religious Violence: Secular Ideology and the Roots of Modern Conflict* (Oxford: Oxford University Press, 2009).

4. Andrew Bell-Fialkoff, 'A Short History of Ethnic Cleansing', *Foreign Affairs* 72.3 (1992): 110–121.

5. Samantha Power, *A Problem from Hell: America and the Age of Genocide* (New York: Basic Books, 2002) 282.

6. Robert D. Kaplan, *Balkan Ghosts: A Journey Through History* (New York: St. Martin's Press, 1993).

7. Elizabeth Drew, *On the Edge: The Clinton Presidency* (New York: Simon & Schuster, 1995) 157. Kaplan was a supporter of intervention and disclaimed responsibility for the use Clinton had made of his book. See his exchange with Timothy Garton Ash, 'The Foul Balkan Sky', *New York Review of Books*, 21 Mar. 1996, following the latter's review in 'Bosnia in our Future', *New York Review of Books*, 21 Dec. 1995.

8. Robert Kaplan, 'The Coming Anarchy', *The Atlantic Monthly*, February 1994. On Clinton's approval see Toby Lester, 'Beyond "The Coming Anarchy"', *The Atlantic Online*, Aug. 1996. Available: http://www.theatlantic.com/past/docs/issues/96aug/proport/kapsid.htm

9. Katharine Q. Seelye, 'Clinton Blames Milosevic, Not Fate, for Bloodshed', *New York Times*, 14 May 1999. Available: http://www.nytimes.com/1999/05/14/world/crisis-in-the-balkans-washington-clinton-blames-milosevic-not-fate-for-bloodshed.html

10. Benjamin A. Valentino, 'Why We Kill: The Political Science of Political Violence against Civilians', *Annual Review of Political Science* 17 (2014): 189–103.

11. John Mueller, 'The Banality of "Ethnic Conflict"', *International Security* 25.1 (2000) 47.

12. Warren Zimmerman, *Origins of a Catastrophe: Yugoslavia and its Destroyers* (New York: Times Books, 1996) 152.

13. V. P. Gagnon, 'Ethnic Nationalism and International Conflict', *International Security* 19.3 (1994/95) 164.

14. Samantha Powers, *A Problem from Hell: America and the Age of Genocide* (New York: Basic Books, 2002).

15. James Gow, 'After the Flood: Literature on the Context, Causes and Course of the Yugoslav War: Reflections and Refractions' *The Slavonic and East European Review* 75.3 (1997): 446–484. For a thorough review of the literature see Dutch Institute for War Documentation (NIOD), Srebrenica, *A 'Safe' Area: Reconstruction, Background, Consequences And Analyses Of The Fall Of A 'Safe Area'*, November 1996, *Appendix VI The Background of the Yugoslav crisis: A review of the literature*. Available: http://www.niod.knaw.nl/nl/srebrenica-rapport. Thus, John Zametica, in a paper emphasising the need for disinterested policy analysis, attributed the problems of Bosnia to it being hijacked by a Muslim-Croat coalition and wrote of the legitimacy of Serb demands. John Zametica, *The Yugoslav Conflict* (London: International Institute for Strategic Studies, 1992). Not long after its publication John became Jovan and re-emerged as a senior adviser and spokesperson for the Bosnian Serb leader Radovan Karadžić. For background, including the influence of Zametica's paper, see Brendan Simms, *Unfinest Hour: Britain and the Destruction of Bosnia* (London: Allen Lane, The Penguin Press, 2001) 228.

16. James Gow, *The Serbian Project and Its Adversaries: A Strategy of War Crimes* (London: Hurst & Co., 2003). For an argument that the rhetoric of ethnic conflict was

used for elite political purposes see Gagnon, 'Ethnic Nationalism and International Conflict'.

17. Toft, 'The Origins of Ethnic Wars'.

18. Joseph Young, 'Repression, Dissent, and the Onset of Civil War', *Political Research Quarterly* 66.3 (2012): 516–32, and also his chapter 'Antecedents of Civil War Onset', in Mason and Mitchell, *What Do We Know about Civil Wars?* 33–42.

19. NIE 15-90, 'Yugoslavia Transformed,' 18 October 1990, in *Yugoslavia from National Communism to National Collapse: US Intelligence Community Estimative Products on Yugoslavia, 1948–1990* (NOIC 2006-004), (Washington DC: US Government Printing Office, 2006).

20. Gregory Treverton and Renanah Miles, 'Unheeded warning of war: why policymakers ignored the 1990 Yugoslav estimate', *Intelligence and National Security*, 32:4 (2017), 506–522.

21. Benedict Anderson, *Imagined Communities: Reflections on the Origin and Spread of Nationalism* (London: Verso, 1991).

22. Lee J. M. Seymour and Kathleen Gallagher Cunningham, 'Identity Issues and Civil war', in Mason and Mitchell 43–57.

23. J. Wucherpfennig et al., 'Ethnicity, the State, and the Duration of Civil War', *World Politics* 64.1 (2012): 79–115.

24. Hironaka, *Neverending Wars*.

25. Kaplan, 'The Coming Anarchy' 54.

26. *The Economist*, 11 May 2000. David T. Burbach and Christopher J. Fettweis cite other examples of this gloom: Chris Allen, 'Warfare, Endemic Violence, and State Collapse in Africa', *Review of African Political Economy* 26.81 (1999): 367–84; James D. Fearon and David D. Laitin, 'Neotrusteeship and the Problem of Weak States', *International Security* 28.4 (2004): 5–43; Peter Schwab, *Africa: A Continent Self-Destructs* (New York: Palgrave, 2002); and Howard W. French, *A Continent for the Taking: The Tragedy and Hope of Africa* (New York: Vintage Books, 2004).

27. Fearon and Laitin, 'Ethnicity, Insurgency, and Civil War'.

28. John Clark, 'A Constructivist Account of the Congo Wars', *African Security* 4.3 (2011): 147–170.

29. Gerard Prunier, *Africa's World War: Congo, the Rwandan Genocide, and the Making of a Continental Catastrophe* (New York: Oxford University Press, 2008).

30. The numbers and uncertainties connected with counting the costs of these events are huge. When looking at the violence that afflicted Zaire/DRC, the International Rescue Committee (IRC) concluded on the basis of a number of mortality surveys that the war must have cost some 5.4 million lives, largely due to 'infectious diseases, malnutrition and neonatal- and pregnancy-related conditions'. Children had been particularly hard hit: they 'accounted for 47 percent of deaths, even though they constituted only 19 percent of the total population'. Dr Benjamin Coghlan et al., *Mortality in the Democratic Republic of Congo: An ongoing crisis* (International Rescue Committee, 2007). Available: https://www.rescue.org/sites/default/files/migrated/where/g_belgium /2006-7_congomortalitysurvey_a4.pdf. This estimate was contested by the Human Security Report Project (HSP), who argued that the original surveys were not carried out scientifically, relying too much on the most badly affected regions. In addition, any estimate depended on the baseline mortality-rate figure, and that the IRC's figure, based on an average for sub-Saharan Africa, was too low. Instead of 2.83 million excess deaths, the HSP argued a better number would be 860,000 (Human Security Report Project, *The Human Security Report 2009/2010: The Causes of Peace and the Shrinking Costs of War,* Part 2, (New York: Oxford University Press, 2011) 123–31).

31. Jack Hirshleifer, 'The dark side of the force', *Economic Inquiry* 32 (1994): 3. For a survey of the economic literature on civil wars, see Christopher Blattman and Edward Miguel, 'Civil War', *Journal of Economic Literature* 48.1 (2010): 3–57.

32. Michael Ross, 'A closer look at oil, diamonds, and civil war', *Annual Reviews of Political Science* 9 (2006): 265–300.

33. See Abiodun Alao, *Natural Resources and Conflict in Africa: The Tragedy of Endowment* (Rochester: University of Rochester Press, 2007).

34. Fearon and Laitin, 'Ethnicity, Insurgency, and Civil War', 88. They acknowledged that grievances could be produced by civil wars.

35. Paul Collier and Anke Hoeffler, 'Economic causes of civil conflict and their implications for policy' in *Managing Global Chaos*, ed. Chester A. Crocker, et al. (Washington, DC: United States Institute of Peace, 2000).

36. Paul Collier et al., *Breaking the Conflict Trap: Civil War and Development Policy* (Washington DC: World Bank and Oxford University Press, 2003). See also Paul Collier, Anke Hoeffler, and Dominic Rohner, 'Beyond greed and grievance: feasibility and civil war', *Oxford Economic Papers* 61 (2009): 1–27.

37. Collier et al., *Conflict Trap* 53–4.

38. Paul Collier and Anke Hoeffler, 'Greed and grievance in civil war', *Oxford Economic Papers* 56.

39. C. Cramer, '*Homo Economicus* goes to war: methodological individualism, rational choice, and the political economy of war', *World Development* 30 (2002): 1849.

40. Paul Collier, 'The Cultural Foundations of Economic Failure: A Conceptual Toolkit', *Journal of Economic Behavior & Organization*, 126, (2016), 5-24.

41. M. Humphreys, 'Natural resources, conflict, and conflict resolution: uncovering the mechanisms', *Journal of Conflict Resolution* 49 (2005): 508–37.

42. Ross, 'A closer look at oil, diamonds, and civil war'. He found more statistical significance in the occasional cases of 'primary' diamond extraction from deep-shaft mines, controlled by large firms and governments, than with 'secondary' diamonds, near the surface and commonly mined by unskilled workers.

43. Michael L. Ross, 'What Have We Learned about the Resource Curse?' *Annual Review of Political Science* 18 (2015): 239–59.

44. In making this point, Humphreys refers to Angell 513.

45. Jeremy M. Weinstein, 'Resources and the Information Problem in Rebel Recruitment', *The Journal of Conflict Resolution* 49:4 (2005): 598–624.

46. David Keen, *The Economic Functions of Violence in Civil Wars*, Adelphi Paper no. 320 (London: Taylor & Francis for IISS, 1998).

47. Dennis Rodgers and Robert Muggah, 'Gangs as Non-State Armed Groups: The Central American Case', *Contemporary Security Policy* 30.2 (2009): 301–17; Jeffrey Gettleman, 'Forever Wars: Why the Continent's Conflicts Never End', *Foreign Policy* 178 (2010): 73–5; and John Mueller, *The Remnants of War* (Ithaca, NY: Cornell University Press, 2004).

CHAPTER 15

1. Prime Minister Tony Blair, Speech to Economic Club of Chicago, PBS, 22 April 1999, http://www.pbs.org/newshour/bb/international-jan-june99-blair_doctrine4-23/

2. Nicholas Wheeler, *Saving Strangers: Humanitarian Intervention in International Society* (Oxford: Oxford University Press, 2000).

3. Michael Walzer, *Just and Unjust Wars: A Moral Argument with Historical Illustrations*, (New York: Basic Books, 1977)

4. On 15 February 1991, President Bush invited the Iraqi people to "take matters into their own hands, to force Saddam Hussein the dictator to step aside." Margaret Dowd, 'War in the Gulf: The President; Bush, Scorning Offer, Suggests Iraqis Topple Hussein', *New York Times*, 16 February 1991, http://www.nytimes.com/1991/02/16/world/war-in-the-gulf-the-president-bush-scorning-offer-suggests-iraqis-topple-hussein.html.

5. *The Times*, 18 August 1992, cited in Martin Bell, *In Harm's Way* (London: Hamish Hamilton, 1995) 137. At the time this was described as the 'CNN Effect'. See Piers Robinson, 'The CNN effect: can the news media drive foreign policy?', *Review of International Studies*, 25:2 (1999) 301–09. The original CNN Effect referred to the ubiquity of the channel (so that all sides were using the same information source) as much as to the particulars of its effects. The term itself originated during the Gulf War and was naturally promoted by CNN's owner, Ted Turner. See Thomas Allen, F. Clifton Berry, and Norman Polmar, *CNN: War in the Gulf* (Atlanta, GA: Turner Broadcasting, 1999).

6. *Document of The Moscow Meeting of the Conference on the Human Dimension Of The CSCE*, Organization for Security and Co-operation in Europe, 4 Oct. 1991. Available: http://www.osce.org/odihr/elections/14310

7. Albrecht Schnabel and Ramesh Thakur, eds., *Kosovo and the Challenge of Humanitarian Intervention: Selective Indignation, Collective Action, and International Citizenship* (New York: United Nations University Press, 2000), and Ivo Daalder and Michael O'Hanlon, *Winning Ugly: NATO's War to Save Kosovo* (Washington DC: Brookings Institution, 2000).

8. Blair, Chicago speech (fn 1). For background to the speech, to which the author contributed, see Lawrence Freedman 'Force and the International Community: Blair's Chicago Speech and the Criteria for Intervention', *International Relations*, 21:3 (2017), 1-17.

9. John McKinley, ed., *A Guide to Peace Support Operations* (Providence, RI: The Thomas J. Watson Jr. Institute for International Studies, Brown University, 1996), and Alex J. Bellamy, 'The "Next Stage" in Peace Operations Theory?' *International Peacekeeping* 11:1 (2004): 17–38.

10. Lawrence Freedman, 'Bosnia: Does Peace Support Make Any Sense?', *NATO Review*, 43: 6 (1995), 19-23.

11. For a sample of the literature, see Nigel Rodley, ed., *To Loose the Bands of Wickedness* (London: Brassey's, 1992); Lawrence Freedman, ed., *Military Intervention in European Conflicts* (London: Blackwell, 1994); and Stephen A. Garrett, *Doing Good and Doing Well: An Examination of Humanitarian Intervention* (Westport, CT: Greenwood Press, 1999).

12. See discussion by Adam Roberts, "The Civilian in Modern War", in Strachan and Scheipers 373.

13. International Commission on Intervention, *The Responsibility to Protect: The Report of the International Commission on Intervention and State Sovereignty* (Ottawa: International Development Research Centre [IDRC], November 2002); and Thomas G. Weiss, *Military-Civilian Interactions: Humanitarian Crises and the Responsibility to Protect* (New York: Rowman & Littlefield, 2004).

14. High-Level Panel on Threats, Challenges and Change, *A More Secure World: Our Shared Responsibility* (New York: United Nations, 2004), 66 (pt. 3, para 203).

15. *Resolution Adopted by the General Assembly*, 2005 World Summit Outcome Document, 24 Oct. 2005, http://www.un.org/womenwatch/ods/A-RES-60-1-E.pdf. The resolution notably did not refer to Chapter 7 so it did not in principle authorise force in support of this responsibility.

16. UN, Security Council Resolution 1270 (Sierra Leone), S/RES/1270, 22 Oct. 1999.

17. Cited by Mats Berdal, 'The State of UN Peacekeeping: Lessons from Congo', *Journal of Strategic Studies* 39 (2016): 1–30.

18. Simone Haysom and Jens Pedersen, 'Robust peacekeeping in Africa: the challenge for humanitarians', *Humanitarian Practice Network*, online, Oct. 2015. Available: http://odihpn.org/magazine/robust-peacekeeping-in-africa-the-challenge-for-humanitarians.

19. This became the subject of a Security Council meeting in 2001. UN Security Council, 'Security Council Meets on HIV/Aids and Peacekeeping Operations; Hears

from Peacekeeping Under-Secretary-General, UNAIDS', (19 January 2001), http://
www.un.org/press/en/2001/sc6992.doc.htm. On efforts to educate forces on the dangers see: UNAIDS, 'Fact Sheet: HIV/AIDS and Peace-Keeping', (June 2004), http://data
.unaids.org/Topics/Security/fs_peacekeeping_en.pdf?preview=true

20. Emily Paddon Rhoads, *Taking Sides in Peacekeeping* (Oxford: Oxford University Press, 2016).

21. Andrew M. Dorman, *Blair's Successful War: British Military Intervention in
Sierra Leone* (Farnham: Ashgate Publishing, 2009).

22. Virginia Page Fortna, *Does Peacekeeping Work? Shaping Belligerents' Choices
After Civil* War (Princeton: Princeton University Press, 2008). Michael Gilligan and
Stephen Stedman, 'Where Do the Peacekeepers Go?' *International Studies Review* 5.4
(2003): 37–54.

23. Paul Diehl and Daniel Druckman, *Evaluating Peace Operations* (Boulder, CO:
Lynne Rienner, 2010).

24. Roland Paris, 'Saving Liberal Peacebuilding', *Review of International Studies*,
36:2 (2010), 337-365

25. Jean-Marie Guéhenno, *The Fog of Peace: A Memoir of International Peacekeeping in the 21st Century* (Washington DC: Brookings Institution Press, 2015).

26. UN, *Report of the Panel on United Nations Peace Operations*, 'Brahimi Panel
Report', S/2000/809, 21 Aug. 2000.

27. By early 2017 there were 16 current operations with over 107,000 personnel
deployed by the UN. Peacekeeping Fact Sheet, United Nations, http://www.un.org/en
/peacekeeping/resources/statistics/factsheet.shtml.

28. Berdal, 'The State of UN Peacekeeping', 6.

29. Guéhenno, Epilogue.

CHAPTER 16

1. Tim O'Brien, *Going after Cacciato*, (New York: Delacorte Press, 1978), 225–6.

2. Mark Taylor, *The Vietnam War in History, Literature and Film*, (Edinburgh: Edinburgh University Press, 2003), 51. This was loosely based on Robin Moore, *The
Green Berets*, (New York: Crown, 1965).

3. Lawrence H. Suid. *Guts & Glory: The Making of the American Military Image
in Film* (Lexington: The University Press of Kentucky 2002), 248.

4. Suid, 356, 332. *Apocalypse Now* was a free adaption of Joseph Conrad's *Heart
of Darkness* which had been set in the 1890s.

5. Suid, 514.

6. C D B Bryan, 'Barely Suppressed Screams', *Harper's*, (1 June 1984).

7. Albert Auster & Leonard Quart, *How the War was Remembered: Hollywood &
Vietnam*, (New York: Prager, 1988).

8. This is a recurring theme in Linda Dittmar and Gene Michaud, eds., *From Hanoi
to Holywood: The Vietnam War in American Film*, (New Brunswick, NJ: Rutgers University Press, 1990).

9. The US intervention in Beirut is described in my *Choice of Enemies: America
Confronts the Middle East* (New York: PublicAffairs, 2009).

10. George Shultz, *Turmoil and Triumph: My Years as Secretary of State*, (New
York: Charles Scribner's Sons, 1993), p. 648.

11. Caspar Weinberger, "The Uses of Military Power," Speech to National Press
Club, November 28, 1984, at www.pbs.org/wgbh/pages/frontline/shows/military/force
/weinberger.html.

12. Mark Bowden, *Black Hawk Down: A Story of Modern War* (New York: Atlantic
Monthly Press, 1999). Theo Farrell, "Sliding into War: The Somalia Imbroglio and U.S.
Army Peace Operations Doctrine," *International Peacekeeping* 2:2 (1995). 194–214.

13. See Powers, *A Problem from Hell*. Arguably, Rwanda was a rare situation in
which there was an established obligation to intervene, as this was genocide. The

genocide convention had come into force in 1948 in reaction to the Nazi holocaust against the Jews. Genocide was defined as acts committed with the 'intent to destroy, in whole or in part, a national, ethnical, racial or religious group'. States had a duty to prevent or punish these acts, an exception to the UN Charter's obligation not to intervene. As Clinton did not want to take on another African intervention, his administration went to some lengths to deny that Rwanda was genocide.

14. *The Carnegie Commission for the Prevention of Deadly Conflict* (New York: Carnegie Corporation, 1998). For a contrary view see Alan J. Kuperman, *The Limits of Humanitarian Intervention: Genocide in Rwanda* (Washington DC: Brookings Institution Press, 2001).

15. Transcript of Osama Bin Ladin interview by Peter Arnett, March 1997, http://news.findlaw.com/cnn/docs/binladen/binladenintvw-cnn.pdf.

16. See John Esposito, *The Islamic Threat: Myth or Reality* (New York: Oxford University Press, 1992), and Fawaz Gerges, *America and Political Islam: Clash of Cultures or Clash of Interests* (New York: Cambridge University Press, 1999).

17. Bernard Lewis, 'The Roots of Muslim Rage', *The Atlantic*, September 1990. https://www.theatlantic.com/magazine/archive/1990/09/the-roots-of-muslim-rage/304643/

18. Huntington, 'The Clash of Civilizations?' 31.

19. Anthony J. Dennis, *The Rise of the Islamic Empire and the Threat to the West* (Ohio: Wyndham Hall Press, 1996).

20. Tom Clancy, *The Sum of all Fears* (New York: Berkely Mass market publishing, 1992), p. 913.

21. Gavin Cameron, *Nuclear Terrorism: A Threat Assessment for the 21st Century*, (London: Macmillan, 1999).

22. Brian M. Jenkins, *Will Terrorists Go Nuclear?* (Santa Monica, CA: RAND, 1975).

23. The 1993 attack on the World Trade Center left six killed and 1,000 wounded. The intent was to topple one tower on to the other, which would have caused mass casualties. On 7 August 1998, the US embassies in Kenya and Tanzania were bombed, killing 300 people, including 12 Americans, and injuring 5,000 more. In December 1999 attacks on millennium celebrations in Israel and the United States were thwarted.

24. Remarks by Director of Central Intelligence George J. Tenet on the 'World-wide Threat 2001: National Security in a Changing World', 7 Feb. 2001). http://u2.lege.net/avalon.law.yale.edu/21st_century/tenet_001.asp.

25. US Commission on National Security/21st Century, *New World Coming: American Security in the 21st Century* (Washington DC: US Government printing Office, 1999) 48. For a similar emphasis, see also National Commission on Terrorism, *Countering the Changing Threat of International Terrorism* (Washington DC: US Congress, 2000). Pursuant to Public Law 277, 105th Congress. The issue of attacks using nuclear, chemical, or biological weapons had been addressed in a number of studies prior to 9/11: Richard A. Falkenrath, Robert D. Newman, and Bradley Thayer, *America's Achilles' Heel: Nuclear, Biological, and Chemical Terrorism and Covert Attack* (Cambridge, MA: MIT Press, 1998); Peter R. Lavoy, Scott D. Sagan, and James J Wirtz, eds., *Planning the Unthinkable: How New Powers Will Use Nuclear, Chemical and Biological Weapons* (Ithaca, NY: Cornell University Press, 2000); Jan Lodal, *The Price of Dominance: The New Weapons of Mass Destruction and Their Challenge to American Leadership* (New York: Council on Foreign Relation, 2001); and Jessica Stern, *The Ultimate Terrorists* (Cambridge, MA: Harvard University Press, 1999).

26. Hassner, *Religion on the Battlefield* 3–5.

27. Richard K. Betts, 'The New Threat of Weapons of Mass Destruction', *Foreign Affairs* 77.1 (1998): 26-41.

CHAPTER 17

1. DoD News Briefing—Secretary of Defense Donald H. Rumsfeld, 12 Feb. 2002. http://archive.defense.gov/Transcripts/Transcript.aspx?TranscriptID=2636.

2. John J. Mearsheimer, *Conventional Deterrence*. (Ithaca, NY: Cornell University Press, 1983).

3. André Beaufre, 'Battlefields of the 1980s', in Nigel Calder, ed., *Unless Peace Comes: A Scientific Forecast of New Weapons*, (London: Allen Lane, 1968), 19.

4. Mark Clodfelter, *The Limits of Air Power: The American Bombing of North Vietnam* (New York, Free Press, 1989).

5. Richard Burt, *New Weapons Technologies: Debate and Directions*, Adelphi Paper no. 126 (London: IISS, 1976) 3.

6. Alvin and Heidi Toffler, *The Third Wave* (New York: Morrow, 1980).

7. Alvin and Heidi Toffler, *War and Anti-War: Survival at the Dawn of the 21st Century* (New York: Little Brown, 1993). This provides a thorough guide to the debates on military technology of the time.

8. Basil Liddell Hart, *The Revolution in Warfare* (London: Faber, 1946).

9. Richard Simpkin, *Race to the Swift: Thoughts on Twenty-first Century Warfare* (London: Brassey's, 2000).

10. Alan Campen, ed., *The First Information War: The Story of Communications, Computers, and Intelligence Systems in the Persian Gulf War* (Fairfax, VA: AFCEA International Press, 1992), and Edward Mann, 'Desert Storm: The First Information War?', *Airpower Journal* (1994): 4–14.

11. On the origins and development of the Revolution in Military Affairs, see Freedman, *Strategy*, Chapter 16.

12. Admiral William Owens, 'The Emerging System of Systems', *US Naval Institute Proceedings* (1995): 35–39.

13. Robert H. Scales, *Yellow Smoke: The Future of Land Warfare for America's Military* (Lanham, MD.: Rowman & Littlefield, 2003).

14. Ben Lambeth, 'The Technology Revolution in Air Warfare', *Survival* 39.1 (1997): 72, and John A. Warden III, 'The Enemy as a System', *Airpower Journal* 9.1(1995): 40–55.

15. Martin Libicki, 'DBK and its Consequences', *Dominant Battlespace Knowledge*, eds. Stuart Johnson and Martin Libicki (Washington DC: National Defense University, April 1996) 18.

16. Edward Luttwak, 'Towards Post-Heroic Warfare', *Foreign Affairs* 74.3 (1995): 109–122.

17. Eric V. Larson, *Casualties and Consensus: The Historical Role of Casualties in Domestic Support for U.S. Military Operations* (Santa Monica, CA: RAND, 1996); Steven Kull and Clay Ramsay, 'The Myth of the Reactive Public: American Public Attitudes on Military Fatalities in the Post-Cold War Period', *Public Opinion and the International Use of Force*, eds. Philip Everts and Pierangelo Isernia (London: Routledge, 2001); and Peter D. Feaver and Christopher Gelpi, 'A Look at Casualty Aversion: How Many Deaths Are Acceptable? A Surprising Answer', *Washington Post*, 7 Nov. 1999. Available: http://www.washingtonpost.com/wp-srv/WPcap/1999-11/07/061r-110799-idx.html.

18. US Department of Defense, *Joint Military Net Assessment* (Washington DC: Department of Defense, 1993) 3. Quoted in Keith Payne, 'Post-Cold War Deterrence and Missile Defense', *Orbis* 39.2 (1995) 203.

19. Jeffrey Record, 'Force-Protection Fetishism: Sources, Consequences, and (?) Solutions', *Aerospace Power Journal* (Summer 2000); Andrew Erdmann, 'The U.S. Presumption of Quick, Costless Wars', *Orbis* (Summer 1999).

20. Michael O'Hanlon, *Technological Change and the Future of Warfare* (Washington DC: Brookings Institution, 2000) 197.

21. Ralph Peters, 'Our Soldiers, Their Cities', *Parameters*, (1996), 43–50.

22. Barry R. Posen 'Urban Opertions: Tactical Realities and Strategic Ambiguities' in Michael C. Desch, ed. *Soldiers in Cities: Military Operations on Urban Terrain* (Carlisle, PA: U.S. Army War College, 2001) 153-4.

23. Michael Evans, Future War in Cities: Urbanization's challenge to strategic studies in the 21st century', *International review of the Red Cross*, 98:1 (2016) 37-5.

24. Major General Robert H. Scales, Jr. 'The Indirect Approach: How U.S. Military Forces Can Avoid the Pitfalls of Future Urban Warfare', *Armed Forces Journal International*, 136:3 (1998).

25. Secretary of Defense Donald Rumsfeld, 'A New Kind of War', *New York Times*, 27 Sept. 2001. Available: http://www.nytimes.com/2001/09/27/opinion/a-new-kind -of-war.html

26. For an early use of the term, in a Vietnam context, see Andrew Mack, 'Why Big Nations Lose Small Wars: The Politics of Asymmetric Conflict', *World Politics* 27.2 (1975): 175–200. See Steven Metz and Douglas V. Johnson, *Asymmetry and U.S. Military Strategy: Definition, Background, and Strategic Concepts* (Carlisle, PA: Strategic Studies Institute, US Army War College, 2001).

27. Steven Metz, *Iraq and the Evolution of American Strategy* (Washington DC: Potomac Books, 2008).

28. See Freedman, *Choice of Enemies* 431–2.

29. "President and Prime Minister Blair Discussed Iraq, Middle East, The East Room" 12 November 2004, http://www.whitehouse.gov/news/ releases/2004/11/2004 1112-5.html.

30. Conrad C. Crane, *Cassandra in Oz: Counterinsurgency and Future War* (Annapolis: Naval Institute Press, 2016).

31. Conrad C. Crane, *Avoiding Vietnam: The U.S. Army's Response to Defeat in Southeast Asia* (Carlisle Barracks, PA: Strategic Studies Institute, U.S. Army War College, 2002)

32. Conrad C. Crane and W. Andrew Terrill, *Reconstructing Iraq: Insights, Challenges, and Missions for Military Forces in a Post-Conflict Scenario* (Carlisle Barracks, PA: US Army War College, Strategic Studies Institute, Feb. 2003).

33. A literate group of officers was involved: John A. Nagl, *Counterinsurgency Lessons from Malaya and Vietnam: Learning to Eat Soup with a Knife* (Westport, CT: Praeger, 2002); David Kilcullen, *The Accidental Guerrilla: Fighting Small Wars in the Midst of a Big One* (London: Hurst & Co., 2009); and Lieutenant General David H. Petraeus, 'Learning Counterinsurgency: Observations from Soldiering in Iraq', *Military Review* (2006): 2–12.

34. *U.S. Army/Marine Corps Counterinsurgency Field Manual* (FM 3–24) (Chicago: University of Chicago Press, 2007).

35. See the exchange between Robert J. Gonzalez, 'Toward Mercenary Anthropology?' and Montgomery McFate, 'Building Bridges or Burning Heretics?', *Anthropology Today* 23:3 (2007): 14–21. See also Montgomery McFate and Janice Laurence, eds., *Social Science Goes to War: The Human Terrain System in Iraq and Afghanistan* (London: Hurst, 2015).

36. Stathis N. Kalyvas, 'The New U.S. Army/Marine Corps Counterinsurgency Field Manual as Political Science and Political Praxis', *Perspectives on Politics* 6.2 (2008): 351.

37. David Galula, *Counterinsurgency Warfare: Theory and Practice* (Westport, CT: Praeger, 1964).

38. The distinction between kinetic and non-kinetic was noticed in Bob Woodward's, *Bush at War*, (New York: Simon & Schuster, 2002). See Timothy Noah, 'Birth of a Washington Word: When warfare gets "kinetic"', *Slate*, 20 Nov. 2002. Available: http:// www.slate.com/articles/news_and_politics/chatterbox/2002/11/birth_of_a_washington _word.html. However, the word was introduced during the development of concepts for destroying missiles in space as part of President Reagan's Strategic Defense Initiative (including a Kinetic Kill Vehicle). The kinetic energy of an object is the energy that it possesses due to its motion.

39. M. L. R. Smith and David Martin Jones, *The Political Impossibility of Modern Counterinsurgency: Strategic Problems, Puzzles and Paradoxes* (New York: Columbia University Press, 2015).

40. Colonel Gian Gentile, *Wrong Turn: America's Deadly Embrace of Counterinsurgency* (New York: The New Press, 2013).

41. Ralph Peters 'Progress and Peril, New Counterinsurgency Manual Cheats on the History Exam,' *Armed Forces Journal International*, 144 (2007), http://armedforces journal.com/progress-and-peril.

42. Carter Malkasian, *Illusions of Victory: The Anbar Awakening and the Rise of the Islamic State,* (New York: Oxford University Press, 2017).

43. Smith and Jones 182.

44. Edward Luttwak, 'Dead end: Counterinsurgency warfare as military malpractice', *Harpers*, February 2007, 33–42.

CHAPTER 18

1. Martin Barker, *A 'Toxic Genre': The Iraq War Films,* (London: Pluto Press, 2011), p. 32–3.

2. Brian Castner, *All the Ways We Kill and Die,* (New York: Arcade, 2016). Castner's previous book, *The Long Walk: A Story of War and the Life That Follows,* (New York: Doubleday, 2012), chronicled his struggles with Post-Traumatic Stress Disorder (PTSD), which he called his 'Crazy', after returning from the war. On the killing of bin Laden see Robert O'Neill, *The Operator: Firing the Shots that killed Osama Bin Laden,* (New York: Scribner, 2017); Mark Owen, *No Easy Day: The Firsthand Account of the Mission that Killed Osama Bin Laden,* (New York: Dutton, 2014).

3. The definitive account, confirming both the high cost of waging strategic bombing campaigns and their limited achievements is Richard Overy, *The Bombing War: Europe 1939–1945,* (London, Allen Lane, 2013).

4. For a historical survey see Beatrice Heuser, 'Atrocities in Theory and Practice: An Introduction', *Civil Wars*, 14:1, (2012), 2–28.

5. James Corum and Wray Johnson, *Airpower in Small Wars: Fighting Insurgents and Terrorists* (Lawrence, KS: University Press of Kansas, 2003), p. 58 It was in Iraq that Arthur Harris as a Squadron Leader developed his ideas of strategic bombing which he later applied ruthlessly as Head of Bomber Command against German cities. Aylmer Haldane, *The Insurrection in Mesopotamia, 1920* (Edinburgh, Blackwood, 1922; Mark Jacobsen 'Only by the sword': British counter insurgency in Iraq, 1920, *Small Wars & Insurgencies*, 2:2, (1991) 323-363,

6. Sahr Conway-Lanz, *Collateral Damage: Americans, Noncombatant Immunity, and Atrocity after World War II* (New York: Routledge, 2006) 2.

7. Matthew Evangelista and Henry Shue, *The American Way of Bombing; Changing Ethical and Legal Norms from Flying Fortress to Drones* (Ithaca, NY: Cornell University Press, 2004).

8. Thomas Smith, *Human Rights and War Through Civilian Eyes* (Philadelphia, PA: University of Pennsylvania Press, 2016).

9. Charles J. Dunlap, Jr., 'Lawfare Today... and Tomorrow', *International Law and the Changing Character of War*, eds. Raul A. 'Pete' Pedrozo and Daria P. Wollschlaeger, vol. 87 (Newport, RI: US Naval War College International Law Studies, 2011); and Charles Dunlap, *Law and Military Interventions: Preserving Humanitarian Values in 21st Conflicts* (Cambridge, MA: Carr Center for Human Rights Policy Kennedy School of Government, Harvard University, 2001).

10. Stephen Saideman, *The Ties That Divide: Ethnic Politics, Foreign Policy, and International Conflict* (New York: Columbia University Press, 2001).

11. James Gow and James Tilsey, 'The Strategic Imperative for Media Management', *Bosnia by Television*, eds. James Gow, Richard Paterson, and Alison Preston (London: British Film Institute, 1996) 107.

12. Ivan Arreguin-Toft, 'How the Weak Win Wars: A Theory of Asymmetric Conflict', *International Security* 26.1 (2001): 93–128.

13. Gil Merom, *How Democracies Lose Small Wars* (Cambridge: Cambridge University Press, 2003) 15.

14. Mao Zedong, *On Guerrilla Warfare*, trans. Samuel B. Griffith (Urbana: University of Illinois Press, 2000).

15. Beatriz Manz, *Paradise in Ashes: A Guatemalan Journey of Courage, Terror, and Hope* (Oakland, CA: University of California Press, 2005), and Jennifer Schirmer, *The Guatemalan Military Project: A Violence Called Democracy* (Philadelphia, PA: University of Pennsylvania Press, 1998).

16. Schirmer 45.

17. Alex de Waal, *The Real Politics of the Horn of Africa: Money, War and the Business of Power* (London: Jon Wiley, 2015).

18. Ian Fisher, 'Playing by the Rules: From an Old Fashioned War, a Very Modern Calamity', *New York Times Week in Review*, 4 June 2000, 5; and Ian Fisher, 'Awful War, Real Peace: The Model of Eritrea', *New York Times*, 6 April 2001, A3.

19. Benjamin Valentino, Paul Huth, and Dylan Balch-Lindsay, '"Draining the Sea": Mass Killing and Guerrilla Warfare', *International Organization* 58 (2004): 375–407.

20. Benjamin A. Valentino, *Final Solutions: Mass Killing and Genocide in the Twentieth Century* (Ithaca, NY: Cornell Studies in Security Affairs, 2005).

21. VK Shashikumar, 'Lessons from Sri Lanka's War', *Indian Defence Review* 24.3 (2009). Available: http://www.indiandefencereview.com/spotlights/lessons-from -the-war-in-sri-lanka.

22. Niel A. Smith, 'Understanding Sri Lanka's Defeat of the Tamil Tigers', *Joint Forces Quarterly* 59 (2010): 40-44 Samir Puri points out that this 'cruel affair' followed attempts by the government to combine dialogue with coercion, *Fighting and Negotiating with Armed Groups: The Difficulty of Securing Strategic Outcomes* (London: Taylor & Francis for IISS, 2016), 36.

23. Amy Knight, 'Finally, We Know About the Moscow Bombings', *New York Review of Books*, 22 Nov. 2012, review of John Dunlop, *The Moscow Bombings of September 1999: Examinations of Russian Terrorist Attacks at the Onset of Vladimir Putin's Rule* (Stuttgart: Ibidem, 2012).

24. Jason Lyall, 'Are Coethnics More Effective Counterinsurgents? Evidence from the Second Chechen War', *American Political Science Review* 104 (2010): 1–20.

25. Timothy L. Thomas, 'Grozny 2000: Urban Combat Lessons Learned', *Military Review* (July–August 2000): 50-59.

26. Mark Galeotti, 'Putin is Playing by Grozny Rules in Aleppo', *Foreign Policy*, 29 Sept. 2016.

27. Jason Lyall, 'Does Indiscriminate Violence Incite Insurgent Attacks? Evidence from Chechnya', *Journal of Conflict Resolution* 53.3 (2009): 331–362. Lyall was clearly uncomfortable with his findings: 'The article clearly should not be read as endorsing the use of random violence against civilians as a policy instrument. Such actions are morally abhorrent and are rightly regarded as war crimes under both international law and Russia's own legal system'.

28. Emil Aslan Souleimanov and David Siroky, 'Random or Retributive?: Indiscriminate Violence in the Chechen Wars', *World Politics*, 68:4 (2016), 677–712.

29. Luke N. Condra and Jacob N. Shapiro, 'Who Takes the Blame? The Strategic Effects of Collateral Damage', *American Journal of Political Science* 56:1 (2012): 167–187.

30. Jason Lyall, Graeme Blair, and Kosuke Imai, 'Explaining Support for Combatants during Wartime: A Survey Experiment in Afghanistan', *American Political Science Review* 107.4 (2013).

31. Valentino *Final Solutions*, 68, and Stathis Kalyvas *The Logic of Violence in Civil War*, (Cambridge: Cambridge University Press, 2006), 388.

32. Seth Jones, *Waging Insurgent Warfare: Lessons from the Vietcong to the Islamic State* (New York: Oxford University Press, 2017) 11.

33. Christopher Paul, Colin Clarke, and Beth Grill, *Victory Has a Thousand Fathers: Sources of Success in Counterinsurgency* (Santa Monica, CA: RAND, 2010) xxiv.

34. Austin Long, *The Soul of Armies: Counterinsurgency Doctrine and Military Culture in the US and UK* (Ithaca, NY: Cornell University Press, 2016) 225.

CHAPTER 19

1. Deborah Scroggins, *Emma's War: Love, Betrayal and Death in the Sudan* (New York: Vintage Books, 2004) 427. I found the quote in Kalyvas, 'Civil Wars', in Boix and Stokes, *The Oxford Handbook of Comparative Politics*, which led me to read the book.

2. *The State Failure Task Force Report: Phase III Findings* (McLean, VA: Science Applications International Corporation, 30 Sept. 30, 2000).

3. Charles Call, 'The Fallacy of the "Failed States"', *Third World Quarterly* 29.8 (2008): 1491–1507.

4. Carnegie Commission on Preventing Deadly Conflict, *Preventing Deadly Conflict* (New York: Carnegie Corporation, 1997) xviii. Available: http://www.dtic.mil/dtic/tr/fulltext/u2/a372860.pdf.

5. Francis Fukuyama, *State-Building: Governance and World Order in the 21ˢᵗ Century* (Ithaca, NY: Cornell University Press, 2004).

6. Stephen D. Krasner and Carlos Pascual, 'Addressing State Failure', *Foreign Affairs* 84:4 (2005): 153–163.

7. Wendy Brown, 'The New U.S. Army/Marine Corps Counterinsurgency Field Manual as Political Science and Political Praxis', *Perspectives on Politics* 6.2 (2008): 351.

8. Walter C. Ludwig II, 'Influencing Clients in Counterinsurgency: U.S. Involvement in El Salvador's Civil War, 1979–92', *International Security* 41.6 (2016): 99.

9. Virginia Page Fortna and Reyko Huang, 'Democratization after Civil War: A Brush-Clearing Exercise', *International Studies Quarterly* 56 (2012): 801–08.

10. John Clark, 'The Decline of the African Military Coup', *Journal of Democracy* 18.3 (2007): 144–155.

11. Jennifer M. Welsh, 'Introduction', *Humanitarian Intervention and International Relations*, ed. Jennifer M Welsh (Oxford: Oxford University Press, 2004) 7. For some candid musings about a new imperialism, undertaken for defensive reasons, see Robert Cooper, *The post-modern state and world order* (London: Demos and the Foreign Policy Centre, 2000).

12. Richard Cockett, *Sudan: The Failure and Division of an African State* (New Haven: Yale University Press, 2016) for more background on the conflict. Emma McCone is also the model for a fictional character in Philip Caputo, *Acts of Faith* (New York: Knopf, 2005).

13. BBC News: '"I'm going to return to Soiuth Sudan", says Riek Machar (18 October 2016) http://www.bbc.co.uk/news/world-africa-37689235.

14. 'Why South Sudan is still at war', *The Economist*, 3 Oct. 2016. Available: http://www.economist.com/blogs/economist-explains/2016/10/economist-explains-0 *The Economist* was also scathing about a memoir of the person who was at the head of the UN mission, Hilde Johnson: *South Sudan: The Untold Story from Independence to Civil War* (London: I.B. Tauris, 2016). ("From hope to horror", *The Economist*, 16 July 2016.) Available: http://www.economist.com/news/books-and-arts/21702158-hope-horror.

15. Monica Duffy Toft, *Securing the Peace: The Durable Settlement of Civil Wars* (Princeton: Princeton University Press, 2010) 17.

16. Ian Morris, *War: What Is It Good For? The Role of Conflict in Civilisation, From Primates to Robots* (London: Profile Books, 2014).

17. Charles Tilly, 'War Making and State Making as Organized Crime', *Bringing the State Back In*, eds. Peter Evans, Dietrich Rueschemeyer, and Theda Skocpol (Cambridge: Cambridge University Press, 1985) 169–191.

18. Edward Luttwak, 'Give War a Chance', *Foreign Affairs* 78.4 (1999): 36-44

19. Roy Licklider, 'The Consequences of Negotiated Settlements in Civil Wars, 1945–1993', *American Political Science Review* 89.3 (1995): 681–690.

20. Monica Duffy Toft, 'Peace Through Victory: The Durable Settlement of Civil Wars', Unpublished Manuscript, Harvard University, 2003.

21. Robert Harrison Wagner, 'The Causes of Peace', *Stopping the* Killing, ed. Licklider (New York: New York University Press, 1993). For a slightly different mechanism, see Toft, "Peace Through Victory'. Herbst argued that the fundamental problem confronting African leaders was (and continues to be) how to extend power over vast, inhospitable territories with low population densities. See Jeffrey Herbst, *States and Power in Africa: Comparative Lessons in Authority and Control* (Princeton, NJ: Princeton University Press, 2000).

22. Jeremy M. Weinstein, 'Autonomous Recovery and International Intervention In Comparative Perspective', Center for Global Development, Working Paper Number 57, April 2005.

23. Sebastian Mallaby, *The World's Banker: A Story of Failed States, Financial Crises, and the Wealth and Poverty of Nations* (New York: Penguin, 2004).

24. David T. Burbach and Christopher J. Fettweis, 'The Coming Stability? The Decline of Warfare in Africa and Implications for International Security', *Contemporary Security Policy* 35.3 (2014): 421–445.

25. See Jonathan M. Powell and Clayton L. Thyne, 'Global Instances of Coups from 1950 to 2010: A New Dataset', *Journal of Peace Research* 48.2 (2011): 249–259.

26. Paul D. Williams, 'Continuity and Change in War and Conflict in Africa', *PRISM* 6: 4 (2017), 33-45; Williams, 'Continuity and Change in War and Conflict in Africa'; Barbara Walter, 'Why Bad Governance Leads to Repeat Civil Wars', *Journal of Conflict Resolution*, 59:7 (2015), 1242–72.

27. Scott Gates, Havard Mokleiv Nygard, Havard Strand, and Henrik Urdal, *Trends in Armed Conflict, 1946–2014*, (Oslo: Peace Research Institute Oslo, 2016).

28. Max Berak and Laris Karklis, 'Starving to Death', *Washington Post*, 11 April 2017.

29. Christopher Chivvis, *Toppling Qaddafi: Libya and the Limits of Liberal Intervention* (Cambridge: Cambridge University Press, 2013).

30. Barbara Walter, 'The New New Civil Wars', Annual Review of Political *Science*, 20-25, (2017) 1–18.

CHAPTER 20

1. David W. Barno, 'Military Adaptation in Complex Operations', *PRISM* 1:1 (2009): 30.

2. Christopher Elliott, *High Command: British Military Leadership in the Iraq and Afghanistan Wars* (London: Hurst & Co., 2015).

3. Charles Krulak, "The Three Block War: Fighting in Urban Areas," in *Vital Speeches of the Day*, 64:5 (15 December 1997), 139–141.

4. Frank G. Hoffman and James N. Mattis. "Future Warfare: The Rise of Hybrid Wars," in *Naval Institute Proceedings*, 132:11 (November 2005).

5. Frank G. Hoffman, *Conflict in the 21ˢᵗ Century: The Rise of Hybrid Wars* (Arlington, VA: The Potomac Institute for Policy Studies, 2007). In a similar concept, Thomas Huber identified 'compound war' as a developing form of warfare. In 2002, he described it as the 'systematic, deliberate combining of regular and irregular forces'. Thomas M. Huber, 'Compound Warfare: A Conceptual Framework', *Compound Warfare: That Fatal Knot*, ed. Thomas M. Huber (Fort Leavenworth, MS: US Army Command and General Staff College Press, 2002).

6. Frank G. Hoffman, 'Hybrid vs. Compound War: The Janus Choice of Modern War: Defining Today's Multifaceted Conflict', *Armed Forces Journal* (2009): 1–2. Erin Simpson used the term 'hybrid warfare' to describe a type of conflict that would become more prevalent. 'Thinking about Modern Conflict: Hybrid Wars, Strategy, and

War Aims', *Paper Presented at the Annual Meeting of The Midwest Political Science Association*, 7 April 2005.

7. Russell W. Glenn, *All Glory is Fleeting: Insights from the Second Lebanon War* (Santa Monica, CA: RAND, 2008) 3.

8. Sam Jones, 'Ukraine: Russia's new art of war', *Financial Times*, 28 Aug. 2014, and Paul Goble, 'Putin's Actions in Ukraine Following Script by Russian General Staff a Year Ago,' *The Interpreter*, 20 June 2014, http://www.interpretermag.com/putins -actions-in-ukraine-following-script-by-russian-general-staff-a-year-ago/. This was a speech of late January 2013 to the annual general meeting of the Russian Academy of Military Science on 'The Role of the General Staff in the Organization of the Defense of the Country in Correspondence with the New Statute about the General Staff Confirmed by the President of the Russian Federation.'

9. Frank Hoffman discussed Ukraine as an example of hybrid warfare in 'On Not-So-New Warfare: Political Warfare vs. Hybrid Threat', *War on the Rocks*, 28 July 2014, http://warontherocks.com/2014/07/on-not-so-new-warfare-political-warfare-vs-hybrid-threats.

10. I discuss this in 'Ukraine and the art of limited war', *Survival* 56.6 (2014): 7–38.

11. Mark Galeotti, 'The west is too paranoid about Russia's information war', *Guardian*, 7 July 2015. https://www.theguardian.com/world/2015/jul/07/russia-propaganda -europe-america

12. Timothy McCulloh and Richard Johnson, *Hybrid Warfare*, JSOU Report 13–4 (MacDill AFB, FL.: Joint Special Operations University, 2013).

13. For historical examples see Williamson Murray and Peter R. Mansoor, eds., *Hybrid Warfare: Fighting Complex Opponents from the Ancient World to the Present* (New York: Cambridge University Press, 2012).

14. Keynote speech by NATO Secretary-General Jens Stoltenberg at the opening of the NATO Transformation Seminar, 25 March 2015. Available: http://www.nato.int /cps/en/natohq/opinions_118435.htm?selectedLocale=en

15. Frank G. Hoffman, 'Hybrid Warfare and Challenges', *Joint Forces Quarterly* 52 (2009): 34–39.

16. Lincoln A. Mitchell, *The Color Revolutions* (Philadelphia, PA: University of Pennsylvania Press, 2012).

17. Maria Snegovaya, *Putin's Information Warfare in Ukraine: Soviet Origins of Russia's Hybrid Warfare*, (Washington DC: Institute for the Study of War, 2015).

18. John Arquilla and David Ronfeldt, eds., *Networks and Netwars: The Future of Terror, Crime, and Militancy* (Santa Monica, CA: RAND, 2001) 3–4. Available: www .rand.org/publications/MR/MR1382/.

19. David Kilcullen, 'Twenty-Eight Articles: Fundamentals of Company-Level Counterinsurgency', *Military Review* 83:3 (2006): 105–107. This began as an e-mail that was widely distributed around the US Army. See also Emile Simpson, *War from the Ground Up: Twenty-First-Century Combat as Politics* (London: Hurst & Co., 2012) 233.

20. G. J. David and T. R. McKeldin III, *Ideas as Weapons: Influence and Perception in Modern Warfare* (Washington DC: Potomac Books, 2009).

CHAPTER 21

1. William Gibson, *Neuromancer* (New York: Ace Books, 1984) 69. Science fiction writer Gibson is credited with introducing the word 'cyberspace', first in a 1982 short story and then in this novel. Wikipedia draws attention to other uses before Gibson's, but they were not in a computer context: https://en.wikipedia.org/wiki/Cyberspace.

2. Jean-Loup Samaan, 'Cyber Command', *RUSI Journal* 195.6 (2010): 16–21.

3. The first reference appears to have been: 'Science: Push-Button War', *Time Magazine*, 23 June 1947.

4. Thomas Rid, *Rise of the Machines: A Cybernetic History* (New York: W. W. Norton, 2016) 95–6.

5. Scott Brown, '*WarGames*: A Look Back at the Film That Turned Geeks and Phreaks Into Stars', *Wired Magazine*, 21 July 2008. For a highly critical view of the movie, noting the criminality of the hacking and the total unreality of the plot, see Suid, 446-452.

6. Fred Kaplan, *Dark Territory: The Secret History of Cyber War* (New York: Simon & Schuster, 2016) 1–2.

7. This term was first used in connections with space exploration, and the possibility of 'artifact-organism systems which would extend man's unconscious, self-regulatory controls'. See Manfred E. Clynes and Nathan S. Kline 'Cyborgs and Space', *Astronautics* (Sept. 1960). Reprinted in *New York Times*, (26 February 1997), https://partners .nytimes.com/library/cyber/surf/022697surf-cyborg.html.

8. P. W. Singer, Wired *for War: The Robotics Revolution and Conflict in the 21st Century*, (New York: Penguin Books, 2009). 66, 416.

9. M. W. Thring, 'Robots on the March' in Calder, *Unless Peace Comes*, 180, 190.

10. Owen Davies, 'Robotic Warriors Clash in Cyberwars', *Omni* 9.4 (1987): p. 76. Cited by Rid 301.

11. Eric Arnett, 'Hyperwar', *Bulletin of the Atomic Scientists* 48.7 (1992): 14-21. Cited in Rid 303.

12. Kaplan, *Dark Territory* 31–2.

13. National Research Council, *Computers at Risk: Safe Computing in the Information Age* (Washington DC: National Academies Press, 1991).

14. See Rid 308. The original article was Winn Schwartau, 'Fighting Terminal Terrorism', *Computerworld*, 28 Jan. 1991. As this was the start of the year, the claim appears to be stronger than that of RSA Data Security President D. James Bidzos, credited by Scott Berinato in 'The Future of Security', *Computerworld*, 30 Dec. 2003, cited in Jon R. Lindsay, 'Stuxnet and the Limits of Cyber Warfare', *Security Studies* 22.3 (2013): 365-404.

15. Winn Schwartau, *Terminal Compromise* (Old Hickory, TN: Interpact Press, 1991). Available: http://www.gutenberg.org/files/79/79.txt.

16. Tofflers, *War and Anti-War* 195.

17. Bruce Berkowitz, *The New Face of War: How War Will Be fought in the 21ˢᵗ Century* (New York: The Free Press, 2003) 138–140.

18. Rid 310.

19. Anna Mulrine, 'CIA Chief Leon Panetta: The Next Pearl Harbor Could Be a Cyberattack', *Christian Science Monitor*, 9 June 2011. Adm. Mike Mullen, quoted in Marcus Weisgerber, 'DoD to Release Public Version of Cyber Strategy', *Defense News*, 8 July 2011. Both cited by Lindsay.

20. Berkowitz 143.

21. Kim Zetter, *Countdown to Zero Day: Stuxnet and the Launch of the World's First Digital Weapon* (New York: Crown, 2014).

22. Kaplan 275.

23. Cited in Aaron Franklin Brantly, *The Decision to Attack: Military and Intelligence Cyber-Decision-Making* (Athens, GA: University of Georgia Press, 2016) 39.

24. Thomas Rid and Ben Buchanan, 'Attributing Cyber Attacks', *Journal of Strategic Studies* 38. (2015): 1–2.

25. Kaplan 283.

26. John Arquilla and David Ronfeld, 'Cyberwar is Coming!', *Comparative Strategy* 12.2 (1993): 141–165.

27. I deal with this in *Strategy: A History*.

28. John Arquilla, 'The Computer Mouse that Roared: Cyberwar in the Twenty-First Century', *The Brown Journal of World Affairs*, 18:1 (2011), 42.

29. Lt. Gen. Richard P. Mills, US Marine Corps, cited by Raphael Satter, 'US General: We Hacked the Enemy in Afghanistan', *Associated Press*, 24 Aug. 2012, cited in Lindsay.

30. Ben Buchanan, *The Cybersecurity Dilemma: Hacking, Trust and Fear Between Nations* (Oxford: Oxford University Press, 2017).

31. Gadi Evron, 'Battling Botnets and Online Mobs: Estonia's Defense Efforts During the Internet War', *Georgetown Journal of International affairs*, 9:1 (1991), 121-6.

32. George Lucas, *Ethics and Cyber Warfare: The Quest for Responsible Security in the Age of Digital Warfare* (New York: Oxford University Press, 2017).

CHAPTER 22

1. Isaac Asimov, 'Runaround', *Foundation* (New York: Gnome Press, 1951). 'Runaround' was originally published in 1942.

2. *Star Wars: Episode IV—A New Hope* (1977). The prequel *Rogue One* (2016) showed that the flaw was deliberate, introduced by a designer sympathetic to the rebels, and also that the Death Star was successfully tested on another planet.

3. *Star Wars: Episode VI—Return of the Jedi* (1983).

4. Dan Ward, 'Don't Come to the Dark Side: Acquisition Lessons from a Galaxy Far, Far Away', Defense *AT&L: Better Buying Power*, 70, (September–October 2011), http://www.thedanward.com/resources/Build+Droids+Not+Death+Stars.pdf.

5. Paul Shawcross, 'This Isn't the Petition Response You're Looking For', *Wired*, (11 January 2013), https://www.wired.com/2013/01/white-house-death-star.

6. Norman R Augustine, *Augustine's Laws*, (New York: Viking, 1987), 143.

7. Paul Scharre, *Robotics on the Battlefield Part II The Coming Swarm*, (Washington DC: Center for New American Security, 2014), p. 6.

8. Richard Whittle, *Predator: The Secret Origins of the Drone Revolution* (New York: Henry Holt, 2014).

9. Michael Ignatieff, *Virtual War: Kosovo and Beyond* (New York: Metropolitan Books, 2000).

10. Peter L. Bergen and Daniel Rothenberg, eds., *Drone Wars: Transforming Conflict, Law, and Policy* (Cambridge: Cambridge University Press, 2015); Hugh Gusterson, *Drone: Remote Control Warfare* (Cambridge, MA: MIT Press, 2016); and Sarah Kreps, *Drones: What Everyone Needs to Know* (New York: Oxford University Press, 2016).

11. Patrick Johnston, 'Does Decapitation Work? Assessing the Effectiveness of Leadership Targeting in Counterinsurgency Campaigns', *International Security* 36.4 (2012): 47–79.

12. Daniel Byman, 'Do Targeted Killings Work?', Foreign Affairs 85 (2006): 95–111, and Johnson, 'Does Decapitation Work?' 47–79. Jenna Jordan in 'When heads roll: Assessing the effectiveness of leadership decapitation', *Security Studies* 18.4 (2009) suggests that ideological groups are more vulnerable to decapitation than religious groups, and are hierarchical more than decentralised, and also that the tactic can be counterproductive. Stephanie Carvin, 'The Trouble with Targeted Killing', *Security Studies* 21:5, (2012), 29–555.

13. Avery Plaw, Matthew S. Fricker, and Carlos R. Colon, *The Drone Debate: A Primer on the U.S. Use of Unmanned Aircraft Outside Conventional Battlefields* (Lanham, MD: Rowman & Littlefield, 2015). It's hard to know exactly how many civilians have been killed by drones, since insurgents inevitably insist that the victims were innocent noncombatants, while the US government has tended to count most of those killed as combatants. For an idea of scale, the administration put the numbers killed outside the recognized war zones of Afghanistan, Iraq, and Syria between January 2009 and December 2015 as between 2,372 and 2,581 combatants and between 64 and 116 civilians, while the London-based Bureau of Investigative Journalism estimated that as of August 2016 US drone strikes had killed between 492 and 1,138 civilians in Pakistan, Somalia, and Yemen.

14. See Chris Woods, *Sudden Justice: America's Secret Drone Wars* (Oxford: Oxford University Press, 2015), and Jeremy Scahill and the staff of *The Intercept, The*

Assassination Complex: Inside the Government's Secret Drone Warfare Program (New York: Simon & Schuster, 2016).

15. The Trump Administration sought to ease restrictions on drone strikes. Greg Jaffe and Karen deYoung, 'Trump administration reviewing ways to make it easier to launch drone strikes', *Washington Post*, (13 March 2017).

16. Gordon Johnston of Pentagon's Joint Forces Command quoted in Singer, *Wired for War*: 63.

17. Remarks by Deputy Secretary of Defense Robert Work at the Center for New American Security Defense Forum, 14 Dec. 2015. Available: https://www.defense.gov/News/Speeches/Speech-View/Article/634214/cnas-defense-forum. See also James R. McGrath, 'Twenty-First Century Information Warfare and the Third Offset Strategy', *Joint Forces Quarterly* 82 (2016): 16–23.

18. Louis A. Del Monte, *Nanoweapons: A Growing Threat to Humanity* (Lincoln, NE: Potomac Books, 2017).

19. For a sceptical take, see Christopher Coker, *Future* War (Cambridge: Polity Press, 2015), 100–105.

20. These two paragraphs draw upon Mary L. Cummings, *Artificial Intelligence and the Future of Warfare*, Research Paper (London: Royal Institute of International Affairs, Jan. 2017).

21. 'Flight of the Drones: Why the Future of Air Power Belongs to Unmanned Systems', *The Economist*, 8 Oct. 2011. Matthew Rosenberg and John Markoff, 'At Heart of U.S. Strategy, Weapons That Can Think', *New York Times*, 26 October 2016. A Terminator-like machine was said to be a decade away.

22. Thomas G. Mahnken, *Technology and the American Way of War Since 1945* (New York: Columbia University Press, 2008).

23. Benjamin Wittes and Gabriella Blum, *The Future of Violence – Robots and Germs, Hackers and Drones: Confronting the New Age of Threat* (New York: Basic Books, 2015).

24. John Arquilla and David Ronfeldt, *Swarming and the Future of Conflict*, (Santa Monica: RAND Corporation, 2005).

25. Scharre.

26. David Kilcullen, *Blood Year: Islamic State and the Failures of the War on Terror* (London: Hurst 2016).

27. Michael O'Hanlon, *The Future of Land Warfare* (Washington DC: Brookings Institution, 2015) 163–4.

28. Sharon Weinberger, *The Imagineers of War: The Untold Story of DARPA, the Pentagon Agency That Changed the World* (New York: Alfred A. Knopf, 2017) 496.

29. President Bush, *Addresses the 89th Annual National Convention of the American Legion*, Reno, Nevada, 28 Aug. 2007.

30. President Barack Obama, 'Remarks by the President', Joint Base McGuire-Dix-Lakehurst, NJ, 15 Dec. 2014. For Obama, the moment of truth had come in Syria in 2013 when, despite the Assad regime having apparently crossed a 'red line' he had set when it used chemical weapons, he decided not to intervene in the conflict. Jeffrey Goldberg, 'The Obama Doctrine', *The Atlantic Monthly*, April 2016. Available: https://www.theatlantic.com/magazine/archive/2016/04/the-obama-doctrine/471525.

31. Patrick Porter, *The Global Village Myth: Distance, War, and the Limits of Power* (London: Hurst, 2015).

32. The classic analysis of raiding strategies is found in Archer Jones, *The Art of War in the Western World* (Urbana and Champaign, IL: University of Illinois Press, 2001).

33. Efraim Inbar and Eitan Shamir, 'What after counter-insurgency?' *International Affairs* 92.6 (2016): 1427–1441.

34. Bernard I. Finel, 'An Alternative to COIN', *Armed Forces Journal*, (February 2010) http://armedforcesjournal.com/an-alternative-to-coin.

35. Peter Cole and Brian McQuinn, eds, *The Libyan Revolution and Its Aftermath*, (Oxford: Oxford University Press, 2015).

36. H. R. McMaster, 'Discussing the Continuities of War and the Future of Warfare: The Defense Entrepreneurs Forum', *Small Wars Journal* (2014). McMaster became President Trump's National Security Advisor in February 2017.

37. Developments of this sort loom large in Coker, *Future War*.

38. P. W. Singer and August Cole, 'How to Write About World War III: Can Fiction Help Prevent Another Conflict Between Great Powers?' *The Atlantic Monthly*, 30 June 2015. Also see P. W. Singer and August Cole, *Ghost Fleet: A Novel of the Next World War* (New York: Houghton Mifflin, 2015).

39. 'Chronicle of a war foretold: The story of a conflict between America and China makes a fine example of future-war fiction', *The Economist*, 27 June 2015. Available: http://www.economist.com/news/books-and-arts/21656124-story-conflict-between-america-and-china-makes-fine-example-future-war.

40. August Cole, ed., *War Stories from the Future* (Washington DC: The Atlantic Council Art of Future Warfare Project, 2015). Available: http://www.atlanticcouncil.org/images/publications/War_Stories_from_the_Future.pdf. General Martin. Dempsey, the former Chairman of the Joint Chiefs of Staff, praised the work, noting how the stuff of science fiction in the past, such as directed energy weapons, electromagnetic pulse, and autonomous warfare, were beginning to materialize. 'Science fiction allows us to model future possibilities and explore the practical and tactical possibilities of emerging or future technologies.'

CHAPTER 23

1. Fukuyama, *The End of History* 148.

2. Julia Dunn, 'Los Angeles Crips and Bloods: Past and Present', *Poverty & Prejudice: Gangs of All Color*, Stanford University Edge. Available: https://web.stanford.edu/class/e297c/poverty_prejudice/gangcolor/lacrips.htm

3. Newman, 'Conflict research and the 'Decline' in Civil wars', 263.

4. Wendy MacClinchy, 'Violence Today', *States of Fragility* (Paris: OECD, 2016) 31-67, and Krause, 'From Armed Conflict to Political Violence'.

5. Lothar Brock et al., *Fragile States: Violence and the Failure of Intervention* (Cambridge: Polity Press, 2012).

6. United Nations, 'The World's Cities in 2016'. Available: http://www.un.org/en/development/desa/population/publications/pdf/urbanization/the_worlds_cities_in_2016_data_booklet.pdf

7. Robert Muggah, 'Fixing Fragile Cities: Solutions for Urban Violence and Poverty', *Foreign Affairs* (2015): https://www.foreignaffairs.com/articles/africa/2015-01-15/fixing-fragile-cities; Robert Muggah, *Fragile Cities Rising* (Global Observatory, International Peace Institute, 2013); and João Pontes Nogueira, *From Fragile States to Fragile Cities: Redefining Spaces of Humanitarian Practices*, HASOW Discussion Paper 12, Oct. 2014. Available: https://igarape.org.br/wp-content/uploads/2016/04/From-Fragile-States-to-Fragile-Cities.pdf

8. Coker, *Future War* 189. The quote comes from Mike Davis.

9. Richard J. Norton, 'Feral Cities', *Naval War College Review* 56.4 (2003): 97–106.

10. Jennifer M. Hazen, 'Understanding gangs as armed groups', *International Review of the Red Cross* (2010): 369–386.

11. David Kilcullen, *Out of the Mountains: The Coming Age of the Urban Guerrilla* (New York: Oxford University Press, 2013).

12. Chief of Staff of the Army, Strategic Studies Group, *Megacities and the United States Army Preparing for a Complex and Uncertain Future*, June 2014. Available: https://www.army.mil/e2/c/downloads/351235.pdf.

13. Puri, *Fighting and Negotiating with Armed Groups*.

14. Phil Williams, 'Transnational Criminal Organizations and International Security', *Survival* 36.1 (1994): 96–113, and Moises Naim, 'Mafia States: Organised Crime Takes Office', *Foreign Affairs* 91:3 (2012): 100–111.

15. Robert Muggah, 'A War by Any Other Name', *Small Wars Journal*, (2017).

16. Phil Williams, 'The Terrorism Debate Over Mexican Drug Trafficking Violence', Terrorism and Political *Violence*, 24:2, (2012) 259–278. Cockayne concluded, after looking at the American and Sicilian mafias, that their conflicts were properly understood as war. James Cockayne, *Hidden Power: The Strategic Logic of Organised Crime* (London: Hurst, 2016).

17. Michael T. Klare, *Rising Powers, Shrinking Planet: The New Geopolitics of Energy* (New York: Metropolitan Books, 2008).

18. Pavel Baev, *Russian Energy Policy and Military Power: Putin's Quest for Greatness* (London: Routledge, 2008).

19. Jeff D. Colgan, 'Fueling the Fire: Pathways from Oil to War', *International Security* 38.2 (2013): 147–80.

20. Tim Boersma, 'The end of the Russian energy weapon (that arguably was never there)', Brookings, online, 5 Mar. 2015. Available: https://www.brookings.edu/blog/order-from-chaos/2015/03/05/the-end-of-the-russian-energy-weapon-that-arguably-was-never-there.

21. Roger J. Stern, 'Oil Scarcity Ideology in US Foreign Policy, 1908–97', *Security Studies* 25.2 (2016): 214–257.

22. Rosemary A. Kelani, 'The Petroleum Paradox: Oil, Coercive Vulnerability, and Great Power Behavior', *Security Studies* 25.2 (2016): 181–213, and Llewelyn Hughes and Austin Long, 'Is There an Oil Weapon? National Security Implications of Changes in the Structure of the International Oil Market', *International Security* 39.3 (2014/15): 152–189.

23. Emily Meierding, 'Dismantling the Oil Wars Myth', *Security Studies* 25.2 (2016): 258-288

24. Thomas F Homer-Dixon, 'Environmental Scarcities and Violent Conflict: Evidence from Cases', *International Security* 19.1(1994): 5–40. See also his *Environment, Scarcity, and Violence* (Princeton, NJ: Princeton University Press, 1999).

25. For a bleak example see Harald Welzer, *Climate Wars: What People Will Be Killed for in the 21st Century*, (Cambridge: Polity Press, 2012).

26. Ban Ki Moon, 'A Climate Culprit in Darfur', *Washington Post*, (16 June 2007) http://www.washingtonpost.com/wp-dyn/content/article/2007/06/15/AR2007061501857.html

27. Bradford Plummer, 'Global Warring', *New Republic*, 20 Nov. 2009.

28. Henk-Jan Brinkman and Cullen S. Hendrix, 'Food Insecurity and Violent Conflict: Causes, Consequences, and Addressing the Challenges', *World Food Programme*, July 2011.

29. Julie Hirschfeld Davis, Mark Landler, and Coral Davenport, 'Obama on Climate Change: The Trends Are "Terrifying"', *New York Times*, 8 Sept. 2016. https://www.nytimes.com/2016/09/08/us/politics/obama-climate-change.html?_r=0.

30. *Presidential Memorandum—Climate Change and National Security,* (The White House: Office of the Press Secretary, (21 September 2016) https://www.whitehouse.gov/the-press-office/2016/09/21/presidential-memorandum-climate-change-and-national-security.

31. *Implications for US National Security of Anticipated Climate Change*, NIC WP 2016-01(Washington DC: National Intelligence Council 21, Sept. 2016).

32. A. T. Wolf, 'Conflict and Cooperation Along International Waterways' *Water Policy*, 1:2 (1998), 251; Nils Petter Gleditsch, 'Armed conflict and the environment: A critique of the literature', *Journal of Peace Research* 35.3 (1998): 363–380.

33. Halvard Buhaug, 'Climate not to blame for African civil wars', *Proceedings of the National Academy of Sciences* 107.1 (2010):16477–16482.

34. Wenche Hauge and Tanja Ellingsen, 'Beyond environmental scarcity: Causal pathways to conflict', *Journal of Peace Research* 35.3 (1998): 299–317; Vally Koubi, Gabriele Spilker, Tobias Böhmelt and Thomas Bernauer, "Do natural resources matter for interstate and intrastate armed conflict?", *Journal of Peace Research* 51 (2014): 227; and Mark Notaras, 'Does Climate Change Cause Conflict?' *Our World*, 27 Nov. 2009, online. Available: https://ourworld.unu.edu/en/does-climate-change-cause -conflict.

35. Peter Gleick, 'Water, Drought, Climate Change, and Conflict in Syria', *Weather, Climate, and Society* (2014).

36. Williams, 'Continuity and Change in War', 37–8; Discussed in *Human Security Report Project. Human Security Report 2012: Sexual Violence, Education, and War*, Vancouver: Human Security Press, 2012, 195–7.

CHAPTER 24

1. Thucydides, *The History of the Peloponnesian War* (London: Penguin, 1972) 407.

2. Major General Bob Scales, *Scales on War* (Annapolis, MD: U.S. Naval Institute Press, 2016) 37.

3. Harlan K. Ullman and James P. Wade, *Shock and Awe: Achieving Rapid Dominance* (Washington DC: NDU Press Book, 1996).

4. On the role of scenarios, with some examples, see Michael F. Oppenheimer, *Pivotal countries, alternate futures: using scenarios to manage American strategy* (Oxford: Oxford University Press, 2016).

5. Paul Kennedy, *The Rise and Fall of the Great Powers* (New York: Vintage, 1988).

6. See George Friedman and Meredith Lebard, *The Coming War with Japan* (New York: St. Martin's Press, 1991).

7. James Fallows, 'Is Japan the Enemy?' *New York Review of Books*, 30 May 1991. http://www.nybooks.com/articles/1991/05/30/is-japan-the-enemy.

8. Michael Crichton, *Rising Sun* (New York: Knopf, 1992).

9. Tom Clancy, *Debt of Honor* (New York: Putnam, 1994). The book came largely to be remembered because—before 9/11—it included a crazed Japanese pilot flying his Boeing 747 into Capitol Hill while Congress was in a special session.

10. George Friedman and Meredith LeBard, *The Future of War: Power, Technology and American World Dominance in the Twenty-first Century*, (New York: St. Martin's Griffin, 19980, 102, 419.

11. George Friedman, *The Next 100 Years: A Forecast for the 21st Century* (New York: Anchor Books, 2010).

12. Caspar Weinberger and Peter Schweizer, *The Next War*, foreword by Lady Thatcher (Washington DC: Regnery, 1998).

13. Jed Babbin and Edward Timperlake, *Showdown: Why China Wants War with the United States* (Washington DC: Regnery, 2006). For a more moderate scenario see also Ted Galen Carpenter, *America's Coming War with China: A Collision Course Over Taiwan* (New York: Palgrave, 2005).

14. Geoffrey Till, *Seapower: A Guide for the Twenty-First Century*, 3rd Edition, (London: Routledge, 2013); Peter Haynes, *Toward a New Maritime Strategy: American Naval Thinking in the Post-Cold War Era*, (Annapolis, MD: Naval Institute Press, 2015).

15. Sam J. Tangredi, *Anti-Access Warfare: Countering A2/AD Strategies*, (Annapolis, MD: Naval Institute Press; 2013).

16. Stephen Biddle and Ivan Oelrich, 'Future Warfare in the Western Pacific: Chinese Antiaccess/ Area Denial, US Air/Sea Battle and Command of the Commons in East Asia', *International Security*, 41:1 (2016)7–48.

17. Chief of Naval Operations Adm. John Richardson, 'Deconstructing A2AD', *The National Interest*, (October 2016), http://nationalinterest.org/feature/chief-naval -operations-adm-john-richardson-deconstructing-17918. Paul Kennedy made these

points in a preface to a new edition of his classic *The Rise and Fall of British Naval Mastery,* (London: Penguin, 2017).

18. Andrew F. Krepinevich, *7 Deadly Scenarios: A Military Futurist Explores War in the 21st Century* (New York: Bantam Dell, 2007).

19. David A. Shlapak and Michael Johnson, *Reinforcing Deterrence on NATO's Eastern Flank: Wargaming the Defense of the Baltics* (Santa Monica, CA: RAND Corporation, 2016).

20. General Sir Richard Shirreff, *War with Russia* (London: Coronet, 2016). Also his article on this subject in *The Daily Mail,* available: http://www.dailymail.co.uk/news /article-3601918/Why-war-Russia-year-apocalyptic-vision-British-General-Nato-chief -threatened-sack-blasting-Tory-defence-cuts.html#ixzz4ADrCHKi7.

21. Douglas Cohn, *World War 4* (Washington DC: The Lyons Press, 2016).

22. Cohn 194.

23. Peter Schwartz, *Inevitable Surprises: A Survival Guide for the 21st Century* (New York: Free Press, 2003). His view was affected by a very gloomy reading of the impact of the AIDS pandemic, which was one area where things did not continue as badly as they had started.

24. Adrian Levy and Catherine Scott-Clark, *Deception: Pakistan, the United States and the Global Nuclear Weapons Conspiracy,* (London: Atlantic Books, 2007).

25. Graham Allison, *Nuclear Terrorism: The Ultimate Preventable Catastrophe,* (New York: Henry Holt, 2004), p. 15. Matthew Bunn, 'A Mathematical Model of the Risk of Nuclear Terrorism', *Annals, AAPSS,* 607:1 (September 2006), 103-120, concluded that there was a 29 percent probability of an act of nuclear terrorism over the coming decade. For a calm assessment of the risks of bioterrorism, appearing just after Allison's book, see Jeanne Guillemin, *Biological Weapons: From the Invention of State-Sponsored Programs to Contemporary Terrorism,* (New York Columbia University Press, 2005). On radiological weapons see Charles Ferguson and Michelle Smith, 'Assessing Radiological Weapons: Attack Methods and Estimated Effects', *Defence Against Terrorism Review,* 2:2 (2009), 15–34.

26. Michael Levi, *On Nuclear Terrorism,* (Cambridge, Mass; Harvard University Press, 2007), p.141. There is an interesting debate between Allison and Levi in 2007 'How Likely is a Nuclear Terrorist attack on the United States?' http://www.cfr.org /weapons-of-mass-destruction/likely-nuclear-terrorist-attack-united-states/p13097.

27. Joe Cirincione, 'Nuclear terrorist threat bigger than you think', *CNN,* 1 April 2016, http://edition.cnn.com/2016/04/01/opinions/nuclear-terrorism-threat-cirincione/; Martin Malin, Matthew Bunn, Nickolas Roth and William H. Tobey. "Will the Nuclear Security Summit Help Stop Terrorists from Getting the Bomb?" *The National Interest,* 31 March 2016. http://nationalinterest.org/blog/the-buzz/will-the-nuclear-security-summit -help-stop-terrorists-15644?page=show.

28. Graham Allison, *Destined for War: America, China, and Thucydides's Trap,* (New York: Houghton Mifflin, 2017), xvii.

29. Edward N. Luttwak, *The Grand Strategy of the Soviet Union* (New York: St. Martin's, 1983). Amalrik had also anticipated a war with China.

30. Kiyoshi Takenaka, 'Abe sees World War One echoes in Japan-China tensions', *Reuters,* 23 Jan. 2014. Available: http://www.reuters.com/article/us-japan-china-idUS BREA0M08G20140123.

31. 'India and China, A Himalayan rivalry', *The Economist,* 19 August 2010.

32. Edward N. Luttwak, *The Rise of China vs The Logic of Strategy* (Cambridge, Mass: Harvard University Press, 2012*).* For an argument that China is bound to become the world's leading power see Gideon Rachman, *Easternisation: War and Peace in the Asian Century,* (London: Bodley Head, 2016).

33. The successive documents can be found on the Director of National Intelligence's webpage: https://www.dni.gov/index.php/about/organization/national-intelligence -council-global-trends.

34. Office of the Director of National Intelligence, *Global Trends 2010*, revised edition (Washington DC: National Intelligence Council, February 1997). Available: https://www.dni.gov/index.php/about/organization/national-intelligence-council-global-trends/global-trends-2010. On the influence of 'black swan' as unexpected events see Nassim Nicholas Taleb, *Black Swan: The Impact of the Highly Improbable*, (London: Penguin, 2008).

35. Office of the Director of National Intelligence, *Global Trends 2015: A Dialogue About the Future with Nongovernment Experts* (Washington DC: National Intelligence Council, December 2000).

36. Office of the Director of National Intelligence, *Mapping the Global Future: Report of the National Intelligence Council's 2020 Project* (Washington DC: National Intelligence Council, December 2004).

37. Office of the Director of National Intelligence, *Global Trends 2025: A Transformed World*, (Washington DC: National Intelligence Council, November 2008).

38. Office of the Director of National Intelligence, *Global Trends 2030: Alternative Worlds* (Washington DC: National Intelligence Council, December 2012).

39. Office of the Director of National Intelligence, *Global trends: Paradoxes of Progress* (Washington DC: National Intelligence Council, January 2017).

CHAPTER 25

1. Friedman was recalling his time stuck in an Israeli outpost in Southern Lebanon in the late 1990s. Matti Friedman, *Pumpkinflowers: A Soldier's Story* (Chapel Hill, NC: Algonquin, 2016) 222.

2. John Stoessinger, *Why Nations Go to War* (New York: St. Martin's Press, 1997). For a similar thought see Geoffrey Blainey, *The Causes of War* (New York: Free Press, 1988) 246.

3. Dominic Tierney and Dominic Johnson, 'The Rubicon Theory of War How the Path to Conflict Reaches the Point of No Return', *International Security* 36.1 (2011): 7-40.

4. David Betz, *Carnage and Connectivity: Landmarks in the Decline of Conventional Military Power* (London: Hurst, 2015) 5.

5. H. R. McMaster, 'Discussing the Continuities of War and the Future of Warfare'.

6. Colin S. Gray, *Another Bloody Century: Future Warfare* (London: Weidenfeld & Nicholson, 2005).

7. Richard Rosencrance and Steven Miller, ed., *The Next Great War? The Roots of World War 1 and the Risk of U.S.-China Conflict*, (Cambridge, MA: MIT Press, 2015). See also David C. Gompert, Hans Binnendijk, Bonny Lin, *Blinders, Blunders, and Wars* (Santa Monica, Calif: RAND Corporation, 2014).

8. James Goodby and George P. Shultz, eds., *The War That Must Never Be Fought* (Stanford: Hoover Press, 2015).

9. Brad Roberts, *The Case for U.S. Nuclear Weapons in the 21st Century* (Stanford: Stanford University Press, 2016).

10. President Putin's September 2014 comment is noted in Tom Parfitt, 'Ukraine crisis: Putin's nuclear threats are a struggle for pride and status', *The Telegraph*, 26 Sept. 2014. Available: http://www.telegraph.co.uk/news/worldnews/europe/russia/11064978/Ukraine-crisis-Putins-nuclear-threats-are-a-struggle-for-pride-and-status.html.

11. Mark Fitzpatrick, *The World After: Proliferation, Deterrence and Disarmament if the Nuclear Taboo is Broken* (Paris: IFRI, 2009).

12. Philip Bobbitt, *Terror and Consent: The Wars for the Twenty-first Century*, (London: Allen Lane, 2008).

13. Max Boot, *War Made New: Technology, Warfare, and the Course of History, 1500 to Today* (New York: Gotham, 2006), and Rosa Brooks, *How Everything Became War and the Military Became Everything: Tales from the Pentagon* (New York: Simon & Schuster, 2016).

14. Hal Brands, 'Paradoxes of the Gray Zone', *Foreign Policy Research Institute* (2016); http://www.fpri.org/article/2016/02/paradoxes-gray-zone/ and Frank G. Hoffman, 'The Contemporary Spectrum of Conflict: Protracted, Gray Zone, Ambiguous, and Hybrid Modes of War', *Heritage Foundation Index of Military Power* (2016): 25–36.

15. David Rothkopf, 'The Cool War', *Foreign Policy* (2013). http://foreignpolicy.com/2013/02/20/the-cool-war/ Also see Noah Feldman *Cool War: The Future of Global Competition* (New York: Random House, 2013).

16. The stream of books on future war is unlikely to dry up. As this book went to press, two new books appeared. Paul Cornish and Kingsley Donaldson, both with military and think-tank experience, published *2020: World of War* (London: Hodder & Stoughton, 2017), dedicated to the memory of Sir John Hackett and taking his *The Third World War* as their starting point, and with a similar short-term focus. The authors looked at a number of scenarios: the challenges posed by Russia, and then by climate change, resource scarcity and health security, before offering a number of scenarios, covering the most troubled regions, then terrorism and cyber security before considering an 'omni-scenario'—the possibility that a number of these challenges might arrive together. The scenarios were intended to be illustrative not predictive, using the worst cases to help identify areas of strategic risk and possibilities for their management. Former Air Force general Robert Latiff's *Future War: Preparing for the New Global Battlefield*, (New York: Alfred Knopf, 2107) compared the pace of technological change and the complexity of security challenges to the tendency to resort to platitudes and flag-waving. His book was a demand for more honesty from politicians and engagement from the public.

BIBLIOGRAPHY

Ahlström, Christer, and Kjell-Åke Nordquist. *Casualties of Conflict: Report for the World Campaign for the Protection of Victims of War.* Uppsala: Department of Peace and Conflict Research, 1991.

Ajala, Adekunle. 'The Nature of African Boundaries'. *Afrika Spectrum* 83 (1983): 180.

Alao, Abiodun. *Natural Resources and Conflict in Africa: The Tragedy of Endowment.* Rochester: University of Rochester Press, 2007.

Alexander, Amanda, 'The Genesis of the Civilian'. *Leiden Journal of International Law* 20.2 (2007): 364.

Alfrey, Anthony, *Man of Arms: The Life and Legend of Sir Basil Zaharoff.* London: Thistle Publishing, 2013.

Allen, Chris. 'Warfare, Endemic Violence, and State Collapse in Africa'. *Review of African Political Economy* 26.81 (1999): 367–84.

Allen, Thomas, F. Clifton Berry, and Norman Polmar. *CNN: War in the Gulf.* Atlanta, GA: Turner Broadcasting, 1999.

Allison, Graham. *Nuclear Terrorism: The Ultimate Preventable Catastrophe.* New York: Henry Holt, 2004.

_____. *Destined for War: Can America and China Escape Thucydides's Trap?* New York: Houghton Mifflin, 2017.

Amalrik, Andrei. *Will the Soviet Union Survive Until 1984?* New York: HarperCollins, 1981.

An Agenda for Peace: Preventive diplomacy, peacemaking and peace-keeping. Report of the Secretary-General pursuant to the statement adopted by the Summit Meeting of the Security Council, 31 Jan. 1992.

Anderson, Benedict. *Imagined Communities: Reflections on the Origin and Spread of Nationalism.* London: Verso, 1991.

Angell, Norman. *The Great Illusion: A Study of the Relation of Military Power to National Advantage.* London: G. P. Putnam's, 1910.

Arendt, Hannah. *On Violence.* New York: Harcourt, 1970.

Armitage, David. *Civil Wars: A History in Ideas.* New York: Knopf, 2017.

Arnett, Eric. 'Hyperwar'. *Bulletin of the Atomic Scientists* 48.7 (1992).

Arquilla, John, and David Ronfeldt. 'Cyberwar is Coming!' *Comparative Strategy* 12.2 (1993).

_____ eds. *Networks and Netwars: The Future of Terror, Crime, and Militancy.* Santa Monica, CA: RAND, 2001. Available: www.rand.org/publications/MR/MR1382/.

_____. *Swarming and the Future of Conflict,* Santa Monica: RAND Corporation, 2005.

Arquilla, John. 'The Computer Mouse that Roared: Cyberwar in the Twenty-First Century'. *The Brown Journal of World Affairs* 18.1 (2011): 39–48

Arreguín-Toft, Ivan. 'How the Weak Win Wars: A Theory of Asymmetric Conflict'. *International Security* 26.1 (2001): 93–128.

Ashford, Oliver M. *Prophet or Professor? The Life and Work of Lewis Fry Richardson.* Bristol: Adam Hilger, 1985.

Asimov, Isaac. 'Runaround'. *Foundation.* New York: Gnome Press, 1951.

Atwood, Margaret. *Morning in the Burned House.* New York: Houghton Mifflin, 1995.

Atzili, Boaz. 'When Good Fences Make Bad Neighbors: Fixed Borders, State Weakness, and International Conflict'. *International Security* 31.3 (2006/07): 139–173.

Augustine, Norman R. *Augustine's Laws*. New York: Viking, 1987.

Auster, Albert, and Leonard Quart. *How the War was Remembered: Hollywood & Vietnam*. New York: Praeger, 1988.

Babbin, Jed, and Edward Timperlake. *Showdown: Why China Wants War with the United States*. Washington DC: Regnery, 2006.

Baden-Powell, Robert. *Scouting for Boys: A Handbook for Instruction in Good Citizenship*. London: H. Cox, 1908.

Baev, Pavel. *Russian Energy Policy and Military Power: Putin's Quest for Greatness*. London: Routledge, 2008.

Baker, James A., III. *The Politics of Diplomacy: Revolution, War, and Peace, 1989–1992*. New York: G. P. Putnam's Sons, 1995.

Barker, Martin. *A 'Toxic Genre': The Iraq War Films*. London: Pluto Press, 2007.

Barnett, Michael. *Empire of Humanity: A History of Humanitarianism*. Ithaca: Cornell University Press, 2011.

Barno, David W. 'Military Adaptation in Complex Operations'. *Prism 1* 1 (2009): 30.

Barot, O. *Lettres sur la Philosophie de l'Histoire*. Paris: Germer-Baillière, 1864.

Barth, Boris. *The Democratic Peace Controversy: A Critical Survey*. Oslo files on Defence and Security, 2008.

Beaufre, André. 'Battlefields of the 1980s'. *Unless Peace Comes: A Scientific Forecast of New Weapons*. Ed. Nigel Calder. London: Allen Lane, 1968.

Bechhoefer, Bernhard G. *Postwar Negotiations for Arms Control*. Washington DC: Brooking Institution, 1961.

Bell, Martin. *In Harm's Way*. London: Hamish Hamilton, 1995.

Bellamy, Alex J. 'The "Next Stage" in Peace Operations Theory?' *International Peacekeeping* 11:1 (2004): 17–38.

Bellamy, Christopher. '"Civilian Experts" and Russian Defence Thinking: The Renewed Relevance of Jan Bloch'. *RUSI Journal* (1992): 50–56.

Bell-Fialkoff, Andrew. 'A Short History of Ethnic Cleansing'. *Foreign Affairs* 72.3 (1992).

Berdal, Mats. 'The "New Wars" Thesis Revisited'. *The Changing Character of War*. Eds. Hew Strachan and Sibylle Scheipers. Oxford: Oxford University Press, 2011. 109–133.

_____. 'The State of UN Peacekeeping: Lessons from Congo'. *Journal of Strategic Studies* (2016).

Bergen, Peter L., and Daniel Rothenberg, eds. *Drone Wars: Transforming Conflict, Law, and Policy*. Cambridge: Cambridge University Press, 2015.

Berinato, Scott. 'The Future of Security'. *Computerworld*, 30 Dec. 2003.

Berkowitz, Bruce. *The New Face of War: How War Will Be Fought in the 21st Century*. New York: The Free Press, 2003.

Best, Geoffrey. *Humanity in Warfare*. London: Methuen, 1980.

Betts, Richard K. *Surprise Attack: Lessons for Defense Planning*. Washington DC: Brookings Institution, 1982.

_____. 'The New Threat of Weapons of Mass Destruction'. *Foreign Affairs* 77.1 (1998).

Betz, David. *Carnage and Connectivity: Landmarks in the Decline of Conventional Military Power*. London: Hurst, 2015.

Bew, John. *Realpolitik: A History*. New York: Oxford University Press, 2016.

Biddle, Stephen, and Ivan Oelrich. 'Future Warfare in the Western Pacific: Chinese Antiaccess/ Area Denial, US Air/Sea Battle and Command of the Commons in East Asia'. *International Security* 41.1 (2016): 7–48.

Biddle, Tami Davis. *Rhetoric and Reality in Air Warfare: The Evolution of British and American Ideas about Strategic Bombing*. Princeton: Princeton University Press, 2002.

Bidwell, Shelford, ed. *World War 3*. London: Hamlyn, 1978.

Black, Jeremy. *The Age of Total War, 1860–1945*. Westport, Conn.: Praeger Security International, 2006.

Blainey, Geoffrey. *The Causes of War*. New York: Free Press, 1988.

Blair, Prime Minister Tony. Speech to Economic Club of Chicago. PBS, 22 April 1999. Available: http://www.pbs.org/newshour/bb/international-jan-june99-blair_doctrine 4-23/.

Blattman, Christopher, and Edward Miguel. 'Civil War'. *Journal of Economic Literature* 48.1 (2010): 3–57.

Blight, James. *The Shattered Crystal Ball: Fear and Learning in the Cuban Missile Crisis.* New York: Rowman & Littlefield, 1990.

Bloch, I. S. *Is War Now Impossible? Being an Abridgment of The War of the Future in Its Technical Economic and Political Relations.* London: Grant Richard, 1899. Available: https://archive.org/details/iswarnowimpossib00bloc.

_____. 'The Wars of the Future'. *The Contemporary Review* 8 (1901): 305–32.

_____. 'The Transvaal War: Its Lessons in Regard to Militarism and Army Reorganisation'. *Journal of the Royal United Service Institute* 45 (1901): 1316–1344.

Bobbitt, Philip. *The Shield of Achilles: War, Peace and the Course of History.* New York: Knopf, 2002.

_____. *Terror and Consent: The Wars for the Twenty-First Century*, London: Allen Lane, 2008.

Boix, Carles. 'Democracy, development, and the international system'. *American Political Science Review* 105.4 (2011): 809–828.

Bond, Brian. 'Doctrine and Training in the British Cavalry 1870–1914'. *The Theory and Practice of War.* Ed. Michael Howard. London: Cassell, 1965.

Boot, Max. *War Made New: Technology, Warfare, and the Course of History, 1500 to Today.* New York: Gotham, 2006.

Boulding, Kenneth. *Conflict and Defense: A General Theory.* New York: Harper & Bros., 1962.

Bowden, Mark. *Black Hawk Down: A Story of Modern War.* New York: Atlantic Monthly Press, 1999.

Brands, Hal. 'Paradoxes of the Gray Zone'. *Foreign Policy Research Institute* (2016).

Brantly, Aaron Franklin. *The Decision to Attack: Military and Intelligence Cyber-Decision-Making.* Athens, GA: University of Georgia Press, 2016.

Brians, Paul. *Nuclear Holocausts: Atomic War in Fiction 1895–1984.* Kent, OH: Kent State University Press, 1987.

Brinkman, Henk-Jan, and Cullen S. Hendrix. 'Food Insecurity and Violent Conflict: Causes, Consequences, and Addressing the Challenges'. World Food Programme, July 2011.

Brock, Lothar, et al. *Fragile States: Violence and the Failure of Intervention.* Cambridge: Polity Press, 2012.

Brooks, Rosa. *How Everything Became War and the Military Became Everything: Tales from the Pentagon.* New York: Simon & Schuster, 2016.

Brown, Archie. *The Gorbachev Factor.* Oxford: Oxford University Press, 1996.

Brown, Scott. '*WarGames*: A Look Back at the Film That Turned Geeks and Phreaks Into Stars'. *Wired Magazine*, 21 July 2008.

Brown, Wendy. 'The New U.S. Army/Marine Corps Counterinsurgency Field Manual as Political Science and Political Praxis'. *Perspectives on Politics* 6.2 (2008): 351.

Bryan, C. D. B. 'Barely Suppressed Screams'. *Harper's*. 1 June 1984. 67–72.

Bryant, Peter. *Red Alert.* Rockville, MD: Black Mask, 1958.

Buchanan, Ben. *The Cybersecurity Dilemma: Hacking, Trust and Fear Between Nations.* Oxford: Oxford University Press, 2017.

Buhaug, Halvard. 'Climate not to blame for African civil wars'. *Proceedings of the National Academy of Sciences* 107.1 (2010): 16477–16482.

Bull, Hedley. 'Disarmament and the International System'. *Australian Journal of Politics & History* 5.1 (1959): 41–50.

Bunn, Matthew. 'A Mathematical Model of the Risk of Nuclear Terrorism'. *Annals, AAPSS*, 607.1 (2006): 103–120.

Burbach, David T., and Christopher J. Fettweis. 'The Coming Stability? The Decline of Warfare in Africa and Implications for International Security'. *Contemporary Security Policy* 35.3 (2014): 421–445.

Burdick, Eugene, and Harvey Wheeler. *Fail-Safe*. New York: McGraw-Hill, 1962.

Burt, Richard. *New Weapons Technologies: Debate and Directions*, Adelphi Paper no. 126. London: IISS, 1976.

Bush, President George, and Brent Scowcroft. *A World Transformed*. New York: Knopf, 1998.

Bush, President George. *Addresses the 89th Annual National Convention of the American Legion*. Reno, Nevada, 28 Aug. 2007.

Byman, Daniel. 'Do Targeted Killings Work?' *Foreign Affairs* (2006): 95–111.

Bywater, Hector. *Great Pacific War: A History of the American-Japanese Campaign of 1931–33*. New York: Applewood Books, 2002.

Call, Charles. 'The Fallacy of the "Failed States"'. *Third World Quarterly* 29.8 (2008): 1491–1507.

Callwell, Colonel Charles. *Small Wars: Their Principles and Practice*. London: HMSO, 1886.

Cameron, Gavin. *Nuclear Terrorism: A Threat Assessment for the 21st Century*. London: Macmillan, 1999.

Campen, Alan, ed. *The First Information War: The Story of Communications, Computers, and Intelligence Systems in the Persian Gulf War*. Fairfax, VA: AFCEA International Press, 1992.

Caputo, Philip. *Acts of Faith*. New York: Knopf, 2005.

Carnesale, Albert, et al. *Living with Nuclear Weapons*. Cambridge, MA: Harvard University Press, 1983.

Carpenter, Ted Galen. *America's Coming War with China: A Collision Course Over Taiwan*. New York: Palgrave, 2005.

Carr, E. H. *The Twenty Years' Crisis*. London: Macmillan, 1939.

Carr, Matthew. *Sherman's Ghosts: Soldiers, Civilians, and the American Way of War*. New York: New Press, 2015.

de Castella, Tom. 'Arthur Conan Doyle's eerie vision of the future of war'. BBC News Magazine, 28 August 2014. Available: http://www.bbc.co.uk/news/magazine-28954510.

Castner, Brian. *The Long Walk: A Story of War and the Life That Follows*. New York: Doubleday, 2012

_____. *All the Ways We Kill and Die*. New York: Arcade, 2016.

Cavanaugh, William. *The Myth of Religious Violence: Secular Ideology and the Roots of Modern Conflict*. Oxford: Oxford University Press, 2009.

Ceadel, Martin. *Living the Great Illusion: Sir Norman Angell, 1872–1967*. Oxford: Oxford University Press, 2009.

Center for the Study of Intelligence. *At Cold War's End: US Intelligence on the Soviet Union and Eastern Europe, 1989–1991*. Langley: CIA, 1999.

Cesa, Marco. 'Realist Visions of the End of the Cold War: Morgenthau, Aron and Waltz'. *The British Journal of Politics and International Relations* 11 (2009): 177–191.

Checkel, Jeffrey. *Transnational Dynamics of Civil War*. 2013. New York: Cambridge University Press, 2013.

Chesney, George. 'The Battle of Dorking: Reminiscences of a Volunteer'. *Blackwood's Magazine*, May 1871. Available: http://gutenberg.net.au/ebooks06/0602091h.html.

Chief of Staff of the Army Strategic Studies Group. *Megacities and the United States Army Preparing for a Complex and Uncertain Future*. June 2014.

Chivvis, Christopher. *Toppling Qaddafi: Libya and the Limits of Liberal Intervention*. Cambridge: Cambridge University Press, 2013.

'Chronicle of a war foretold: The story of a conflict between America and China makes a fine example of future-war fiction'. *The Economist*, 27 June 2015.

Clancy, Tom. *Red Storm Rising*. New York: Putnam Publishing, 1986.

_____. *The Sum of All Fears*. New York: Berkeley Mass Market Publishing, 1992.

_____. *Debt of Honor*. New York: Putnam, 1994.

Clark, Christopher. *The Sleepwalkers: How Europe Went to War in 1914*. New York: Harper, 2012.

Clark, John. 'A Constructivist Account of the Congo Wars'. *African Security* 4.3 (2011): 147–170.

_____. 'The Decline of the African Military Coup'. *Journal of Democracy* 18.3 (2007): 144–155.

Clarke, I. F. *Voices Prophesying War: Future Wars, 1763–3749.* Oxford: Oxford University Press, 1972.

Clarke, Peter. *The Locomotive of War: Money, Empire, Power and Guilt.* London: Bloomsbury, 2017.

Clinton, David. 'Francis Lieber, Imperialism, and Internationalism'. *Imperialism and Internationalism in the Discipline of International Relations.* Eds. David C. Long and Brian Schmidt. New York: SUNY Press, 2005.

Clodfelter, Mark. *The Limits of Air Power: The American Bombing of North Vietnam.* New York: Free Press, 1989.

Close, Robert. *Europe Without Defence?: 48 Hours That Could Change The Face of the World.* Brussels: Editions Arts and Voyages, 1976.

Clynes, Manfred E., and Kline, Nathan S. 'Cyborgs and Space'. *Astronautics*, Sept. 1960.

Cockayne, James. *Hidden Power: The Strategic Logic of Organised Crime.* London: Hurst, 2016.

Cockett, Richard. *Sudan: The Failure and Division of an African State.* New Haven: Yale University Press, 2016.

Cohn, Douglas. *World War 4.* Washington DC: The Lyons Press, 2016.

Coker, Christopher. *Future War.* Cambridge: Policy, 2015.

Cole, August, ed. *War Stories from the Future.* Washington DC: The Atlantic Council Art of Future Warfare Project, 2015. Available: http://www.atlanticcouncil.org/images/publications/War_Stories_from_the_Future.pdf

Colgan, Jeff D. 'Fueling the Fire: Pathways from Oil to War'. *International Security* 38.2 (2013): 147–80.

Collier, Paul, et al. *Breaking the Conflict Trap: Civil War and Development Policy.* World Bank and Oxford University Press, 2003.

Collier, Paul, Anke Hoeffler, and Dominic Rohner. 'Beyond greed and grievance: feasibility and civil war'. *Oxford Economic Papers* 61 (2009): 1–27.

Collier, Paul, and Anke Hoeffler. 'Economic Causes of Civil Conflict and Their Implications for Policy'. *Managing Global Chaos.* Ed. Chester A. Crocker, et al. Washington DC: United States Institute of Peace, 2000.

_____. 'Greed and grievance in civil war'. *Oxford Economic Papers* 56 (2004).

Collier, Paul. 'The Cultural Foundations of Economic Failure: a Conceptual Toolkit'. *Journal of Economic Behavior & Organization* 126 (2016): 5–24.

Colomb, Rear-Admiral P., et al. *The Great War of 189_: A Forecast.* London: Heinemann, 1893. Available: https://archive.org/details/greatwarof18900colorich.

Comaroff, John L., and Paul C. Stern. 'New Perspectives on Nationalism and War'. *Theory and Society* 23.1 (1994): 35–45.

Conan Doyle, Arthur. 'Danger! Being the log of Captain John Sirius'. *The Strand Magazine*, July 1914.

Condra, Luke N., and Jacob N. Shapiro, 'Who Takes the Blame? The Strategic Effects of Collateral Damage'. *American Journal of Political Science* 56.1 (2012): 167–187.

Conetta, Carl. *The Wages of War: Iraqi Combatant and Noncombatant Fatalities in the 2003 Conflict: Project on Defense Alternatives.* Research Monograph # 8, 20 Oct. 2003. Appendix 2: Iraqi Combatant and Noncombatant Fatalities in the 1991 Gulf War. Available: http://www.comw.org/pda/0310rm8ap2.html.

_____. 'Disappearing the Dead: Iraq, Afghanistan, and the Idea of a "New Warfare"'. *Project on Defense Alternatives.* 18 Feb. 2004.

Conrad, Joseph. 'Autocracy and War'. *Note on Life and Letters.* Cambridge: Cambridge University Press, 2004.

Conway-Lanz, Sahr. *Collateral Damage: Americans, Noncombatant Immunity, and Atrocity after World War II.* New York: Routledge, 2006.

Cooper, Robert. *The post-modern state and world order.* London: Demos and the Foreign Policy Centre, 2000.

Cooper, Sandi E. *Patriotic Pacifism: Waging War on War in Europe, 1815–1914.* Oxford: Oxford University Press, 1991.

Cornish, Paul and Kingsley Donaldson, *2020: World of War* (London: Hodder & Stoughton, 2017),

Cortright, David. *Peace: A History of Movements and Ideas*. Cambridge: Cambridge University Press, 2008.

Corum, James, and Wray Johnson. *Airpower in Small Wars: Fighting Insurgents and Terrorists*. Lawrence, KS: University Press of Kansas, 2003.

Cousins, Norman. 'Electronic Brain on War and Peace: A report of an Imaginary Experiment'. *St. Louis Post-Dispatch*, 13 Dec. 1953.

_____. 'Editorial'. *Saturday Review*, 4 April 1954.

_____. *In Place of Folly*. New York: Harper, 1961.

Cox, Mick. *1989 and why we got it wrong*. Working Paper Series of the Research Network 1989 1 (2008): 5.

Cramer, Christopher. '*Homo Economicus* goes to war: methodological individualism, rational choice, and the political economy of war'. *World Development* 30 (2002): 1849.

_____. *Civil War is Not a Stupid Thing: Accounting for Violence on Developing Countries*. London: C. Hurst & Co., 2006.

Crane, Conrad C., and W. Andrew Terrill. *Reconstructing Iraq: Insights, Challenges, and Missions for Military Forces in a Post-Conflict Scenario*. Annapolis: US Army War College, Strategic Studies Institute, Feb. 2003.

Crane, Conrad C. *Avoiding Vietnam: The U.S. Army's Response to Defeat in Southeast Asia* (Carlisle Barracks, PA: Strategic Studies Institute, U.S. Army War College, 2002).

_____. *Cassandra in Oz: Counterinsurgency and Future War*. Annapolis: Naval Institute Press, 2016.

Creasy, Sir Edward. *The Fifteen Decisive Battles of the World: From Marathon to Waterloo*. Boston: IndyPublish, 2002.

van Creveld, Martin. *Nuclear Proliferation and the Future of Conflict*. New York: The Free Press, 1993.

Crichton, Michael. *Rising Sun*. New York: Knopf, 1992.

Cummings, Mary L. *Artificial Intelligence and the Future of Warfare*. Research Paper. London: Royal Institute of International Affairs, Jan. 2017.

Daalder, Ivo, and Michael O'Hanlon. *Winning Ugly: NATO's War to Save Kosovo*. Washington DC: Brookings Institution, 2000.

Dadrian, Vahakn N. 'Ottoman Archives and Denial of the Armenian Genocide'. *The Armenian Genocide: History, Politics, Ethics*. Ed. R. G. Hovannisian. New York: St. Martin's Press, 1992.

Daley, Paul. 'Why the number of Indigenous deaths in the frontier wars matters'. *Guardian*, 15 July 2014.

Daponte, Beth Osborne. 'A Case Study in Estimating Casualties from War and Its Aftermath: The 1991 Persian Gulf War'. *Medicine & Global Survival* 3 (1993).

_____. "Wartime estimates of Iraqi civilian casualties", *International Review of the Red Cross*, 89:868 (Dec. 2007), 943–957.

David, G. J., and T. R. McKeldin III. *Ideas as Weapons: Influence and Perception in Modern Warfare*. Washington DC: Potomac Books, 2009.

Davenport, Christian. 'State Repression and Political order'. *Annual Review of Political Science* 10 (2007).

Davies, Owen. 'Robotic Warriors Clash in Cyberwars'. *Omni* 9.4 (1987).

Davis, Paul K. *100 Decisive Battles: From Ancient Times to the Present*. Oxford: Oxford University Press, 1999.

Davis, Julie Hirschfeld, Mark Landler, and Coral Davenport. 'Obama on Climate Change: The Trends Are "Terrifying"'. *New York Times*, 8 Sept. 2016.

Decalo, Samuel. *Coups and Army Rule in Africa*. New Haven: Yale University Press, 1976.

'Declaration on the Granting of Independence to Colonial Countries and Peoples'. Adopted by General Assembly Resolution 1514 (XV). 14 Dec. 1960.

Del Monte, Louis A. *Nanoweapons: A Growing Threat to Humanity*. Lincoln, NE: Potomac Books, 2017.

Dennis, Anthony J. *The Rise of the Islamic Empire and the Threat to the West*. Ohio: Wyndham Hall Press, 1996.

Deutsch, Karl W. 'Quincy Wright's contribution to the study of war: a preface to the second edition'. *Journal of Conflict Resolution* 14 (1970): 473.

Diehl, Paul, and Daniel Druckman. *Evaluating Peace Operations*. Boulder, CO: Lynne Rienner, 2010.

Dittmar, Linda, and Gene Michaud, eds. *From Hanoi to Hollywood: The Vietnam War in American Film*. New Brunswick, NJ: Rutgers University Press, 1990.

Dobrynin, Anatoly. *In Confidence: Moscow's Ambassador to Six Cold War Presidents*. New York: Times Books/Random House, 1995.

Document of the Moscow Meeting of the Conference on the Human Dimension Of The CSCE. Organization for Security and Co-operation in Europe, 4 Oct. 1991. Available: http://www.osce.org/odihr/elections/14310.

Dorman, Andrew M. *Blair's Successful War: British Military Intervention in Sierra Leone*. Farnham: Ashgate Publishing, 2009.

Douhet, Giulio. *The Command of the Air*. Trans. Dino Ferrari. Washington DC: Office of Air Force History, 1983. Available: http://www.au.af.mil/au/awc/awcgate/readings/command _of_the_air.pdf.

Doyle, Michael. 'Kant, liberal legacies, and foreign affairs'. Part II, *Philosophy & Public Affairs* 12.4 (1983): 23–353.

_____. 'Liberalism and World Politics'. *American Political Science Review* 80 (1986): 1151–69.

Drew, Elizabeth. *On the Edge: The Clinton Presidency*. New York: Simon & Schuster, 1995.

Dumas, Samuel, and K. O. Vedel-Petersen. *Losses of Life Caused by War*. Ed. Harald Westergaard. Oxford: Clarendon Press, 1923. Available: https://archive.org/stream/lossesof lifecaus00samu#page/n4/mode/1up.

Dunant, Henry. *A Memory of Solferino*. 1862. Online, International Committee of the Red Cross, 31 Dec. 1986. Available: https://www.icrc.org/eng/resources/documents/publication /p0361.htm.

Dunlap, Charles J., Jr. 'Lawfare Today... and Tomorrow'. *International Law and the Changing Character of War*. Eds. Raul A. 'Pete' Pedrozo and Daria P. Wollschlaeger. Vol. 87. Newport, RI: US Naval War College International Law Studies, 2011.

_____. *Law and Military Interventions: Preserving Humanitarian Values in 21st Conflicts*. Washington DC: Carr Center for Human Rights Policy Kennedy School of Government, Harvard University, 2001.

Dunlop, John. *The Moscow Bombings of September 1999: Examinations of Russian Terrorist Attacks at the Onset of Vladimir Putin's Rule*. Stuttgart: Ibidem, 2012.

Dunn, David. *The Politics of Threat: Minuteman Vulnerability in American National Security Policy*. London: Palgrave, 1997.

Dunn, Julia. 'Los Angeles Crips and Bloods: Past and Present'. *Poverty & Prejudice: Gangs of All Color*. Stanford University Edge, no date. Available: https://web.stanford .edu/class/e297c/poverty_prejudice/gangcolor/lacrips.htm.

Durant, Will and Ariel. *The Lessons of History*. New York: Simon & Schuster, 1968.

Dutch Institute for War Documentation (NIOD). *Srebrenica, A 'Safe' Area: Reconstruction, Background, Consequences and Analyses Of The Fall Of A 'Safe Area'*. November 1996. *Appendix VI the Background of the Yugoslav crisis: A review of the literature*. Available: http://www.niod.knaw.nl/nl/srebrenica-rapport.

Earle, Edward Mead. 'H. G. Wells, British Patriot in Search of a World State'. *World Politics* 2.2 (1950): 181–208.

Echevarria, Antulio. *Imagining Future War: The West's Technological Revolution and Visions of Wars to Come, 1880–1914*. Westport, CT: Praeger, 2007.

Eck, Kristine, and Lisa Hultman. 'One-Sided Violence Against Civilians in War: Insights from New Fatality Data'. *Journal of Peace Research* 44.2 (2007): 233–246.

Eck, Kristine. *A Beginner's Guide to Conflict Data: Finding and Using the Right Dataset*. Uppsala: Uppsala Conflict Data Programme, December 2005.

Eckhardt, William. 'Civilian Deaths in Wartime'. *Bulletin of Peace Proposals* 20.1 (1989): 89–98.

Edwards, Valerie. 'How Ronald Reagan based his foreign policy on Tom Clancy books: President told Margaret Thatcher to read Red Storm Rising thriller to understand Russia'. *Daily Mail* 30 Dec. 2015. Available: http://www.dailymail.co.uk/news/article -3378683/Ronald-Reagan-advised-Margaret-Thatcher-read-Tom-Clancy-s-thriller-Cold -War-strategy.html.

Elias, Norbert. *The Civilizing Process: Sociogenetic and Psychogenetic Investigations*. Eds. Eric Dunning et al. Malden, MA: Blackwell, 2000.

Elliott, Christopher. *High Command: British Military Leadership in the Iraq and Afghanistan Wars*. London: Hurst & Co., 2015.

Ellis, John. *The Social History of the Machine Gun*. London: Cresset, 1975.

Ellman, Michael, and S. Maksudov. 'Soviet Deaths in the Great Patriotic War: a note—World War II'. *Europe Asia Studies* (1994).

Enzensberger, Hans Magnus. *Civil War*. Trans. Piers Spence and Martin Chalmers. London: Granta Books, 1994.

Epstein, Katherine C. *Torpedo: Inventing the Military-Industrial Complex in the United States and Great Britain*. Cambridge, MA: Harvard University Press, 2014.

Erdmann, Andrew. 'The U.S. Presumption of Quick, Costless Wars'. *Orbis*. Summer 1999.

Esposito, John. *The Islamic Threat: Myth or Reality*. New York: Oxford University Press, 1992.

Evangelista, Matthew, and Henry Shue. *The American Way of Bombing; Changing Ethical and Legal Norms from Flying Fortress to Drones*. Ithaca, NY: Cornell University Press, 2004.

Evans, Raymond, and Robert Ørsted-Jensen. 'I Cannot Say the Numbers that Were Killed': Assessing Violent Mortality on the Queensland Frontier'. Paper given to the 2014 Australian Historical Association Conference.

Evans, Richard. *The Third Reich at War: How the Nazis Led Germany from Conquest to Disaster*. London: Allen Lane, 2008.

Evron, Gadi. 'Battling Botnets and Online Mobs: Estonia's Defense Efforts During the Internet War'. *Georgetown Journal of International Affairs* 9.1 (1991): 121–6.

Faber, David. *Munich, 1938: Appeasement and World War II*. New York: Simon & Schuster, 2009.

Fallows, James. 'Is Japan the Enemy?' *New York Review of Books*. 30 May 1991.

Falkenrath, Richard A., Robert D. Newman, and Bradley Thayer. *America's Achilles' Heel: Nuclear, Biological, and Chemical Terrorism and Covert Attack*. Cambridge, MA: MIT Press, 1998.

Farrell, Theo. 'Sliding into War: The Somalia Imbroglio and U.S. Army Peace Operations Doctrine'. *International Peacekeeping* 2.2 (1995): 194–214.

Fazal, Tanisha M. *State Death: The Politics and Geography of Conquest, Occupation, and Annexation*. Princeton: Princeton University Press, 2007.

_____. Secessionism and Civilian Targeting'. *Annual Meeting of the American Political Science Association*. Chicago: American Political Science Association, 2013.

_____. 'Dead Wrong? Battle Deaths, Military Medicine, and Exaggerated Reports of War's Demise'. *International Security* 39.1 (2014): 95–125.

_____. 'Rebellion, War Aims & the Laws of War'. *Daedalus* 146:1 (2017): 71–82.

Fearon, James, and David D. Laitin. 'Ethnicity, Insurgency, and Civil War'. *American Political Science Review* 97.1 (2003): 75–90.

_____. 'Neotrusteeship and the Problem of Weak States'. *International Security* 28.4 (2004): 5–43.

Feaver, Peter D., and Christopher Gelpi. 'A Look at Casualty Aversion: How Many Deaths Are Acceptable? A Surprising Answer'. *Washington Post,* 7 Nov. 1999.

Feir, Gordon D. *H. G. Wells at the End of His Tether: His Social and Political Adventures* (Lincoln, NE: iUniverse, 2005).

Feldman, Noah. *Cool War: The Future of Global Competition*. New York: Random House, 2013.

Ferguson, Charles and Michelle Smith, 'Assessing Radiological Weapons: Attack Methods and Estimated Effects'. *Defence Against Terrorism Review*, 2:2 (2009), 15–34.

Fink, Carole. 'The search for peace in the interwar period'. *The Cambridge History of War*. Vol. IV. Eds. Chickering et al. 285–309.

Fitzpatrick, Mark. *The World After: Proliferation, Deterrence and Disarmament if the Nuclear Taboo is Broken*. Paris: IFRI, 2009.

'Flight of the Drones: Why the Future of Air Power Belongs to Unmanned Systems'. *The Economist*, 8 Oct. 2011.

Foley, Robert. *German Strategy and the Path to Verdun: Erich von Falkenhayn and the Development of Attrition, 1870–1916*. Cambridge: Cambridge University Press, 2005.

Förster, Stig. 'The Prussian Triangle of Leadership in the Face of a People's War: A Reassessment of the Conflict Between Bismarck and Moltke, 1870–71'. *On The Road to Total War: The American Civil War and the German Wars of Unification, 1861–1871*. Eds. Stig Förster and Jorg Nagler. Cambridge: Cambridge University Press for the German Historical Institute, 1997. 115–140.

Fortna, Virginia Page, and Reyko Huang. 'Democratization after Civil War: A Brush-Clearing Exercise'. *International Studies Quarterly* 56 (2012): 801–08.

Fortna, Virginia Page. *Does Peacekeeping Work? Shaping Belligerents' Choices After Civil War*. Princeton: Princeton University Press, 2008.

Fox, William T. R. *The Super-Powers: The United States, Britain, and the Soviet Union—Their Responsibility for Peace*. New York: Harcourt Brace, 1944.

_____. '"The truth shall make you free": one student's appreciation of Quincy Wright'. *Journal of Conflict Resolution* 14 (1970): 449.

Freedman, Lawrence, ed. *Military Intervention in European Conflicts* (London: Blackwell, 1994)

_____. 'Bosnia: Does Peace Support Make Any Sense?', *NATO Review*, 43: 6 (1995), 19-23.

_____. *Kennedy's Wars: Berlin, Cuba, Laos and Vietnam*. New York: Oxford University Press, 2000.

_____. 'Social Science and the Cold War'. *Journal of Strategic Studies* 38:4 (2015): 554–574.

_____. *Choice of Enemies: America Confronts the Middle East*. New York: PublicAffairs, 2009.

_____. *Strategy: A History*. New York: Oxford University Press, 2013.

_____. 'Ukraine and the art of limited war'. *Survival* 56.6 (2014): 7–38.

_____. 'Force and the International Community: Blair's Chicago Speech and the Criteria for Intervention'. *International Relations* (2017): 1–17.

Frei, Christoph. *Hans J Morgenthau: An Intellectual Biography*. Baton Rouge: Louisiana State University Press, 2001.

French, Howard W. *A Continent for the Taking: The Tragedy and Hope of Africa*. New York: Vintage Books, 2004.

Friedman, George, and Meredith Lebard. *The Coming War with Japan*. New York: St. Martin's Press, 1991.

_____. *The Future of War: Power, Technology and American World Dominance in the 21st Century*. New York: St. Martin's Griffin, 1998. 102, 419.

Friedman, George. *The Next 100 Years: A Forecast for the 21st Century*. New York: Anchor Books, 2010.

Friedman, Matti. *Pumpkinflowers: A Soldier's Story*. Chapel Hill, NC: Algonquin, 2016.

'From hope to horror'. *The Economist*, 16 July 2016.

Fukuyama, Francis. 'The End of History'. *The National Interest* (1989).

_____. *The End of History and the Last Man*. New York: Free Press, 1992.

_____. *State-Building: Governance and World Order in the 21st Century*. Ithaca, NY: Cornell University Press, 2004.

Fuller, J. F. C. *The Decisive Battles of the Western World and Their Influence Upon History*. Vol. 1–3. London: Eyre & Spotiswood, 1963.

Gaddis, John Lewis. *The Long Peace: Inquiries into the History of the Cold War*. London: Oxford University Press, 1989.

_____. 'International Relations Theory and the End of the Cold War'. *International Security* 17.3 (1992/93): 5–58.

_____. *The Cold War*. London: Penguin, 2007.

Gagnon, V. P. 'Ethnic Nationalism and International Conflict'. *International Security* 19.3 (1994/95): 164.

Galeotti, Mark. 'Putin Is Playing by Grozny Rules in Aleppo'. *Foreign Policy*, 29 Sept. 2016.

_____. 'The west is too paranoid about Russia's information war'. *Guardian*, 7 July 2015. Available: https://www.theguardian.com/world/2015/jul/07/russia-propaganda-europe -america

Gannon, Charles E. *Rumors of War and Infernal Machines: Technomilitary agenda-setting in American and British Speculative Fiction*. Lanham, MD: Rowman & Littlefield, 2005.

von der Goltz, Colmar. *The Nation in Arms*. Trans. Philip A. Ashworth. London: W. H. Allen, 1883. Available: https://archive.org/details/nationinarms00ashwgoog.

Galula, David. *Counterinsurgency Warfare: Theory and Practice*. Westport, CT: Praeger, 1964.

Garrett, Stephen A. *Doing Good and Doing Well: An Examination of Humanitarian Intervention*. Westport, CT: Greenwood Press, 1999.

Garthoff, Ray. *A Journey Through the Cold War*. Washington DC: Brookings Institution, 2001.

Gat, Azar. *War in Human Civilization*. Oxford: Oxford University Press, 2008.

_____. 'Is War Declining and Why?' *Journal of Peace Research* 50.2 (2013): 149–157.

_____. *Causes of War and the Spread of Peace: But Will War Rebound?* (New York: Oxford University Press, 2017).

Gates, Scott, et al. *Trends in Armed Conflict, 1946–2014*. Oslo: Peace Research Institute Oslo, 2016.

Gates, Scott, Torbjørn L. Knutsen, and Jonathan W. Moses. 'Democracy and peace: A more skeptical view'. *Journal of Peace Research* 33.1 (1996): 1–10.

Gentile, Colonel Gian. *Wrong Turn: America's Deadly Embrace of Counterinsurgency*. New York: The New Press, 2013.

George, Peter. *Dr Strangelove or How I Learned to Stop Worrying and Love the Bomb*. Cardiff: Candy Jar Books, 2015.

Gerges, Fawaz. *America and Political Islam: Clash of Cultures or Clash of Interests*. New York: Cambridge University Press, 1999.

Gerlach, Christian. 'The Wannsee Conference, the Fate of German Jews, and Hitler's Decision in Principle to Exterminate All European Jews'. *The Journal of Modern History* 70.4 (1998): 759–812.

Gerwarth, Robert. *The Vanquished: Why the First World War Failed to End*. London: Allen Lane, 2016.

Gettleman, Jeffrey. 'Forever Wars: Why the Continent's Conflicts Never End'. *Foreign Policy* 178 (2010): 73–5.

Ghamari-Tabrizi, Sharon. *The Worlds of Herman Kahn: The Intuitive Science of Thermonuclear War*. Cambridge, MA: Harvard University Press, 2005.

Ghobarah, Hazem Adam, Paul Huth, and Bruce Russett. 'Civil Wars Kill and Main People— Long After the Shooting Stops'. *American Political Science Review* 97.2 (2003): 189–202.

Gibler, Douglas, and Jaroslav Tir. 'Settled Borders and Regime Type: Democratic Transitions as Consequences of Peaceful Territorial Transfers'. *American Journal of Political Science* 54.4 (2010): 951–68.

Gibler, Douglas M., Steven V. Miller, and Erin K. Little. 'An Analysis of the Militarized Interstate Dispute (MID) Dataset, 1816–2001'. *International Studies Quarterly* 60:4 (2017) 719–730.

Gibler, Douglas. 'The Implications of a Territorial Peace'. *What Do We Know About War?* Ed. John Vasquez. 2nd ed., Lanham, MD: Rowman & Littlefield, 2012.

Gibson, William. *Neuromancer*. New York: Ace Books, 1984.

Gilligan, Michael, and Stephen Stedman. 'Where Do the Peacekeepers Go?' *International Studies Review* 5.4 (2003): 37–54.

Gittings, John. *The Glorious Art of Peace: From the Iliad to Iraq*. London: Oxford University Press, 2012.

Gleditsch, Nils Petter. 'Armed conflict and the environment: A critique of the literature'. *Journal of Peace Research* 35.3 (1998): 363–380.

_____. 'The Decline of War—The Main Issues'. *International Studies Quarterly* 15.3 (2013).

Gleick, Peter. 'Water, Drought, Climate Change, and Conflict in Syria'. *Weather, Climate, and Society* 6 (2014): 331–340.

Glenn, Russell W. *All Glory Is Fleeting: Insights from the Second Lebanon War*. Santa Monica, CA: RAND, 2008.

Godfrey, Hollis. *The Man Who Ended War*. New York: Little Brown & Co., 1908.

Goldberg, Jeffrey. 'The Obama Doctrine'. *The Atlantic Monthly*, April 2016. Available: https://www.theatlantic.com/magazine/archive/2016/04/the-obama-doctrine /471525.

Goldman, Marshall I. *Gorbachev's Challenge: Economic Reform in the Age of High Technology*. New York: W. W. Norton, 1978.

Goldstein, Lyle J. 'Return to Zhenbao Island: Who Started Shooting and Why It Matters'. *The China Quarterly* 168 (2001): 985–997.

Goldstein, Joshua. *Winning the War: The Decline of Armed Conflict*. New York: Dutton, 2011.

Golovine, M. N. *Conflicts in Space: A Pattern of War in a New Dimension*. New York: St. Martin's Press, 1962.

Gompert, David C., Hans Binnendijk, and Bonny Lin. *Blinders, Blunders, and Wars*. Santa Monica, CA: RAND Corporation, 2014.

Gonzalez, Robert J. 'Toward Mercenary Anthropology?' *Anthropology Today*, 13 (2007).

Goodby, James, and George P. Shultz, eds. *The War That Must Never Be Fought*. Stanford: Hoover Press, 2015.

Gordon, Michael, and Gen. Bernard Trainor. *The General's War: The Inside Story of the Conflict in the Gulf*. Boston: Little, Brown, & Company, 1995.

Gow, James, and James Tilsey. 'The Strategic Imperative for Media Management'. *Bosnia by Television*. Eds. James Gow, Richard Paterson, and Alison Preston. London: British Film Institute, 1996.

Gow, James. 'After the Flood: Literature on the Context, Causes and Course of the Yugoslav War: Reflections and Refractions'. *The Slavonic and East European Review* 75.3 (1997): 446–484.

_____. *The Serbian Project and Its Adversaries: A Strategy of War Crimes*. London: Hurst & Co., 2003.

Grachev, Andrei. *Gorbachev's Gamble: Soviet Foreign Policy and the End of the Cold War*. Cambridge: Polity, 2008.

Grahame-White, Claude, and Harry Harper. *Air Power: Naval, Military, Commercial*. London: Chapman & Hall, 1917.

Gray, Colin S. *Another Bloody Century: Future Warfare*. London: Weidenfeld & Nicholson, 2005.

Grayzel, Susan R. *At Home and under Fire: Air Raids and Culture in Britain from the Great War to the Blitz*. Cambridge: Cambridge University Press, 2012.

Greenhill, Kelly M. 'Counting the Cost'. *Sex, Drugs, and Body Counts: The Politics of Numbers in Global Crime and Conflict*. Eds. Peter Andreas and Kelly M. Greenhill. Ithaca: Cornell University Press, 2010.

_____. 'Nigeria's Countless Casualties, The Politics of Counting Boko Haram¹s Victims', *Foreign Affairs*, February 9, 2015.

Grey, Viscount of Fallodon, KG. *Twenty-Five Years, 1892–1916*. Vol. 1. London: Hodder & Stoughton, 1925.

Guéhenno, Jean-Marie. *The Fog of Peace: A Memoir of International Peacekeeping in the 21st Century*. Washington DC: Brookings Institution Press, 2015.

Guetzkow, Harold. 'Long Range Research in International Relations'. *American Perspective* 4 (1950): 421–40.

Guillemin, Jeanne. *Biological Weapons: From the Invention of State-Sponsored Programs to Contemporary Terrorism*. New York: Columbia University Press, 2005.

Gurr, Ted Robert. *Why Men Rebel*. Princeton, NJ: Princeton University Press, 1970.

_____. *Minorities at Risk: A Global View of Ethnopolitical Conflicts*. Washington DC: United States Institute of Peace Press, 1993.

Gusterson, Hugh. *Drone: Remote Control Warfare*. Cambridge: MIT Press, 2016.

Haass, Richard. *War of Necessity, War of Choice: A Memoir of Two Iraq Wars*. New York: Simon & Schuster, 2009.

Hacker, J. David. 'A Census-Based Count of the Civil War Dead'. *Civil War History* 57.4 (2011): 307–348.

Hackett, General Sir John. 'A Third World War'. Third Jubilee Lecture, Imperial College of Science and Technology, University of London, 13 Mar. 1979.

_____. *The Third World War: The Untold Story*. New York: Macmillan, 1982.

Hagopian, Amy, et al. 'Mortality in Iraq Associated with the 2003–2011 War and Occupation: Findings from a National Cluster Sample Survey by the University Collaborative Iraq Mortality Study'. *PLOS* 15 (2013).

Haldane, James Aylmer. *The Insurrection in Mesopotamia, 1920*. Edinburgh: Blackwood, 1922.

Hanson, Victor Davis. *Carnage and Culture: Landmark Battles in the Rise of Western Power*. New York: Doubleday, 2001.

Harari, Yuval N. 'The Concept of "Decisive Battles" in World History'. *Journal of World History* 18.3 (2007): 251–266.

Hartmann, Christian. *Operation Barbarossa: Nazi Germany's War in the East, 1941–1945*. Oxford: Oxford University Press, 2015.

Haslam, Jonathan. *The Vices of Integrity: E. H. Carr, 1892–1982*. London; New York: Verso, 1999.

_____. *Russia's Cold War*. New Haven: Yale University Press, 2011.

Hassner, Ron. *Religion on the Battlefield*. Ithaca: Cornell University Press, 2016.

Hastings, Max. *Catastrophe: Europe Goes to War 1914*. London: Collins, 2013.

Hauge, Wenche, and Tanja Ellingsen. 'Beyond environmental scarcity: Causal pathways to conflict'. *Journal of Peace Research* 35.3 (1998): 299–317.

Havel, Václav. *Open Letters: Selected Prose* (London: Faber & Faber, 1992).

Hawkins, William. 'New Enemies for Old'. *The National Review* 42.18 (1990): 28–29.

Haynes, Michael. 'Counting Soviet Deaths in the Great Patriotic War: a Note'. *Europe Asia Studies* 55.2 (2003): 300–309.

Haynes, Peter. *Toward a New Maritime Strategy: American Naval Thinking in the Post-Cold War Era*. Annapolis, MD: Naval Institute Press, 2015.

Haysom, Simon, and Jens Pedersen. 'Robust peacekeeping in Africa: the challenge for humanitarians'. *Humanitarian Practice Network*. Oct. 2015. Available: http://odihpn.org/magazine/robust-peacekeeping-in-africa-the-challenge-for-humanitarians/.

Hazen, Jennifer M. 'Understanding gangs as armed groups'. *International Review of the Red Cross* (2010).

Hearne, R. P. *Aerial Warfare*. London: John Lane, The Bodley Head, 1909.

Hegre, Håvard, et al. 'Predicting Armed Conflict, 2010–2050'. *International Studies Quarterly* 57 (2013): 250–270.

Hegre, Håvard. 'Democracy and armed conflict'. *Journal of Peace Research* 51.2 (2014): 159–172.

Helman, Gerald, and Steven Ratner. 'Saving Failed States'. *Foreign Policy* (1992–93).

Henderson, Errol A., and David J. Singer. 'Civil War in the Post-colonial world, 1946–92'. *Journal of Peace Research* 37.3 (2000): 275–299.

_____. '"New Wars" and Rumors of "New Wars"'. *International Interactions: Empirical and Theoretical Research in International Relations* 28.2 (2002): 165–190.

Henderson, Errol A., and Richard Tucker. 'Clear and Present Strangers: The Clash of Civilizations and International Conflict'. *International Studies Quarterly* 45 (2001): 317–338.

Hensel, Paul. 'The More Things Change'. *Conflict Management and Peace Science* 19.1 (2002): 48.

Herbst, Jeffrey. 'The Creation and Maintenance of National Boundaries in Africa'. *International Organization* 43.4 (1989): 673–692.

_____. *States and Power in Africa: Comparative Lessons in Authority and Control*. Princeton, NJ: Princeton University Press, 2000.

Hersey, John. 'Hiroshima'. *New Yorker*, 31 August 1946. Available: http://www.newyorker.com/magazine/1946/08/31/hiroshima.

Herz, John H. *Political Realism and Political Idealism*. Chicago: Chicago University Press, 1951.

Heuser, Beatrice. 'Atrocities in Theory and Practice: An Introduction'. *Civil Wars*, 14:1, (2012), 2–28.

High-Level Panel on Threats, Challenges and Change. *A More Secure World: Our Shared Responsibility*. New York: United Nations, 2004. 66, pt. 3, para 203.

Hill, Maj. Lewis D., Doris Cook, and Aron Pinker. *Gulf War Air Power Survey: Statistical Compendium*. Washington DC: Department of the Air Force, 1993.

Hironaka, Ann. *Neverending Wars: The International Community, Weak States, and the Perpetuation of Civil War*. Cambridge, MA: Harvard University Press, 2005.

Hirshleifer, Jack. 'The dark side of the force'. *Economic Inquiry* 32 (1994): 3.

Hoagland, Jim. 'From Yalta To Malta'. *Washington Post*. 9 Nov. 1989.

Hobson, J. A. *Imperialism: A Study*. New York: James Pott & Co., 1902. Available: http://files.libertyfund.org/files/127/0052_Bk.pdf.

Hoffman, Frank G., and James N. Mattis. 'Future Warfare: The Rise of Hybrid Wars'. *Naval Institute Proceedings* 132.11 (2005).

Hoffman, Frank G. *Conflict in the 21st Century: The Rise of Hybrid Wars*. Arlington, VA: The Potomac Institute for Policy Studies, 2007.

_____. 'Hybrid Warfare and Challenges'. *Joint Forces Quarterly* 52 (2009): 34–39.

_____. 'Hybrid vs. Compound War: The Janus Choice of Modern War: Defining Today's Multifaceted Conflict'. *Armed Forces Journal* (2009): 1–2.

_____. 'On Not-So-New Warfare: Political Warfare vs. Hybrid Threat'. *War on the Rocks*. 28 July 2014. Available: http://warontherocks.com/2014/07/on-not-so-new-warfare-political-warfare-vs-hybrid-threats/.

_____. The Contemporary Spectrum of Conflict: Protracted, Gray Zone, Ambiguous, and Hybrid Modes of War'. *Heritage Foundation Index of Military Power* (2016).

_____. *Foresight into 21st Century Conflict: End of the Greatest Illusion*. Philadelphia: Foreign Policy Research Institute, 2016.

Holman, Brett. *The Next War in the Air: Britain's Fear of the Bomber, 1908–1941*. London, Ashgate: 2014.

Holsti, Kalevi J. *Armed Conflicts and International Order: 1648–1989*. Cambridge: Cambridge University Press, 1991.

_____. *The State, War, and the State of War*. Cambridge: Cambridge University Press, 1996.

Homer-Dixon, Thomas F. 'Environmental Scarcities and Violent Conflict: Evidence from Cases'. *International Security* 19.1(1994): 5–40.

_____. *Environment, Scarcity, and Violence*. Princeton, NJ: Princeton University Press, 1999.

Honan, W. H. *Visions of Infamy: The untold story of how journalist Hector C. Bywater devised the plans that led to Pearl Harbor*. New York: St. Martin's Press, 1991.

Horgan, John. *The End of War*. San Francisco: McSweeney's, 2012.

Horne, John N., and Alan Kramer. *German Atrocities of 1914: A History of Denial*. New Haven: Yale University Press, 2001.

Howard, Michael. *Studies in War & Peace*. London: Temple Smith, 1970.

_____. *War and the Liberal Conscience*. London: Temple Smith, 1978.

_____. *The Invention of Peace*. London: Profile Books, 2000.

Huber, Thomas M. 'Compound Warfare: A Conceptual Framework'. *Compound Warfare: That Fatal Knot*. Ed. Thomas M. Huber. Fort Leavenworth, MS: US Army Command and General Staff College Press, 2002.

Hughes, Llewelyn, and Austin Long. 'Is There an Oil Weapon? National Security Implications of Changes in the Structure of the International Oil Market'. *International Security* 39.3 (2014/15).

Hull, Isabel V. *Absolute Destruction: Military Culture and The Practices of War in Imperial Germany*. Ithaca, NY: Cornell University Press, 2005.

Human Security Report Project. *The Human Security Report 2005*. Oxford: Oxford University Press, 2005.

_____. *Human Security Report 2009/2010: The Causes of Peace and The Shrinking Costs of War*. New York: Oxford University Press, 2011.

_____. *Human Security Report 2012: Sexual Violence, Education, and War*. Vancouver: Human Security Press, 2012.

_____. *Human Security Report 2013: The Decline in Global Violence: Evidence, Explanation, and Contestation*. Vancouver: Human Security Press, 2013.

Humphreys, M. 'Natural resources, conflict, and conflict resolution: uncovering the mechanisms'. *Journal of Conflict Resolution* 49 (2005): 508–37.

Huntington, Samuel. *The Third Wave: Democratization in the Late Twentieth Century*. Norman, OK: University of Oklahoma Press, 1991.

_____. 'The Clash of Civilizations?' *Foreign Affairs* 72:3 (1993), 22–49.

_____. *The Clash of Civilizations and the Remaking of World Order*. New York: Simon & Schuster, 1996.

Hutton, Paul. *Phil Sheridan and His Army*. Norman, OK: University of Oklahoma Press, 1999.

Ignatieff, Michael. *Virtual War: Kosovo and Beyond*. New York: Metropolitan Books, 2000.

Implications for US National Security of Anticipated Climate Change. NIC WP 2016–01. Washington DC: National Intelligence Council 21, Sept. 2016.

Inbar, Efraim, and Eitan Shamir. 'What after counter-insurgency?' *International Affairs* 92.6 (2016): 14409.

International Commission on Intervention. *The Responsibility to Protect: The Report of the International Commission on Intervention and State Sovereignty*. Ottawa: International Development Research Centre [IDRC], Nov. 2002.

Jackson, Robert H. *The Global Covenant: Human Conduct in a World of States*. Oxford: Oxford University Press, 2000.

Jackson, Robert H., and Carl G. Rosberg. 'Why Africa's Weak States Persist: The Empirical and the Juridical in Statehood'. *World Politics* 35 (1982): 1–24.

Jacobsen, Mark. 'Only by the sword': British counter-insurgency in Iraq, 1920'. *Small Wars & Insurgencies* 2.2 (1991): 323–363.

Jenkins, Brian M. *Will Terrorists Go Nuclear?* Santa Monica, CA: RAND, 1975.

Jesse, Richards. *The Secret Peace: Exposing the Positive Trend of World Events*. New York: Book & Ladder, 2010.

Johnson, Hilde. *South Sudan: The Untold Story from Independence to Civil War*. London: I.B. Tauris, 2016.

Johnston, Alastair Iain. 'How New and Assertive Is China's New Assertiveness?' *International Security* 37.4 (2013): 7–48.

Johnston, Patrick. 'Does Decapitation Work? Assessing the Effectiveness of Leadership Targeting in Counterinsurgency Campaigns'. *International Security* 36.4 (2012): 47–79.

de Jomini, Baron Antoine-Henri. *The Art of War*. London: Greenhill Books, 1992.

Jones, Archer. *The Art of War in the Western World*. Urbana and Champaign, IL: University of Illinois Press, 2001.

Jones, Daniel M., Stuart A. Bremer, and J. David Singer. 'Militarized Interstate Disputes, 1816–1992'. *Conflict Management and Peace Science* 15.2 (1996): 163–213, 169.

Jones, Sam. 'Ukraine: Russia's new art of war'. *Financial Times*, 28 Aug. 2014.

Jones, Seth. *Waging Insurgent Warfare: Lessons from the Vietcong to the Islamic State*. New York: Oxford University Press, 2017.

Jongman, B., and H. van der Dennen. 'The Great "War Figures" Hoax: An investigation in polemomythology'. *Security Dialogue* 19.2 (1988): 197–202.

Jordan, Jenna. 'When heads roll: Assessing the effectiveness of leadership decapitation'. *Security Studies* 18.4 (2009): 719–755.

'Justice Report: Bosnia's Book of the Dead'. *Balkan Investigative Reporting Network*, 21 June 2007. Available: http://www.birn.eu.com/ en/88/10/3377/.

Kagan, Donald. *On the Origins of War and the Preservation of Peace*. New York: Doubleday, 1995.

Kahn, Herman. *On Thermonuclear War*. Princeton: Princeton University Press, 1960.

Kakutani, Michiko. 'Critic's Notebook; The Writers Who Shook a Government'. *New York Times*, 8 Feb. 1990.

Kaldor, Mary. *New and Old Wars: Organized Violence in a Global Era*. Cambridge: Polity Press, 1999.

Kalyvas, Stathis N. '"New" and "Old" Wars: A Valid Distinction?' *World Politics* 54.1 (2001): 99–118.

_____. 'Civil Wars'. *The Oxford Handbook of Comparative Politics*. Eds. Carles Boix and Susan C. Stokes. Oxford: Oxford University Press, 2007.

_____. 'The New U.S. Army/Marine Corps Counterinsurgency Field Manual as Political Science and Political Praxis'. *Perspectives on Politics* 6.2 (2008): 351.

_____. 'The Changing Character of Civil Wars'. *The Changing Character of War*. Eds. Hew Strachan and Sibylle Scheipers. Oxford: Oxford University Press, 2011. 202–219.

Kant, Immanuel. *Political Writings*. Cambridge: Cambridge University Press, 1991.

Kaplan, Fred. *Wizards of Armageddon*. Stanford: Stanford University Press, 1983.

_____. *Dark Territory: The Secret History of Cyber War*. New York: Simon & Schuster, 2016.

Kaplan, Robert D. *Balkan Ghosts: A Journey Through History*. New York: St. Martin's Press, 1993.

_____. 'The Coming Anarchy'. *The Atlantic Monthly*, February 1994.

Karber, Phillip A. *The Impact of New Conventional Technologies on Military Doctrine and Organization in the Warsaw Pact*. Adelphi Paper no. 144. London: International Institute for Strategic Studies, 1978.

Karklins, Rasma. *Ethnic Relations in the USSR: The View from Below*. Boston, MA: Unwin Hyman, 1986.

Karnow, Stanley. *In Our Own Image: American Empire in the Philippines*. New York: Random House, 1989.

Kaufman, Stuart J. 'An "International" Theory of Inter-ethnic War'. *Review of International Studies* 22.2 (1996): 153.

Kaysen, Carl. 'Is War Obsolete?: A Review Essay'. *International Security* 14.4 (1990): 42–64.

Keaney, Thomas, and Eliot Cohen. *Gulf War Air Power Survey: Summary Report*. Washington DC: Department of the Air Force, 1993.

Keegan, John. *A History of Warfare*. New York: Knopf, 1993.

Keen, David. *The Economic Functions of Violence in Civil Wars*. Adelphi Paper no. 320. London: Taylor & Francis for IISS, 1998.

Kegley, Charles, and Martin Hermann. 'Putting military intervention into the democratic peace'. *Comparative Political Studies* 30.1 (1997): 78–107.

Kelani, Rosemary A. 'The Petroleum Paradox: Oil, Coercive Vulnerability, and Great Power Behavior'. *Security Studies* 25.2 (2016), 181–213.

Kennedy, Paul. *The Rise and Fall of the Great Powers*. New York: Vintage, 1988.

_____. *The Rise and Fall of British Naval Mastery*, (London: Penguin, 2017).

Keohane, Robert O., ed. *Neorealism and Its Critics*. New York: Columbia University Press, 1986.

Kerman, Cynthia. 'Kenneth Boulding and the Peace Research Movement'. *American Studies* 13.1 (1972): 149–165.

Kevorkian, Raymond. *The Armenian Genocide: A Complete History*. London: I. B. Tauris, 2011.

Kilcullen, David. 'Twenty-Eight Articles: Fundamentals of Company-Level Counterinsurgency'. *Military Review* (2006): 105–107.

_____. *The Accidental Guerrilla: Fighting Small Wars in the Midst of a Big One*. London: Hurst & Co., 2009.

_____. *Out of the Mountains: The Coming Age of the Urban Guerrilla*. New York: Oxford University Press, 2013.

_____. *Blood Year: Islamic State and the Failures of the War on Terror*. London: Hurst 2016.

Kirkwood, Patrick M. 'The Impact of Fiction on Public Debate in Late Victorian Britain: The Battle of Dorking and the "Lost Career" of Sir George Tomkyns Chesney'. *The Graduate History Review* 4.1 (2012): 3.

Kissane, Bill. *Nations Torn Asunder: The Challenge of Civil War*. Oxford: Oxford University Press, 2016.

Kissinger, Henry. *Diplomacy*. New York: Simon & Schuster, 1994.

Klare, Michael T. *Rising Powers, Shrinking Planet: The New Geopolitics of Energy*. New York: Metropolitan Books, 2008.

Knight, Amy. 'Finally, We Know About the Moscow Bombings'. *New York Review of Books*. 22 Nov. 2012.

Knightley, Philip. *The Second Oldest Profession*. New York: W. W. Norton, 1987.

Korb, Lawrence J., and Stephen Biddle. 'Violence by the Numbers in Iraq: Sound Data or Shaky Statistics?' *Council on Foreign Relations*. 25 Sept. 2007.

Korol, V.E., "The price of victory: Myths and reality", *Journal of Slavic Military Studies*, 9:2 (1996), 417–426.

Kotkin, Stephen. *Armageddon Averted: Soviet Collapse since 1970*. Updated Edition. New York: Oxford University Press, 2009.

Koubi, Vally, et al. 'Do natural resources matter for interstate and intrastate armed conflict?' *Journal of Peace Research* 51 (2014): 227.

Krasner, Stephen D., and Carlos Pascual. 'Addressing State Failure'. *Foreign Affairs*, 84:4 (2005), 153-163

Krause, Keith. 'From Armed Conflict to Political Violence: Mapping and Explaining Conflict Trends'. *Daedalus: Journal of the American Academy of Arts & Sciences* (2016): 117.

Krepinevich, Andrew F. *7 Deadly Scenarios: A Military Futurist Explores War in the 21ˢᵗ Century*. New York: Bantam Dell, 2007.

Kreps, Sarah. *Drones: What Everyone Needs to Know*. Oxford University Press, 2016.

Kreutz, Joakim. 'How Civil Wars End (and Recur)'. *Routledge Handbook of Civil Wars*. Eds. Edward Newman and Karl DeRouen, Jr. London: Routledge, 2014.

Krivosheev, G. I. *Soviet Casualties and Combat Losses*. London: Greenhill, 1997.

Krugman, Paul. 'The Great Illusion'. *New York Times*, 14 Aug. 2008.

Kuisong, Y. 'The Sino-Soviet Border Clash of 1969: From Zhenbao Island to Sino-American Rapprochement'. *Cold War History* 1.1 (2000): 21–52.

Kull, Steven, and Clay Ramsay. 'The Myth of the Reactive Public: American Public Attitudes on Military Fatalities in the Post-Cold War Period'. *Public Opinion and the International Use of Force*. Eds. Philip Everts and Pierangelo Isernia. London: Routledge, 2001.

Kuperman, Alan J. *The Limits of Humanitarian Intervention: Genocide in Rwanda*. Washington DC: Brookings Institution Press, 2001.

Lacina, Bethany, and Nils Petter Gleditsch. 'Monitoring Trends in Global Combat: A New Dataset of Battle Deaths'. *European Journal of Population* 21.2–3 (2005): 145–166.

Lambeth, Ben. 'The Technology Revolution in Air Warfare'. *Survival* 39.1 (1997): 72.

Lanouette, William. *Genius in the Shadows: A Biography of Leo Szilard, the Man Behind the Bomb*. Chicago: University of Chicago Press, 1994.

Larson, Eric V. *Casualties and Consensus: The Historical Role of Casualties in Domestic Support for U.S. Military Operations*. Santa Monica, CA: RAND, 1996.

Latiff, Robert, *Future War: Preparing for the New Global Battlefield*, (New York: Alfred Knopf, 2107.

Lavoy, Peter R., Scott D. Sagan, and James J Wirtz, eds. *Planning the Unthinkable: How New Powers Will Use Nuclear, Chemical and Biological Weapons*. Ithaca, NY: Cornell University Press, 2000.

Layne, Christopher. 'Kant or Cant. The Myth of the Democratic Peace'. *International Security* 19 (1994).

Le Bon, Gustave. *The Crowd: A Study of the Popular Mind*. New York: The Macmillan Co, 1896.

Lebow, Richard Ned. 'The Long Peace, the End of the Cold War, and the Failure of Realism'. *International Organization* 48.2 (1994): 249–277.

Lebow, Richard Ned, and Janice Gross Stein. 'Reagan and the Russians: The Cold War ended despite President Reagan's arms buildup, not because of it—or so former President Gorbachev told the authors'. *The Atlantic Monthly*, 1994.

Leigh, David. 'Iraq War Logs Reveal 15,000 Previously Unlisted Civilian Deaths'. *Guardian*, 22 Oct. 2010.

Leitenberg, Milton. *Deaths in Wars and Conflicts in the Twentieth Century*. Cornell University Peace Studies Program, Occasional Paper #29, 3rd ed., 2006.

Lemarchand, René. 'Patterns of State Collapse and Reconstruction in Central Africa'. *African Studies Quarterly* 1.3 (1997): 5–6.

Lester, Toby. 'Beyond "The Coming Anarchy"'. *The Atlantic Online*, Aug. 1996. Available: http://www.theatlantic.com/past/docs/issues/96aug/proport/kapsid.htm.

Levi, Michael. *On Nuclear Terrorism*. Cambridge, MA: Harvard University Press, 2007.

Levy, Jack S. 'Domestic Politics and War'. *The Origin and Prevention of Major Wars*. Eds. Robert I. Rotberg and Theodore K. Rabb. Cambridge: Cambridge University Press, 1989.

Lewis, Bernard. 'The Roots of Muslim Rage'. *The Atlantic*, September 1990.

Libicki, Martin. 'DBK and its Consequences'. *Dominant Battlespace Knowledge*. Eds. Stuart Johnson and Martin Libicki. Washington DC: National Defense University, April 1996.

Licklider, Roy. 'The Consequences of Negotiated Settlements in Civil Wars, 1945–1993'. *American Political Science Review* 89.3 (1995): 681–690.

Liddell Hart, Basil. *Paris or the Future of War*. New York: E. P. Dutton, 1925.

———. *Europe in Arms*. London: Faber & Faber, 1937.

———. *The Revolution in Warfare*. London: Faber, 1946.

Lindsay, Jon R., 'Stuxnet and the Limits of Cyber Warfare'. *Security Studies* 22.3 (2013).

Lischer, S. K. 'Security and displacement in Iraq: responding to the forced migration crisis'. *International Security* 33.2 (2008): 95–119.

Livermore, Thomas. *Numbers and Losses in the Civil War in America, 1861–65*. Boston: Houghton Mifflin & Co., 1900.

Lodal, Jan. *The Price of Dominance: The New Weapons of Mass Destruction and Their Challenge to American Leadership*. New York: Council on Foreign Relation, 2001.

Long, Austin. *The Soul of Armies: Counterinsurgency Doctrine and Military Culture in the US and UK*. Ithaca, NY: Cornell University Press, 2016.

Lucas, George. *Ethics and Cyber Warfare: The Quest for Responsible Security in the Age of Digital Warfare*. New York: Oxford University Press, 2017.

Ludendorff, Erich. *The Nation at War*. Trans. A.S. Rapaport. London: Hutchinson, 1936.

Ludwig II, Walter C. 'Influencing Clients in Counterinsurgency: U.S. Involvement in El Salvador's Civil War, 1979–92'. *International Security* 41.6 (2016): 99.

Luttwak, Edward. *The Grand Strategy of the Soviet Union*. New York: St. Martin's, 1983.

———. 'Towards Post-Heroic Warfare'. *Foreign Affairs* 74.3 (1995): 109–122.

———. 'Give War a Chance'. *Foreign Affairs* 78.4 (1999).

———. 'Dead end: Counterinsurgency warfare as military malpractice'. *Harper's*, Feb. 2007, 33–42.

———. *The Rise of China vs. the Logic of Strategy*. Cambridge, MA: Harvard University Press, 2012.

Luvaas, Jay. *The Military Legacy of the Civil War: The European Inheritance*. Lawrence, KA: University Press of Kansas, 1959.

Lyall, Jason. 'Does Indiscriminate Violence Incite Insurgent Attacks? Evidence from Chechnya'. *Journal of Conflict Resolution* 53.3 (2009): 331–362.

———. 'Are Coethnics More Effective Counterinsurgents? Evidence from the Second Chechen War'. *American Political Science Review* 104 (2010): 1–20.

Lyall, Jason, Graeme Blair, and Kosuke Imai. 'Explaining Support for Combatants during Wartime: A Survey Experiment in Afghanistan'. *American Political Science Review* 107.4 (2013): 679–705.

MacClinchy, Wendy. 'Violence Today'. *States of Fragility*. OECD: 2016.

Mack, Andrew. 'Why Big Nations Lose Small Wars: The Politics of Asymmetric Conflict'. *World Politics* 27.2 (1975): 175–200.

MacMillan, Margaret. *Peacemakers Six Months that Changed the World: The Paris Peace Conference of 1919 and Its Attempt to End War.* London: John Murray, 2011.

_____. *The War That Ended Peace: The Road to 1914.* New York: Random House, 2013.

McPherson, James. 'Was It More Restrained Than You Think?' *New York Review of Books,* 14 Feb. 2008.

de Madariaga, Salvador. *Disarmament.* New York: Coward-McCann, 1929.

Mahnken, Thomas G. *Technology and the American Way of War Since 1945.* New York: Columbia University Press, 2008.

Maiolo, Joseph. *Cry Havoc: How the Arms Race Drove the World to War, 1931–1941.* New York: Basic Books, 2010.

Malin, Martin, Matthew Bunn, Nickolas Roth, and William H. Tobey. 'Will the Nuclear Security Summit Help Stop Terrorists from Getting the Bomb?' *The National Interest,* 31 Mar. 2016. Available: http://nationalinterest.org/blog/the-buzz/will-the-nuclear -security-summit-help-stop-terrorists-15644.

Malkasian, Carter. *Illusions of Victory: the Anbar Awakening and the Rise of the Islamic State,* New York: Oxford University Press, 2017.

Mallaby, Sebastian. *The World's Banker: A Story of Failed States, Financial Crises, and the Wealth and Poverty of Nations.* New York: Penguin, 2004.

Mann, Edward. 'Desert Storm: The First Information War?' *Airpower Journal* (1994): 4–14.

Mansfield, Edward D., and Jack Snyder. *Electing to Fight: Why Emerging Democracies Go to War.* Cambridge, MA: MIT Press, 2007.

Manz, Beatriz. *Paradise in Ashes: A Guatemalan Journey of Courage, Terror, and Hope.* Oakland, CA: University of California Press, 2005.

Maoz, Zeev, and Bruce M. Russett. 'Normative and structural causes of democratic peace, 1946–1986'. *American Political Science Review* 87.3 (1993): 624–638.

Mason, T. David and Sara McLaughlin Mitchell, *What Do We Know about Civil Wars?* (New York: Rowman & Littlefield, 2016)

McCarthy, Justin. The End of Ottoman Anatolia'. *Muslims and Minorities: The Population of Ottoman Anatolia and the End of the Empire.* New York: New York University Press, 1983.

McCulloh, Timothy, and Johnson, Richard. *Hybrid Warfare.* JSOU Report 13–4. MacDill AFB, FL: Joint Special Operations University, 2013.

McFate, Montgomery, and Janice Laurence, eds. *Social Science Goes to War: The Human Terrain System in Iraq and Afghanistan.* London: Hurst, 2015.

McFate, Montgomery. 'Building Bridges Or Burning Heretics?' *Anthropology Today* (2007).

McGowan, Patrick J. 'African Military Coups d'Etat, 1956–2001: Frequency, Trends and Distribution'. *Journal of Modern African Studies* 41 (2003): 339–70.

McGrath, James R. 'Twenty-First Century Information Warfare and the Third Offset Strategy'. *Joint Forces Quarterly* 82 (2016).

McKinley, John, ed. *A Guide To Peace Support Operations.* Providence, RI: The Thomas J. Watson Jr. Institute for International Studies, Brown University, 1996.

McMaster, H. R. 'Discussing the Continuities of War and the Future of Warfare: The Defense Entrepreneurs Forum'. *Small Wars Journal* (2014).

Mearsheimer, John. *Conventional Deterrence.* Ithaca, NY: Cornell University Press, 1983.

_____. 'Back to the Future: Instability in Europe after the Cold War'. *International Security* 15.1 (1990).

Meierding, Emily. 'Dismantling the Oil Wars Myth'. *Security Studies* 25.2 (2016).

Merom, Gil. *How Democracies Lose Small Wars.* Cambridge: Cambridge University Press, 2003.

de Mesquita, Bruce Bueno, et al. 'An institutional explanation of the democratic peace'. *American Political Science Review* 93.4 (1999): 791–807.

Metz, Steven, and Douglas V. Johnson. *Asymmetry and U.S. Military Strategy: Definition, Background, and Strategic Concepts.* Carlisle, PA: Strategic Studies Institute, US Army War College, 2001.

Metz, Steven. *Iraq and the Evolution of American Strategy*. Washington DC: Potomac Books, 2008.

Michaels, Jeff. 'Revisiting General Sir John Hackett's *The Third World War*'. *British Journal for Military History*, 3:1, (2016), 88–104.

Ministry of Defence. *Strategic Trends Programme: Global Strategic Trends—Out to 2045*. Shrivenham: Doctrine, Concepts and Development Center, 2014.

Mitchell, Lincoln A. *The Color Revolutions*, (Philadelphia, PA: University of Pennsylvania Press, 2012).

Mitter, Rana. *China's War with Japan, 1937–1945: The Struggle for Survival*. London: Allen Lane, 2013.

Moore, Robin. *The Green Berets*. New York: Crown, 1965.

Morgenthau, Hans J. 'The Four Paradoxes of Nuclear Strategy'. *American Political Science Review* 581 (1964): 23–35.

_____. *Politics Among Nations: The Struggle for Power and Peace*. 5th ed. New York: Alfred A. Knopf, 1978.

Morris, Ian. *War: What Is It Good For? The Role of Conflict in Civilisation, From Primates to Robots*. London: Profile Books, 2014.

Mousseau, Michael. 'A Market-Capitalist or a Democratic Peace'. *What Do We Know About War?* 2nd ed. Ed. John Vasquez. Lanham, MD: Rowman & Littlefield, 2012.

Mueller, John. *Retreat from Doomsday: The Obsolescence of Major War*. New York: Basic Books, 1989.

_____. 'The Banality of "Ethnic Conflict"'. *International Security* 25.1 (2000): 47.

_____. *The Remnants of War*. Ithaca, NY: Cornell University Press, 2004.

Muggah, Robert. *Fragile Cities Rising*. Global Observatory, International Peace Institute, 2013.

_____. 'Fixing Fragile Cities: Solutions for Urban Violence and Poverty'. *Foreign Affairs* (2015).

_____. 'A War by Any Other Name'. *Small Wars Journal* (2017).

Mulligan, William. *The Great War for Peace*. New Haven: Yale University Press, 2014.

Mulrine, Anna. 'CIA Chief Leon Panetta: The Next Pearl Harbor Could Be a Cyberattack'. *Christian Science Monitor*, 9 June 2011.

Münkler, Herfried. *The New Wars*. Cambridge: Polity, 2005.

Murray, Williamson, and Peter R. Mansoor, eds. *Hybrid Warfare: Fighting Complex Opponents from the Ancient World to the Present*. New York: Cambridge University Press, 2012.

Murray, Williamson, and Wayne Wei-Siang Hsieh. *A Savage War: A Military History of the Civil War*. Princeton: Princeton University Press, 2016.

Nagl, John A. *Counterinsurgency Lessons from Malaya and Vietnam: Learning to Eat Soup with a Knife*. Westport, CT: Praeger, 2002.

Naim, Moises. 'Mafia States: Organised Crime Takes Office'. *Foreign Affairs* 91:3 (2012).

Narang, Vipin. *Nuclear Strategy in the Modern Era: Regional Powers and International Conflict*. Princeton: Princeton University Press, 2014.

National Commission on Terrorism. *Countering the Changing Threat of International Terrorism*. Washington DC: US Congress, 2000.

National Research Council. *Computers at Risk: Safe Computing in the Information Age*. Washington DC: National Academies Press, 1991.

Neely, Mark E., Jr. *The Civil War and the Limits of Destruction*. Cambridge: Harvard University Press, 2007.

Neff, Stephen. *War and the Law of Nations*. Cambridge: Cambridge University Press, 2005.

Nelson, Craig. *Pearl Harbor From Infamy to Greatness*. New York: Simon & Schuster, 2016.

Newman, Edward. 'Conflict Research and the 'Decline' of Civil War'. *Civil Wars* 11.3 (2009): 255–278.

Newman, James. *The Rule of Folly*. London: Allen & Unwin, 1962.

Nicholson, Michael. 'Lewis Fry Richardson and the Study of the Causes of War'. *British Journal of Political Science* 29.3 (1999): 541–563.

Nixon, Richard. *1999—Victory Without War*. New York: Simon & Schuster, 1988.

Noah, Timothy. 'Birth of a Washington Word: When warfare gets "kinetic"'. *Slate*, 20 Nov. 2002. Available: http://www.slate.com/articles/news_and_politics/chatterbox/2002/11/birth_of_a_washington_word.html.

Noel-Baker, Philip. 'Peace and the Arms Race'. Nobel Lecture, 11 Dec. 1959.

Nogueira, João Pontes. *From Fragile States to Fragile Cities: Redefining Spaces of Humanitarian Practices*. HASOW Discussion Paper 12, Oct. 2014. Available: https://igarape.org.br/wp-content/uploads/2016/04/From-Fragile-States-to-Fragile-Cities.pdf.

Nolan, Cathal J. *The Allure of Battle: A History of How Wars Have Been Won and Lost*. Oxford: Oxford University Press, 2017.

Notaras, Mark. 'Does Climate Change Cause Conflict?' *Our World*, 27 Nov. 2009. Available: https://ourworld.unu.edu/en/does-climate-change-cause-conflict.

Norton, Ray. *The Vanishing Fleets*. London: Forgotten Books, 2015.

Norton, Richard J. 'Feral Cities'. *Naval War College Review* 56.4 (2003): 97–106.

Nunn, Sam, and Dewey F. Bartlett. *NATO and the New Soviet Threat*. US Senate, Armed Services Committee, 95th Congress, First Session. Washington DC: US Government Printing Office, 1977.

Nye, Joseph S., Jr., Graham T. Allison, Jr., and Albert Carnesale, eds. *Fateful Visions: Avoiding Nuclear Catastrophe*. New York: Harper & Row, 1988.

Obama, President Barack. 'Remarks by the President'. Joint Base McGuire-Dix-Lakehurst, NJ. 15 Dec. 2014.

O'Brien, Phillips Payson. *How the War Was One: Air-Sea Power and Allied Victory in World War II*. Cambridge: Cambridge University Press, 2015.

O'Brien, Tim. *Going After Cacciato*. New York: Delacorte Press, 1978.

Office of the Director of National Intelligence. *Global Trends 2010*. Revised edition. Washington DC: National Intelligence Council, Feb. 1997. Available: https://www.dni.gov/index.php/about/organization/national-intelligence-council-global-trends/global-trends-2010.

_____. *Global Trends 2015: A Dialogue About the Future with Nongovernment Experts*. Washington DC: National Intelligence Council, Dec. 2000.

_____. *Mapping the Global Future: Report of the National Intelligence Council's 2020 Project*. Washington DC: National Intelligence Council, Dec. 2004.

_____. *Global Trends 2025: A Transformed World*. Washington DC: National Intelligence Council, Nov. 2008.

_____. *Global Trends 2030: Alternative Worlds*. Washington DC: National Intelligence Council, Dec. 2012.

_____. *Global trends: Paradoxes of Progress*. Washington DC: National Intelligence Council, Jan. 2017.

O'Hanlon, Michael. *Technological Change and the Future of Warfare*. Washington DC: Brookings Institution, 2000.

_____. *The Future of Land Warfare*. Washington DC: Brookings Institution, 2015.

O'Neill, Barry. 'Policy folklorists and evolutionary theory'. *Proceedings of the National Academy of Scientists of the United States* 111.3 (2014).

O'Neill, Robert. *The Operator: Firing the Shots That killed Osama Bin Laden*. New York: Scribner, 2017.

Oppenheimer, Michael F. *Pivotal countries, alternate futures: using scenarios to manage American strategy*. Oxford: Oxford University Press, 2016.

Orwell, George. 'Wells, Hitler and the World State'. *Horizon*, Aug. 1941.

Osmanczyk, Edmund. *Encyclopaedia of the United Nations and International Agreements*. 3rd ed. Ed. Anthony Mango. London: Routledge, 2003.

Otte, Thomas. *July Crisis: The World's Descent into War, Summer 1914*. Cambridge: Cambridge University Press, 2014.

Overy, Richard. *The Bombing War: Europe 1939–1945*. London: Allen Lane, 2013.

Owen, Mark. *No Easy Day: The Firsthand Account of the Mission that Killed Osama Bin Laden*. New York: Dutton, 2014.

Owens, Admiral William. 'The Emerging System of Systems'. *US Naval Institute Proceedings* (1995): 35–39.

Pakenham, Thomas. *The Boer War*. New York: Random House, 1979.

Parfitt, Tom. 'Ukraine crisis: Putin's nuclear threats are a struggle for pride and status'. *The Telegraph*, 26 Sept. 2014.

Paris, Michael. *Winged Warfare: Literature and Theory of Aerial Warfare in Britain, 1859–1917*. Manchester: Manchester University Press, 1992.

Paris, Roland. 'Saving Liberal Peacebuilding'. *Review of International Studies* 36.2 (2010): 337–365.

Partington, John S. 'The Pen as Sword: George Orwell, H. G. Wells and Journalistic Parricide'. *Journal of Contemporary History* 39.1 (2004): 45–56.

Paul, Christopher, Colin Clarke, and Beth Grill. *Victory Has a Thousand Fathers: Sources of Success in Counterinsurgency*. Santa Monica, CA: RAND, 2010.

Payne, Keith. 'Post-Cold War Deterrence and Missile Defense'. *Orbis* 39.2 (1995): 203.

Peceny, Mark, Caroline C. Beer, and Shannon Sanchez-Terry. 'Dictatorial peace?' *American Political Science Review* 96.1 (2002): 15–26.

Perrie, Maureen. *The Cambridge History of Russia: The twentieth century*. Cambridge: Cambridge University Press, 2006.

Peters, Ralph. 'Our Soldiers, Their Cities'. *Parameters* (1996): 43–50.

_____. 'Progress and Peril, New Counterinsurgency Manual Cheats on the History Exam'. *Armed Forces Journal International* 144 (2007).

Petraeus, Lieutenant General David H. 'Learning Counterinsurgency: Observations from Soldiering in Iraq'. *Military Review* ((2006): 2–12.

Pettersson, Therese, and Peter Wallensteen. 'Armed Conflicts, 1946–2014'. *Journal of Peace Research* 52.4 (2015): 536–540.

Pick, Daniel. *Faces of Degeneration: A European disorder, c.1848–c.1918*. Cambridge: Cambridge University Press, 1989.

Pinker, Steven. *The Better Angels of Our Nature: Why Violence Has Declined*. London: Penguin Books, 2011.

Plaw, Avery, Matthew S. Fricker, and Carlos R. Colon. *The Drone Debate: A Primer on the U.S. Use of Unmanned Aircraft Outside Conventional Battlefields*. Lanham, MD: Rowman & Littlefield, 2015.

Plummer, Bradford. 'Global Warring'. *New Republic*, 20 Nov. 2009.

Porter, Patrick. *The Global Village Myth: Distance, War, and the Limits of Power*. London: Hurst, 2015.

Posen, Barry R. 'The Security Dilemma and Ethnic Conflict'. *Survival* 35.1 (1993): 27–47.

_____. 'Urban Operations: Tactical Realities and Strategic Ambiguities'. *Soldiers in Cities: Military Operations on Urban Terrain*. Ed. Michael C. Desch. Carlisle, PA: US Army War College, 2001.

Powell, Jonathan M., and Clayton L. Thyne. 'Global Instances of Coups from 1950 to 2010: A New Dataset'. *Journal of Peace Research* 48.2 (2011): 249–259.

Power, Samantha. *A Problem from Hell: America and the Age of Genocide*. New York: Basic Books, 2002.

Preston, Diana. *A Higher Form of Killing: Six Weeks in World War One That Forever Changed the Nature of Warfare*. New York: Bloomsbury Press, 2015.

Prunier, Gerard. *The Rwanda Crisis: History of a Genocide*. London: Hurst & Company, 1998.

_____. *Africa's World War: Congo, the Rwandan Genocide, and the Making of a Continental Catastrophe*. New York: Oxford University Press, 2008.

Puri, Samir. *Fighting and Negotiating with Armed Groups: The Difficulty of Securing Strategic Outcomes*. London: Taylor & Francis for IISS, 2016.

'Quantifying carnage'. *The Economist*, 20 Feb. 2016. Available: http://www.economist.com /news/middle-east-and-africa/21693279-how-many-people-has-syrias-civil-war-killed -quantifying-carnage.

Quataert, Jean. 'War-making and restraint by law'. *The Cambridge History of War*, Vol. IV, *War and the Modern World*. Eds. Roger Chickering et al. Cambridge: Cambridge University Press, 2012.

Le Queux, William, *The Great War in England in 1897*. London: Tower, 1894. Available: http://www.gutenberg.org/files/37470/37470-h/37470-h.htm.

_____. *The Invasion of 1910: With A Full Account of the Siege of London*. London: Nash, 1906. Available: http://www.gutenberg.org/ebooks/36155.

_____. *Spies of the Kaiser: Plotting the Downfall of England*. London: Hurst & Blackwell, 1909.

Quinlan, Michael. *Thinking About Nuclear Weapons: Principles, Problems, Prospects*. (London: OUP, 2009).

Rachman, Gideon. *Easternisation: War and Peace in the Asian Century*. (London: Bodley Head, 2016).

Record, Jeffrey. 'Force-Protection Fetishism: Sources, Consequences, and (?) Solutions'. *Aerospace Power Journal*. Summer 2000.

_____. *A War It was Always Going to Lose: Why Japan Attacked America in 1941*. Washington DC: Potomac Books, 2011.

Reid, Brian Holden. 'A Signpost That Was Missed? Reconsidering British Lessons from the American Civil War'. *The Journal of Military History* 70.2 (2006): 385–414.

'Report puts Iraqi dead at 1500'. *Jane's Defence Weekly*, 13 Mar. 1993.

Resolution adopted by the General Assembly. 2005 World Summit Outcome Document. 24 Oct. 2005. Available: http://www.un.org/womenwatch/ods/A-RES-60-1-E.pdf.

Rhoads, Emily Paddon. *Taking Sides in Peacekeeping*. Oxford: Oxford University Press, 2016.

Rice, Condoleezza. 'Promoting the National Interest'. *Foreign Affairs* 79.1 (2000): 53.

Richard, Rhodes. *The Making of the Atomic Bomb*. New York: Simon & Schuster, 1986.

Richardson, Adm. John, Chief of Naval Operations, 'Deconstructing A2AD'. *The National Interest*, Oct. 2016. Available: http://nationalinterest.org/feature/chief-naval-operations-adm-john-richardson-deconstructing-17918.

Richardson, Lewis Fry. *Arms and Insecurity: A Mathematical Study of the Causes and Origins of War*. Pittsburgh, PA: Boxwood Press, 1960.

_____. *Statistics of Deadly Quarrels*. Pittsburgh, PA: Boxwood Press, 1960.

Rid, Thomas, and Ben Buchanan. 'Attributing Cyber Attacks'. *Journal of Strategic Studies* 38 (2015): 1–2.

Rid, Thomas. *Rise of the Machines: A Cybernetic History*. New York: W. W. Norton, 2016.

Roberts, L. et al. 'Mortality before and after the 2003 invasion of Iraq: cluster sample survey'. *Lancet* 364 (2004): 1857–1864.

Roberts, Adam. 'Lives and Statistics: Are 90% of War Victims Civilians?' *Survival: Global Politics and Strategy* 52.3 (2010): 115–136.

_____. 'The Civilian in Modern War'. *The Changing Character of War*. Eds. Hew Strachan and Sibylle Scheipers. Oxford: Oxford University Press, 2011.

Roberts, Andrew. *The Storm of War: A New History of the Second World War*. London: Penguin, 2009.

Roberts, Brad. *The Case for U.S. Nuclear Weapons in the 21st Century*. Stanford: Stanford University Press, 2016.

Robin, Ron. *The Cold War They Made: The Strategic Legacy of Roberta and Albert Wohlstetter*. Cambridge, MA: Harvard University Press, 2016.

Robinson, Linda et al. *Improving Strategic Competence: Lessons from 13 Years of War*. Santa Monica, CA: RAND Corporation, 2014.

Robinson, Piers. 'The CNN effect: can the news media drive foreign policy?' *Review of International Studies* (1999): 301–09.

Rodgers, Dennis, and Muggah, Robert. 'Gangs as Non-State Armed Groups: The Central American Case'. *Contemporary Security Policy* 30.2 (2009): 301–17;

Rodley, Nigel, ed. *To Loose the Bands of Wickedness*. London: Brassey's, 1992.

Rosato, Sebastian. 'The flawed logic of democratic peace theory'. *American Political Science Review* 97.4 (203): 585–602.

Rosencrance, Richard and Steven Miller, eds. *The Next Great War? The Roots of World War 1 and the Risk of U.S.-China Conflict*. Cambridge, MA: MIT Press, 2015.

Ross, Michael. 'A closer look at oil, diamonds, and civil war'. *Annual Reviews of Political Science* 9 (2006): 265–300.

_____. 'What Have We Learned about the Resource Curse?' *Annual Review of Political Science* 18 (2015): 239–59.

Rothkopf, David. 'The Cool War'. *Foreign Policy* (2013).

Rummel, R. J. *Death by Government*. New Brunswick, NJ: Transaction Publishers, 1994.

Russett, Bruce. 'Alliance, contiguity, wealth, and political stability'. *International Interactions* 18.3 (1992): 245–267.

Russett, Bruce M., and John R. O'Neal. *Triangulating Peace: Democracy, Interdependence, and International Organizations*. New York: W. W. Norton, 2001.

Sabin, Philip. *The Third World War Scare in Britain*. London: Macmillan, 1986.

Saideman, Stephen. *The Ties That Divide: Ethnic Politics, Foreign Policy, and International Conflict*. New York: Columbia University Press, 2001.

Saki. *The Complete Saki*. London: Penguin, 1982.

Samaan, Jean-Loup. 'Cyber Command'. *RUSI Journal* 195.6 (2010).

Sarkees, Meredith Reid, Frank Whelon Wayman, and David J. Singer. 'Inter-State, Intra-State, and Extra-State Wars: A Comprehensive Look At Their Distribution Over Time, 1816–1997'. *International Studies Quarterly* (2003): 47, 49–70.

Satter, Raphael. 'US General: We Hacked the Enemy in Afghanistan'. *Associated Press*, 24 Aug. 2012.

Scahill, Jeremy and the staff of *The Intercept*. *The Assassination Complex: Inside the Government's Secret Drone Warfare Program*. New York: Simon & Schuster, 2016.

Scales, Major General Robert. *Yellow Smoke: The Future of Land Warfare for America's Military*. Lanham, MD: Rowman & Littlefield, 2003.

_____. *Scales on War*. Annapolis, MD: U.S. Naval Institute Press, 2016.

Scharre, Paul. *Robotics on the Battlefield Part II: The Coming Swarm*. Washington DC: Center for New American Security, 2014.

Schelling, Thomas. 'Meteors, Mischief, and War'. *Bulletin of the Atomic Scientists* 16 (1960): 292–296, 300.

Schirmer, Jennifer. *The Guatemalan Military Project: A Violence Called Democracy*. Philadelphia, PA: University of Pennsylvania Press, 1998.

Schlosser, Eric. 'Deconstructing "Dr. Strangelove"'. *New Yorker*, 18 Jan. 18 2014. Available: http://www.newyorker.com/News/News-Desk/Deconstructing-Dr-Strangelove.

Schnabel, Albrecht, and Thakur, Ramesh, eds. *Kosovo and the Challenge of Humanitarian Intervention: Selective Indignation, Collective Action, and International Citizenship*. New York: United Nations University Press, 2000.

Schwab, Peter. *Africa: A Continent Self-Destructs*. New York: Palgrave, 2002.

Schwartau, Winn. 'Fighting Terminal Terrorism'. *Computerworld*, 28 Jan. 1991.

_____. *Terminal Compromise*. Old Hickory, TN: Interpact Press, 1991. Available: http://www.gutenberg.org/files/79/79.txt.

Schwartz, Peter. *Inevitable Surprises: A Survival Guide for the 21st Century*. New York: Free Press, 2003.

'Science: Push-Button War'. *Time Magazine*, 23 June 1947.

Sclove, Richard E. 'From Alchemy to Atomic War: Frederick Soddy's "Technology Assessment" of Atomic Energy, 1900–1915'. *Science, Technology, & Human Values* 14.2 (1989): 163–194.

Scroggins, Deborah. *Emma's War: Love, Betrayal and Death in the Sudan*. New York: Vintage Books, 2004.

Seelye, Katharine Q. 'Clinton Blames Milosevic, Not Fate, for Bloodshed'. *New York Times*, 14 May 1999.

Seung-Whan, Choi. 'Re-evaluating capitalist and democratic peace models'. *International Studies Quarterly* 55.3 (2011): 759–769.

Seybolt, Taylor, et al. *Counting Civilian Casualties: An Introduction to Recording and Estimating Nonmilitary Deaths in Conflict*. Oxford: Oxford University Press, 2013.

Seymour, Lee J. M., and Kathleen Gallagher Cunningham. 'Identity Issues and Civil war'. *What Do We Know about Civil Wars?* Eds. T. David Mason and Sara McLaughlin Mitchell. New York: Rowman & Littlefield, 2016.

Shashikumar, VK. 'Lessons from Sri Lanka's War'. *Indian Defence Review* 24.3 (2009).

Shawcross, Paul. 'This Isn't the Petition Response You're Looking For'. *Wired*, Jan. 2013.

Shirreff, General Sir Richard. *War With Russia*. London: Coronet, 2016.

Shlapak, David A., and Michael Johnson. *Reinforcing Deterrence on NATO's Eastern Flank: Wargaming the Defense of the Baltics*. Santa Monica, CA: RAND Corporation, 2016.

Shultz, George. *Turmoil and Triumph: My Years as Secretary of State*. New York: Charles Scribner's Sons, 1993.

Shy, John. 'Jomini'. *Makers of Modern Strategy from Machiavelli to the Nuclear Age*. Ed. Peter Paret. Princeton: Princeton University Press, 1986.

Simms, Brendan. *Unfinest Hour: Britain and the Destruction of Bosnia*. London: Allen Lane, The Penguin Press, 2001.

Simpkin, Richard. *Race to the Swift: Thoughts on Twenty-first Century Warfare*. London: Brassey's, 2000.

Simpson, Emile. *War from the Ground Up: Twenty-First-Century Combat as Politics*. London: Hurst & Co., 2012.

Simpson, Erin. 'Thinking about Modern Conflict: Hybrid Wars, Strategy, and War Aims'. *Paper Presented at the Annual Meeting of The Midwest Political Science Association*, 7 April 2005.

Singer, J. David, and Paul Diehl, eds. *Measuring the Correlates of War*. Ann Arbor: University of Michigan Press, 1990.

Singer, J. David, and Melvin Small. *The Wages of War, 1816–1965: A Statistical Handbook*. New York: John Wiley, 1972.

Singer, Peter W., and August Cole. *Ghost Fleet: A Novel of the Next World War*. New York: Houghton Mifflin, 2015.

_____. 'How to Write About World War III: Can Fiction Help Prevent Another Conflict Between Great Powers?' *The Atlantic Monthly*, 30 June 2015.

Singer, Peter. *Wired For War: The Robotics Revolution and Conflict in the 21ˢᵗ Century*. London: Penguin Group, 2009.

_____. 'Robots at War: The New Battlefield'. *The Changing Character of War*. Eds. Hew Strachan and Sibylle Scheipers. Oxford: Oxford University Press, 2011.

Sivard, Ruth Leger. *World Military and Social Expenditures 1991*. Washington DC: World Priorities, 1991.

Small, Melvin, and J. David Singer. *Resort to Arms: International and Civil War, 1816–1980*. Beverly Hills: Sage, 1982.

Smith, Bruce L. R. *The RAND Corporation; Case Study of a Nonprofit Advisory Corporation*. Cambridge, MA: Harvard University Press, 1966.

Smith, General Sir Rupert. *The Utility of Force: The Art of War in the Modern World*. London: Allen Lane, 2005.

Smith, M. L. R., and David Martin Jones. *The Political Impossibility of Modern Counterinsurgency: Strategic Problems, Puzzles and Paradoxes*. New York: Columbia University Press, 2015.

Smith, Niel A. 'Understanding Sri Lanka's Defeat of the Tamil Tigers'. *Joint Forces Quarterly* 59 (2010).

Smith, P. D. *Doomsday Men: The Real Dr Strangelove and the Dream of the Superweapon*. London: Allen Lane, 2007.

Smith, Thomas. *Human Rights and War Through Civilian Eyes*. Philadelphia, PA: University of Pennsylvania Press, 2016.

Snegovaya, Mari. *Putin's Information Warfare in Ukraine: Soviet Origins of Russia's Hybrid Warfare*. Washington DC: Institute for the Study of War, 2015.

Snow, C. P. 'The Moral Un-Neutrality of Science'. *American Association for the Advancement of Science* (1960).

Snyder, Jack L. *The Ideology of the Offensive: Military Decision Making and the Disasters of 1914*. Ithaca: Cornell University Press, 1984.

_____. *From Voting to Violence: Democratization and Nationalist Violence*. New York: W. W. Norton, 2000.

Soddy, Frederick. *The interpretation of radium: being the substance of six free popular experimental lectures delivered at the University of Glasgow*. London: John Murray, 1908.

Söderbaum, Fredrik, and Rodrigo Tavares. 'Problematizing Regional Organizations in African Security'. *African Security* 2.2–3 (2009): 69–81.

Sokolov, B.V. 'The Cost of War: Human Losses for the USSR and Germany, 1939–1945'. *The Journal of Slavic Military Studies* 9.1 (1966): 151–193.

Souleimanov, Emil Aslan, and David Siroky. 'Random or Retributive?: Indiscriminate Violence in the Chechen Wars'. *World Politics* 68.4 (2016): 677–712.

Soviet Military Power 1985. Washington DC: Department of Defense, 1985.

Soviet Military Power 1990. Washington DC: Department of Defense, 1990.

Spieir, Hans. 'Ludendorff: The German Concept of Total War'. *Makers of Modern Strategy: Military Thought from Machiavelli to Hitler*. Ed. Edward Mead Earle. Princeton: Princeton University Press, 1943.

Sprinzak, Ehud. 'Rational Fanatics'. *Foreign Policy* (2000).

Standards for Casualty Recording. London: Every Casualty Worldwide, 2016.

Stanton, Jessica. *Violence and Restraint in Civil War: Civilian Targeting in the Shadow of International Law*. New York: Cambridge University Press, 2016.

Stern, Jessica. *The Ultimate Terrorists* Cambridge, MA: Harvard University Press, 1999.

Stern, Roger J. 'Oil Scarcity Ideology in US Foreign Policy, 1908–97'. *Security Studies* 25.2 (2016).

Stevenson, David. 'Strategic and Military Planning, 1871—1914'. *The Fog of Peace and War Planning: Military and Strategic Planning under Uncertainty*. Eds. Talbot Imlay and Monica Duffy Toft. London: Routledge, 2006.

Stoessinger, John. *Why Nations Go to War*. New York: St. Martin's Press, 1997.

Stone, John. 'George Orwell on politics and war'. *Review of International Studies* 43.2 (2016): 221–239.

Strachan, Hew. *European Armies and the Conduct of War*. London: Allen & Unwin, 1983.

Stromseth, Jane. *The Origins of Flexible Response: Nato's Debate over Strategy in the 1960s*. London: Palgrave, 1988.

Suid, Lawrence H. *Guts and Glory: The Making of the American Military Image in Film*. Lexington: University of Kentucky Press, 2002.

Suri, Jeremi. 'America's Search for a Technological Solution to the Arms Race: The Surprise Attack Conference of 1958'. *Diplomatic History* 21.3 (1997): 41–86.

Szymborska, Wislawa. 'Hunger Camp at Jaslo'. Trans. Grazyna Drabik and Austin Flint. *Against Forgetting: Twentieth Century Poetry of Witness*. Ed. Carolyn Forché. New York: W. W. Norton, 1993.

Takenaka, Kiyoshi. 'Abe sees World War One echoes in Japan-China tensions'. *Reuters*, 23 Jan. 2014.

Tamm, Henning. 'The Origins of Transnational Alliances: Rulers, Rebels, and Political Survival in the Congo Wars'. *International Security* 41.1 (2016).

Tangredi, Sam J. *Anti-Access Warfare: Countering A2/AD Strategies*. Annapolis, MD: Naval Institute Press, 2013.

Taylor, Brendan. *Sanctions as Grand Strategy*. London: Routledge, for the International Institute of Strategic Studies, 2010.

Taylor, Mark. *The Vietnam War in History, Literature and Film*. Edinburgh: Edinburgh University Press, 2003.

Tenet, Director of Central Intelligence George J. 'World-wide Threat 2001: National Security in a Changing World'. 7 Feb. 2001.

The Carnegie Commission for the Prevention of Deadly Conflict. New York: Carnegie Corporation, 1998.

The Federation of American Scientists. *One World or None: A Report to the Public on the Full Meaning of the Atomic Bomb*. Ed. Dexter Masters. New York: New Press, 2007.

The International Committee of the Red Cross. *Arms Availability and the Situation of Children in Armed Conflict*. Geneva: ICRC, 1999.

The National Security Strategy of the United States of America. Washington DC: September 2002.

The State Failure Task Force Report: Phase III Findings. McLean, VA: Science Applications International Corporation, 30 Sept. 30, 2000.

Thomas, Daniel C. *The Helsinki Effect: International Norms, Human Rights and the Demise of Communism*. Princeton: Princeton University Press, 2001.

Thomas, Timothy L. 'Grozny 2000: Urban Combat Lessons Learned'. *Military Review* (2000).

Thring, M. W. 'Robots on the March'. *Unless Peace Comes: A Scientific Forecast of New Weapons*. Ed. Nigel Calder. London: Allen Lane, 1968.

Thucydides. *The History of the Peloponnesian War*. London: Penguin, 1972.

Tierney, Dominic, and Dominic Johnson. 'The Rubicon Theory of War How the Path to Conflict Reaches the Point of No Return'. *International Security* 36.1 (2011).

Till, Geoffrey. *Seapower: A Guide for the Twenty-First Century*. 3rd Edition. London: Routledge, 2013.

Tilly, Charles. 'War Making and State Making as Organized Crime'. *Bringing the State Back In*. Eds. Peter Evans, Dietrich Rueschemeyer, and Theda Skocpol. Cambridge: Cambridge University Press, 1985.

Titterton, Ernest. *Facing the Atomic Future*. London: Macmillan, 1956.

Toffler, Alvin and Heidi. *The Third Wave*. New York: Morrow, 1980.

_____. *War and Anti-War: Survival at the Dawn of the 21ˢᵗ Century*. New York: Little Brown, 1993.

Toft, Monica Duffy 'Peace Through Victory: The Durable Settlement of Civil Wars'. Unpublished Manuscript. Harvard University, 2003.

_____. 'The Origins of Ethnic Wars: An Historical and Critical Account'. *Handbook of War Studies III*. Ed. Manus Midlarsky. Ann Arbor, MI: University of Michigan Press, 2008.

_____. *Securing the Peace: The Durable Settlement of Civil Wars*. Princeton: Princeton University Press, 2010.

_____. 'Territory and War'. *Journal of Peace Research* 51 (2014): 185–198.

Touval, Saadia. *The Boundary Politics of Independent Africa*. Cambridge, MA: Harvard University Press, 1972.

Travers, T. H. E. 'Future Warfare: H. G. Wells and British Military Theory'. *War and Society: A Yearbook of Military History*. Eds. Brian Bond and Ian Roy. London: Croom Helm, 1975.

_____. 'Technology, Tactics, and Morale: Jean de Bloch, the Boer War, and British Military Theory, 1900–1914'. *The Journal of Modern History* 51.2 (1979): 264–286.

Treverton, Gregory and Renanah Miles, `Unheeded warning of war: why policymakers ignored the 1990 Yugoslav estimate'. *Intelligence and National Security*, 32:4 (2017), 506–522.

Trevithick, Joseph. 'Bizarre weapons never left the drawing board: The U.S. Army's Gun-Toting Space Soldiers'. *War is Boring*. 9 Nov. 2015. Available: https://warisboring.com/the-u-s-army-s-gun-toting-space-soldiers-ea9f1f1d48d0#.5u0wb9fyb.

Twomey, Steve. *Countdown to Pearl Harbor: The Twelve Days to the Attack*. New York: Simon & Schuster, 2016.

Ullman, Harlan K., and James P. Wade. *Shock and Awe: Achieving Rapid Dominance*. Washington DC: NDU Press Book, 1996.

UN. Report of the Panel on United Nations Peace Operations. 'Brahimi Panel Report'. S/2000/809. 21 Aug. 2000.

UNHCR Iraq fact sheet—December 2011. United Nations High Commissioner for Refugees. Geneva, 2011.

United Nations Commission of Experts Established to Security Council Resolution 935 on Rwanda, Final Report. Geneva: UN, 25 Nov. 1994.

U.S. Army/Marine Corps Counterinsurgency Field Manual (FM 3–24). Chicago: University of Chicago Press, 2007.

US Department of Defense. *Joint Military Net Assessment*. Washington DC: Department of Defense, 1993.

US Commission on National Security/21st Century. *New World Coming: American Security in the 21ˢᵗ Century* (Washington DC, 1999).

US-Soviet Basic Principles Agreement. May 1972.

Valentino, Benjamin A. *Final Solutions: Mass Killing and Genocide in the Twentieth Century*. Ithaca, NY: Cornell Studies in Security Affairs, 2005.

_____. 'Why We Kill: The Political Science of Political Violence against Civilians'. *Annual Review of Political Science* 17 (2014): 189–103.

Valentino, Benjamin A., Paul Huth, and Dylan Balch-Lindsay. '"Draining the Sea": Mass Killing and Guerrilla Warfare'. *International Organization* 58 (2004): 375–407.

Vandervort, Bruce. 'War and Colonial Expansion'. *The Cambridge History of War*, Vol. IV, *War and the Modern World*. Eds. Roger Chickering et al. Cambridge: Cambridge University Press, 2012.

Vasquez, John A. *The War Puzzle*. Cambridge: Cambridge University Press, 1993.

_____. *The War Puzzle Revisited*. Cambridge: Cambridge University Press, 2009.

_____. *What Do We Know About War?* 2nd ed. Lanham, MD: Rowman & Littlefield, 2012.

Väyrynen, Raimo, ed. *The Waning of Major War: Theories and Debates*. London: Routledge, 2006.

Verpoorten, Marijke. 'Le coût en vies humaines du génocide rwandais : le cas de la province de Gikongoro'. *Population* 60 (2005).

Verne, Jules. *The Clipper of the Clouds*. London: Sampson Low, 1887. 233–4. Available: https://archive.org/details/clipperclouds00verngoog.

_____. *Master of the World*. London: Sampson Low, 1904. Available: http://www.gutenberg .org/cache/epub/3809/pg3809.txt.

de Waal, Alex. *The Real Politics of the Horn of Africa: Money, War and the Business of Power*. London: Jon Wiley, 2015.

Wagar, W. Warren. 'H. G. Wells and the Genesis of Future Studies'. *World Future Society Bulletin* (1983): 25–29.

Wagner, Robert Harrison. The Causes of Peace'. *Stopping the Killing*. Ed. Roy Licklider. New York: New York University Press, 1993.

Wallensteen, Peter, and Margareta Sollenberg. 'Armed Conflict, 1989–98'. *Journal of Peace Research* 36.5 (1999): 593–606.

Walter, Barbara, 'Why Bad Governance Leads to Repeat Civil Wars'. *Journal of Conflict Resolution*, 59:7 (2015), 1242–72.

_____. 'The New New Civil Wars'. *Annual Review of Political Science*, 20:25, (2017), 1–18.

Waltz, Kenneth N. *Theory of International Politics*. New York: Random House, 1979.

_____. *The Spread of Nuclear Weapons: More May Better*. Adelphi Paper no. 171. London: International Institute for Strategic Studies, 1981.

Walzer, Michael. *Just and Unjust Wars: A Moral Argument with Historical Illustrations*. New York: Basic Books, 1977.

Ward, Dan. 'Don't Come to the Dark Side Acquisition Lessons from a Galaxy Far, Far Away'. *Defense AT&L: Better Buying Power* 70 (2011).

Warden, John A., III. 'The Enemy as a System'. *Airpower Journal* 9.1 (1995): 40–55.

Watt, Donald Cameron. *Too Serious a Business: European Armed Forces and the Approach to the Second World War*. Berkeley: University of California Press, 1975.

Wawro, Geoffrey. *The Franco-Prussian War: The German Conquest of France in 1870–1871*. Cambridge: Cambridge University Press, 2003.

Weber, Max. *The Vocation Lectures: 'Science as a Vocation'; 'Politics as a Vocation'*. Indianapolis: Hackett, 2004.

Weeks, Jessica, and Cohen, Dara Kay. 'Fishing Disputes, Regime Type, and Interstate Conflict a Research Note'. Stanford University, Stanford International Relations Workshop, 7 Mar. 2006. Available: http://citation.allacademic.com//meta/p_mla_apa_research_citation/0/9/8/1/0/pages98104 /p98104-1.php.

Weinberger, Caspar. 'The Uses of Military Power'. Speech to National Press Club, 28 Nov. 1984. Available: www.pbs.org/wgbh/pages/frontline/shows/military/ force/weinberger. html.

Weinberger, Caspar, and Peter Schweizer. *The Next War*. Foreword by Lady Thatcher. Washington DC: Regnery, 1998.

Weinberger, Sharon. *The Imagineers of War: The Untold Story of DARPA, the Pentagon Agency That Changed the World*. New York: Alfred A. Knopf, 2017.

Wiener, Anthony J. *The Year 2000. A Framework for Speculation on the Next Thirty-Three Years*. New York: Macmillan, 1967.

Weinkauf, Mary. *Sermons in Science Fiction: The Novels of S. Fowler Wright*. Rockville, MA: Wildside Press, 2006.

Weinstein, Jeremy M. 'Autonomous Recovery and International Intervention in Comparative Perspective'. *Center for Global Development*. Working Paper Number 57, April 2005.

_____. 'Resources and the Information Problem in Rebel Recruitment'. *The Journal of Conflict Resolution* 49:4 (2005): 598–624.

Weisgerber, Marcus. 'DoD to Release Public Version of Cyber Strategy'. *Defense News*, 8 July 2011.

Weiss, Leonard. 'Atoms for Peace'. *Bulletin of the Atomic Scientists* 59.6 (2003): 34–44.

Weiss, Thomas G. *Military-Civilian Interactions: Humanitarian Crises and the Responsibility to Protect*. New York: Rowman & Littlefield, 2004.

Welch, Michael. 'The Centenary of the British Publication of Jean de Bloch's *Is War Now Impossible?* (1899–1999)'. *War in History* 7.3 (2000): 273–294.

Wells, H. G. *Anticipations of the Reaction of Mechanical and Scientific Progress upon Human Life and Thought*. London: Chapman & Hall, 1902. Available: http://www.gutenberg.org/files/19229/19229-h/19229-h.htm.

_____. *The War in the Air*. London: George Bell & Sons, 1908. Available: http://www.free classicebooks.com/H.G.%20Wells/The%20War%20in%20Twentiethe%20Air.pdf.

_____. *The War That Will End War*. London: Frank & Cecil Parker, 1914.

_____. *The World Set Free*. London: Macmillan, 1914.

Welsh, Jennifer M. 'Introduction'. *Humanitarian Intervention and International Relations*. Ed. Jennifer M. Welsh. Oxford: Oxford University Press, 2004.

Welzer, Harald. *Climate Wars: What People Will Be Killed for in the 21st Century*. Cambridge: Polity Press, 2012.

Werner, Suzanne. 'The effects of political similarity on the onset of militarized disputes, 1816–1985'. *Political Research Quarterly* 53.2 (2000): 343–374.

Westad, Odd Arne. 'The wars after the war, 1945–1954'. *The Cambridge History of War*, Vol IV, *War and the Modern World*. Eds. Chickering et al. Cambridge: Cambridge University Press, 2012.

Whaley, Barton. *Codeword Barbarossa*. Cambridge, MA: MIT Press, 1974.

Wheeler, Nicholas. *Saving Strangers: Humanitarian Intervention in International Society*. Oxford: Oxford University Press, 2000.

Whitman, James Q. *The Verdict of Battle: The Law of Victory and the Making of Modern War*. Cambridge, MA: Harvard University Press, 2012.

Whitman, Walt. *Complete Prose Works*. Philadelphia, PA: David Mckay, 1892.

Whittle, Richard. *Predator: The Secret Origins of the Drone Revolution*. New York: Henry Holt, 2014.

'Why South Sudan is still at war'. *The Economist*, 3 Oct. 2016.

Wich, Richard. *Sino-Soviet Crisis Politics: A Study of Political Change and Communication*. London: Council on East Asian Studies, Harvard University, 1980.

Williams, Paul D. *War and Conflict in Africa*. (Cambridge: Policy, 2nd edition, 2016).

_____. 'Continuity and Change in War and Conflict in Africa'. *PRISM* 6: 4 (2017), 33–45

Williams, Phil. Transnational Criminal Organizations and International Security'. *Survival* 36.1 (1994): 96–113.

_____. 'The Terrorism Debate Over Mexican Drug Trafficking Violence'. *Terrorism and Political Violence*, 24:2, (2012): 259–278.

Wilson, Woodrow. Address to Congress, 11 Feb. 1918.

Witt, John Fabian. *The Laws of War in American History*. New York: The Free Press, 2012.

Wittes, Benjamin, and Gabriella Blum. *The Future of Violence – Robots and Germs, Hackers and Drones: Confronting the New Age of Threat*. New York: Basic Books, 2015.

Wohlstetter, Albert, Fred Hoffman, R. J. Lutz, and Henry S. Rowen. *Selection and Use of Strategic Air Bases*. Santa Monica, CA: RAND Corporation, 1954. Available: http://www.rand.org/pubs/reports/R0266.html.

Wohlstetter, Albert. 'The Delicate Balance of Terror'. *Foreign Affairs* 37.2 (1959): 211–234.

Wohlstetter, Roberta. *Pearl Harbor: Warning and Decision*. Stanford, CA: Stanford University Press, 1962.

A. T. Wolf, 'Conflict and Cooperation along International Waterways'. *Water Policy*, 1–2 (1998) 251–265.

Wood, Graeme. 'What Isis Really Wants'. *The Atlantic*, March 2015.

Woods, Chris. *Sudden Justice: America's Secret Drone Wars*. Oxford: Oxford University Press, 2015.

Woodward, Bob, *Bush at War.*, New York: Simon & Schuster, 2002.

Woolf, Leonard, ed. *The Intelligent Man's Way to Prevent War*. London: Victor Gollancz, 1933.

Work, Deputy Secretary of Defense Robert. Remarks at the Center for New American Security Defense Forum. 14 Dec. 2015.

Wright, Quincy. *A Study of War*, 2nd ed. Chicago: University of Chicago Press, 1965.

Wright, S. Fowler *Prelude in Prague: A Story of the War of 1938*. London: George Newnes, 1935.

_____. *Four Days War*. London: George Newnes, 1936.

_____. *Megiddo's Ridge*. London: George Newnes, 1937.

Wucherpfennig, J. et al. 'Ethnicity, the State, and the Duration of Civil War'. *World Politics* 64.1 (2012): 79–115.

Yakovlev, Alexander N. *A Century of Violence in Soviet Russia*. New Haven: Yale University Press, 2002.

Young, Joseph. 'Antecedents of Civil War Onset'. *What Do We Know about Civil Wars?* Eds. T. David Mason and Sara McLaughlin Mitchell. New York: Rowman & Littlefield, 2016. 33–42.

_____. 'Repression, Dissent, and the Onset of Civil War'. *Political Research Quarterly* 66.3 (2013): 516–32.

Yugoslavia from 'National Communism to National Collapse: US Intelligence Community Estimative Products on Yugoslavia, 1948–1990 (NOIC 2006-004), (Washington DC: US Government Printing Office, 2006).

Zametica, John. *The Yugoslav Conflict*. London: International Institute for Strategic Studies, 1992.

Zantovsky, Michael. *Havel: A Life*. London: Atlantic Books, 2014.

Zarate, Robert, and Henry Sokolski, eds. *Nuclear Heuristics: Selected Writings of Albert and Roberta Wohlstetter*. Strategic Studies Institute: US Army War College, 2009.

Zartman, William. *Collapsed States: The disintegration and restoration of legitimate authority*. Boulder, CO: Lynne Rienner, 1995.

Zedong, Mao. *On Guerrilla Warfare*, trans. Samuel B. Griffith. Urbana: University of Illinois Press, 2000.

Zetter, Kim. *Countdown to Zero Day: Stuxnet and the Launch of the World's First Digital Weapon*. New York: Crown, 2014.

Zimmerman, Warren. *Origins of a Catastrophe: Yugoslavia and its Destroyers*. New York: Times Books, 1996.

Zwierzchowski, Jan, and Ewa Tabeau. 'The 1992–95 War in Bosnia and Herzegovina: Census-based Multiple System Estimation of Casualties' Undercount'. *Paper for International Research Workshop on 'The Global Economic Costs of Conflict'*. Berlin, 1–2 Feb. 2010, pp. 1 and 18–21. Available: http://www.diw.de/sixcms/detail. php?id=diw_01.c.338475.en.

ACKNOWLEDGMENTS

The issues discussed in this book have been topics for discussion through my professional career and I have benefitted enormously in particular from all my colleagues in the Department of War Studies at King's College London. I have also learnt much from my newer colleagues in the twitter community where a lively debate on all national security issues can be found. I am especially grateful to a number of people for specific advice and comments: John Bew, Ryan Evans, Sam Freedman, Matthew Harries, Beatrice Heuser, Frank Hoffman, Stathis Kalyvas, Milton Leitenberg, Jack Macdonald, Jeff Michaels, Robert Muggah, Funmi Olinasakin, and Monica Toft. I am grateful for the excellent advice from my agents Catherine Clarke and George Lucas, and to two of the best editors in the business—Clive Priddle and Stuart Proffit—who have pushed me hard to make the most of this topic. Thanks also to Marco Pavia and his team for getting the book in a fit state to be published. To my wife Judith who had harboured some hope that retirement from King's would mean that I would not spend so much time in my study writing I can only—once again—apologise.

INDEX

military necessity, laws of war and, 30–31, 33
military preparedness, US and, 270
Milošević, Slobodan, 155–157, 156, 168
Minorities at Risk (report), 117
Mitchell, Billy, 56
modern states, state failure and, 210–211
Molander, Roger, 235
von Moltke, Helmuth, 3, 7, 8, 37, 39
Moore, Gordon, 185
morale, 14–15
  Pearl Harbor and, 66
  total war and, 56–57
  See also motivation
Morgenthau, Hans, 109
Morris, Ian, 216
Morsi, Mohamed, 218–219
Mosul, 219
motivation, future war and, 22
Mousseau, Michael, 140
Mubarak, Hosni, 218, 261
Mueller, John, xi
Muggah, Robert, 256, 258
Munro, Hector (Saki), 23
Museveni, Yoweri, 218
mutually assured destruction (MAD), 89–90, 232

Nagasaki, bombing of, 71–72
Namibia, 161
nanotechnology, 244
Napoleon, 5, 8, 33
Napoleon III, 2
Napoleonic Wars, 4, 8
  See also Austerlitz, Battle of
narratives, information warfare and, 228–229
national liberation, wars of, 146
national minorities, self-determination and, 47
National Security Agency (NSA), 234
nationalism, 51, 275
  democracy and, 138, 141
  Germany and, 51–52
  liberalism and, 46–47
  Yugoslavia, former and, 155–157
nationhood, statehood and, 151
NATO. *See* North Atlantic Treaty Organization
natural resources, 161–164, 195
  See also diamonds; energy resources; oil; resource wars
naval battle, Pacific War and, 63–66
  See also submarines
navy, China, 268
navy, US, 63–66, 268
  See also Anti-Access/Area Denial

Nazis, xx, 51–52, 62–63, 67, 126–127
  See also "Final Solution to the Jewish Problem"; Holocaust
negotiated settlements, civil war and, 217
netwars, 227–228
New Wars, 143
Newman, Edward, 255
Nicholas II (Tsar), 25
Nigeria, 129, 150, 172, 219
Nixon, Richard, 99, 106
Noel-Baker, Philip, 83–85
North American Aerospace Defense Command (NORAD), 232
North Atlantic Treaty Organization (NATO), 95–96, 140–141
  hybrid war and, 226
  nuclear war and, 93–94, 97
  Warsaw Pact and, 186–187
  West Germany and, 82
  Yugoslavia and, 168, 202–203
North Korea, 257, 279
  state failure and, 210
  US and, 120, 182, 236–237, 267–269, 281
Norton, Richard, 256
Norton, Roy, 20
NSA. *See* National Security Agency
nuclear stalemate, deterrence and, 84–86, 92
nuclear war, xi, xviii, 69–92, 280–281
  accidental war and, 76–77, 231–233
  conventional forces and, 93–94, 96–97
  cyberwar and, 232–233
  defence against, 88–89
  deterrence and, 79–80, 200
  disarmament and, 83–84
  fallout and, 72–74
  fiction and, 74–76, 94–98, 232–233
  knockout blow and, 76, 78–79
  NATO and, 93–94, 97
  Pearl Harbor and, 82, 90
  reason and, 75–76
  surprise attack and, 82–83, 86–87, 90
  terrorism and, 181, 271–272
  total war and, 72
  war, abolition of, and, 70
  world government and, 83
  World War II and, xx
  See also atomic bombs; cobalt bombs; Cuban Missile Crisis; dirty bombs; doomsday machine; hydrogen bombs; intercontinental ballistic missiles; mutual assured destruction

OAU. *See* Organization of African Unity
Obama, Barack, xvi, 119, 249, 261–262, 269
Obama Administration, drones and, 242–244

Lawrence Freedman is emeritus professor of War Studies at King's College London. Elected a fellow of the British Academy in 1995 and awarded the CBE in 1996, he was appointed official historian of the Falklands Campaign in 1997. He was awarded the KCMG in 2003. In June 2009, he was appointed to serve as a member of the official inquiry into Britain and the 2003 Iraq War. Professor Freedman has written extensively on nuclear strategy and the Cold War as well as commentating regularly on contemporary security issues. His most recent book, *Strategy*, was a best book of 2013 in the *Financial Times* and *A Choice of Enemies: America Confronts the Middle East* won the 2009 Lionel Gelber Prize and Duke of Westminster Medal for Military Literature.

PublicAffairs is a publishing house founded in 1997. It is a tribute to the standards, values, and flair of three persons who have served as mentors to countless reporters, writers, editors, and book people of all kinds, including me.

I. F. STONE, proprietor of *I. F. Stone's Weekly*, combined a commitment to the First Amendment with entrepreneurial zeal and reporting skill and became one of the great independent journalists in American history. At the age of eighty, Izzy published *The Trial of Socrates*, which was a national bestseller. He wrote the book after he taught himself ancient Greek.

BENJAMIN C. BRADLEE was for nearly thirty years the charismatic editorial leader of *The Washington Post*. It was Ben who gave the *Post* the range and courage to pursue such historic issues as Watergate. He supported his reporters with a tenacity that made them fearless and it is no accident that so many became authors of influential, best-selling books.

ROBERT L. BERNSTEIN, the chief executive of Random House for more than a quarter century, guided one of the nation's premier publishing houses. Bob was personally responsible for many books of political dissent and argument that challenged tyranny around the globe. He is also the founder and longtime chair of Human Rights Watch, one of the most respected human rights organizations in the world.

. . .

For fifty years, the banner of Public Affairs Press was carried by its owner Morris B. Schnapper, who published Gandhi, Nasser, Toynbee, Truman, and about 1,500 other authors. In 1983, Schnapper was described by *The Washington Post* as "a redoubtable gadfly." His legacy will endure in the books to come.

Peter Osnos, *Founder*

CPSIA information can be obtained
at www.ICGtesting.com
Printed in the USA
LVHW092044281019
635601LV00002B/3/P